THE LEGEND OF
ALBERT JACKA

Also by Peter FitzSimons and published by Hachette Australia

Kokoda
Burke and Wills
Monash's Masterpiece
Mutiny on the Bounty
The Catalpa Rescue
James Cook
Breaker Morant
The Incredible Life of Hubert Wilkins
The Opera House
The Battle of Long Tan
The Last Charge of the Australian Light Horse

PETER FITZSIMONS

THE LEGEND OF
ALBERT JACKA

hachette
AUSTRALIA

hachette
AUSTRALIA

Published in Australia and New Zealand in 2024
by Hachette Australia
(an imprint of Hachette Australia Pty Limited)
Gadigal Country, Level 17, 207 Kent Street, Sydney, NSW 2000
www.hachette.com.au

The authorised representative
in the EEA is
Hachette Ireland
8 Castlecourt Centre
Dublin 15, D15 XTP3, Ireland
(email: info@hbgi.ie)

Hachette Australia acknowledges and pays our respects to the past, present and future Traditional Owners and Custodians of Country throughout Australia and recognises the continuation of cultural, spiritual and educational practices of Aboriginal and Torres Strait Islander peoples. Our head office is located on the lands of the Gadigal people of the Eora Nation.

Copyright © Peter FitzSimons 2024

This book is copyright. Apart from any fair dealing for the purposes of private study, research, criticism or review permitted under the *Copyright Act 1968*, no part may be stored or reproduced by any process without prior written permission. Enquiries should be made to the publisher.

A catalogue record for this book is available from the National Library of Australia

ISBN: 978 0 7336 4670 6 (paperback)

Cover design by Luke Causby/Blue Cork
Cover images courtesy of the Australian War Memorial. Front cover, top, and back cover: scattered Australian graves, Pozières (AWM E00998); middle: studio portrait of Second Lieutenant (later Captain) Albert Jacka (AWM A03408); bottom: on the road near Petit Pont behind Hill 63, during the Battle of Messines (AWM E00607).
Thanks to Anne Carroll for her assistance on behalf of the C. E. W. Bean Estate
Maps by Jane Macaulay
Author photo courtesy of Peter Morris/Sydney Heads
Siegfried Sassoon poetry on pages 335, 366 and 399 copyright Siegfried Sassoon by kind permission of the Estate of George Sassoon
Rudyard Kipling poetry on pages 50, 58 and 171 reproduced with the kind permission of National Trust UK
Typeset in 11.2/15.1 pt Sabon LT Pro by Bookhouse, Sydney
Printed and bound in Great Britain by Clays Ltd, Elcograf S.p.A.

To Albert Jacka VC. What an extraordinary soldier, and great Australian, you were.

Jacka should have come out of the war the most decorated man in the A.I.F. One does not usually comment on the giving of decorations, but this was an instance in which something obviously went wrong. Everyone who knows the facts, knows that Jacka earned the Victoria Cross three times.[1]

Charles Bean

Captain Jacka was a super-soldier, a born leader, with an instinct to do the right thing in a critical situation. A company under his leadership was as good as an additional battalion.[2]

Brigadier General Charles Brand, Commanding Officer of the 4th Brigade

All of us had grown accustomed to hearing, as we marched along the roads of France, 'Hello, here's Jacka's mob.' But to those of us who were privileged to claim his friendship – and to call him 'Bert' – he was a constant urge to greater efforts ... Fate seemed to lead him to where desperate situations required desperate remedies, and stories of his audacity will be handed on to generations of Australians.[3]

Captain Ted Rule, *Jacka's Mob*

The recollection of his splendid courage, high personal honour, and outstanding manhood – equal to that of the greatest heroes of antiquity – will stir the blood of Australians for all time, and will serve as a beacon light to illuminate the future of Australia, that native land that he loved so well and served so nobly.[4]

Newton Wanliss, *Reveille*, 31 January 1931

CONTENTS

Dramatis personae		xi
Introduction and acknowledgements		xiii
One	Jacka v Jacko	1
Two	Death or glory	29
Three	The days of their discontent	58
Four	From Cairo to Calais	84
Five	The Valley of the Somme	121
Six	Attack!	140
Seven	Glittering prizes	165
Eight	Recover, return, revenge	189
Nine	Bullecourt blunders	220
Ten	'Come on, boys!'	247
Eleven	The aftermath	278
Twelve	The Battle of Polygon Wood	308
Thirteen	Journey's end	335
Fourteen	Home is the soldier	366
Epilogue		399
Notes		413
Bibliography		443
Index		453

DRAMATIS PERSONAE

Captain Albert Jacka. Forestry worker from regional Victoria who became the first winner of the Victoria Cross from Australia in the Great War.

Lieutenant Colonel John Peck. Commanded the 14th Battalion, from December 1916 to June 1917.

General Sir John Monash. Initially commanded the 4th Brigade, later taking command of the 3rd Division and finally the Australian Corps.

General Sir Hubert Gough. Commanded the British Fifth Army.

Brigadier General Charles Brand. Commanded the 4th Brigade from July 1916 to the end of the war.

Lieutenant Colonel Charles Dare. Commanded the 14th Battalion from August 1915 to December 1916.

Major William Watson. Commanding Officer of the tank company participating in the First Battle of Bullecourt.

Major Percy Black. Rose to command B Company of the 16th Battalion.

Lieutenant Colonel 'Mad Harry' Murray. Commander of A Company of the 13th Battalion, before being promoted to the rank of Lieutenant Colonel, commanding the 4th Australian Machine Gun Battalion.

Captain Ted Rule. Served throughout the Great War, with the 14th Battalion.

Charles Bean. Famed journalist, and later Official Australian Historian, who was embedded with the AIF during the war.

INTRODUCTION AND ACKNOWLEDGEMENTS

Albert Jacka VC?
I had 'met him' many times before. In seven previous books covering either the First World War or parts thereof, his name and derring-do had come up again and again, and I remember being particularly transfixed when I stumbled across a funeral account, noting that his coffin had been borne by eight fellow recipients of the Victoria Cross.

What kind of man must he have been to have garnered that level of respect from his fellow VC awardees?

Starting out on this book, I already had a fair idea of the sheer horror he had endured and triumphed over, given the books I had done on Gallipoli and the battles of Fromelles and Pozières, together with the battles of Villers-Bretonneux and Hamel.

It was fascinating to research and write as I kept discovering devastating detail that put flesh on the bones of the story and showed it in all its gory glory, its wonder, its desperation and inspiration.

What a man!

What a soldier!

What an emblematic Australian character, of an extraordinary time.

Inevitably, when trawling through letters, diaries and contemporary accounts one feels like one actually gets to know the subject, even though he is long dead. Allow me to say how much I came to like and admire Jacka the deeper I went – and how amazed I was that he managed to survive, given the risks he took and the furious fire he faced. He was an extraordinary soldier – surely the finest Australia has produced.

Happily, as I uncovered ever more about what he had accomplished, and how he had not only overcome amazing odds in battle to triumph, but also against efforts that were made against his attempts to rise in a system ill-disposed to allow a man with strong opinions on how things should be run on the battlefield to prosper, I also became entranced with other characters from Jacka's life who leapt from the page and deserved further exploration. I particularly cite Harold Wanliss, 'Mad Harry' Murray and Percy Black – while going back to the life of my previous obsession, the great Sir John Monash, was once again rewarding.

My principal researcher for this book was my friend Barb Kelly, who digitally trawled as mightily as ever to bring to the surface long-lost treasures of previously unrevealed detail to the account. It continues to stun both of us just how much can be uncovered from archives around the world; how, with judicious clicking, you can go down ever deeper through layer after layer until you get to gold – contemporary reports and accounts of *what happened*. It provided crucial material to help bring to life previously obscure and unknown episodes in Jacka's life. As with previous books I've done with Barb, it was wonderful that her son Lachlan – who in my book on Breaker Morant, single-handedly blew away an endlessly repeated century-old myth – was able to lend valuable assistance, finding letters, reports and death notices that had previously escaped the rest of us.

As to my long-time researcher and cousin, Angus FitzSimons, he was brilliant as ever. It helps that we are from the same familial storytelling tradition and he often knows exactly how I will want to recount a particular episode before I have even got to it, and is able to provide the necessary material accordingly!

My warm thanks also to Dr Peter Williams, the Canberra military historian who has worked with me on 13 books now. As ever, I relied on the depth and width of his military knowledge and lore, to inform my writing and military maps – not to mention his extensive library of wartime literature and contacts, including the excellent Lieutenant Colonel Renfrey Pearson (Retired) of the British Army who was able to dig out much valuable documentation in London from the National Army Museum, National Archives and the Liddell Hart Centre for Military Archives.

Thanks, too, to Gregory Blake for his expert advice on all things to do with the weapons of the time, and my friend Dr Michael Cooper for his expertise in matters medical and how things were done in the Great War. In similar fashion, the Reverend Dr Michael P. Jensen of St Mark's, Darling Point, was kind in helping source detail on the lives and work of the Reverends Gillison and Rolland, and religious practice. Meantime, a decade ago, one of my *Herald* readers, Bryce Abraham – who did a PhD on Jacka – provided material that was useful in getting me started down the whole saga of his life.

As I always recount at the beginning of my historical writing, I have tried to bring the *story* part of this history alive, by putting it in the present tense, and constructing it in the manner of a novel, albeit with a thousand or so footnotes as the pinpoint pillars on which the story rests.

For the sake of the storytelling, I have occasionally created a direct quote from reported speech in a journal, diary or letter, and changed pronouns and tenses to put that reported speech in the present tense. When the story required generic language – as in the words used when commanding movements in battle, I have taken the liberty of using that dialogue, to help bring the story to life, just as very occasionally I have tweaked the chronological order of scenes to help with flow.

Always, my goal has been to determine what were the words used, based on the primary documentary evidence presented, and what the feel of the situation was. All books used are listed in the Bibliography, but I relied particularly on the incomparable first-hand accounts of Charles Bean, John Monash, George Mitchell and William Watson – while the Official 14th Battalion History by Newton Wanliss, which relied on so many contemporary accounts, was invaluable. The most valuable source of all, of course, was done by Jacka's comrade and friend who fought alongside him, Ted Rule, whose book *Jacka's Mob* is a classic and a rich treasure trove of colour and anecdotes for all of us trying to recapture Jacka and his times. I not only relied on it heavily, I loved it!

In terms of more contemporary work, I particularly cite Ian Grant's *Jacka, VC: Australia's Finest Fighting Soldier*, and Robert Macklin's *Jacka VC, Australian Hero* – the latter of which I found a wonderful tool for sorting chronology and characters.

Even more than Dr Michael Lawriwsky's books, *Hard Jacka* and *Return of the Gallipoli Legend: Jacka VC*, I found his YouTube video interview, *Michael Lawriwsky on Captain Albert Jacka VC MC and Bar*, valuable guidance – as was an article he wrote in *Quadrant*, 'The Truth about Albert Jacka, Our First War Hero'.

To bring Percy Black and 'Mad Harry' Murray to life, the book written by the Vietnam vet Jeff Hatwell, *No Ordinary Determination: Percy Black and Harry Murray of the First AIF*, was simply wonderful – and Jeff was most generous in sharing his knowledge over the phone.

As to Jacka's own family, I was grateful to meet and talk with Jacka's nephew, Ken Jacka. I thank him for his time, generosity and patience.

Meanwhile my long-time sub-editor, Harriet Veitch, took her usual fine-tooth comb to the whole thing, untangling sentences, twisted hopelessly as be they might, eliminating many of my grammatical errors and giving my work a sheen which does not properly belong to it. She has strengthened my stuff for three decades now, and I warmly thank her.

In all my books, I give a draft of the near finished product to the eldest of my six siblings, David, who has the toughest red pen in the business. When Davo's interest flags, it is a fair bet so too will that of the reader, and I slash what doesn't grab him, so long as it is not key to the story. In this book, he was typically astute, and I record my deep fraternal gratitude.

My thanks also to my highly skilled editor, Deonie Fiford, who has honoured my request that she preserve most of the oft esoteric – I'm told – way I write, while only occasionally insisting that something come out because it just doesn't work.

I am also grateful to my friend and publisher, Matthew Kelly of Hachette, with whom I have worked many times over the last three decades, and who was as enthusiastic and supportive as ever. This book has been quite the journey for me, and my chief hope is that it does justice to Jacka's extraordinary story.

Peter FitzSimons
Neutral Bay, Sydney
May 2024

CHAPTER ONE

JACKA v JACKO

This is the first time I have been brought into contact with the Australian troops, and they certainly create an excellent impression with their fine physique and general bearing. A truly magnificent body of men; but their ideas of discipline are very different from those of our old regular army. The men seem to discipline themselves, and the officers have very little authority over them through the holding of military rank – personality plays a much more important role.[1]

English journalist Ellis Ashmead-Bartlett, on meeting the Diggers just before they head to Gallipoli

April 1915, Gallipoli, upon the fatal shore

Of course Australia is in this war.

As the loyal offspring of Great Britain, the Australian Government has been with the Motherland from the beginning of her conflict with Germany, few questions asked. It is *blood*. The new Prime Minister, Andrew Fisher, had even made clear in the leadup to his election that Australia would rally to the Mother Country, and that when it came to actual battle, 'I am in favour of defending this country with the last man and the last shilling against anyone who would try and take it.'[2]

It is just that at the time of the declaration of war, no-one could have envisioned that the first battle would be here, at Gallipoli.

But now, it has come to this.

Just before dawn on calm seas, the senior Australian officers on these boats, being towed to the Turkish shores by steamboats, are confused. For their briefings had been clear. They will be landing on a flat sandy beach, with 150 to 200 yards of gently rising ground behind it. But even in this dim light it is clear there is nothing like that ahead. Instead, the lightly frothing white water of the lapping shore here looks to be practically at the foot of massive hills, one jutting knoll of which looks all of 200 feet high.

'Tell the Colonel,' Flotilla Commander Charles Dix hisses, 'that the damn fools have taken us a mile too far north!'[3]

True or not, it is too late now to alter course.

'This landing farther north than was intended naturally caused some temporary difficulties,' Field Marshal Sir William Birdwood, the English commander of the Australian and New Zealand Army Corps at Gallipoli, will later acknowledge. 'For these I must take the blame, for they were caused by my insistence on landing before daylight.'[4]

At 75 yards from the shore, the boats are let loose from the steamboats, as now the four seamen allotted to each boat take up an oar each and begin hauling hard, no easy task in such heavy boats.

And *pull*. And *pull*. And *pull*.

Floating phantoms on the water, gliding to their goal . . .

And now it happens. A single shot rings out in the silent stillness . . . as nerves jangle and soldiers instinctively hold their own rifles closer.

Is it a random shot in the dark, or something else?

'Look at that!'[5] whispers a son of South Australia, Captain Raymond Leane, in one of the forward boats bearing the men of the 11th Battalion, now approaching the Turkish shore. Against the ethereal glow of the eastern sky, on the clifftop, stands the ghostly silhouette of a man.

A male voice rings out, in a foreign language . . .

God knows what he is saying, but it doesn't sound good.

And sure enough.

The dawn is shattered by shots, as bullets start flying over their heads.

'Hullo!' one Digger yells, 'Now we're spotted.'[6]

No sooner spot than shot, as the bullets grow in number and accuracy. The first boats of Australians are just drifting into range of a platoon of 50 Turks which soon sees 50 rifles trained upon them. The water spits around them, a vertical rain summoned by metal, and it is obvious these moments will be the last for some.

The next sound is strange indeed. To calm their nerves, a clutch of Diggers begin to sing a song that drips in irony, a music hall ditty called 'This Bit of the World Belongs to Us'.[7]

The Turks disagree, and their counter-melody fires fast.

Sing, boys!

> *We'll all stand together, boys,*
> *If the foe wants a flutter or a fuss,*
> *And we're hanging out the sign,*
> *From the Leeuwin to the line,*
> *this bit of the world belongs to us!*

The singers are game but they are being drowned out by fire, thicker now. 'They want to cut that shooting out,' a wag yells 'somebody might get killed.'[8]

Somebody is, for, look there, the fellow in the first boat has fallen forward, blood weeps from his head as his body becomes a rag doll – his comrades propping him up for a few pointless seconds before letting the corpse rest among them. He is the first to die at Gallipoli, his body will lie upon it forever, in a land he never set foot on. And now another groans, two soldiers clutch their bodies in one strange motion as the same bullet cuts through both and the casualties become casual; so frequent that you stop watching them and start watching the beach. Reach that, and our part of the battle can begin.

The air sings with bullets now; they whistle past, unceasing. Private 'Combo' Smith of the 11th Battalion nudges the man next to him Lieutenant 'Snowy' Howe.

'Just like little birds, ain't they, Snow?'[9]

And Snowy, despite himself, starts laughing; and the laughter spreads through the boat. The little birds fly on by, but surely the swansong is coming for the man next to you in a moment. 'Constantinople by night'[10] had been the cry of their commanders. Right now they would settle for being alive by sundown. The shore of Gallipoli is here; time to get your boots wet and leap on to Turkish land. Go!

In short order, the Australians are hitting the shores of Gallipoli *en masse* – soon to be followed by the New Zealanders.

Some fall, and die on the spot. Others fall, maimed. Most of the rest push on, and the emblematic attitude is the one displayed by Lieutenant John Peck of the 11th Battalion, who cries out to his men, 'Come on, boys! By God, I'm frightened.'[11]

Within hours they have at least secured a toe-hold on the peninsula, with the challenge being to turn it into a large footprint.

•

Some miles away on this morning, Colonel Mustafa Kemal, who commands the Ottoman 19th Division, is putting his troops through exercises when the word comes that there has been a landing. For a short time, Kemal tries to reach the German officer that the Turkish Government has placed in command of the 5th Ottoman Army, seeking permission to take his troops forward, but is unsuccessful.

So, *Allah belanı versin,* the hell with it.

Colonel Kemal decides to rush forward anyway, personally leading the men of his finest unit, the 57th Infantry Regiment, towards the sound of the crashing artillery. They arrive by mid-morning, in time to see Turkish troops of the 9th Division's 27th Regiment streaming back from where the landing has been made.

'Why are you running away?' he shouts.

'They come, they come,' the rattled soldiers reply. 'Our ammunition is finished.'[12]

'You cannot run away. You have bayonets.'

It has the desired effect, as the receding tide of Turkish soldiers is halted, and they fix bayonets.

Colonel Mustafa now gives an order that will become the stuff of legend:

'I don't order you to attack,' he says. 'I order you to *die.* In the time which passes until we die other troops and commanders can take our places.'[13]

His men stream forward with a commitment, he will later note to his wife, that may well have come from their expectation of – if the worst comes to the worst – at least shortly meeting 72 virgins in heaven.[14]

With the arrival of the 57th – ordered by Kemal to control the high ground at all costs – the tone of the battle for the marauding

Australians changes, as heavier punishment than ever pours and roars down upon them – withering fire and a shellacking of shrapnel from the highly trained and committed soldiers and gun crews now occupying the high ground.

It is true, they are not much to look at, these Turks, with their mostly slight frames covered in rag-tag uniforms, but that is not the measure of them. For their bravery is beyond all doubt, and even beyond all reason, as waves of them charge at the Australians and New Zealanders, shouting – what is that word, again? – *'Allah! Allah! ALLAH!'*

No matter that the first wave is cut to pieces, the second wave comes on, running over their own dead and dying.

'Allah! Allah! ALLAH!'

The Australians and New Zealanders are shocked.

•

Back at the island of Lemnos the night before – their last port of call before landing at Gallipoli – there had been bitter disappointment among the men of the 14th Battalion of the AIF's 4th Brigade of the 1st Division to find out that they were not only not in the first wave of Australians to hit the shores, but were only in the reserve of the *second* wave.

Right now, however, in the late afternoon, gazing at the shore from the deck of the *Seang Choon* – 'a dirty boat full of cockroaches, fleas and rats'[15] – some of them are not so sure.

It doesn't look . . . too good.

'Every now and again above the fiendish din of battle came the WOOM-PAH, at which ground, sea and sky seemed to get up and sit down again,' one Digger notes.[16]

'It was Big Lissie [HMS *Queen Elizabeth*], arguing with her 15-inch toys. And when her shells landed – suffering sinner, they shifted a hill – arms, legs and other curios flying in all directions . . .'

The sheer shattering roar from this end takes your breath away, as does the visible results on yonder hills.

Not that everyone is *that* impressed.

Up near the stern, on the deck, small groups of country chaps are playing cards and chortling, while sipping big mugs of tea, and only occasionally glancing to the shore.

As the Commanding Officer of the 4th Brigade, Colonel John Monash, notes approvingly, when watching them from up on the bridge, 'What do they care if the greatest naval bombardment in history is going on? When the job comes, there will be time enough to sit up and take notice.'[17]

And he's right. It's just that what they will be facing when they do land looks to be grim and getting grimmer, as the sound of Turkish fire becomes overwhelming and it is clear from the many exploding plumes of sand on the shore that the defenders do not lack artillery.

Could it be they had underestimated the Turks?

Look, none of them had reckoned they would be in Constantinople by nightfall. That was obvious madness. They had been much more realistic, and as the Official History of the 14th Battalion will record, 'Bets at short odds were freely made that they would be in Constantinople within three days of the landing, whilst the more cautious who were only prepared to bet on being there within a week could obtain almost any odds they wished to lay.'[18]

For Lance Corporal Albert Jacka's part, while disappointed not to be in the first wave, he is still hopeful that he will be able to catch up before they actually reach Constantinople.

In contemplation of what awaits now, though, as the shelling and machine-gun fire becomes even more intense, some of Jacka's comrades are overwhelmed by great feelings of mortality, and are soon seen in quiet conversation – or hurried prayer – with the 14th Battalion's beloved pastor, the Captain Reverend Andrew Gillison. Nudging towards 60, the Scottish-born man of God with the thick burr has a way of talking, of praying, of *caring* about them – and assuring them that, whatever happens, the Lord is by their side – that calms.

Albert Jacka is a believer in the Lord himself but has no need right now of spiritual solace. He somehow has an innate sense that he will be alright.

For his part, Monash – in civilian life a brilliant engineer from Melbourne – does not share the disappointment. For the last two weeks this citizen soldier of 30 years standing – the one-time dux of Scotch College, from a Jewish German family, boasting three degrees that rest on his towering intellect – has been so frantically engaged in the organisation of getting away that he has fallen ill.

But now that they have actually made it to the shores of Gallipoli without mishap, he cannot help but feel relief, as his sickness lifts.

For all that, there is no doubt, as the afternoon wears on that things on shore are dim and grim.

The Turks certainly have firepower, as shells continue to burst among the Australians and New Zealanders on the shore, and they are exacting a toll from those who would dare invade their turf.

'Can hear terrible gunfire,'[19] Jacka writes in his diary. And now, more than ever, he can see up close the results of much of that gunfire.

Already barges and boats are coming back with the wounded, and worse – for some had expired since leaving the shore – and to look down upon such barges is to see hell on earth.

'Eight boat loads of wounded,' Jacka writes, 'arrived at our boat.'[20]

So extreme is the situation that the Medical Officer gives orders to some of the soldiers and sailors to climb down and bring the worst cases up. They must *make* room.

But the wounded just keep coming!

And the stories the wounded tell are appalling.

At dawn, 1500 of them had hit the shores, expecting to find easy slopes leading up to the high ground, only to be confronted by the need to climb cliffs under withering fire of Turkish machine guns.[21]

As the eventide falls, the flow of wounded gets ever thicker, as do stories of chaos on the beach as the too few stretcher-bearers fall to exhaustion or bullets or shrapnel. They need help. As it happens, Albert Jacka is one of those dispatched to lend a hand.

'Going ashore with 30 A Coy men to help with the wounded,'[22] he writes in his diary.

Approaching the shore, Jacka cannot help but reflect on how far he has come. Was it really only a little over half a year ago, just after the war had broken out, that he had been farewelled from his quiet life around Wedderburn in country Victoria? There was a ceremony at the local Rechabite chapter, where he and two other soldier recruits from the Rechabites had been wished well, and reminded of their sacred pledge to never drink. And then, just a day later, he and the others had been farewelled on the platform of Wedderburn Railway Station, where the brass band had played 'Australia Will Be There', and the Reverend's daughter, sweet Elsie Raff, had *kissed him on the lips*. Yes, the blue-eyed boy of Wedderburn had blushed furiously, but all that had been so warm, so sunny, so, *so* happy.

But now this.

'In amongst the warships ready to go ashore. Some sight this. Shells from warships bursting all over the island. Troops landing on the beach: heavy rifle and machine-gun fire. All the hills covered in smoke, reminds me of a bush fire.'[23]

Jacka is one of a hundred men who are tasked today not with battle but with rescuing and tending the wounded. At 7 pm he and 30 men are ferried to the beach and set foot on Gallipoli – which is no easy thing.

Only a short time before, two mates in the 16th Battalion, Lance Corporal Percy Black and Private Harry Murray, had been close to the shore and, in the midst of heavy fire, Black had jumped into the water the moment he felt the boat touch bottom – only to find that the boat had merely scraped a stray jutting rock, and he had gone straight to the bottom! Heavily laden with boots, gun, ammunition and rations, it had been touch and go to get him out before drowning but, mercifully, Murray managed.

While Black and Murray push to the heights with their Maxim gun, Jacka is soon immersed in the rows of wounded and screaming men on shore as a terrible triage is underway to determine who is worth transporting and who will die here on the shore.

You! Don't stand there! Lift and carry! A bloodied body is Jacka's cargo as he and another shocked private move a twisting soldier back towards the boats. It is a baptism of blood not of fire, and until night falls Jacka and his fellows will be dealing with the aftermath of battle; the men who fought it, the men who will die of it before the next sun rises. Strangely, despite the horror all around, Jacka feels calm, committed, cold in his calculations. (Beyond everything else, it is good to be off that damn *ship*, allowing him to get over his wretched seasickness. The only thing worse he has experienced in this war so far had been the inoculations he faced early on. Now, *they* were terrifying.)

There is work to be done. He is the man to do it. And there are things he can do to maximise his chances of survival. Grabbing one end of a stretcher from a man who has just been shot, Jacka is like a machine, ferrying the wounded to the shore, managing to bend himself nearly double, to make his already diminutive five foot six inch frame even smaller. It is only when he is done that the sights and sounds of the horror start to sink in. This is his new world, and there is no man alive who has seen anything like it.

•

In all the chaos, one older man stands out for his calm, his care, his leadership – as his words alone start to restore order through orders. He projects a sense that he knows what must be done, and only needs the men to follow him.

Few soldiers know him personally. Nearly all of them know of him, and are more than happy to do what he says.

For this is, don't you see, Colonel Neville Howse VC, the first man serving with the Australian forces to become a recipient of the Victoria Cross, which was awarded to him for his staggering derring-do in the Boer War. Yes, don't you remember the story?

On 24 July 1900, six months before Australia became a federation, during the battle at Vredefort, Howse – then a young Lieutenant of the Medical Corps, a British man who'd emigrated to Australia when he was 26 – had seen a trumpeter fall to the ground in the midst of a bitter clash. Disregarding the Boer bullets pinging all around, the highly trained doctor turned officer had ridden his horse out to try to save the trumpeter, and even when that horse was shot from under him, had continued on foot, bandaged the trumpeter's wounds on the spot, and *carried* him back to safety!

Such experience is desperately needed right now. For it turns out there is no plan for evacuating the wounded capable of coping with the flood of blood, so Howse – who is quietly appalled and actively disgusted by the lack of foresight displayed by the Imperial authorities – has taken the matter into his own hands. Setting up a system of triage, he is getting those most likely to be saved onto the ships as quickly as possible.

As Jacka follows his instruction, Howse intersperses his orders with gentle cheer as he passes his hands over grievously wounded soldiers, does what he can to stabilise them, and then sends them on their way. Jacka, though shocked with what he is seeing, feels eerily composed. Once or twice while wood-chopping he has seen accidents that have caused blood, but never anything remotely like this, as he carries men with missing limbs, men whose hands are holding in their own intestines, men who are screaming with pain, from as many as five bullets, shrapnel or even bayonet wounds. It is *infernal*. And yet as shells are still landing on the beach, and bullets from far-flung guns regularly dropping the upright and further wounding the prone, whatever it is in a man that can remain steady amid horror and danger, Jacka finds he has it.

•

Throughout the battered night, the evacuation of the wounded goes on as they are crammed into every small vessel that can be commandeered. Initially the boats head for the ships with green lights, indicating they are hospital ships, but it does not take long before those vessels can take no more, at which point the men must search wider, coming alongside every ship with crammed cargoes of broken bodies, looking for ways to unload.

'Wounded alongside, sir!' a voice from a barge rings out to those on high, on the *Seang Choon*.

'I cannot take any more,' the Medical Officer calls down. 'I've got my quota, 250, and a battalion of troops [the 14th] is still on board.'

'It cannot be helped, sir. I've been dragging these unfortunate men from ship to ship and there's no room anywhere.'[24]

One glance over the side reveals the ghastly cargo, and just how desperate their situation is. As the barge is now alongside the ship, every swell on the Aegean Sea – and it is heavy tonight – causes big bumps against the iron hull, unleashing fresh wails of agony from the wounded.

One soldier, unable to bear it any longer, cries out.

'For God's sake, cobber, take me off this barge.'[25]

The sailors and soldiers do exactly that, despite the fact that 'the swell, the stench, and the slippery blood-washed deck, combined, made the handling of the slings difficult and nauseating'.[26]

They are hauled up on deck, where 'one stepped warily over their bodies as they slept the sleep of utter exhaustion which brought with it a merciful unconsciousness of their wounds'.[27]

•

Into the night, the noise of the Aegean Sea slapping the shore is drowned by the sound of rifle and machine-gun fire rolling over those by the beach where the landing has taken place, together with the regular boom of artillery, which begets exploding shells and the moans of yet more dying men and the shouts for medics to *come quickly!* because this one has not got long.

The chaos on shore is as appalling as it is unforgivable.

'The medical arrangements were awful,' the English journalist Ellis Ashmead-Bartlett will document, 'and terribly mismanaged. There seemed to be no-one in charge, in supreme authority, to direct the stream of wounded for whom no accommodation could be found, to any particular ship.'[28]

As Jacka continues to haul desperately wounded and oft dying men to the beach, a key meeting is taking place no more than 100 yards away, in a tent in yonder gully, just visible by the glow of a lantern whose light shines through the entrance – a tiny chink of cheer in the blackness with death, destruction and chaos reigning all around.

Inside the tent, however, there is no cheer whatsoever.

The day is done, the battle lost, the bloody fiasco of the whole thing obvious to all. Major General William Bridges and Major General Sir Alexander Godley, the commanders of the Australian 1st Division and New Zealand and Australian Division, use the suitable euphemisms; but their meaning is clear. The Commander of the Corps their divisions belong to, General Sir William Birdwood, listens to both, his face falling by the minute as they make the case for withdrawal. It is time to pull up stumps and fight another day. To do otherwise is to embark on a long defeat. Victory can be won in another place; not this one.

General Sir William Birdwood is being asked to make happen what must happen: an evacuation.

Birdwood is shocked; he has just landed, and now he is to order all to withdraw?

But what choice can there be? This landing has not established anything except a surge in Turkish confidence; tens of thousands have surely been ordered to advance towards our position and our position is *hopeless*. Their shocked faces say it even more than their words. Birdy must see that there is no other choice. No fewer than 500 of our soldiers are confirmed dead, 2000 are missing and will be dead once hope is lost; and at least 2500 are wounded. Do you have it, little Birdy? We are 5000 men down, after one day!

This was not the spot to land and it is not the spot to fight. It has been a mistake; pure and simple. The choice is now whether we learn from it or compound it? Even if we were to stay, we do not have enough fit men to secure the ground we currently hold and the Turks have the high ground, the high numbers and the will to press any advantage they have – which is all of them. The front line? That is half a mile yonder and it will be falling back by morning. And the morning is when the Turks will begin their attack in full.

Sir William listens and says nothing. Finally, he nods and speaks. *General Godley, take this down.* Quickly, Godley grabs the nearest serviceable paper, the back of a white signal form, and writes down every word:

'General Hamilton,' Birdwood begins, 'Both my divisional generals and brigadiers have represented to me that they fear their men are thoroughly demoralised by shrapnel fire to which they have been subjected all day after exhaustion and gallant work in morning.'

Birdy's stately words do not come close to capturing the catastrophe, but are still clear enough.

'Numbers have dribbled back from firing line and cannot be collected in this difficult country. Even New Zealand Brigade which has been only recently engaged lost heavily and is to some extent demoralised. If troops are subjected to shell fire again tomorrow morning there is likely to be a fiasco.'

Another fiasco would be more accurate, but they can see Sir William is with them as he continues: 'I have no fresh troops with which to replace those in firing line. I know my representation is most serious but if we are to re-embark it must be done at once.'[29]

Add my name and send it at once. Sir! No order has been more happily followed on this day.

•

If the great Australian adjective is indeed 'bloody', never can it have been more suitably applied than to Private Albert Jacka right now. It has been a shocking eight hours since landing and he has done his best to save as many men as he can, or at least done what he can to ease their passage to the next world.

Completely covered in blood and gore, he has kept going until the early hours, when he drops his swag near the base of the cliffs to snatch a couple of hours rest before what will be a challenging day on the morrow.

•

General Sir Ian Hamilton is abed. And asleep. Well, having already finished his diary, what else is there to stay awake for? His entry, after the first day at Gallipoli, can best be described as sanguine, a word that Sir Ian is particularly fond of: 'I feel sanguine in the spirit of the men; sanguine in my own spirit; sanguine in the soundness of my scheme.'

Is there perhaps room for one more sanguine? Sadly, no, but at least one can go to the land of nod knowing that '. . . our fellows are steadily pouring ashore'.[30] The *Queen Elizabeth* bobs in the water soothingly and BLOODY HELL! Who has the gall to wake the commander at this time? It proves his bloody chief of staff, Major General Walter Braithwaite. Yes?

'Sir Ian, you've got to come right along,' Braithwaite gasps, 'a question of life and death – you *must* settle it!'[31]

Life and death is their bloody profession, but a bleary Sir Ian rolls out of bed, dons dressing gown and slippers and goes to an impromptu if bizarre Council of War in the dining room. Admiral John de Robeck is here, as is Rear Admiral Cecil Thursby, as is Commodore Roger Keyes and they are all dressed to the nines and look as though they are about to pose for a painting. One glance and Sir Ian knows, cold fate has murdered his sanguine hopes; this is a hanging jury and the life of the Gallipoli campaign is about to be cut short. Birdy's note is given to him and Sir Ian reads it twice before speaking.

'This is a difficult business . . . What are we to do about it?'[32]

Retreat. Ignominiously. Rear Admiral Thursby has already worked out the firm logistics of defeat. 'It will take the best part of three days to get that crowd off the beaches.'

Hmm.

'And where are the Turks?' asks Sir Ian.

'On top of 'em,' replies Cecil.

'Well, then, tell me, Admiral, what do you think?'

A buck is to be passed, but damn me if Thursby won't take it.

'What do I think?' Yes! 'Well . . . I think, myself . . . They will stick it out if only it is put to them that they *must*.'[33]

True. You can beat a retreat from defeat, *only* if given the means to do so. Why evacuate over three messy days when you can stay where you are straight away?

Hamilton, in the middle of the room where it happens, takes out a red pencil he uses to mark troop positions on maps, and scrawls a message of reply for those ashore: '*Your news is indeed serious. But there is nothing for it but to dig yourselves right in and stick it out. It would take at least two days to re-embark you, as Admiral Thursby will explain to you . . . Hunter-Weston despite his heavy losses will be advancing tomorrow which should divert pressure from you. Make a personal appeal to your men and Godley's to make a supreme effort to hold their ground. (Sd.) Ian Hamilton P.S. You have got through the difficult business, now you have only to dig, dig, dig, until you are safe. Ian H.*'[34]

Dig? Dig, dig, dig? It is not a very . . . *sanguine* strategy, but it is an order. Sir Ian goes back to bed; Admiral Thursby goes to the boat. By 2 am he places Hamilton's note in Birdy's hands. Well then, Diggers, you know what to do. Shovels begin to scrape out furrows, furrows become trenches and the Australians become . . . entrenched. Gallipoli is not a disaster; it is just the site of a future triumph. The difficult part is done. As they dig it starts to rain heavily, a sound that is quite soothing when hitting in flurries against a porthole on the *Queen Elizabeth*, but ashore, it is just bloody wet.

Dig. Dig, dig, dig!

Using the trench model first developed by the War Office in 1911, the trenches will not be straight, as that would expose all in to enfilade fire from just one breakthrough. Instead, a cunning sort of zig-zag is used, with lengths, bays and traverses protecting you from a flow of attack, just as a ship is protected from sinking by clever compartments.

Most of the trenches are to be a little over two feet wide, and go the appropriate depth of six feet under, making many men feel like they are fighting from their own graves – and many are right.

•

To judge from the shrapnel still falling all around on this morning of 26 April, the endless cracks of rifles and clatter of machine guns coming from on high as the invaders try to hold their ragged line atop the ridges of the first range of hills . . . things have little improved overnight.

And yet?

And yet, tragically, the killing is far from done.

At mid-morning Jacka is standing on the shore with the rest of the advance party, ready to help the rest of the 14th Battalion alight with their gear. For every boat coming their way with the fresh troops, there are yet more heading out loaded with wounded – scores of them – and every shell-burst continues to bring showers of shrapnel, though mercifully most of it is bursting too high or too wide to do damage.

But oh, the terror!

'I heard *zzz-zzz-zzz* over my head!' one Digger will describe the experience. 'Oh God, I thought, that's bullets. They were bullets all right.'[35]

And now, in the leading boat Jacka spies one of D Company's favourites, Sergeant William Patrick Murphy of Warracknabeal, a jolly old soul with the Royal Naval Air Service at Great Yarmouth before arriving in Australia and soon joining the AIF. Alas, from somewhere on high behind Jacka, a Turkish sharp-shooter has lined him up and pulled the trigger. Before Jacka's very eyes, a red splotch appears on Murph's chest, and he drops like a sack of spuds right into crystal-clear water.

'First man killed,'[36] the Wedderburn man will regretfully note in his diary.

Most of the battalion will spend the day on the beach in reserve, getting as close to the shelter of the cliffs as they can, all while organising themselves back into companies, platoons and sections. By lunch-time the 14th Battalion has 928 men on shore.

The arrival of Colonel Monash on shore helps impose more order among the men of the wider 4th Brigade and Jacka is soon back with his own battalion bivouacking on the beach until such time as they are called into action.

•

Now this is the army all over. On paper, everything is so organised.

You, Albert Jacka, are a Lance Corporal in D Company of the 14th Battalion of the 4th Brigade, which is part of the Australian and New Zealand Division, which is in turn part of the Australian and New Zealand Army Corps.

All is structured, and your every action is ordained or ordered.

But here on the ground, in the middle of a battle, fighting for your life?

Things are not so organised.

On 27 April, just two days after landing, the 14th Battalion has been pulled out of reserve and assigned to the front lines of the ground gained. It proves to be at the apex of the ridge that borders the northern end of freshly christened Monash Valley. In the time since the landing, the Australians who have advanced this far, and lived, have done exactly what Hamilton had suggested they do – which was to 'dig, dig, dig' – all with such enthusiasm that as a breed they are well on their way to becoming known as 'Diggers'.

Many of those first ones – the men of Australia's 11th Battalion who had stormed this position and held it for two days – now lie dead at their feet and Jacka and the 14th must take over their nascent trenches, to dig deeper, and hold back the hordes of Turks coming their way.

As Jacka climbs up what is already known as 'Shrapnel Gully', all around him are dead men, dying men, moaning men and the quiet ones, with not long to live. Those who are judged as still a chance of living are loaded onto donkeys, their blood covering the little beasts' flanks, and led back towards the beach. Machine guns are chattering, bombs are exploding, and a quick glance over the parapet reveals masses of extraordinarily brave Turkish soldiers coming their way. They are doing so, seriously, to the tune of endless bugles.

'Some say,' one soldier will recount, 'that "morse calls" were being blown on it, at all events the sound which travelled rapidly about was eerie in the extreme.'[37]

While Jacka and most of the soldiers of the 14th fire at them, others keep digging. Every shovelful they put on the parapet makes them all just that bit safer, as a labyrinthine series of trenches continues to expand all around the position of their landing. (Yes, this whole exercise had been designed to get *away* from the trench warfare of the Western Front, where so many had been killed, but the truth of it is that when both you and your enemy have machine guns and are close to each other, the same imperative applies: DIG.)

The 4th Brigade is now holding a series of 'posts' – distinctive defensive positions, all linked to each other by trenches – named for the 4th Brigade commanders whose responsibility they are, ergo 'Pope's Hill', 'Quinn's Post', 'Courtney's Post' and 'Steele's Post'. Nearly all of them are so close to the opposing Turkish trenches that the two groups of soldiers can hear each other – and the Turks can lob small bombs on the Diggers. (The Australians don't have any yet.)

In all the chaos, confusion and catastrophe, Albert Jacka remains remarkably at peace. Somehow, despite only having had eight weeks of military training at Broadmeadows Camp outside Melbourne once the war had broken out, followed by a little learning on the ship on the way over and nine weeks training around the Pyramids, he instinctively *knows* what to do. No matter that all around him, fellow soldiers are falling from Turkish snipers positioned *they know not where*, even as there is a regular shrill shrieking getting ever louder before there is an explosion somewhere near generating a billowing cloud of dust and scything shrapnel which you can only survive if it hits one of your mates first. Everywhere you look, men gurgle and die, as the blizzard of bullets grows thicker.

Others survive against all odds and some of them cover themselves in glory. A little further over from the 14th's position in the freshly dug trenches of Courtney's Post, two of the Maxim gunners of the 16th Battalion – Private Harry Murray and Lance Corporal Percy Black – have been able to keep the surging Turks back by keeping constant fire on their snipers and machine-gunner. The two had never met before joining up six months before, but now work like twins, Black firing, while Murray – who had signed his enlistment papers under occupation as 'Bushman', meaning there is no problem so great that enough elbow grease and fencing wire can't fix it – feeds the belt in. The fact that both men are in their mid-thirties, while most of their comrades are a good decade and a half younger, makes them natural partners.

The Turks, inevitably, bring heavy fire back on them, but despite Black being shot through the ear and hand, and bullets hitting the Maxim, still they keep going!

'It was an inspiration to watch the fight that gallant fellow put up,'[38] Murray will note of his mate. Black returns the admiration in kind. When, after the intensity of the battle and 24 hours with no sleep, Murray starts to nod off, Black presses some rum on him. Murray declines at first, as he is a teetotaller. But Black insists, Murray swigs and . . . *in vino veritas*. Before, Murray had wanted to fight the Turks. Now, he insists on it, climbing out of the trench to take down a *shniper thatsh been giving him the shits!* Black grabs him by the collar and hauls him back down before disaster.

Meanwhile, some of the unluckiest of the Australian soldiers are wounded in such a manner – a bullet through the stomach or the chest – that though they cannot live, nor can they die quickly. Some plead with comrades to kill them, to end it, or at least pass them a rifle or pistol so they can do it themselves. If not obliged they just lie there in an expanding pool of their own rapidly congealing blood, emitting an oddly sickly sweet smell.

At one point while under severe fire, one of their officers, Captain Bill Hoggart – a married 38-year-old who only nine months before had been a teacher at Melbourne Grammar School, telling the class to turn to page 54 of their Cadet Corps textbook – dares to stand up to get a better bead on where the Turks are situated. He is one of Victoria's finest marksmen, and is confident he can shoot many Tur—

He is instantly struck down, riddled by no fewer than eight bullets from a machine gun.

'He had his usual smile on his lips when they buried him after the fight,'[39] one of the Diggers will recall.

Another time, Lance Corporal Bill Howard of A Company is with 60 of his brethren, waiting to replace those in the front line, when Lieutenant Keith Wallace Crabbe – a clerk from St Kilda – interrupts the anxious conversation he is having with the red-headed bloke next to him to ask Howard to escort one of the soldiers who has been wounded back to a Regimental Aid Post.

'I did so,' Howard will recount, 'and during my absence a machine gun was trained on the position; and the result was that the whole of the 60 were either killed or wounded.'[40]

Christ Almighty. And the red-headed bloke he'd been talking to, just minutes before? His dead body, missing part of the head, is being 'rolled out of the trenches',[41] before Howard's very eyes, right now. After all, it is no use in the trench, and can now form part of the parapet.

Amid the shrieks and death-rattles, one man is seen to take quick action. It is Lance Corporal Albert Jacka, who gathers some fellow soldiers and manages to outflank the Turkish gun crew, and get close enough to hurl some jam-tin bombs at them, which destroys the threat for the moment.

('Jam-tin bombs'? Yes, in a superb bit of innovation that Jacka has enthusiastically embraced, the Australians, lacking handy little bombs like the Turks boast, have taken to filling empty jam-tins and cans of bully beef with explosive, before squeezing in old cartridge cases, bits of barbed wire and scrap metal, and even pebbles. Now add a short fuse, and who's your uncle? Bob is. With a ciggie in your mouth, you have a few seconds after lighting the bastard before it explodes and the dinkum skill is to time your throw so it explodes either just as it lands, or, even better, just above the lot of 'em.)

Dig, dig, dig!

Still, 'Jacko' – as the Australians often refer to the Turks, when not calling him 'Abdul' – keeps coming, keeps attacking, firing shells and bullets and hurling bombs at the attackers, even through the nights – though, strangely, it is not the prospect of imminent death that most troubles Jacka, as he records in his diary: 'Having hard time in the trenches. Terribly cold at nights, without overcoats or blankets of any description.'[42]

Mercifully, after two solid days of fighting in the front-line trenches, the 14th Battalion are given some respite, only to find themselves back there two days later again – 'Going into trenches tonight to relieve the 13th Bn'[43] – where the situation is still ... fluid. By now the Turkish reinforcements have arrived in full, and are hurling themselves in wave after wave against the positions of the Anzacs – which has become the acronym of choice to describe the Australian and New Zealand Army Corps.

Every hour of every day is still filled with life-and-death battles which sees battle teetering every which way – and Albert Jacka is nothing if not busy. While the 14th Battalion is atop one ridge, another one lies some 500 yards further inland. From just behind this the Turks have their artillery set up, and are shelling the Anzac positions, to give their men some cover.

'As the Turks came in open order across the little plain at the foot of the hills, we potted them with machine guns,' Jacka will recount. 'Those who got across attained safety in the "dead" ground under our own hill, and there got ready to storm our position.'[44]

Right beside Jacka at Courtney's Post on the high point of the ridge from the 14th Battalion machine-gun section is Lieutenant John Rutland, who is firing his Maxim gun at the Turks as they continue to advance in short bursts. Yes, many of them go down, but there are still so many, they just keep coming. And wouldn't you know it?

Right when they are just 50 yards away, Rutland's Maxim gun jams.[45]

'No-one could have blamed Rutland had he thrown the useless thing down,' Jacka will recount. 'The Turks were shelling his position from the next ridge, and he was defenceless against the advance.'[46]

But Rutland does not do that.

In an act of bravery that Jacka will never forget, and will often cite as the bravest thing he saw, Rutland just *gets on with it*, doing what needs to be done, regardless. Coolly, his tongue poking out one side of his mouth – the way some do when they must concentrate on a difficult task – he pulls the gun to pieces, cleaning what he can, before re-assembling and rattling off more bursts of deadly fire against the Turks who approach. They fall dead before him, leaving their yelling German officer to continue the charge, a ragged remnant behind him. The German lunges for Rutland now, his sword raised and now rending the air with a massive swipe that just misses ... even as the German now falls. A second later Turkish bullets from the remnant pour into Rutland and he drops to the dirt, dead.

One Turk actually gets close enough to Jacka that he is able to deal with him with his bayonet, but finally the attack is beaten off ... at least for the moment.

But how long can it be before one of these endless Turkish waves crashing on their shores bursts over the top and into the Allied trenches?

'In the trenches. Hardest fighting we have had yet,' Jacka records in his diary on 1 May. 'Turks making great attack on our trenches. They are brave, but are going to certain death. Mowing them down in hundreds.'[47]

Alas, there are *thousands* more that just keep coming, and it can only be a matter of time.

'9 pm. Battle has been won by us. Can hear Turks out in front collecting their wounded.'[48]

•

The strange thing?

Jacka is growing, both in his own estimation, and that of his fellow Diggers. While some men placed on the Dardanelles are like fish on the sand, Jacka is like a bird who has just found the sky; a man in his element. It is strange indeed to feel comfortable in such a ghastly environment, but somehow, that is him. Moreover, his is a purposeful poise that settles and inspires his comrades. To have a man beside you who is perpetually stoical, no matter how extreme the situation, is a precious thing and the regard in which this quiet wood-chopper is held grows accordingly.

And so it goes on, as the 14th Battalion fights for its life, trying to hold on to its section of ridge as its four companies are constantly rotated through front-line trench duty.

Jacka's D Company has been holding on through the daylight hours and, as the sun sets, gives way to the relieving A Company. Exhausted, Jacka and his brethren make their way back to their support trenches, where some cavities dug into the walls and the floors will have to serve as a place to drop their kit, wolf down their iron rations, and get some scattered sleep.

The following morning at dawn Jacka is fast asleep when he awakes to the sound – *good morning* – of a whistling, getting so loud it becomes a screeching and now, squealing.

Is this it?

He has had near misses before with Turkish shells, and knows that the higher the pitch, the closer it is. This one is the highest pitch he has heard and he involuntarily flexes his whole body, as if that might save him.

The shell explodes just above his trench, sending out shrapnel in all directions. From the heavens and heading straight to hell, two large pieces of shrapnel – one, the nose-cap of the shell that has exploded above them – slice off the left leg of the man lying next to him, Lieutenant Quinton Smith, while badly wounding the right leg. The blood pours out of him like an open tap on full force, and it is all Jacka can do to try to get a belt around the left leg, to stem the flow.

The good lieutenant – a clerk from Essendon – dies a very short time later from loss of blood, and shock, despite Jacka's urgent ministration.

'I was unscathed,'[49] Jacka writes incredulously.

The fighting goes on, with the 14th Battalion leaching between five and ten men a day, through being killed, wounded or becoming so sick they must be evacuated. It is no easy matter to keep up to full strength of about 20 officers and 750 soldiers, but the arrival of a slew of 'reinstoushments' in early May helps. The attrition for the Turks is even worse.

By the time the 14th Battalion is withdrawn completely, the area in front of Quinn's Post has so many Turkish dead that, according to Major Charles Dare, the second-in-command of 14th Battalion, 'it looked as though a battalion was sleeping in the open'.[50]

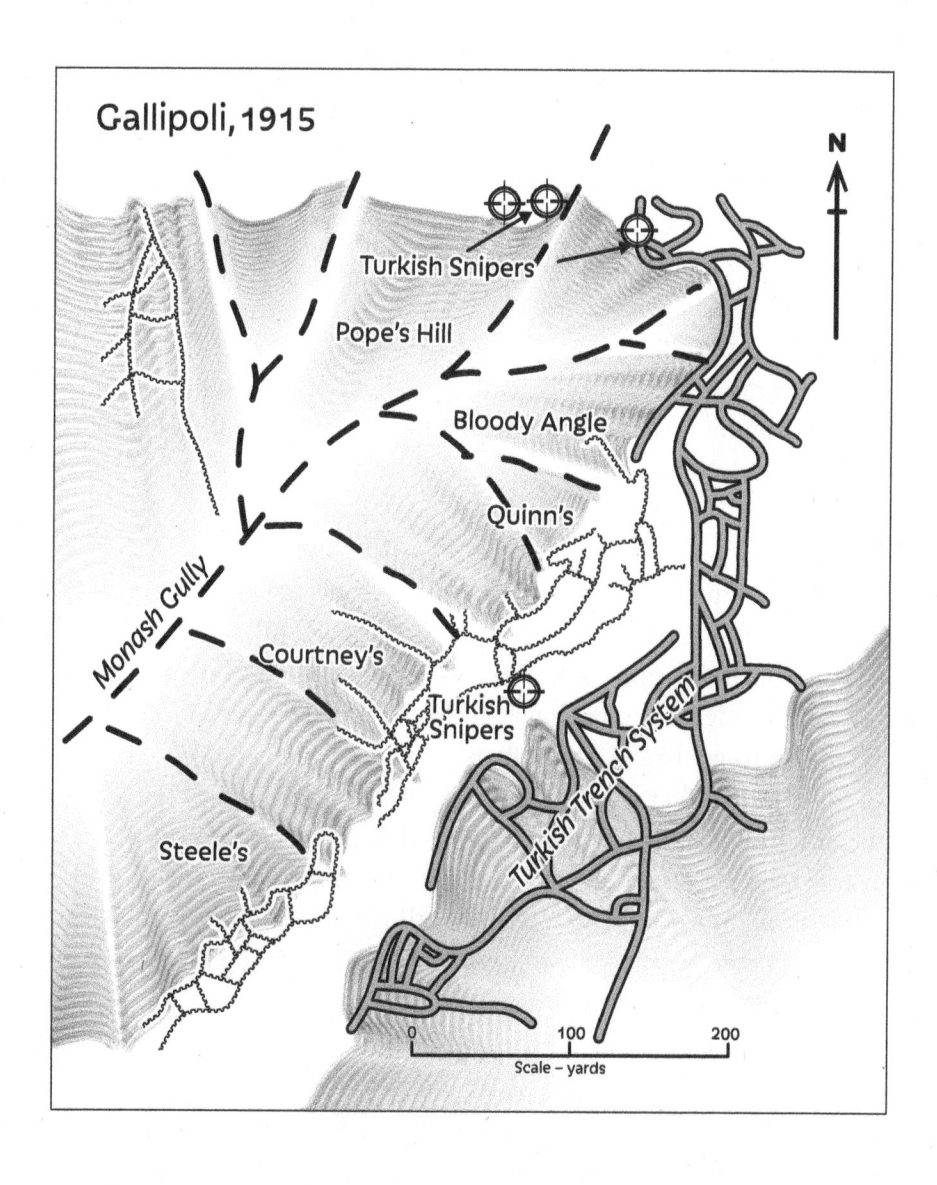

8 May 1915, from above Anzac Cove, attack of the wild Turks

Colonel Mustafa Kemal, Commander of 19th Division, is restless, roaming...

The Minister of War, General Enver, has made clear after his visit to the peninsula that nothing less than the infidel enemy being pushed off the Turkish homeland is acceptable to the government in Constantinople.

The objective aim of the attack, regardless of losses, is really quite simple, 'Attack before daybreak, drive the ANZAC troops from their trenches, and follow them down to the sea.'[51]

On 10 May, the well-trained and fresh Turkish 2nd Division arrive from Constantinople and are carefully placed in position. Now with 42,000 soldiers secretly amassed in coming days and suddenly on the charge, they should be able to dislodge the invaders, who number just a little more than 17,000. After all, they only need to break through at one strategic point, say Quinn's Post, and the rest of the Allied defences should fold in on themselves.

God help the Anzacs, because Allah won't.

It is simply a question of how long it will take to amass the required men and munitions and have them all in position. If all goes well, in about 10 days they should be ready to launch.

•

In all of Gallipoli there is neither a more likely trench to fall – nor a more crucial one to hold.

For Courtney's Post is at the crest of a ridge and on the Turkish side of the ridge is a scrubby slope that offers the best approach that Jacko has to get to the Australians.

And on the other side, the gully right behind it leads all the way to the beach! It is no exaggeration to say that if it falls, the entire Anzac grip on the peninsula risks falling with it. More than just a Turkish breakthrough, it will be practically a fall-through as there can be little to prevent them getting to the shore, completely splitting the Australian line, and the Australian forces.

•

Things are quiet.

Maybe a little *too* quiet?

In the late afternoon of 17 May, Charles Bean is down near the beach of Anzac Cove, attending the burial of Major Villers-Stuart, General Birdwood's Chief Intelligence Officer, who had died while sketching near the cove.

'It was almost too dark to see,' Bean will recount, 'the exquisite last lights of sunset were just fading over Imbros – the old volcano cone showing dark grey against them. Above, along path, mules going past in the half dark clanking. Indians leading.'

But you can *hear* that clanking. For once there is little shelling from on high, almost as if the Turks are girding their loins, and stockpiling their ammunition for a mighty push? The rest is much as usual.

'New moon hanging over Imbros. Ships out there floating like toy things on sea . . . Continual whistle of bullets overhead . . . Man passes below along beach path whistling . . . whistling stops when he heard the service. The voice of the parson, "Now the battle day is o'er, Jesus in thy gracious keeping, Leave we here thy servant sleeping."'[52]

Bean moves back to his dugout, his sense growing that things might be building to another storm. As it happens, the following morning, Bean is far from alone, and Albert Jacka is just one of many others who are suddenly wary . . .

For some reason the Turks are not firing at them today. No bullets, no booms, no constant explosions of shells all around them. You can hear the birds singing.

(Well, mostly anyway. In the mid-morning, a flock of storks is unwise enough to fly over the Australian trenches, at which point furious firing skywards breaks out. Two of the birds fall in positions where they can be recovered by the Diggers, meaning a welcome change from bully beef tonight.)

But now, the silence returns.

'The day was unusually quiet,' Bean documents. 'As quiet as a lazy holiday afternoon in summer . . .'[53]

There can be no mistake.

'Sniping almost ceased, and so quiet was the day that in the Australian and New Zealand lines it was repeatedly asked what the Turks were planning.'[54]

Visiting the 8th Light Horse Regiment HQ, one of the officers comments to Bean, 'Turks are up to some devilment, I suppose.'

When Bean in turn makes comment to Colonel White, that officer and gentleman replies:

'Yes, I wonder what it means ... General HQ sent out to say that an aeroplane had seen a division landing ... just opposite us on the Dardanelles coast this side of the Straits ... So we shall probably be attacked tonight.'[55]

Their suspicions are confirmed when a pilot of the Royal Naval Air Service flies over the peninsula at a safe height and sees 'two of the valleys east of the ANZAC line are packed with Turkish troops, densely crowded upon the sheltered slopes'.[56]

But it gets worse. For when a second plane is sent up to confirm the report, its pilot not only sees the same masses of troops, but also spots four steamers unloading even *more* soldiers on the European shore of the Dardanelles. Reports roll in throughout the day, bringing news of 'considerable bodies of mounted troops and guns'.[57] Just what on earth are the Allies about to face? Against the 17,500 men the Anzacs can muster, it looks as though there must be 40,000 of the brutes about to come at them. Can it really be that bad?[58]

They are not long in finding out.

On the Anzac perimeter, at 5 pm, the air is suddenly filled with a distant boom, closely followed by a whistling sound, before a weird screeching comes in with an ever higher crescendo and then ... a massive explosion. And then another and another and another. More shells than ever before start falling 'chiefly on the Australian line from the Pimple northwards to Courtney's'.[59] And it is not just those at Anzac Cove who can hear it.

Just after dark, it happens. Behind the Turkish trenches closest to Courtney's Post, three Turkish soldiers load a howitzer and follow their strict routine, with their Sergeant shouting '*Hazirol!* Ready,' and then '*Ates!* Fire!'

An instant later the howitzer erupts and the shell heads skywards as a searing streak of flame, before lobbing towards the Australian lines. Of course, the Turks have no idea exactly where it will land, only that it will be right among those who have been raining exactly the same kind of devastation on them.

In their trenches at Courtney's Post, the soldiers are just about to settle down for evening grub, when, even over the sound of so many other exploding shells all around, they now hear a louder whistling, getting louder still, screeching now, squealing . . . *is this it?*

Time . . . is . . . momentarily . . . sus . . . pended.

The shell explodes just a few yards from them, but not in their actual trench.

In his dugout Bean records that the sound of Turkish fire is so overwhelming, it has 'grown to a roar like that of a great stream over a precipice'.[60]

As his position is close to the signals office – the communications nerve centre for all of Anzac Cove – he heads over to seek more information. The office is doing exactly that as he arrives, checking with all the brigades and their battalions on the front line. All, bar 2nd Battalion, have reported in that, despite the unprecedented barrage, everything is under control. Bean waits, as they all do, for an operator to track the battalion down.

Soon a report comes crackling down the line.

All is 'OK'.

'Tell him I wanted to know,' Brigadier General 'Hooky' Walker says, 'whether in view of the firing there is anything to report.'[61]

'He says it's only the Turks firing.'[62]

Barely worth mentioning, when you put it like that, and it continues into the darkest hours. Just after midnight, Bean goes back to bed. But the shelling on the Australian front lines, particularly around Quinn's, Walker's and Courtney's posts, only intensifies.

In the expectation of an attack, all of the Diggers are instructed to 'Stand to arms at 3 am'[63] instead of the usual 3.30 am. Oh, and start stockpiling ammo up in the front trenches, as this might be a long night and day ahead. Lance Corporal Bill Howard is one of those from the 14th Battalion's A Company assigned to start hauling the boxes of bullets and extra rifles up the hill into the front-line trenches, where C and D Companies are holding the fort. Those in the front line are ordered to clean their rifles to prevent jamming, sharpen their bayonets and get ready.

Here we go again. The 14th Battalion had landed with 930 officers and men only a little over three weeks ago – and have already lost over 400 men to battle or sickness. It's clear to Bert Jacka that they are about to lose a whole lot more.

But the strangest thing? Despite the horror of what the men are experiencing, as the barrage still grows in intensity, more than a few soldiers are struck by the beauty of what they are witnessing.

'The scene during this shelling was a wild but beautiful sight,' one soldier will recount, 'a mass of bursting shells, our own & the Turks' & as they burst they threw out different coloured flashes, some golden, some pink, yellow, blue, dark & light red & all different shades from the different sorts of explosives they were using.'[64]

It is all more spectacular than the fireworks on Empire Day back home!

Suddenly, however, it stops and there is a strong sense that something big is about to happen.

Positions, everyone . . .

CHAPTER TWO

DEATH OR GLORY

> *He [Jacka] is a bundle of paradoxes – the state's greatest fighter yet abnormally sensitive, blunt to a degree, yet peculiarly susceptible to kindness.*[1]
>
> Official 14th Battalion historian Newton Wanliss replies to Bean,
> 5 March 1923

20 May 1915, Gallipoli, danger before dawn
Everyone ready?

Among the first wave of the four divisions of Turks readying to charge, the soldiers crouch, waiting for the moment, which is due to come at 3.30 am.

'The plan,' one of them, Kiazim Pasha, will recall, 'was to attack before day-break, drive the Anzac troops from their trenches, and follow them down to the sea.'[2]

The particular post the Turks have chosen to attack is distinctive for the fact that it lies no more than 50 yards from their own lines, with a gully behind it that goes all the way to the beach. If they can break through here, there will be little to prevent them completely smashing the entire Anzac occupation of their sacred soil.

And suddenly a piercing bugle call cleaves the night.

It is followed by the guttural cries of *'Allah! Allah! Allah!'* coming from thousands of Turks, spectres rising from the ground in front at first, and now suddenly looming large, as the first wave of soldiers rush towards the Anzac trenches ... now illuminated as the Australians send up white flares – 'Verey lights' – which adds enough strength to the tepid moonlight that they can see No Man's Land clearly and the rush of phantom figures across it.

And *now* ...

The shout goes up, the triggers are pulled, and the night is filled with the roar of dozens of machine guns and thousands of rifles, together with the boom of the mountain guns, followed by the screams and groans of instantaneously mown-down Turks.

Bizarrely, even above such uproar and such agony, the strangled sounds of Turkish bands playing martial tub-thumpers can be heard as whole lines of Turkish soldiers continue to run forward.

'Instantly across the whole [of our line],' George Mitchell of the 10th Battalion will chronicle, 'there was a leaping, flickering sheet of flame. The roar of musketry was like nothing else I ever heard.'[3]

As the attackers push forth *en masse*, it is all but impossible for the Australian defenders to fire a shot in their direction and not hit anyone.

'The firing was so furious,' the troops will record, 'that the woodwork of some rifles became almost too hot to hold.'[4]

It is slaughter, pure and simple. With such a mass of men coming at them, at such a close range, the Anzacs in the front line simply cannot miss and most bullets billet in a Turk. Soon the succeeding waves of attackers tumble over the bodies of the dead men who have gone before.

So fearful is the damage being done by the Allied front-line soldiers that those behind plead with them for a go.

'Come on down and give us a go,' they beg. 'I'm a miles better shot than you.'[5]

When that doesn't work, in one trench so crammed that not everyone could get up on the fire step, one bloke behind and below is heard to offer '5 quid to any of youse who will give me your spot'.[6]

Over at Pope's Hill, no-one is doing more devastating work than Harry Murray. With fatal accuracy he keeps pouring fire into the waves of Turks trying to charge across the short space between their own trenches and Quinn's Post, as wave after wave is simply cut down.

Observing him, his superior officer Captain John Rose will file a report to the Brigade Commander, lauding Murray's 'initiative and energy' while observing that he is 'an ideal machine-gunner and the class of man that is required to take charge of machine-gun work'.[7]

There is no doubting the courage of the Turks. It is their technique that is lacking.

'The Turks did not seem well trained,' Charles Bean chronicles. 'There was no attempt at covering fire so our men could sit right out on the traverses of the trench, or even on the parapet, and shoot for all they were worth. The Turks would lead out all along the same path, one after another – simply inviting death.'[8]

As to Allah, no-one has the least sympathy for either the deity or the men who are endlessly shouting his name, as they continue to charge forward. *'Allah! Allah! Mohammed! Allah!'*

'Yes,' an infantrymen roars, as he shoots the Turkish soldiers down, 'you can bring them along too!'[9]

It is all just 'dead easy – just like money from home'.[10]

•

Alas, over at Courtney's Post, it is a lot less like money from home – and more like some kind of insane cracker night gone wrong.

'A pall of smoke from the bursting shells continuously hangs over the gully,' one Digger records. 'There were terrific bursts of rifle fire, so loud was it that one had to yell into a man's ear to make himself audible.'[11]

For such is the sheer weight of Turkish numbers that it seems no matter how many the Diggers shoot, there are so many waves of succeeding soldiers that – just as had happened on 1 May – it is inevitable that the biggest of those waves will flood them.

Albert Jacka, like all of the Diggers, is simply stunned at the way the Turks just keep coming. And yet there are so many of them that the only thing keeping the defenders of Courtney's Post in it is the artillery fire roaring out from such enormous Allied battleships as the *Triumph*, *Queen Elizabeth*, *Prince George*, *Lord Nelson* and *Agamemnon*, which – with staggering accuracy from a distance of 4000 yards – are lobbing shells just beyond the Australian trenches, and blowing wave after wave of the Turks apart. Such shells cannot account for them all, of course, and survivors are soon getting close enough to lob bombs of their own into the defensive trenches, exacting a terrible toll.

Nearing 4 am, just as the first dull lustre of dawn is starting to illuminate the masses of dead bodies in front of the Australian trenches, it happens . . .

First their hurled bombs land, and now the Turks themselves, feet first.

Explosions, shots, yells, imprecations, unearthly shrieks and death rattles fill the night. And for the first time the Australians in the front lines of Courtney's Post can hear a foreign language – clearly Turkish – just along from them, not out front!

There has been a breach – 'Turks are in the trench!'[12] – and it must be isolated.

Nearby, Lieutenant Henry Boyle, with Lieutenant Bill Hamilton a few yards behind him, rush forth, their pistols drawn. And yet, no sooner has Boyle put his head round the corner than, as he will recount, 'I was fired on by a Turk guarding the opening about six paces away.'[13] Immediately, the mere 19-year-old officer cries out, 'They got me!'[14]

Boyle reels back, with blood streaming from his ear.

Hamilton – who hails from Bendigo, and had joined the Australian Imperial Force straight from Duntroon when the war broke out – does not hesitate. Only an hour or so ago he had commented to a friend that 'Tomorrow will be my 21st birthday, and I only hope to live long enough to enjoy it,'[15] but now he charges towards the corner to go at the Turks himself, firing his revolver twice in the gloom of the smoke and dust that fills the trench.

The Turks on the parapet fire at the flashes, and in a split instant Hamilton slumps dead, shot through the head.

Reacting quickly, and on his own initiative, D Company's Albert Jacka is the first soldier to rush forward in support, coming up the communication trench that leads to the traverse beside that part of the trench that has been over-run. Yes, he takes a chance jumping across the trench to get into the traverse, but once he is in it, he is able to fire some shots at an angle, into the wall – to indicate that if they try to come this way, they will be *shot*![16]

There had been 10 Diggers of the 14th in that section, and though Jacka calls out to them, none of them calls back. They are either dead or wounded – he can certainly hear what sounds like *Australian* groaning – and it is clear that the Turks are in occupation.

Well, let them come this way, and Jacka will blow their heads off.

Despite the momentary stand-off, the situation remains extreme.

He is one man, and the Turks must be at least half-a-dozen, but if one of them puts so much as a nose around that corner – which he can dimly see from the ethereal if wavering glow of the ongoing Verey lights, which throw endless seeping shadows – they now know he will shoot. Further back, along the trench, just south of the Turkish incursion, the two 14th Battalion machine guns keep chattering, ensuring that the waves of Turkish soldiers who keep coming are prevented from making another breakthrough.

But Jacka is now alone in protecting those machine-gunners from the Turks on their left flank, and in preventing the breach from widening further. Even as he gathers up all the .303s of his mates that he can – ready for a donnybrook to beat them all, resolute that no Turks will get past him – he knows he needs help, and shouts, 'Officer wanted on the left!'[17]

The shout is passed on, and reaches 14th Battalion HQ just back from Courtney's Post, and right beside Monash's 4th Brigade HQ.

The Commander of A Company of the 14th Battalion, Major Robert Rankine, sends one of his best officers, Lieutenant Keith George Wallace-Crabbe (known as Lieutenant Wallace Crabbe, because the army doesn't like hyphens, unless with *very* senior officers) to investigate. Crabbe, already familiar with the situation as he has been in charge of the A Company party assigned to bring fresh munitions forward to D Company in the front lines, does not hesitate and moves quickly towards the firing and screams. The first thing he sees is Lieutenant Bill Hamilton, who he'd been chatting to only a short time before, slumped like a discarded doll, with his back to the trench wall, dead.

And there is Jacka ahead, crouching behind the traverse in the firing line. Well, that is one good thing. On the field, Jacka is the man most likely to lead a charge, and off the field a man quite likely to get one. For, yes, Jacka can be a bit rough around the edges – and only a couple of months before Sergeant Jim Cowey had charged him *twice* in a single day for insolence – but it is already obvious that he is a hell of a soldier, and never better than when under heavy fire.

For Jacka's part, he feels both great relief at the sight of Crabbe coming his way down the communication trench – and alarm, shouting: 'Look out, sir! Turks are in there!'[18]

'What's the situation?' Crabbe yells back.

'I am the only one left in the trench. The others have been [knocked out] by the bombs the enemy threw before rushing this section of the trench. I've been holding the Turks back from advancing further into our trenches for a quarter of an hour.'[19]

'If you are given support,' Crabbe shouts to Jacka over the continuing cacophony of fire, exploding grenades and shrieking men, 'will you charge the Turks?'[20]

'YES! I want two or three.'[21]

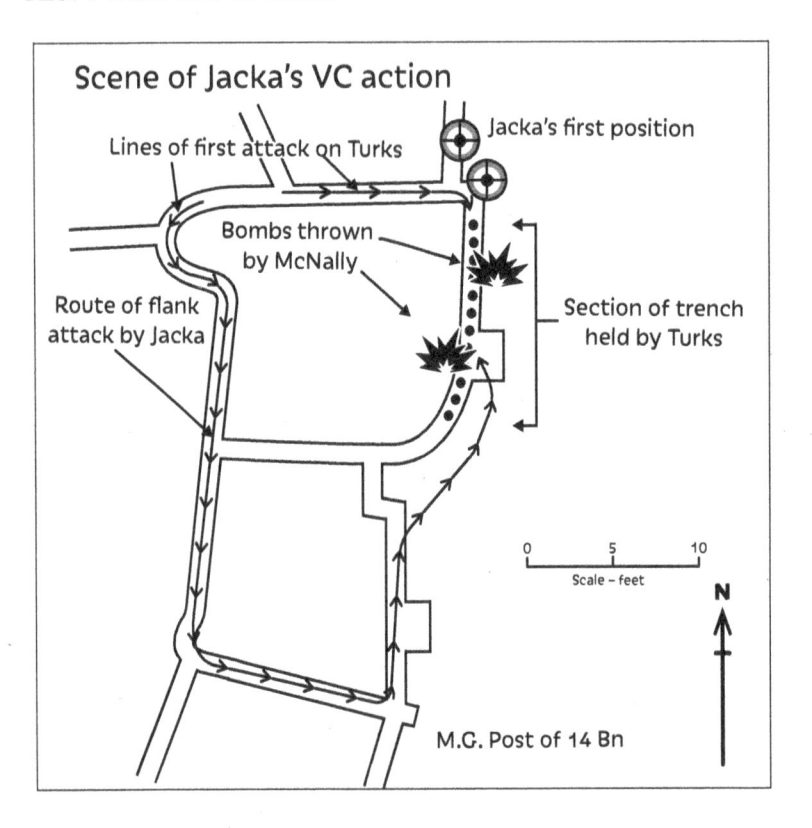

Scene of Jacka's VC action

- Jacka's first position
- Lines of first attack on Turks
- Bombs thrown by McNally
- Route of flank attack by Jacka
- Section of trench held by Turks
- M.G. Post of 14 Bn
- Scale – feet (0, 5, 10)
- N

Jacka must hold on till they get here, and with a deathly calm that surprises even him – a man never knows how he will go until an actual crisis hits, but the Victorian is pleased at his own reaction, feeling on top of it – he continues to keep the Turks in the next bay pinned down, firing at the first sign of any rifle appearing around the corner. For good measure, he thuds irregularly timed bullets into the trench wall beyond the corner, so that the Turks know that the first man who attempts to make a rush on him risks collecting one of those bullets. No, he can't kill them all, but he will certainly kill the first one or two if they rush him.

Back, you bastards! BACK, I say!

The other end of the Turkish breakthrough is equally blocked by an Australian communications trench that leads into the traverse on the right, and another group of the 14th Battalion is regularly firing down it, as warning that any Turk who tries to jump across will cop it.

•

In his 4th Brigade HQ, which is situated in a dugout very close to where the Turkish incursion has occurred, John Monash remains stoical, monitoring the reports coming in, and for the most part allowing his senior staff to compose the orders going out – only intervening sometimes.

'You will scarcely believe it,' Monash will write to his wife, 'but I read the greater part of [your letters] during a severe battle. The firing line at one point was not more than 100 yds from Head Quarters, and I just kept reading my letters in the intervals between the long streams of inward and outward despatches, orderlies and messengers . . .'[22]

It is Monash at his best. Project calm at all times. He has confidence in his officers, and in his men. They will stay on top of this, and the worst thing he could do would be to show panic, which would inevitably infect his whole brigade.

•

Hurrying back to one of the support trenches, Crabbe asks for volunteers from A Company to come and help Jacka.

'Will you back Jacka up?' he calls over the ferocious fire of the machine guns and constant explosions, before adding unnecessarily, 'It's a tough job.'

Three hands immediately go up, all of them mates from around Bendigo: Lance Corporal Stephen De Arango, Lance Corporal Bill Howard and Private Frank Poliness. Since their first days leaving Bendigo, the three have taken a vow to stick tight to each other come what may – from brothers in farms, to brothers in arms – and have stuck to it through Broadmeadows, Cairo and Gallipoli. So naturally they are side by side, now, and volunteer together.

'It's sink or swim,' Lance Corporal De Arango says on behalf of them all. 'We will come, sir.'[23]

Excellent. (And it is typical of De Arango. At six foot one he is likely the tallest man in the battalion, with only the former Carlton star, Lieutenant Alf 'Lofty' Williamson, able to argue the toss with him, and he and his mates are always happy to volunteer for anything.)

They now hurry back down the communication trench, where, hopefully, Jacka is still holding the fort. Crabbe is all but certain he will be. Of all the men in his command, Crabbe could not have hoped to be relying on a better soldier than Jacka.

As they come towards him down the communication trench, Jacka is delighted to see they are three men he knows well, from his own neck of the woods, not far from Wedderburn.

'Hello, Bendigo!' he sings out. 'Will you follow me?'

'Yes!' Bill Howard calls back.

And ... now!

Alas, though Poliness manages to leap across the gap to join Jacka in his traverse, on the very instant that Lance Corporal Howard follows him, a shot rings out, and the Bendigo man is first struck in the left side with 'an explosive bullet, fired at close range',[24] and another bullet shatters his right hand. As he goes down hard, Jacka and Poliness are at least able to grab the groaning, bleeding man, and drag him to safety, back into the communications trench, where it is time to regroup around Lieutenant Crabbe, who has just come up with another soldier, Private James McNally.

Jacka and Lieutenant Crabbe must decide on a new plan, their faces illuminated by the flickering light of exploding shells, their voices having to shout above the continuing roar. Charles Bean will later say of Jacka that he was 'strong, completely confident, entirely fearless, bluntly outspoken, not given to hiding his light under a bushel ... '[25] and this is just such an occasion.

For, though of lower rank, it is Jacka who comes up with a plan that no senior officer would dare to suggest in the first place.

Here is what we are going to do Lieutenant. You and the other three can stay here to hold off any further advance down this trench, before feinting an attack from here minutes later to make them convinced that the danger to them is from this end. Meanwhile, I will run down through the maze of trenches until I am coming at the Turks from the other side. And then you blokes must lob some bombs on their noggins, and in the confusion, I will go at them.

Crabbe looks at him with wonderment. For one thing, their entire allocation of the precious jam-tin bombs now being manufactured in a veritable factory down on Anzac Beach comes to just . . . two. But that is the least of it.

For there are plans, there are daring plans, and there are insane plans. Prima facie this one looks to be well north of them all. But what choice do they have? In the extremity of their situation, *something* has to be done, for the worst of all possible things would be for the Turks to consolidate this breach and be joined by other Turks who would push through – in which case all would be lost. So, if Jacka is happy to have a go at this – in all likelihood sacrificing his life – though it is unlikely to work, it might at least take out a few Turks and delay their consolidation.

So, yes, go, Jacka, and let's give this a crack.

In an instant, the 22-year-old – who this time last year had never even seen a bayonet – is gone, haring down the trenches. Always remarkably light on his feet – for while running he moves like a cat in that last burst before pouncing on a bird – Jacka races past the wounded and groaning Howard, who is being tended by another soldier, trying to keep him alive. He continues to scramble along another of the communication trenches, before turning left. And now, very carefully, risking being shot at any moment, Jacka climbs out of the trench and pads over No Man's Land, lying low and waiting momentarily for what he knows is about to come.

•

A minute after Jacka has left, Crabbe nods to Private James McNally, judged to be the best and most accurate thrower among them. Carefully, McNally examines the fuse on the jam-tin bomb, estimating how long before it will burst, lights the fuse with his Woodbine, swings his arm back, holds it there for a few seconds until the fuse is halfway down, with just a few instants until explosion and ... chucks it towards a point where he hopes it will land right on the Turks' noggins.

At this instant Lance Corporal De Arango fires his .303 into the wall to make the Turks think the attack is coming from this way.

And now, 10 seconds after McNally has thrown the first bomb, he hurls the second one.

There is just enough light for Jacka to note that the first one has missed completely, cannoning off in the wrong direction – at least well away from him – before exploding.

The second one nearly misses, too, but at least lands on the parapet above the Turks before exploding, sending a shower of rubble upon them, mixed with a massive cloud of dust.

NOW!

Lieutenant Crabbe has been listening closely.

After the first explosion, there had been nothing different particularly.

After the second one, however, they can hear the screams: the sound of a continuing furious struggle, with several shouts, lots of guttural cries, and many screams. It can only be ... Jacka.

•

Jacka has jumped down *behind* the survivors. After emptying the 10-round magazine of his .303 bolt action rifle into the staggering smoky figures – his right hand a blur of movement as he first pulls the trigger to fire, then pulls back and pushes forward the bolt to eject the used round and put another round in the chamber, before repeating half-a-dozen times – he wades into those still standing to become a whirling dervish with the bayonet. Alternating between using the tip of his bayonet to knock theirs out of the way, and thrusting it forward to stab them, Jacka rips and tears, parries and thrusts, all the while expertly dodging their attempts to get *him*. Jacka is no more than five foot six inches in thick socks. But, as one who had spent years with axe in hand as a forestry worker and competing on the weekends in long-distance amateur cycling races all around Wedderburn and Ballarat, he is powerful in his upper body, strong in his legs and with such excellent lungs his chest expands by two inches with a deep breath. If you had to design a soldier built for blinding bayonet speed, and being able to maintain it, he would look exactly like . . .

Jacka!

Turk after Turk after Turk goes down . . . .

When two try to get away, by climbing up and over the parapet, they are shot by Private Poliness, who has himself carefully got his .303 just enough out of the trenches for this very contingency. Another three give up the ghost and lift their arms in the internationally recognised signal for 'We are *done*.'

•

And now, though the sounds of the rest of the battle go on, with ongoing whirr of machine guns, shells exploding and distant yells, it is clear that whatever has happened in the battle close at hand is over, at least for the moment.

After 15 minutes, just to be sure, with infinite caution Crabbe draws his pistol and ventures forward. With the first glimmers of the actual dawn appearing, he puts his head around the corner of the trench.

'The trench was in a terrible state,' Crabbe will recount, 'literally filled with dead, and the Turks were lying on top of our boys who had been killed by the bombs the Turks threw before rushing.'[26]

And there is Jacka, completely unharmed, surrounded by seven dead Turks. Five have been killed by his shots, two by the bayonet.

The face of the Victorian is flushed, with an unlit cigarette dangling from the corner of his mouth and, impossibly, not falling. He has his .303 – with the bloody bayonet still attached – trained on three terrified Turkish prisoners whose shaking hands are in the air.

'Well, I managed to get the buggers, sir,'[27] he says, simply nodding towards the earthly remains of what had represented the biggest threat to the Anzacs since the beginning of the Gallipoli landing.

'I am going to recommend you [for a medal],'[28] the stunned Lieutenant Crabbe replies.

Elsewhere, the furious battle goes on, as the Australians keep firing at the oncoming Turks, working the bolts of their rifles as fast as they can, while other lads feed endless canvas belts of bullets into the frenzied machine guns.

For no less than an hour the waves of Turks keep coming, only to fall before the withering fire.

In the words of one Australian soldier, 'It was like shooting rabbits coming out of a warren, they were just about as helpless. The chaps almost quarrelled with one another for the right to stand on the platforms so as they could get a good cut at them.'[29]

'*Saida*, goodbye,' one Digger yells as he dispatches yet one more Turk. 'Play you again next Saturday!'[30]

At last, with the coming of the first glow of dawn, the tide turns. Instead of rushing forward, the Turks begin to rush back to their own trenches, pursued by a furious fusillade of fire all the way.

And what is this? From out of the Turkish trenches leaps a Muhammadan priest, 'his white robes flying in the gentle breeze, calling on his men to charge in the name of *Allah*'.[31]

No doubt this fellow is big on religious ceremony. But at least one Australian soldier does not stand on any ceremony at all, and simply lines him up and pulls the trigger, dropping him immediately. Still, one of the Diggers would report, 'he was a brave man and rose twice only to go down each time'.[32]

Rising summer, 1915, Gallipoli, live legend

That's him.

That's Jacka.

Have you heard what he did in the wee hours?

Took on an entire Turkish platoon, they reckon, and bested the lot of 'em!

Look, for one with such a legendary status, up close there doesn't seem to be much to him bar muscle, gristle, bone and remarkably blue eyes – but he dinkum did it.

When a dozen Turks came over the top of Courtney's Post and killed the Diggers there, there was only one man left standing, which was Jacka, and he ended up taking on the lot of them and killing at least half-a-dozen!

As the exhausted Jacka makes his way back from the front line in the mid-morning, it is inevitable that he is being pointed out by the other soldiers. For already his exploit has become famous, and not only is everyone appreciative – he very well might have saved the lot of us – but they are proud to have one like him among their number. If there is any justice in the world, he will be pulled out of the line and given a very big rest.

As it happens, however, Jacka has many things to do before resting, the first of which is to check on Lance Corporal Bill Howard, who had taken two bullets while trying to come to his aid. He finds him, alive, and groaning, in the Regimental Aid Post just a little way down the gully from Courtney's Post. Mercifully, the explosive bullet that would have killed him outright has first exploded against the diary he carried in his pocket.

Doctors with blood all over their khaki smocks are conducting triage on the latest batch of wounded to come in, but their work on Howard is complete and the two are briefly able to converse before the badly wounded Digger is carried down to the shore, to be transported to the hospital at Lemnos.

'I heard about what you did,' Howard groans. 'How could you *do* that?'

'I think I lost my nut,'[33] Jacka replies.

It is nigh on noon before Jacka can get back to his dugout for some precious rest, before going back into the line. Before turning in, the hands that just killed seven men carefully take out a spotless diary and grip a pen to dash off the happenings of the day. Without thought, just memory, his right hand now flies across the page to record in simple, modest prose . . . 'Great battle at 3 am. Turks captured large portion of our trench. D. Coy called into the frontline. Lieut. Hamilton shot dead. I led a section of men and recaptured the trench. I bayoneted two Turks, shot five, took three prisoners and cleared the whole trench. I held the trench alone for 15 minutes against a heavy attack. Lieut. Crabbe informed me that I would be recommended.'[34]

And so for some shut-eye.

But sleep will be some time in coming.

Has all that really just happened? Has he killed seven men, in the space of a minute? And somehow he's still *here*? Visions keep coming back. Their faces. Their shock. Their agony. And he can still hear their screams, no matter how many shells land close, how much the machine guns continue to clatter from both sides. He can still feel that sickening sponginess as he had to walk over two layers of bodies, Australians and Turks, to get out of the trench.

Sleep finally comes.

But late that afternoon, the blue-eyed Digger making his way back to the newly reinforced Courtney's Post is . . . Albert Jacka.

•

It will later be calculated that the Australians had shot out nearly a million rounds of ammunition to stop the charging Turks, which had killed some 7000, and likely wounded twice as many. Most of those dead, mixed with many Australian dead from previous weeks' battles, were still lying out in No Man's Land – together with those who were wounded and had not been able to crawl away.

'The bodies of Turks were lying in heaps,' the Official History of the 14th Battalion will record, 'and the sufferings of the wounded must have been appalling.'

The Australians cannot help but feel for their 'enemies'.

'Doubtless, in the main, our opponents were rough and illiterate men, but they had fought like heroes and given their lives freely in defence of their country.'[35]

But what now?

It is a delegation of Turks coming forward across No Man's Land, under a white flag.

They wish, Albert Jacka records, to arrange, 'an armistice for them to bury their dead from yesterday's battle'.[36]

Five days later, a miraculous if momentary peace breaks out.

At 7.30 am, an amazing silence falls, and for the first time the soldiers can hear the Aegean Sea lulling its way to shore, a sweet ancient sound unbroken by shells or shot.

And now officers with white flags, soon accompanied by their men, rise from the ground and walk to greet each other; No Man's Land now for all men. For Albert Jacka it is an extraordinary thing to be face to face with men whom minutes before you were trying to kill.

This is Jacko? Jacko, *this* is Jacka. And handshakes and foreign pleasantries are exchanged with smiles.

Some Turkish soldiers hoot in laughter as the Australians hold up cigarettes and call out '*Baksheesh!*'[37] Yes, they've learnt that word! Time for the Turks to learn one of theirs.

'One of the first words they taught us,' one Turkish officer will recount, 'was "ANZAC", which was the name given to their group of soldiers.'

'Are you English?' one Turkish soldier asks.

'No, we aren't English. We are Australian and New Zealanders . . .'

'Why are you in this war?'

'The English are our brothers.'[38]

The Anzacs rip buttons and badges off their uniforms and hand them to the Turks, who in turn give them coins and buttons, chocolates and sweets. Turkish delights. *Don't mind if we do.*

For Jacka, as for all the Australians, it is an interlude that will always be treasured.

But now to the task at hand. For the rest of the day, both sides bury their dead.

The bodies that have been lying there for four weeks are the worst, as they are black and bloated and mostly only identifiable by the identification discs around their necks. But at least that lack of identification helps to hide the horror of what you are doing.

Captain Reverend Andrew Gillison is one of those who is frantic all day, providing as Christian a burial as he can for those shoved beneath the sod.

'I never beheld such a sickening sight in my life,' he records in his diary, 'and hope it may not be my lot again.'[39]

When it comes to the more recent corpses, there is no hiding it. These are men – *mates*, who you'd often known for months, who you'd joined up with, trained with, travelled with and fought alongside. And many a man is seen to weep as he finds a beloved friend, a brother, a brother in arms, who he had last seen charging forward only to finish here, with an agonised expression on what remains of his face – his death grimace. There is no time for the smoothing comforts of undertakers at the front; you are buried as you died, unvarnished and terribly true.

On their side, the Turks are doing it even tougher. To begin with, there are so many more of their dead. In the translated words of a Turkish captain, 'At this spectacle even the most gentle must feel savage, and the most savage must weep.'[40]

By late afternoon it is mostly done, and by 4.17 pm the white flag men are retired, after first shaking hands with their counterparts. 'Goodbye, old chap; good luck!'

'*Oghur Ola gule gule gedejekseniz, gule gule gelejekseniz*,'[41] the Turks reply. 'Smiling may you go and smiling come again.'[42]

It is with some regret, then, that the two sides take their leave of each other, shaking hands and waving goodbye as, one by one, they climb back into their trenches, all on the strict understanding that it would be 25 minutes before the battle would begin again.

A strange kind of hush now falls over Anzac Cove.

At 4.45 pm, a single shot rings out, followed shortly afterwards by another, and then a burst of a machine gun, and then another, and then a bomb explodes.

It is on again.

•

Just a few days after the truce, something sails from the Turkish trenches to land just beyond the Australian parapet.

GET DOWN!

From long experience, the Australian soldiers know that it is most likely some kind of bomb . . . and yet . . . strangely, there is no explosion. Very carefully, the sergeant closest to it takes a close look through his telescope. It seems to be . . . some kind of . . . package?

Waving hands now appear from the Turkish trenches, and a grinning head appears.

It seems the Turks are inviting them to have a closer look at the package?

Suddenly, even before the sergeant can give permission, the soldier next to him has jumped over the parapet, round the rolls of barbed wire and has darted out to bring back the packet.

No shot is fired. Just grinning Turks, waving. *Go on, you Australians, open it!*

Oh so carefully, the soldier does exactly that, as his mates crowd around.

Inside is a small packet of cigarettes, together with a pencilled note, scrawled in bad French:

A Notre Herox Ennemis [43]

For their part the Diggers have enough schoolboy French between them to translate: 'To our heroic enemies'.

Who would have thought it? Those kind bastards! And a quick smoke reveals them to be slightly better than the 'Camel dung' cigarettes, as the Anzacs called them, they'd been reduced to smoking in Cairo.

What can the Diggers send them back in return? Perhaps a couple of cans of bully beef?

And so the two cans go sailing over the parapets and are quickly gathered up by the Turkish soldiers. What, the Diggers wonder, will they make of it?

It does not take long before they have an answer.

For now comes another message from the Turks wrapped around a stone:

Bully beef non [44]

No to the awful bully beef. Do the Australians have anything else? And so now the Diggers throw some sweet biscuits and a tin of jam, which are soon replied to with more cigarettes, with more kind notes.

Notre Cher Enemi. Our dear enemy.

Femez A Vee Plessir. Take at your pleasure.

Finally, though, after 45 minutes of such pleasantries, it is time for the day's work to begin – trying to kill each other – and after one of them waves with both hands and shouts '*Finis!*' they get back to it. *Fire!*

•

As Charles Bean will note, the Diggers of Gallipoli take an altogether unusual approach to their Generals, and while they know they're meant to salute whenever they see them, and all that malarkey, in the intensity of fighting for their lives on the front lines, not only do they often forget, but so too is it usually forgiven.

'The Generals and General Bridges used to have a guard, by name Bill, when they went around the trenches,' Bean documents. 'Bill was from Sydney and in one of the trenches he met a Sydney friend. "'Allo, Bill," he said, "who's yer prisoners?" Another batch of men saw the Generals (Walker, Bridges and Birdwood) coming along. "Say, Jim," he was heard to say to his chums, "better put a guard over the biscuits; here's three bloody generals."'[45]

As a breed, the Diggers generally have little time for their superior officers, with the notable exception of John Monash. From the beginning, he has demonstrated notable care of the men, is not pompous in his way of dealing with them, and they respect him in turn.

'As a soldier,' Jacka will later say of Monash, 'he's like one of ourselves, and doesn't like swank.'[46]

Monash seeks Lance Corporal Jacka out to personally congratulate him for his heroics, and to obtain some detail on exactly what occurred. It is the first time that Monash has had more than glancing acquaintance with this extraordinary soldier, and he is nothing if not impressed.

There is a way Jacka carries himself, a self-containment, an assurance, together with an obvious power in his compact body that begets confidence. Nothing is more important than having soldiers in the trenches who make the soldiers around them *believe* that the battle can be won, and Jacka has that quality in spades. Among other things Monash is delighted to report to the Victorian that his derring-do had been noted all across the peninsula, up to and including General Ian Hamilton himself!

Back at his HQ, Monash further examines the report that Lieutenant Crabbe has written, recommending that Jacka get a medal. '*I beg to report that at 5 a.m. May 19, Lance-corporal Jacka, No 4 Company, 14th Battalion, A.I.F. . . . rushed in at one end of the trenches whilst I had a party engaging them at the other end, and shot seven Turks who had forced and obtained a section of our trenches. Lance-corporal Jacka and a party of four had tried a previous bayonet rush, but were repulsed, with two casualties to us. Lance-corporal Jacka had held this trench for a time against the Turks, when the remainder of his party were rendered casualties by the enemy's grenades, thrown before they rushed the trench.*'[47]

All up, Monash is more than happy to make his own recommendation as to what sort of medal the young soldier should receive, and to push it with his superior officers, including the Generals Hamilton and Godley.

(Another soldier who Monash pushes for recognition at the same time is a fellow by the name of Simpson, who, with his donkey, had been remarkable for his courage in retrieving the wounded under fire, only to be killed in this last battle. 'They worked all day and all night throughout the whole period since landing, and the help rendered to the wounded was invaluable. Simpson knew no fear, and moved unconcernedly amid shrapnel and rifle fire, steadily carrying out his self-imposed task day by day, and he frequently earned the applause of the personnel for his many fearless rescues of wounded men from areas subject to rifle and shrapnel fire.'[48])

Getting wind of his own possible recognition, Jacka is able to write to his mother, Elizabeth, soon afterwards. 'I suppose you will be surprised to hear that my name is on the list of men that have been recommended and mentioned in dispatches by General Sir Ian Hamilton. If you hear of Lance-Corporal Jacka getting a distinguished service medal or a military cross or something like that, you will know it is me. Even if I don't get any medal or anything like that, it is a great honour even to get mentioned in dispatches by a great general like Sir Ian Hamilton.'[49]

•

On 25 May, the 12,000-ton British battleship *Triumph* is firing broadsides onto the Turks on Gaba Tepe. Seventy feet below, death awaits them. For *Kapitänleutnant* Otto Hersing has spied them in his telescope and is moving in for the kill. He waits until just 300 yards separates the vessels, then:

'*Rohr eins – los!*' 'Torpedo one – launch!'

The six-yard-long torpedo tears forth at the rate of 35 knots.

Seconds later Otto sees a huge cloud of smoke leap out of the sea. His own sub will shake with the fatal vibration they have created with the 350 pounds of TNT in one strike.

It takes just 12 minutes for the *Triumph*'s disaster to complete. Some Australians standing on the shore watch in shock as the ship capsizes, 'her green bottom upwards in the sunlight. The crews on the neighbouring ships stood to attention as she made her last plunge down to the bottom through clouds of smoke and steam.'[50] Seventy-one souls lost, their bodies joining Davy Jones.

From the heights of Gallipoli, Albert Jacka has seen the whole thing. He is not a man given to drama.

'Went into the trenches at 10 am,' he records in his diary. 'At 12.15 the cruiser *Triumph* was sunk by a German submarine. We saw her go down. Very wet afternoon.'[51]

•

With the approaching summer comes heat, dust and thirst. By now the situation at Gallipoli has settled more into a war of attrition than anything else. On the day that the Anzacs had landed here, they had taken some 400 acres of Turkish territory. Now, in rising summer, they control . . . some 400 acres. Neither side is able to move back or forth. The Turks cannot dislodge the Anzacs. But nor can the Anzacs, and their fellow soldiers of the British Army, dislodge the Turks. It is simply just a day-by-day brutal battle for both sides to stay alive, and keep the position they have. Albert Jacka continues to grow in stature among his fellow soldiers, as does his position of leadership among them, despite the fact that he remains no more than a lance corporal.

Somehow, as his mates come to understand, Bert just has a natural ability in this game. If there is a problem, he will become the solution.

Take tonight, it's the third night he's out on the hunt with Percy Bland. What they are looking for, deep in No Man's Land, is one man, a Turkish machine-gunner, who sits comfortably in safe land every bloody night and sprays, just for a half-dozen deadly seconds, one of the paths that leads down to the beach. His fire is precise, it is fast, and it is over before any man next to the Australian dead can figure out where the bugger is. So for two long nights, Bert and Percy have crawled out into danger and waited for the sound and sight of fire. Twice they have missed Jacko, and Percy is praying that three times is the charm because Jacka will keep crawling out until the end of days to find this gunner if he has to. And he has to. They wait now in silence, doing the strangest thing possible for a Digger, hoping to see and hear Turkish gunfire. At last the blast comes, and ... there!

'A spark,' Percy whispers. A nod, as Jacka's eyes fix on the machine gun with a fatal glance. They will not fire now, their range is too far and they don't want that bastard to know he's spotted – but he's more than that; his position is mapped out in Jacka's head.

They return, and Jacka is able to give the exact co-ordinates on the map where the Turkish machine-gunner is positioned to the ships in the bay.

'Within three days there was no more of him,' Bland will recount. 'A shell had landed right where he was, evidently, and blew him to pieces, or blew him out. There was no more of that firing after that.'[52]

And it means that the Turk's daily harvest of dead Diggers stops.

'That corner was easy to go through again. Jacka, he was a wonderful man.'[53]

Not all of those fighting side by side with Jacka will live to tell the tale, and on 28 May, he loses two of his mates – Sam Wilson and Walter Earle from Wedderburn – both shot in the head. Both had been beside him while they were hauling buckets of water up to the front lines, and yet they had died while he had not a mark upon him.

Jacka records the result in his diary.

'Both died.'[54]

May the Good Lord have mercy on their souls. Jacka can only imagine the pain for the Earle family back home, once they find out.

And as more die – the attrition rate at Gallipoli is over 1000 Australians killed every month – while Jacka survives against all odds, his legend grows.

At one point, Private Bill Fitzpatrick is standing right by Jacka as they make their way from the beach back to the front-line trenches. There is a whistling. Jacka stops.

'Small shell landed between Jacka's legs,' Fitzpatrick will recount. 'A dud.'[55]

Jacka looks down. Looks at Fitzpatrick. Walks on. Maybe Captain Reverend Gillison is right: the Lord really is with them, or at least with him!

Under the circumstances, Jacka might be forgiven for breaking his commitment to being a teetotalling Rechabite, most particularly when, as noted in the NZ & Australian Division war diary on 18 June 1915: 'Issue of rum to all ranks to celebrate centenary of Waterloo approved. Canteen opened on beach.'[56]

But not tonight, Rechabite.

Mid-July 1915, Imbros, gang aft agley

General Hamilton is so tired of the endless barrage of negative voices that greet each new plan to take the Gallipoli Peninsula, he can barely raise a theatrical sigh. Yes, one can always be a Cassandra, but that is not his way: 'After all, is not "nothing venture nothing win" an unanswerable retort?'[57]

New divisions arrive in mid-July and the plan is for them to strengthen the force already assembled at Gallipoli so they will be able to launch a major attack in three weeks' time that will push all the way to the crest of the Sari Bair, take the high ground from the Turks, forge a path from Gallipoli and take us to the Promised Land – Constantinople by Christmas. Yes, yes, there are blatherers, bleaters and bedwetters who bitterly protest that 'the ground between Anzac and the Sari Bair crestline is worse than the Khyber Pass'[58] – but General Hamilton is determined to get things done. Birdy thinks they can do it and that will have to do. Play up, and play the game!

They are Godley's sentiments precisely. This pukka English officer had once roomed at the United Services College with none other than the great English writer Rudyard Kipling and when it comes to dying for the British Empire his views are indeed Kiplingesque:

> *For all we have and are,*
> *For all our children's fate,*
> *Stand up and take the war.*
> *The Hun is at the gate!*
>
> *There is but one task for all—*
> *One life for each to give.*

What stands if Freedom fall?
Who dies if England live?[59]

Giving your life can be a bit unfortunate for a man, but in the overall scheme of things for an Army Corps, or two, not particularly significant – and magnificent for England.

'Quite impossible to foresee casualties,' Hamilton notes blithely, 'but suppose for example, we suffered a loss of 20,000 men; though the figure seems alarming when put down in cold blood, it is not an extravagant proportion when calculated on basis of Dardanelles fighting up to date . . .'[60]

You see? It is only when you put those figures up against the catastrophic casualty figures to date that the virtues of 'August Offensive' truly come into positive perspective.

Right now, the biggest concern to General Birdwood is the overall health of the veteran Anzac troops, as no fewer than 200 men a day at Anzac Cove alone are now being evacuated through sickness, while those who remain are more often than not teetering on it.

Albert Jacka is the exemplar of that deteriorating health. The Diggers themselves call it being able to 'shit through the eye of a needle at 40 paces'. The doctors call it dysentery, and the wood-chopper has it so badly he collapses and has to be evacuated to Lemnos to recuperate. Entirely unbeknownst to him, however, things are happening beyond his horizons. Things that will change his life forever.

●

The news breaks first in London, in a supplement to *The London Gazette*, published on the morning of 23 July 1915:

War Office

His Majesty the King has been graciously pleased to award the Victoria Cross to . . . No. 465 Lance-Corporal Albert Jacka, 14th Battalion, Australian Imperial Forces.

For most conspicuous bravery on the night of the 19th–20th May, 1915 at 'Courtney's Post', Gallipoli Peninsula.

> Lance-Corporal Jacka, while holding a portion of our trench with four other men, was heavily attacked. When all except himself were killed or wounded, the trench was rushed and occupied by seven Turks. Lance-Corporal Jacka at once most gallantly attacked them single-handed, and killed the whole party, five by rifle fire and two with the bayonet.[61]

•

All over Australia it is the same. Letters come every morning with the mailman. Cables come via the telegram boy at any time of the day, usually within an hour of arriving at the local post office.

But these days, whenever you see the telegram boy arrive at the home of a family that has a son overseas with the AIF, everyone holds their breath, fearing the worst of all possible news has arrived.

So it is on this Monday when out of the blue, the telegram boy pulls up on his bicycle outside the modest Jacka home, opposite Wedderburn public school.

Shortly thereafter, amazingly, the sound of cheers can be heard coming from inside. For they have received a telegram from the Minister for Defence, Senator Sir George Foster Pearce:

> I desire to offer you my hearty congratulations upon the signal honor - the award of the Victoria Cross - which has been conferred upon your son for his conspicuous bravery upon the battlefield. Australia has reason to be proud of her many gallant sons who are so nobly fighting in the Empire's service, consequently the selection of Lance-Corporal Jacka as the first Australian recipient of the Victoria Cross in the present war must cause you extreme gratification, in which your fellow citizens share. With the hope that your son may be spared for many years to enjoy the honor conferred upon him by His Majesty, I remain, yours very truly,
> G. F. Pearce.[62]

Not long afterwards, the Prime Minister himself, Andrew Fisher, telegraphs.

It must have thrilled you to learn that your brave soldier
son's gallant conduct on the field won first Australian
Victoria Cross of the war. Hope all Australians proud of him
to-day, and congratulate you who gave him to us. I have asked
Minister for Defence to cable Government's congratulations to
your brave boy.
A. Fisher.[63]

(For Prime Minister Fisher and his cabinet, it is an occasion for vindication. Yes, the death toll at Gallipoli had been fearful. But, now look! An Australian hero, all their own, really is something to celebrate – and the more they celebrate him, the bigger a counter it will be to the nay-sayers.)

Now, though an extremely staunch Labor man, Nathaniel Jacka, for this auspicious occasion, is happy to take a little time off from hating Conservatives like Fisher and Pearce, and is gratified on behalf of his son to receive such messages.

And how proud he is, when the local paper, the *Korong Vale Lance and North West Advertiser*, carries the story on the front page!

FOR VALOUR.

District Soldier Wins

V.C. BRAVO! PTE. JACKA.

[From Our Own Correspondent.]

It is with pride and exultation we announce that one of our Wedderburn boys, Pte. Albert Jacka, has gained the V.C., which is the highest honor for bravery that can be bestowed on a British Soldier. Private Jacka gained this distinction at Gallipoli under the following circumstances...[64]

And those circumstances are repeated again, as they are in every home, every bar, every hall and church; an instant legend of bravery that all know, along with a single name: 'Jacka'.

Though never a strutter by nature, Nathaniel is certainly now seen to walk down the main street of Wedderburn with a certain spring in his step. Within days he and his wife will be guests of honour as the local Patriotic Committee holds an extraordinary meeting at the Korong Shire Hall to commemorate the achievement of Wedderburn, Victoria and Australia's favourite son, Albert Jacka VC! All those in favour of sending warmest congratulations to him at Gallipoli, together with his wounded comrades?

Aye!

I tell you it was a *forest* of hands, with nary a nay!

The locals are also there at their son's old primary school – his *only* school, just over the road from the Jacka homestead – when the principal makes a speech as the kids stand around the flagpole's fluttering Union Jack, and the boys salute it, just before the principal gives the kids the rest of the day off, by way of celebration! And all this, as Reverend Raff's daughter, sweet Elsie, rings the bells of Wedderburn Presbyterian Church to mark that God is great, and Wedderburn's favourite son has done something glorious.

The Wedderburn Rechabites hold their own special meeting, where they toast the town's favoured 22-year-old son with . . . tea and coffee. (Yes, it's a VC, but they are still Rechabites. They will hold the champagne for the Second Coming.) They are not at all surprised, but they beam with pride which, just this day, is no sin. Members of the Christian Endeavour Society feel the same. He is one of theirs, done good! All those who have competed with and against Jacka in many road-cycling races in the area feel the same. Everyone remembers how powerful he had been on the hills, how he must have had the lungs and leg power of an emu to stay so fast for so long!

And, of course, the people of Wedderburn now recall the incidents from Bert Jacka's youth, which – now that they think about it, and remember – point to the fact he was always destined for greatness.

Why, who can forget the time that the very young Albert was with his two brothers on the main street of Wedderburn when they saw a fire break out at the hotel, and, after saying, 'Let's go, boys!', had put the fire out!

And the papers carry news of a bravery bonanza won by Jacka, given by famed Melbourne businessman (and bookmaker, but don't look a gift horse in the mouth . . .) John Wren. Mr Wren has been quick as a bullet to let the papers know how generous he is: 'In pursuance of a promise which he made some time ago, Mr. J. Wren has decided to give £500 and a gold medal to Lance-Corporal Jacka, as he was the first Australian to win the Victoria Cross. Mr. Wren has written to the parents of the young Victorian hero, congratulating them, and asking whether he will forward the cheque for £500 to them on Jacka's behalf. Mr. Wren also sent a cable message to Jacka congratulating him.'[65]

By God! That's more than a man in this town will earn in two years! Won in a day by young Bert!

What will he spend it on when he gets back? One who has asked but doesn't know is Lance Corporal Bill Howard, who has had the honour of being shot in the action where Jacka had won the Victoria Cross.

Once returned to Bendigo, he will be proud to tell *The Bendigonian* of his own role in the exploit and jokes, 'Jacka got the V.C., but I got the bullets.'[66]

Albert Jacka VC is a national hero like Australia has never seen before. He is a common man, a working man, an everyman, who has demonstrated extraordinary bravery in an already iconic campaign. The Australian government, without asking Jacka himself, quickly organises to have the soldier's image placed on recruiting posters encouraging his fellow Australian males to join up.

'Join together, train together, embark together, and fight together.'

To potential recruits, Jacka VC himself – giant in the foreground of an image boasting Australian cricketers, footballers and golfers – seems to be saying, 'Enlist in the Sportsman's Thousand' and 'Show the enemy what Australian sporting men can do'.[67]

In all the AIF, surely no-one is more pleased than the man who has pushed hardest for Jacka to be awarded the VC, General Monash.

'Last night we got a cable announcing the grant of the Victoria Cross to Lance-corporal Jacka, of my 14th battalion,' he delightedly writes to his wife in late July. 'This is the first Victoria Cross in this brigade and this division, and I believe in the whole Army Corps. We are all very jubilant about it. Unfortunately Jacka is away ill, so we can't have a ceremony until he returns to duty.'[68]

And the man himself?

Well, Jacka is indeed in for a surprise from the moment that he arrives back from Lemnos a couple of days later to resume his front-line post.

For the man waiting for him on the beach, midst a heavy assembly of all of the senior officers of the 4th Brigade and the 14th Battalion, is none other than Monash.

The 'ceremony', such as it is, is more of a hurried, rag-tag meeting than a stately occasion as Lance Corporal Jacka stands to attention in front of his fellows and Monash salutes him. Though a formal investiture will come later, this is a ceremony to formalise the fact that the famed Victoria Cross is his, bringing honour to him, his battalion, his division and his country. In terms of background and education, there could be few more unalike men in their country than Brigadier General John Monash and Lance Corporal Albert Jacka, but when their common ground is the same battlefield where they both excel at different levels, they like each other enormously from the first.

Jacka is not much fussed by most of the senior officers as a breed, and back in Cairo had twice been placed on report for not slavishly snapping off salutes to senior Pommy officers. But Monash is not like that, he is like them.

Apart from being lauded by senior officers, Jacka is a hero to his fellow soldiers as news of his VC has now spread across the entire fighting force of the Dardanelles. Every man-jack of them had wondered before landing how they would go in a stoush. Few, if any, had dared imagine they would fight as well as Jacka had done. But he has done it, and deserves every tribute coming his way. So, too, among others who have been honoured, the newly promoted Lance Corporal Harry Murray and Lieutenant Percy Black deserve congratulations for their own Distinguished Conduct Medals for their extraordinary work with their Maxim machine gun – and Jacka is warm in his own praise for them. (For yes, he, too, has heard all the stories, which go well beyond their medals. A 4th Brigade favourite is about the time Mad Harry had ventured out into a scrubby part of No Man's Land, only to be suddenly confronted by a Turk who wielded his bayonet like a sword and clearly wanted to run him through. Murray was happy for the fight, only to find the bloke must have been a fencer before the war, as he is so fast and skilled, so . . . Murray reluctantly shot him instead!)

Now, as Jacka makes his way up and down the trenches, his fellow Diggers get out of his way, stop to have a few words if they are lucky, give him a nod of recognition, and even nudge their mates: *That's Jacka... There goes Albert Jacka VC... Oi, Bluey, that's him, the cove that killed seven Turks on his own, and got the Victoria Cross.*

As it happens, there is little time to offer him more than a handshake and a pat on the back as Jacka has arrived back just 24 hours before the August Offensive is to be launched.

CHAPTER THREE

THE DAYS OF THEIR DISCONTENT

From little towns in a far land we came,
To save our honour and a world aflame,
By little towns in a far land we sleep;
And trust that world we won for you to keep![1]

Rudyard Kipling

Our only home was our unit. Pride in ourselves, in face of a world of friends and enemies, was our sustaining force.[2]

2nd Lieutenant George Mitchell, 16th Battalion, 4th Brigade

5 August 1915, Gallipoli, speech on the beach unto the breach

Monash's 4th Brigade is the finest brigade at Gallipoli. So of course General Hamilton wants them front and centre, prow and bow, of the intended breakthrough. And General Birdwood wants them to know just how important they are to the plan, so you senior officers must gather round.

Today, we – by which I mean you – begin 'our second advance on our way to Constantinople'. True the first advance has not advanced even a mile, but Rome wasn't built in a day and Constantinople will be taken in a bit, with a bit of effort from you lads.

'The whole world has now heard of the action of the Australians and New Zealanders . . . and we therefore have to act up to an extraordinarily high standard to live up to our reputation.'

Don't let the side down by dying or shirking.

'Remember, men, the order of the day must be "shove on and keep shoving on" until we are in complete possession of the heights above us, when we hope we will have the Turks at our mercy.'

Hope and mercy are both devoutly wished. 'We know that we have established a moral superiority over the Turks.'[3]

Yes, the military superiority would be nice, but make no mistake, the Turks 'are terrified of the Australian and New Zealand soldiers in the open'.[4]

Not all Generals have such leisure with their speechifying, as Brigadier General John Monash discovers when next he starts to address his men as they gather around him on the beach at Anzac Cove.

'Men . . .'

BOOM!

A Turkish shell lands and explodes, unsettlingly near. Monash continues to speak, the Turks continue to shell and Monash's men continue to stand! Yes, such is the respect the men have for Monash, they wait until he finishes talking. *But for Christ's sake, hurry up, sir!* Monash races to a quick conclusion drowned BOOM out BOOM by some background noise that is getting BOOM bloody close to the foreground and, with a nod and a lightning-quick salute, Monash is done and all run for cover. BOOM, sod's law takes effect and the blooming BOOMING shrapnel strikes the men as they shelter in 'pigeon-holes' carved out from the cliff side. Safe as houses when you stand in the open, take cover and the lead will somehow take you.

The plan is to go for broke, a vast sweep that will avoid the tedium of trench warfare and break through with a smashing attack that will stun the Turks, capture the peaks of the Sari Bair range, most particularly *the* peak of Chunuk Bair, and establish not just a foothold but a mountain top from which to unfurl future forays. It is a battle plan made to overwhelm the Turks, no half measures, but God help them all if they fail. For now, as they get ready to move, the Diggers busy themselves sharpening bayonets that, for the most part, have already been so sharpened they could cut wood. It is particularly important, as General Monash has given orders to 'march with empty magazines, and fight with the bayonet only'.[5]

The idea is not to risk accidental discharges which would warn the enemy of your approach in the night. Get there undiscovered, and then use the bayonet to do the heavy work once you get among them.

The 61-year-old General Stopford, who was first blooded in battle for England in Egypt in 1882, has tasked himself with the command of this fresh invasion. As Commander of IX Corps, he officially has two divisions under him and has his own stately way of doing things, including being fond of sleeping when his battles begin. (It is important to demonstrate a complete lack of anxiety at such times, and he will hear of the results when he awakes!)

The success of the attack on Lone Pine is crucial, so that General Stopford will have a few hours at least of Turkish distraction to rely on before he takes Suvla. Birdwood is determined to make this feint convincing, as 'getting the Turkish reserves deeply committed on my own front, the opposition at Suvla would be proportionately weakened'.[6]

For the last moments of peace, the sun shines hotly and birdsong is heard. A different sound is about to break when the intensive barrage on Turkish positions begins at 4.30 pm and it will not be sweet.

The 4th Brigade set off as that barrage is in full fire, strangely exhilarated, even liberated, to be out of their usual positions in the trenches and now heading along the road by the beach, before they commence their climb into the hills to get at Jacko. They can breathe, feel like free men, enjoy the evening air but . . .

GET DOWN!

Every now and then the searchlights from the destroyers, which are seeking out Turkish targets to pulverise, swing too low and their entire column is exposed and vulnerable.

Soon enough, their passable road turns into a rickety, winding and narrow path. Albert Jacka, with all of them, does his best, even as the said path turns into a track winding back to God knows where, and . . . all stop in their gobsmacked tracks . . . halted for a moment by a sound in the distance that rolls into a blast of dirty thunder rumbling overhead. What the *hell* is that? On the Abdul Rahman Bair ridge, the men of the 14th crane towards it, but can only see far-off smoke billowing into sudden clouds. Shellfire. A sea of it. It is the sound of a battle at Lone Pine. They are not alone in thanking God they are not there.

At Lone Pine – just 100 yards to the front – the shells fall so thick and fast that all the men can hear is 'one continuous roar'.[7] The barrage is supposed to climax at 5.30 pm, though how it can get any louder than this defies explanation. Jacko answers with equal fury, and the 3000 huddled Australians of the 1st Australian Infantry Brigade have to yell to get to a whisper as they gather in the forward trenches. Over-the-top time is here. It takes guts to even pretend to be brave now, but some can muster up some sangfroid and some French.

'*Au revoir*, Bill,' yells one soldier to his mate, 'meet you over there.'
'So long, Tom,' is the roared reply, 'see you again in half an hour.'[8]
Whether they will be seeing each other in this world or the next remains to be ... seen.

'Five twenty-seven,' says a young officer crouching in the corner of the fire-step gazing at his wristwatch. 'Prepare to go over the parapet.'[9]

With a roar they are all up and over, charging forward, across a front some 200 yards wide, even as the Turkish and German machine guns start their shattering and whole rows of Australian soldiers are mown down, even as the succeeding wave takes their place.

Within a minute, the trenches at Lone Pine are filled with rolling balls of battle bouncing back and forth, a bloody trail marking their course.

The battle soon becomes 'hand to hand',[10] bayonet to bayonet.

Evening, 6 August 1915, Northern Anzac Cove, the silent march to the north

Albert Jacka's 4th Brigade, heads off ... but where are they headed? Rather than striding out with a set purpose and sure destination, there is a certain stumbling forward, and hesitation. The men start to chatter in the ranks and their whispers do not flatter. It looks like another organised folly. They simply don't know where they are going, or even in what direction. God help them when the sun comes up as the view will be fatal. As Jacka glowers and the troops stride forward with strain, Charles Bean walks over to where General Godley is standing just outside his HQ and hears him ask one of his officers: 'Can I tell Army Corps that both the Brigades have cleared this place?'[11]

An officer pops out to check.

'No, no, Sir, the Indian Brigade is only arriving.'

'What, are they behind Monash? Good God!'

What! This is not just a surprise, it is a disaster. To Bean it is obvious and 'rather an elementary part of the attack for the General to have forgotten'.

The officer in front of him knows the same for he splutters, 'But that was the order they were told to go in, sir.'[12]

Godley says nothing, for there is nothing to be said. He simply nods. Bean is shocked at the basic nature of the error, and that it is accepted rather than corrected. Godley offers him a whisky and Bean accepts it; a stiff drink is one order that both can easily follow.

There will be none for the road, as Bean is off now, joining a column of Indian soldiers to catch up with Monash. As Bean goes, Godley yells out after him, in his rich English accent, 'Tell him to hurry up.'[13]

Yes, that should do it. A message passed to a journalist, to pass on to a General, should help the movement of thousands of men into their right position.

Soon enough, Bean hears shots coming from a different direction, from a long way off. From the direction of Suvla Bay?

Likely. The landing of General Stopford's troops must have begun...

And then come more shots, bright and blazing, as Monash sees ahead: 'We had not gone half a mile when the black tangle of hills between the beach road and the main mountain-range became alive with flashes of musketry, and the bursting of shrapnel and star shell, and the yells of the enemy and the cheers of our men as they swept in, to drive in the enemy from molesting the flanks of our march.'[14]

Jacka joins in the roar of those watching, knowing they will be doing the same soon enough. The night is lit by fire and flash as they move forward; the battle plan must be followed to the letter. Don't be distracted by the hellscape, gentlemen.

•

In the murderous maze of trenches at Lone Pine, one cannot be sure who is enemy and who countryman. Screams, curses in different languages and universal death rattles fill the night.

By 8.30 pm the situation at Lone Pine is partly stabilised as the Australians are in possession of the first three rows of Turkish trenches, yet no-one is under any illusions. Everyone knows the battle will continue as the Turks launch counter-attack after counter-attack, and the call for stretcher-bearers is heard throughout a black night now split by the roar of rifles and machine guns, the screams of dying men and the regular explosions of artillery shells and bombs.

The aftermath of the Battle of Lone Pine is so sickening that, when he visits the site shortly after the battle, even General Birdwood is shocked: 'God forbid that I should ever again see such a sight as that which met my eyes when I went up there: Turks and Australians piled four and five deep on one another. The most magnificent heroism had been displayed on both sides.'[15]

Charles Bean, a man whose eye and pen cuts to the quick, reports the scene just as he found it: 'The dead lay so thick that the only respect which could be paid to them was to avoid treading on their faces. Their glories will be painted in prose later; those who are there don't have the stomach for it now.'[16]

This 'feint' at Lone Pine, masterminded by General Sir Herbert Vaughan Cox, has resulted in 2000 dead Australian troops and 6000 Turkish ones.

The Australian position has been advanced by 200 yards.

The 'distractions' for the Turks have become destructions for the British and Anzacs. A further fatal feint is now all but pointlessly performed in the south at Helles, with 4000 British casualties strewn about the killing field.

For the 4th Brigade, things are gang agley by the fact that the man designated as their principal guide, from the New Zealand Rifles, is killed by a stray bit of shrapnel immediately after setting off. His local replacements are deliberately unhelpful: 'Some of the guides were Levantines of doubtful character,' the Official History of the 14th Battalion will record, 'whilst the terrain was so intricate that whole columns lost their way and our men sometimes came under a murderous fire from their own artillery.'[17]

Jacka and the rest of the 14th Battalion, right in the middle of the 4th Brigade, are less than 2000 yards from where a dreadful clash is taking place. At 4 am, a roar drifts up to them from the small ridge of land far below them known as The Nek. For the next 23 minutes they hear the blanket artillery fire coming from the big ships below, aimed at the Turkish trenches. This is followed by seven minutes of silence and now . . . the fearful chattering of machine guns.

How many could live in that roaring tempest?

The few. Very, very few.

Survivors of the 14th Battalion would later find out the dreadful truth. Those four shattering chatterings were Turkish machine guns, all but completely destroying four waves of the 8th and 10th Australian Light Horse. Most of the men are cut down within just 10 paces of the trenches. In a few minutes, no fewer than 234 Australians are killed outright, following insane orders to charge Turkish machine guns across 50 yards, armed with nothing but their bayonets.

Jacka's scrawled diary tells the story of the morning of 7 August: 'Lost count of everything but heavy fighting.'[18]

Fighting now also breaks out among the field commanders of the assaulting column, to the later disgust of John Monash.

'There are some things that don't get into the dispatches,' Monash will write to his wife, 'and perhaps not into history – but it is an undoubted fact that during the first 48 hours after landing at Suvla while there was an open road to the Dardanelles, and no opposition worth talking about . . . a whole army corps sat down on the beach, etc . . . while its leaders were quarrelling about questions of seniority and precedence; and it was just that delay of 48 hours which enabled the Turks to bring up their last strategic reserve . . . and render futile the whole purpose of the landing.'[19]

Dusk, 7 August 1915, somewhere below Hill 971, the impossible must be possible

As the sun fades, bringing welcome relief to Albert Jacka and the parched soldiers of Monash's 4th Brigade – who have spent the day digging with their bayonets to gain shelter from Turkish fire – a supply of picks and shovels belatedly arrives at their front line. Jacka is ailing but he will not complain. Until he falls, assume that he is well. Pass a shovel and get on with it, Digger.

An officer passes Monash two messages from Godley: 'The G.O.C. [General Officer Commanding] wishes you to close the troops . . . well up the slopes towards the enemy during the preliminary bombardment of the position, so as to be ready to reach the crest as soon as the gun-fire stops tomorrow morning. The assault should be carried out with loud cheering.'[20]

Any particular noise the bullets should make? God only knows how Godley can dictate this stuff with a straight face.

He adds in his second message, 'I feel confident that, after today's rest, and starting comparatively fresh, your brigade will make a determined effort to capture the key of the positions . . .'[21]

Monash doesn't share this confidence, and starts to draft his own plan of how to survive the morning.

They are to move out at 3 am.

•

Monash's men are far from their objective.

Move out they do, but the fates conspire against their every plan. The naval bombardment on Hill 971 ceases. And they are nowhere near it!

They are wide of their mark. Lost.

And now they are being fired upon by Turkish machine guns that are well positioned above them. 'Being in no present danger, [the Turks] worked their guns with coolness and decisive effect . . .'[22]

Monash's men are scattered, confused. Their numbers are quickly decimated. The objective of Hill 971 is out of reach. The best they can do is hold on to the line they'd begun to entrench the day before.

•

Late that evening the journalist Ellis Ashmead-Bartlett comes across Sir Ian Hamilton, standing all alone, on the north coast of Suvla Bay, not a staff officer or underling to be seen anywhere near. Just as he had feared, all the ranges around Suvla Bay are now held by whole divisions of Turkish reinforcements that have arrived on this day. The English General has squandered 9000 men in four days, with next to nothing to show for it, bar the squalid flats of Suvla Bay. And for all of the August Offensives, there are 25,000 casualties so far!

Despite the Suvla Bay disaster and the debacle of Hill 971, it remains possible the August Offensive could be a success if the Allies can hold on to just one last thing: the summit of Chunuk Bair. Magnificently, the New Zealanders had held on to it all through 9 August and, as dusk falls on this day, they are relieved by soldiers of the 6th Loyal North Lancashires.

But could it continue to be held?

In the dead of night, Jacka and the few surviving men of D Company head towards the summit, men from the 15th and 16th joining them in the frantic struggle to gain ground before dawn reveals their vulnerability with fatal accuracy. A scramble over hills and valleys from each nook and cranny of cover; Jacka can see now that the cover stops abruptly as they enter a strangely open patch of ground: a cornfield with no protection and only risk. It is a risk Jacka has known before, but now all are forced to know it. Come on now, as one, RUN! They start to race through but are stopped by a blizzard of missiles that fall and explode with blazing haste; men fall aground all round, this foreign field now their last.

The Commanding Officer of the 14th Battalion, Major Rankine, falls too, from illness, his body collapsing in sweat and feverish tremors. Major Charles Dare assumes command and they push on towards the Turks, fighting them back up the hill with Jacka and the D Company men at the fore. This now is the point where the men who have poured through Suvla Bay should meet them and . . . and they do not.

Dare waits anxiously but his men are already resigned to disappointment.

Albert Jacka stands alone, literally, daring fate as the bullets whizz past to see if any fallen comrade might move. But no, they are gone; the shells blasting what remains there are to Kingdom Come. Down, now, take what cover you can for the moment. Surely it will just be a moment before relief. There will be no further advance tonight without a left flank.

And here one comes!

Unfortunately it is made up of Turks, who swoop down upon them, and the fray fractures into a frantic improvised retreat by the Allies. It is left to John Monash to give the bitter formal order: Withdraw! Retreat!

Even now, it will be touch and go – and the 14th look likely to be slaughtered in their retreat, until . . .

Until suddenly, the four crews of the machine-gun sections of the 14th and 16th Battalions, including Lieutenant Percy Black and the newly promoted Sergeant Harry Murray, arrive with their Maxim guns. Quickly, Black and Murray position themselves so as to sweep the crest with such fire that any Turk who ventures over it is immediately cut down. Black pulls the trigger while Murray feeds the belt once more and their machine gun exacts an immediate and heavy toll.

'From that moment there was no anxiety regarding the withdrawal,' one account will run. 'Every attempt by the enemy to move brought him heavy losses and the guns pinned him to his ground.'[23]

Praise the Lord.

'With the enemy pinned down the rest of the brigade gradually withdrew to the position it had occupied that morning, the machine guns covering the retreat.'[24]

Jacka and his men are saved, Sergeant Major Bain of the 14th Battalion chronicling that the gunners 'had worked their guns red hot . . . otherwise it is doubtful if any one of us would have succeeded in getting back'.[25]

The day is done before it's begun. Their comrades who just died before them died for naught. It is a fuming failure. Goddamn Godley, stuff Stopford and to hell with Hamilton. These stupid paper plans burn up in the air of reality; and Jacka is sick of seeing lives squandered. Dying for this? For a half-cocked concoction of some Englishman still fighting the Boer War in his mind? Not again. Trench warfare looks like sober sanity compared with this punch-drunk debacle.

By the time the 14th Battalion are withdrawn after this latest venture, they have, as their War Diary records, 'lost about 300 of 868 men'.[26]

To add atrocity to injury, the dreadful news of the Battle of the Nek reaches them; a slaughter beyond belief, carried out not once but three times full of death. Six hundred Australians charged, 372 casualties, no ground gained unless you count the graves. Madness. *Organised* madness, that's what they are participating in. It can't go on like this.

Australians would not send Australians to their deaths like this. A fury begins to build about the way the Mother Country is smothering her colonials.

General Godley's blithe words to the Australians do not help.

'It is impossible to make an omelette unless you break eggs.'[27]

Yes, Hamilton will quickly sack Stopford, but it is all too late. Sane orders now would be based on an acknowledgement that the plan for 'left and right hook' lies in ruins. But Hamilton persists, ordering still more fresh attacks from the remaining shattered Anzac and British divisions.

21 August 1915, Hill 60, a hill to die on

Another day, another disaster.

There are 150 straining soldiers of the 14th Battalion in this line, their task today is to make their way over a small ridge and over just 70 yards of creek bed. Oh, and they will be carrying 45 pounds of equipment and ammo, and there will be frequent fire. All this to reach the base of Hill 60.

Without taking Hill 60, the northern end of the Sari Bair range cannot be held. Without that, the Suvla landings will simply be a lingering slaughter. They might die to capture Hill 60; they will die if they don't. With a dreadful symmetry of fatal selection, 60 men of the 14th will die before this base is reached. In a small, dank gully, on the way to the real beginning of their task, a single shot is heard and Lieutenant Wallace Crabbe falls to the ground, mortally wounded. Far in front of him, unaware, is the man he recommended for a VC long ago at Courtney's Post, Albert Jacka.

For now, Jacka and the 90 men who make it through to the base of the hill choke on the heat as they wait for Major Dare's next order.

The order?

Wait. They are too small a force to attack and must await reinforcements. Good luck to them, but if the panting men of the 14th had any breath left they would not hold it. Three fresh waves of men are decimated trying to reach them. A scattered remnant of the 13th Battalion and the 10th Hampshire Regiment now join their predicament, but they too have survivors so small in number that . . . reinforcements will be needed! Damn it, they can't just sit here. If they are going to die can they at least die *doing something*?

Over the endless fire of machine guns and roar of incoming shells, Dare yells for the men to prepare a most unexpected weapon: sandbags. Each man is to fill and carry as many as he can; they will use them to construct instant parapets as they make their way up this ridge. Don't worry, things can always get worse. One Turkish shell misses them but hits the scrub, the blast bursting it into a brush fire that leaps towards the dead Australians lying nearby and their bombs and ammunition go off as the fire ignites them!

'Any wounded man who so much as stirred to crawl out of the reach of the flames,' Charles Bean will document, 'was instantly shot by the Turks.'[28]

And yet, surely something can be done to help the grievously wounded lying out in No Man's Land?

Captain Reverend Andrew Gillison is one who is so convinced. For he is just giving a Christian burial to a Digger who has been buried by his mates when he hears some particularly agonised cries floating over his solemn words '. . . thy rod and thy staff they comfort me'.

Finishing the burial service as quickly as he can, the Reverend investigates to find the cries are coming from a wounded Digger, just up on yonder ridge whose agony is being compounded by swarms of ants starting in on him.

Yes, it is madness to go out and try to rescue him, but the Reverend Gillison cannot bear it, and the Lord is his shepherd.

'It is hard,' he had written in his diary only a short time before, 'to see the light of many of our best hopes put out so quickly, and the work only begun.'[29]

If he can possibly keep this light flickering, he at least must try.

Taking two men with him – one of whom is a fellow minister, Corporal Robert Pittendreigh from Lithgow – they crawl towards the wounded man, despite being under heavy fire. Grabbing the wounded Digger by the collar, they start to drag him back when both men of the cloth slump. They have been hit by snipers!

Others now crawl forward and, with extraordinary bravery, are able to drag them all back. But for Reverend Gillison it is too late, and he soon succumbs to his wounds, which sees a deep gloom settle on the 14th Battalion.

For Gillison was liked by all and loved by so many. But he is dead now and if the Lord didn't save *him*, he is certainly unlikely to save *us* if they attack further. Pittendreigh, too, will meet his maker a couple of days later.

News of another death reaches Jacka now. *Lieutenant Keith Wallace Crabbe has bought it*. Crabbe who famously found Jacka guarding a trench full of terrified Turks alone, to whom he had said, 'Well, I managed to get the buggers, sir.'[30] Crabbe who had made the first report which saw the VC awarded.

Well, the beggars have now got sir. *Vale*.

The battle goes on.

It will be a whole, bitter week before the next disastrous attack is begun. Jacka is steaming with angry contempt – a mob of kangaroos in a bushfire is better organised. This is *insane*, and men are dying. In the end, Jacka himself is evacuated with gastritis, a severe stomach complaint that would kill a brown dog.

The next advance will be the only one at Gallipoli that Jacka will miss; he will have to hear the news of the havoc from his bed at the 24th Casualty Clearing Station on the island of Lemnos.

A hundred men of the 14th attack Hill 60 on 27 August, with two-thirds killed or severely wounded. The 14th exists practically only in name, while their wider 4th Brigade is equally suffering. With so many dead, those that remain must rise.

Once again the results are catastrophic.

And once again it is the machine gun of Lieutenant Percy Black and Sergeant Harry Murray that keeps them in it.

After a wild charge that cuts down most of the 4th Brigade, other survivors manage to briefly occupy a small section of enemy trench, before being obliged to retreat. Seeing this, the Turks further along the line stand up on their parapets and start firing willy-nilly.

From across the valley, Lieutenant Percy Black sprays the Turks with his Maxim, firing from a rough distance of 200 yards. As recounted by the 14th's Medical Officer, Captain Loughran, the Turkish trench was 'traversed by a whirlwind – a dust storm apparently swept it from end to end and back again several times. We could hear a machine gun firing furiously across our front and we realised the 16th machine guns . . . had spotted this lovely target.'[31]

The Turks go down, and the survivors of the 14th Battalion escape – though 4th Brigade is now down to just a quarter of its original strength.

Strangely, though, as Captain Loughran records, 'I found the 4th Brigade remnant in nothing like as dejected a state as I expected. The fact was that every surviving Digger, knowing the reception that attack would meet with, had expected that afternoon to be his last on earth, and was pleasantly surprised to find himself alive.'[32]

On 28 August, the still ill Albert Jacka is made a Corporal. If there is a bad way to be promoted – fanned by fatalities and the swathe of deaths of so many of the NCOs and officers above him – this is it. Corporal Jacka VC is determined that he will never follow orders without sense or battle plans that can only be won on paper.

And whatever orders he gives will be as precise as they are concise. There must be a better way to win this war that does not involve uselessly slaughtering soldiers.

'Worst month we ever had,' the infuriated Victorian writes in his diary on 31 August, once he has returned to Gallipoli. 'Practically the whole battalion wiped out in these stunts.'[33]

He is not the only one infuriated with the situation, and disgusted by the British officers who have done this to them.

'Deathly depression reigns . . .' the journalist Ellis Ashmead-Bartlett records. 'The truth is now generally known that we have failed everywhere. The empty tents of the IXth Corps, glistening in the sun, have become tombstones of the dead; at night they appear ghostlike and deserted under the moonlight. Where is that mighty host which occupied them but five days ago?'[34]

Dead. Nearly all dead.

So, too, many of those who had gone into the attacks at Achi Baba and Anzac Cove, Ashmead-Bartlett recording, 'The 29th Brigade also suffered heavily, and our total casualties at Helles alone have not been under 6000.'[35]

Birdwood will soon tell him the shocking truth.

'He said his total losses were 375 officers and 10,138 rank and file in the operations on the left and over 2000 in the taking and holding of Lone Pine Plateau.'[36]

And so it goes on. Stark statistics, one after the other, that confirm catastrophic losses on an unimaginable scale.

The total casualties therefore cannot be much under 28,000, an appalling cost for the gains which, as General Godley expressed it, amounted to some 500 acres of bad grazing ground.

Making matters worse for Ashmead-Bartlett is that, somehow, he has to write an account of the battle at Suvla Bay that will contain something of the truth, while still passing the censor: 'an almost impossible task. It is easy enough to write up a success, but it would defy the genius of Ananias to make a victory out of this affair, either at Helles, Anzac or Suvla. We have landed again and dug another graveyard. That is all.'[37]

General Hamilton has no such problems and manages to put out his own releases, subsequently run in the British press, trumpeting 'a successful attack' by the Anzac troops who had made 'additional gains and further progress'.[38]

Suvla Bay?

Special correspondent General Hamilton reports that, 'the new British artillery beat down row after row of Turkish trenches . . . and the Turks beat a hasty retreat'.[39] Never fear, the readers of the British Empire are told, 'the Turkish troops are getting very demoralised, and the whole population of Constantinople is pessimistic'.[40]

But Ashmead-Bartlett will not have it, and writes a long letter which he smuggles out, in the hope it will be delivered to the British Prime Minister, Lord Asquith.

'The Army is in fact in a deplorable condition,' Ellis Ashmead-Bartlett writes. 'Its morale as a fighting force has suffered greatly and the officers and men are thoroughly dispirited. The muddles and mismanagement beat anything that has ever occurred in our military history.

'... The Commander-in-Chief and his Staff are openly spoken of, and in fact only mentioned at all, with derision ... I am convinced the troops could be withdrawn under cover of the warships without much loss, far less in fact than we suffer in any ordinary attack.'[41]

They *must* be evacuated.

For one thing, their manpower is desperately needed on the Western Front where no fewer than 740,000 Allied soldiers have been killed since the beginning of the war.

•

For his part, General John Monash is in despair. While deeply admiring of the qualities of Albert Jacka VC and his fellow Australian soldiers, not to mention the Australian officers, the same cannot be said for their British counterparts.

'The real cause of the failure [at Gallipoli],' he writes to his wife in early September, 'is the poor quality of the British troops. Over and over again they have allowed themselves to be driven out of positions which have been hardly won by the Australian and New Zealand troops and had been handed over to them to hold while we were taken away to make a push to another part of the line ... and altho' some are better than others, they can't soldier for sour apples.

'They have no grit, no stamina or endurance, poor physique, no gumption, and they muddle along and allow themselves to be shot down because they don't even know how to take cover. It will be a poor look out for the Empire if this is the class of soldier they are going to rely on in Flanders. Over and over again I have had to mix up a few platoons of Australians among them to keep them steady and teach them how to dig trenches, how to prepare their bivouacs, how to cook their food, how to take cover, how to fight, and how to stand their ground. They have a willing enough spirit, and plenty of dull stupid courage, but they simply don't know enough to come in out of the wet.

'Much of the fault lies in the leadership; the officers do not mix with the men as we do, but keep aloof, and most of the officers appear chiefly concerned in looking after themselves and making themselves comfortable.'[42]

November 1915, Anzac Cove, rats of first look

The new arrivals to Gallipoli on this day are more wide-eyed than usual. For while it is one thing to be sent to the most iconic battle site imaginable for an Australian – the place is already a legend, as are the men who have been fighting upon it – it is quite something else when you have been sent there as part of the most famous mob of the lot, the 14th Battalion!

It means they will, surely – *surely* – soon see pretty much the most famous Australian who ever lived, Bert Jacka. Stories about him have been all through the Australian press since the awarding of his VC, and among these new 'reinstoushments' it seems to be all that anyone wants to talk about.

One such new recruit is Edgar (Ted) Rule, a well-educated 29-year-old farmer from around Shepparton, who is quite shocked by what he sees, once on the beach. He had expected to be surrounded by the Anzacs of legend, towering behemoths who had taken the best the Turks could throw at them, and given it back in kind, but makes theirs a double.

But these men are not that.

'They seemed to us more like sewer workers than soldiers,' he will chronicle, frankly. 'They were proud of their rags, their whiskers and the colour of the dirt which stained their clothes and helped to set off their grimy, hairy faces.'[43]

The impression is not Rule's alone as the Official 14th Battalion History will record: 'The majority of the survivors on the Peninsula were worn and haggard with long hair and hollow cheeks, covered with dirt, vermin and sores, wearing brimless hats with uniforms torn and stained. No-one would recognise in the jaded handful of worn and weary men the remnants of that magnificent battalion – bronzed and bursting with vitality – which took part in the famous brigade route march through the streets of Melbourne on 17 December 1914. The old spirit existed in the survivors but the flesh was very, very weak.'[44]

A rag-tag mob, once mighty. Surely, Jacka himself will be different?

Wonderfully, Rule is not long in finding out. For as each of the new arrivals' names are read out down on the beach, they are allotted to a particular company, and by the luck of the draw, Rule's name is read out in D Company.

Jacka's! In fact, none other than the newly promoted Jacka.

'Those of us allotted to D Company felt a thrill of self-esteem,' he notes in his diary. 'Our Sergeant-Major was no less than Jacka VC.'[45]

As Rule and his fellow lucky soldiers begin their climb to Durrant's Post, where the 14th men are situated now, there is growing excitement, more so when they arrive and are assigned different positions. Jacka must be here somewhere!

Inevitably, the new recruits – always identifiable to each other by their clean-shavedness and fresh uniforms – have just one question when they run across each other.

'Have you seen him yet?'[46]

Most haven't, but a lucky few have.

'The man who could point out Jacka seemed to swell with importance.'

Ted Rule himself is pleased to be one of them. And he is not disappointed.

'To me, Jacka looked the part; he had a medium-sized body, a natty figure and a determined face with crooked nose.'[47]

All good. But God help any of the new arrivals if Jacka hears them complaining about the grub, or the water, or cold, or the fact that they were being shot at and shelled.

'I grumbled about something,' one Digger will recall, 'oh, about the food or something, and Jacka heard about it, and by God, didn't he go crook. He said, "You're just arrived in, you're grumbling!"'[48]

As Rule settles in, he comes to admire Jacka VC all the more for the way he goes about things. No matter that he is so famous, so revered. Forget that he is now a Company Sergeant Major – responsible for such things as welfare, discipline, drill and ceremonies. There is *nothing* about him that says he is better than anybody else, and anything other than one of them, who just happens to also be responsible for them on all fronts. So *lift* your fucking game!

'One characteristic above all endeared him to all the under-dogs,' Rule notes. 'Instead of "criming" men and bringing them before the officers, his method was: "I won't crime you, I'll give you a punch on the bloody nose."'[49]

It is bush justice, rough justice, but it works. After all, in a stink with officers for your bad behaviour, there's an outside chance you could make your case and be let off. But win in a blue with Bert Jacka VC? Can't be done, Digger. Better behave.

Another, Private Fred Stanton, notes in his diary, 'Jacka VC is my company sergeant major. I am great pals with him. He is a particularly decent chap, knows the game, and very modest.'[50]

Other officers are less impressive, starting with the newly appointed commander of the 14th Battalion's D Company, a replacement officer.

'My name is Major Belshazaar,' he says to them all one day, while waving his arms around in a curious manner. 'Some call me by it and others call me "an old Jewish bastard".'[51]

And presumably some call him barking mad, for he proceeds to sprinkle his remarks with ever more obscene language, presumably on the reckoning that this is the way hard men speak, to gain respect. But it does nothing for the hardest man among them.

'My gaze rested on Jacka's face,' Ted Rule will recount. 'It was a study, his mouth actually commenced to open in astonishment. The old fellow had evidently arrived among us with the fixed idea that, unless his language was that of the gutter, he would never get along with us. He utterly failed to grasp our mentality, and vanished almost as quickly as he came.'[52]

But to the business at hand! Surviving. Rule and his companions have arrived at a time when the Diggers at Gallipoli have a new enemy, and one that could be very quickly identified, if not necessarily beaten. It is the cold. Winter is coming, and they all know it.

The chill approaches every night, an ache so cold it makes a man think fondly of being in Hell, just for the warmth of the place. You would think that the trenches would help stop the wind, or slow it down, but it seems to encourage it, the breeze brazenly becoming bitter as soon as the light fades. The Dardanelles are never welcoming at the best of times, but in winter all the elements seem to be conspiring to suck the will to live right out of you. The panting frosty breaths of your fellows can be seen cutting through the night in whatever light the moon provides; woe betide the man who loses a glove because he will soon be saying farewell to his fingers. Would you like to be warm? Fire your rifle, five times rapid, then hug the barrel. Remember to aim at the Turks first, otherwise even the dimmest officer will guess your true purpose.

•

What a week!

Since arriving on this fatal shore, Private Ted Rule has been goggle-eyed. The trenches! The Turks! The bullets! The bursts of bombs! The endless sense that at any given second you risk being maimed at best, killed at worst.

Men not only live like this, but some of them have been doing it for six months?

It seems incredible.

And here is one of those men now, the most significant one of the lot, Jacka VC, coming into his bay. He wants a word. With Jacka, Rule already knows, a word or two is all you are likely to get at the best of times, and so it proves this time.

'I've decided to make you a Lance Corporal,' he says without preamble. 'Tonight, I want you to take a party of six men and patrol the battalion frontage from dusk until midnight.'[53]

And with that, he is gone.

It is Jacka all over. Say what needs to be said, get the job done, and move on.

Mercifully, the light of the wan moon that night is insufficient to pick out Rule and his companions as they make their way out into No Man's Land, looking for any signs of Turks, Turkish saps, or listening posts.

Rule's heart is in his mouth, his pulse quickens as his sweat thickens, and there are so many butterflies in his stomach it is a wonder he doesn't float away. The further they go into No Man's Land, the more 'the feeling of loneliness and uncertainty increased'.[54]

At the slightest sound they all go to ground, and many times are nearly sure that yonder clump of scrub must contain a party of Turks about to fire on them.

One of the party, Private Sidney Green, even crawls up to Rule and whispers in his ear that he is *certain* he saw something move in the bushes ahead. If so, there is no question of surrendering. They all know the Turks take no prisoners but slaughter every infidel they find on their land.

But for now, nothing. There is no movement, no sound. It is just another clump of scrub. They keep going, until a hundred yards out from their own line, where Rule calls a halt and . . .

And, good GOD, what is that sickening stench?

Private Granigan, who has been out this way before, whispers that there are six dead Turks lying in a heap, just up ahead.

'I had never realised before that dead men smelt like dead animals and the experience came as a shock to me,' Rule notes. 'Away over the ridge in the Turkish lines, dogs were howling as if kept on the chain; it was a certainty that they were not howling for raw meat.'[55]

Shortly thereafter they find two of their own dead soldiers. In such cases, the orders are clear. They must search for their 'meat tickets' – slang for identity discs – retrieve them, and bring them back. But it is completely beyond Rule to do so. There may come a time when he can accomplish such grisly tasks without blinking, but that time is certainly not now.

Heading back, this time they really do very nearly run into a Turkish patrol and must lie low until they are gone. But which way are our own lines now? In hissed whispers it seems they might have gone the wrong way? If so, it will be Rule's worst nightmare.

His relief is infinite when a voice rings out from the darkness, 'Well, you silly bastards, aren't you coming in? You've been kicking up a hell of a row out there.'[56]

12 December 1915, Gallipoli, the word spreads

Strange, how things work out.

Back at Cairo, after being evacuated from Gallipoli with dysentery, colitis and enteritis, Sergeant Harry Murray had been declared 'unfit for service', and told he was being sent home to Australia. Bugger that for a joke. Murray had felt crook, yes, but not so crook he couldn't go on. So, arriving at the docks in Alexandria, and noting a ship heading to Gallipoli, he had simply jumped upon it and was soon reporting for duty with the 13th Battalion, where his 'CO accepted him back without question'.[57]

But now?

Murray has not been back for five days before the word spreads . . .

Have yers *heard*?

The bastards are going to pull us out. An evacuation! Get us back to Cairo. Yes, the word has no doubt started at that greatest originator of all wild stories, the Furphy water-carts, but that doesn't mean it ain't true. And as this second freezing week of December starts to shut down for lack of circulation, the rumour tears around Gallipoli like wildfire – the only remotely warm thing on the Peninsula – along the saps and trenches, down the gullies all the way to Anzac Cove, where it swirls round and round the aching acres of crosses in the cemeteries, before heading back up again to the front lines at Quinn's Post, Courtney's Post, Russell's Top and beyond.

The first real clue among the lower ranks of the 14th Battalion that it might be dinkum comes when Albert Jacka himself moves round among the men of D Company and tells them they are to 'maintain absolute silence for 48 hours'.[58] The idea of this silence ruse is to get Johnny Turk used to the idea that silence from the Anzac lines does not mean they are gone. Silence just means . . . silence.

From tonight, and for the next two days and nights, *no-one* at Anzac Cove is to move out of their trenches, fire rifles or machine guns, throw jam-tin bombs, or shout out. If you're going to snore, do it quietly. And no farting!

Everybody is to stay silent, on pain of punishment.

For if we can get Johnny Turk to become accustomed to our silence without panicking, we can start to thin our ranks day by day, night by night, as we get men down to the beaches, onto the piers and away by the meandering moonlight over the waves, until with the final silence, we *all* slip away . . .

So, you're saying it's true, Bert?

We *are* scarpering?

Yes, it's bloody well true.

Jacka's men are *appalled*.

'We are sneaking off like whipped curs,' Bill Gayning, Platoon Sergeant of D Company says. 'Why can't we have another bloody go at them!'[59]

Brigadier General Monash had been right.

'I am almost frightened to contemplate the howl of rage and disappointment there will be when the men find out what is afoot, and how they have been fooled,' he had written beforehand. 'And I am wondering what Australia will think at the desertion of her 6000 dead and her 20,000 other casualties.'[60]

After all, when you have paid for every yard of ground gained and held with so much blood, how can you abandon it *willingly*?

It is a disgrace to the memories of the men lost, and the decision must be changed, Bert!

(A likely exception to the general outrage is one of Bert Jacka's younger brothers, Bill, who has no sooner arrived in the 14th Battalion as a reinforcement from Cairo than he has suffered frostbite – such freezing in his extremities that surgical pruning of the frozen flesh is possible. He is evacuated within a week of arrival.)

But it really is true, and along with all the others, the 14th Battalion must make ready to leave.

First, across the board, across all the front lines, those who are wounded and killed are not replaced by fresh reinforcements, and all units must make do with who they have. And now war *materiel* starts being shifted from the front lines down towards the beaches, and then more and more of the heavy guns and cases of ammunition start coming down the hills.

It becomes official on 14 December when all the men are told that it is *on*.

Night after night it goes on. Company after company descends down newly widened tracks, often with steps cut into the frozen soil to make it easier for heavy traffic, carrying their rifles with butt plates covered in cloth, whatever supplies they can carry and whatever animals they can lead, to walk onto piers covered with several layers of blankets to deaden the noise. From there, they climb onto the 10 'motorised lighters', barges and small boats which will take them to the three ferry ships for troops, plus one for animals, one for guns, one for vehicles, just off shore from just after dusk to just before dawn.

With the rising sun, the Turkish observers can see just the same numbers of men disembarking from barges, and just the same number of donkeys hauling boxes of supplies on high. What they don't know is that the sole job of those men disembarking is to do this every morning, and the boxes being hauled by the donkeys have nothing in them.

Every day, the Anzac becomes more 'facade' than 'force'.

Who should go and in what order?

The organiser of the whole evacuation, Colonel Cyril Brudenell White, proceeds by a simple rule – he wants the best, most capable men to be last off. They are the ones deemed most likely to perform well in a rear-guard action, remain calm, and deadly, to allow as many of their comrades to get away as possible. It will be the responsibility of each company commander to select these men, a skeleton of perhaps as few as six soldiers holding the line where 100 once stood, but maintaining the same responsibilities and using the same structures of command and communications as previously. In the meantime, the key remains to maximise visibility, to make it *appear* as though the Allies are still 40,000 strong.

Jacka and his men of the 14th Battalion – who are of course deemed to be among the very last to leave – make sure to leave a nice tin of bully for Johnny Turk and set up a rifle timed to fire an hour after they've left.

18 December 1915, Anzac Cove, the end of the beginning, and the beginning of the end[61]

On this, the day when the final part of the evacuation is due to begin, General Birdwood decides to put out a Special Army Order, to his men: *Remember that in the final retirement silence is essential ... Those left in the front line to the last will, in their turn, quietly and silently leave their trenches, passing through their comrades in the covering positions to their place of embarkation in the same soldierly manner in which the troops have effected their various magnificent landings on the shores of this peninsula during the last eight months . . . W.R. BIRDWOOD, Lieut.-General Commanding Dardanelles Army.*[62]

Tonight it is the turn of the 14th Battalion. Many men go to sorrowfully visit the grave of the Reverend Andrew Gillison before leaving, as well as those of other mates – a bitter farewell and a remembrance mixed with rage. They are leaving them behind.

Four hours after dark on this night of 18 December, the word comes. We're out.

The base of their trenches have already been torn up, just as their boots have been wrapped in 'bed-socks, bags, shirts, sleeves, anything at all, to hush the sound of the marching to the beach'.[63]

It is harder than any can say for these Diggers, on this bitter night, to turn their backs on the trenches that their mates had given their lives to defend. But so they do, to the minute, towards the beckoning Aegean that has seen so many warriors arrive and depart through the ages.

The 14th file silently out of their trenches, making way for the skeleton crew of 'Die-Hards', whose job it will be to hold it through this night, the next day, and the first hours of the next night, before they, too, will leave.

Following White's minutely calibrated plan, the 14th Battalion leave just before midnight and follow the long trails of sugar and flour that have been laid out to show retreating troops the zig-zagging route they must religiously follow to avoid detonating mines that have been buried just below the surface. When the last of the Die-Hards come down tomorrow night, they will trail scrub branches behind them to scatter the sugar and flour trails, so that the first of the pursuing Turks will detonate the landmines.

Reaching the beach, all is different.

'At the sea's edge planks were laid out over the water on trestles like springboards to assist men in getting into the boats if the expected attack came off. Up in the hills the occasional bursting of bombs and the rattle of machine guns intimated that the Turks were unaware of the departure of the bulk of the garrison. The guns, which normally flung occasional shells on to the beach, were silent, and men turned their thoughts to the graveyard on our left where some of the larger wooden crosses were discernible in the night.'[64]

And now come the very last of them, their numbers including the again newly promoted Captain Percy Black and his mate 2nd Lieutenant Harry Murray. After Jacka, Black and the others board the boats that have purred into the shore, they are soon away, heading to the troopships that await.

The mood is grim, at their abandonment of everything they have fought so hard for.

'Never again,' Ted Rule chronicles, 'do I expect to hear such concentrated foul language.'[65]

On this perfect night, a soft breeze caresses from the north, the only movement of nature on an otherwise completely still night. On the Aegean Sea, just off shore, the vessels are gliding on dark glass. Staggeringly, as the 14th take their leave, there are now fewer than 4000 men holding the 11,000 yards of the Anzac front line – against 80,000 Turks.

Gazing back, Albert Jacka is even more taciturn than usual. The grief and waste are mingled in the minds of all the Australians watching this sorry scene. When he had arrived on these shores, it had been in the company of another thousand men of the 14th Battalion. As Jacka takes his leave, there are just 50 of those originals, out of 980 who landed, still standing. Most galling, most *appalling*, is how many of those deaths could have been prevented with some thoughtful leadership. He could do a better job himself. He knows it and is now determined to show it.

CHAPTER FOUR

FROM CAIRO TO CALAIS

When the history comes to be written this battle of Pozières Ridge will certainly rank with the battle of Pozières village and with the landing at Gallipoli and the battle of August, 1915, as the four hardest battles ever fought by the Australian troops – indeed, among the hardest ever fought by any army.[1]

Charles Bean, *The West Australian*, 10 August 1916

We have Australians against us, daring fellows, who want watching.[2]

The German commander of the 27th (Saxon) Division in his diary, at Armentières

12–17 February 1916, Suez side, unsweet sorrow

It is shocking news.

Because the Australian Imperial Force is to be expanded from two to five divisions, it has been decided that, instead of starting new battalions and divisions from scratch, most existing battalions, such as the 14th, must be split into two. That way, the half of veteran officers and soldiers that splits off can form the grizzled foundation of an entirely new battalion, completed with a batch of new recruits, while the half that remains can do the same. In the case of the 14th Battalion, half their number will be hived off to form the nucleus of the newly established 46th Battalion. It is a compulsory divorce and it will be brutal no matter how fairly it is done.

The 14th Battalion has already been transferred from the 2nd Division to the nascent 4th Division, and now pretty much the entire job of choosing who goes where in D Company falls to . . . Company

Sergeant Major Bert Jacka. No, he does not formally command the company, but he is certainly the one who commands most respect, and all lean in to learn their fate.

Brother is to be separated from brother on his whim, and rumour spreads he is going to keep all of his cobbers with him in the 14th and send all the ne'er-do-wells to the daughter battalion of the 46th.

As documented by the also recently promoted Corporal Ted Rule, 'I have no doubt Bert endeavoured to be perfectly fair to both battalions but for a few days our lines were a seething mass of discontent.'[3]

Nothing Jacka can do will fix that, as D Company rages at the very idea of being split up. They are brothers in arms, not brothers at arm's length!

First, he simply does the division himself, providing two lists to the company commander: one of those who are to remain with the 14th, and the other those who are to leave. He tries to do it without fear or favour, ensuring that both lists have an even mix of experience, and those he is especially close to.

When that is rejected on the grounds of favouritism, he provides a new list of those who are to depart, 'containing the names of all his old cobbers with his own name at the top'.[4]

That, too, is rejected. The idea of the 14th losing Jacka VC is absurd. Jacka is the 14th, and the 14th is Jacka.

Finally, a kind of compromise is reached with his superiors, and he does indeed have two lists which are deemed acceptable.

Under a sun that glares nearly as much as some of the old-stagers who can't believe it has come to this, the 14th Battalion is drawn up on the parade ground, and Jacka – his heels set tightly together, steeling himself to do what has to be done – lowers the boom.

With no preamble – for he is Albert Jacka and has as much interest in preambles as he has in ambling itself – he gets right to it.

The following men are to fall out on my right:

'Banyard, Twomey . . .'

There is a sudden burst of shouting out on his left.

'By gum, Bert,' Private Twomey explodes as loudly as if he were Fourmey, 'but this is a bit of all right!'[5]

'No more soldiering for me! You can make out a sick report, because I'm off to hospital. To think that a man has never left the battalion and been in every stunt, and now he's to be chucked out like this. Bah – I thought you were a cobber of mine!'[6]

Sergeant Banyard couldn't agree more. He has, literally, bled for the 14th, and now he is to be cast aside on the whim of one bloke, even if that bloke is Albert Jacka himself? No, no, and No. Not all of his next 50 words start with the letter 'f', but it is at least recorded that his 'language would need recording on asbestos'.[7]

So be it. For the moment, as the two have been great fighters, Jacka ignores them – it is more than possible they will get a punch in the nose, for their trouble, a little later – and no-one else dares utter a peep. For Jacka simply does what Jacka does best: he keeps going, reading out his list of all the others who are to join Banyard and Twomey on the right.

When he is finished, there is a sigh of relief from those still on the left, while the group on the right look like a storm on the horizon, complete with black clouds, rumbling thunder and a few flashes of lightning. But there is no way around it. One way or another, within hours, they will be marching off to join their new battalion, the 46th.

'There were feelings of consternation among all ranks at the news,' one soldier writes. 'The thought of leaving the old battalions whose names we had helped to make famous, during the Gallipoli Campaign, was a very bitter pill to swallow. Also most of us were leaving old friends behind.'[8]

'I felt,' one famed officer would later tell Charles Bean, 'as though I were having a limb amputated without any anaesthetic.'[9]

Another soldier quite agrees.

'It hurt I can tell you,' he writes home, 'when they ripped the old green and white stripe off our arms as already we were proud to be in such a battalion . . . Now we don't care what is going to happen to us.'[10]

Nevertheless, in this man's army, what's done is done and they have to accept. In short order these brothers in arms are torn asunder, and the losing half must bid farewell. They do so to the ringing three cheers of their comrades, who watch them depart with real regret.

Similar scenes are taking place among most of the AIF veterans. In the 16th Battalion, two men who are like brothers, Percy Black and Harry Murray are to be split under the reorganisation, with both men deciding to leave the machine-gun sections behind and go to infantry. From now, the soon-to-be *Major* Black – a staggering rise from Private to Major in not much more than nine months – is to command B Company of the 16th Battalion, while *Captain* Murray is to command A Company of the 13th Battalion.

But to work! For those who have left are at least quickly replaced by new recruits, freshly arrived from Australia. And, as many of these poor bastards look like they barely know their arse from their elbow, let alone one end of a .303 from another, it will be for the veterans to bring them up to speed.

Inevitably, there is some tension between many of the veterans and these latecomers, often referred to as the 'Heavy Ponderers',[11] who had taken their bloody time to join after much Heavy Pondering indeed.

'You're here at last,' snarls a gnarled Gallipoli veteran at a group of Heavy Ponderers who have just marched into the dusty Egyptian training ground of Tel-el-Kebir, 'only 18 months too long in coming. You've been a bloody long while making up yer minds to come.'

Oh, really?

'You came away and thought you was coming to a picnic,' one of the incoming Ponderers says, with some dignity. 'We didn't.'[12]

To *work*, I said!

Start training, and get serious.

For the news has already broken. The 1st and 2nd Australian Divisions will be on their way to France and the Western Front, almost immediately. Lucky bastards! The 4th and 5th Australian Divisions will follow them in due course, once we have completed training to the point it is felt we can hold our own in the entirely new kind of warfare that we will be facing there. The 3rd Division, being raised in Australia, will later join the AIF in France via England.

The fact that their training is done on old battlefields, still littered with spent cartridges, shattered trenches and bits of bone proves to be a part-humbling, part-horrifying reminder for all – the wrong decision means death. Bad luck means an early grave. Vigilance and fate are the two things left to protect them; so train as if your life depended on it, for it does. Back in the camp in time for tea in the mess huts, a new and more pleasant world comes as the twilight fades into night. Ellis observes the evening ritual: 'Then hundreds of lights would twinkle through the night, the booths of the natives would flare with torches, and the men would wander through the lines, visiting and being visited, making new friendships and renewing old ones, or filing away in hundreds to some picture theatre or boxing match.'[13]

If the flick is no good, a fight will do.

•

In the searing sun of the Tel-el-Kebir parade ground, the Australian soldiers are standing to attention, while the General Officer Commanding this training facility, an Englishman, gives them a strong lecture on the need to clean up their language, and specifically cut out such words as 'fuck' and 'c–nt', as in any case he understands that these two words are not frequently used in Australia, so he doesn't want to hear them here, either.

A voice rings out from the back of the parade: 'The fucking c–nt has never been there.'[14]

The explosion of laughter is emblematic of a view that is so widespread among the Diggers, when it comes to officers (and particularly Pommy bastard officers), that even Charles Bean thinks it worthy of note.

'... [W]ith the exception of those British officers who have fought with us,' Bean records, 'the British officer does not generally like us. The Australian doesn't salute him – as a general rule; he is jealous of the praise we get as soldiers and he probably quite honestly fails to understand our discipline.'[15]

As it happens, one British writer, John Masefield, would later record that when a British officer told off an Australian for not saluting him, the friendly Australian reached out, gave him a pat on the shoulder and said, 'Young man, when you go home, you tell your mother that today you've seen a real bloody soldier.'[16]

Now, on the one hand, when it comes to his own attitude towards the brass hats, Sergeant Major Albert Jacka is also not much of an admirer.

But on the other hand?

On the other hand, after much reflection in these weeks back in Egypt, Jacka conceives a new ambition. He wants to rise in the ranks himself, and actually become an officer, maybe, even. It has been fine to be a Sergeant Major, with responsibility for administration, standards and morale, but as this has brought him into ever more contact with the general organisation and planning of operations, he has come to realise that, for the most part, the officers are no better than him in determining tactics, nor strategy, and in many cases they are demonstrably worse.

For too long at Gallipoli he had seen the lives of his men squandered on insanity, on orders that were guaranteed to fail.

There can only be one solution.

'Sir,' he says to Lieutenant Colonel Charles Moreland Montague Dare, the Commanding Officer of the 14th Battalion, in late February, 'I want to apply for the officers' training course.'[17]

Dare, a 27-year-old Melbourne architect by training – and no less than the scion of the Dares of the vast 'Moreland Park' on the edge of Melbourne – demurs, and puts Jacka off. It is one thing to have won the VC for bravery in the field, but quite another for an uneducated working-class man to be so presumptuous as to think he could actually have the intellectual grunt necessary to understand things like weaponry trajectories and military law. Yes, in wartime much is forgiven if a man can lead in such a way that others willingly follow. Further, there is a record in the AIF of working-class men rising. But for goodness' sake, this is a man whose education had finished at primary school! He'd worked with his father on a *dray*, from the age of 13 onwards.

Beyond that, Jacka is abrasive, and has the tendency to question orders from superior officers. It is not the stuff that *officers* are made of. (And incidentally, has any senior officer in the history of the AIF ever had no middle name at all? A wag might say that as his formal name is now Albert Jacka VC, the problem is sorted, but it is not enough.)

Yet Jacka remains insistent, and plays the strongest card he has. If Dare denies him, he will apply to go to a new battalion, and the 14th will be the unit that *formerly* boasted Australia's most famous soldier.

In so denying Jacka, Dare has the support of the man that General Birdwood has newly appointed as the Commanding Officer of the newly created 4th Division, the British blue-blood General Sir Herbert Vaughan Cox – described by John Monash, as 'one of those crotchety, livery old Indian officers whom the climate has dried and shrivelled up into a bag of nerves'.[18]

General Cox, who had been responsible for much of the disaster to his own brigade at Cape Helles, where some 2000 of his men had been killed for no ground gained, and equally botched his command of the left assaulting column during the August Offensive. But no matter. You have to break eggs to make an omelette. And he has *very* strong views on just who might be made of the right stuff for officer material. And he, like Lieutenant Colonel Dare, is philosophically opposed to common men rising from the ranks to become commissioned officers.

After all, Cox insists, 'You couldn't have working-class men leading businessmen and those with university degrees'.[19]

But Monash is equally strong.

'The man concerned is a born leader. He has proved himself on Gallipoli as a fighter. He is responsible, popular and strong. He wants to lead, make decisions and inspire. That's how it is done in the Australian force.'[20]

For you see, General Cox – the views of Lieutenant Colonel Dare notwithstanding – you clearly don't understand the Australian ethos. Things work differently in our country.

Monash's thoughts on this are clear, and he will later record them.

'Privates, corporals and sergeants who displayed, under battle conditions, a notable capacity for leadership were earmarked for preferment. There was thus no officer caste, no social distinction in the whole force. In not a few instances, men of humble origin and belonging to the artisan class rose, during the war, from privates to the command of battalions. The efficiency of the force suffered in no way in consequence. On the contrary, the whole Australian Army became automatically graded into leaders and followers according to the individual merits of every man, and there grew a wonderful understanding between them.'[21]

As Commanding Officer of Jacka's 4th Brigade, Monash carries enough weight that Major Charles Moreland Montague Dare is overruled, and Cox persuaded to at least give him a go – on the reckoning that, as an ill-educated working-class man, Jacka won't get far in the officer training course anyway.

In fact, when Jacka arrives at Zeitoun on the northern edge of Cairo to the Officers School of Instruction – a large white building with wide windows and a veranda leading on to a spacious garden – it is the academic equivalent of a hurricane blitz.

Not only does he dominate against fellow candidates in the physical examination, so too does his experience on actual battlefields shine through in classwork on platoon tactics.

In a practice begun at Gallipoli, he writes down – in a script that is remarkably elegant for one who has left school so young – the academic spine for many things that he has already learnt through experience guided by instinct.

Uses of fire:

1. To facilitate movement.
2. Preparation for assault.
3. Mutual support.
4. Covering fire & support.
5. Gain superiority of fire.
6. Demoralising effect of enemy.
7. Draw enemy's troops in desired direction.
8. Fire is used to help the advance.[22]

But, moving on. How do you organise a platoon into an assault force and what orders should be given? Jacka already knows.

How do you bring covering fire to bear? Next time, give him a hard one.

And so it goes for much of the course, such as where to position bombers as you launch attacks on enemy trenches and how to use this new weapon, the Lewis gun. Learning the administration part, and the paperwork that must be completed, is a little more challenging, but he is nothing if not a quick learner.

When the final results come in, Albert Jacka VC, graduate of Wedderburn Public School, has come second in the class of 20, with an average of 94 per cent. He is duly promoted to the rank of 2nd Lieutenant – now in charge of a platoon – and becomes one of a small wave of Diggers rising to such exalted ranks from a standing start.

13 March 1916, Ismaïlia, I Anzac Corps is needled

With no fewer than 36 men to every flat-bed railway truck, the soldiers of Australia's 2nd Division are leaving by the light of a desert moon. The 1st Division will do the same in seven days, then the En Zeds, and then the I Anzac Corps will be gone.

Albert Jacka and his mates in the 14th Battalion have watched the first departure, with envy. Those lucky bastards are heading off to fight on the Western Front!

In their absence, II Anzac Corps and Jacka's mob must take over many of their duties, including the defence of 25 miles of the Suez Canal, from Ferry Post to Serapeum. The Anzac Mounted Division is holding the fort now, but does not have enough numbers to do it for more than a fortnight.

How can II Anzac Corps get there?

The hard way.

General McCay, the Grafton-born officer recommended for the VC for his bravery at Lone Pine, and now lone commander of the 4th Infantry Battalion, has decided that the men will *march* there, from Tel-el-Kebir to the bloody end, through the desert, 43 miles away, in the heat, over three days.[23] In full kit, in quick time.

No, really. That's the plan.

For God's *sake!*

The sand proves so soft that their boots frequently sink down to their tops, and so hot that the sun does not merely shine, it *beats*. The 4th Brigade soon begins to break apart, as hands steal to water bottles and drain them dry. Onwards they press to a camp that sits somewhere beyond the burning, shimmering and sizzling horizon that refuses to come forward to meet and comfort the men. They are tortured by the fact that 'a fresh water canal runs along a little distance from the route', from which they are 'forbidden to drink, bath or even wash in it as it is found to be contaminated by all sorts of disease germs, the natives being filthy in their habits and all drainage going into the canal'.[24]

The sweat pours out of them, their trousers chafe their thighs, and as soon as the fine sand works its way into their socks and boots, each step is a severe irritation of the skin and spirit.

'All along the route one could see the articles thrown out by the boys,' one Digger will recount. 'The boys lagged and lagged behind, hundreds needing the doctor's attention, and many fainting. Many begged and begged for water.'[25]

When their route takes them up and down sandhills, they only just manage to keep going, with the heat in the hollows like a furnace. The dust is clinging, choking, oppressive and you cannot see further than 20 yards in any direction.

'Some nearly crazy with thirst lurched along with their tongues out like dogs.'[26]

Those few who have water left sip it, only to find it makes their lips drier! Before long, that water becomes so hot they cannot even bring it to their lips. And now stronger blokes start to carry the rifles of weaker blokes, who appear about to drop in their sandy tracks.

'We were ... foaming at the mouth like mad dogs,' Private Henry Williams records, 'with tongues swollen, breath gripping our throats with agonising pain, and legs buckling under us.'[27]

The most frustrating thing for the exhausted Jacka and his men on the third and most shattering day are the two things running either side of their path of sinking sand: a railway, along which empty trains choof by, leaving them behind; and the freshwater canal, from which they are forbidden to drink.

'You'll have a gutful of worms if you touch it,' their adjutant insists, as he rides back and forth beside them on horseback.

'Well, can we drink out of your water-cart, sir?'

'No, you cannot. You shouldn't have emptied your water bottles.'

When, at 3 pm, men start to collapse, someone makes a suggestion.

'Let's rush the canal. He can't stop the lot of us.'[28]

Second Lieutenant Albert Jacka, for one, though he does not participate – and has been remarkable for how he has kept his own platoon of

50 men together, with fewer drop-outs than all others in the battalion – does not object. He has never been one for insane orders, and these orders from McCay have been positively dangerous. So while he has encouraged his men to conserve their water, to suck on pebbles, to help each other along, in the extremity of this situation, it is up to the men to work out how to survive.

And so many of the men in the whole battalion charge the canal and fill their bellies with water, let the devil take the hindmost. Some indeed get sick, but all survive, staggering on towards the finish.

'Within two miles of our destination,' Ted Rule will recount, 'General Monash rode up and tactlessly told some of the stragglers that their sisters could do as well. It was the only time I've heard men curse him.'[29]

25 April 1916, across Egypt and the Western world, the Little Digger digs deep for his Diggers

At dawn a service is to be held.

A year has passed since they landed at Gallipoli, and the veterans of that extraordinary sunrise are asked to pray and parade for those who fell on that day. For the Anzacs, this day will begin by way of solemn commemoration. General John Monash has pushed the idea that all the men in uniform, wherever they stand this crisp morning – be it Moascar, Tel-el-Kebir or Cairo – must bow their heads to commemorate the landing and the lads who had fallen. The service for the 14th Battalion is attended by a bare-headed Jacka. He, like all the Diggers who were at the landing on the day, has a red ribbon hanging from above his left breast pocket, while those who had seen service in the Dardanelles are entitled to a blue ribbon. Once the service is done, the day becomes one of celebration and fun.

No more training, nothing but sports, including swimming in the canal in a 'great Aquatic Carnival',[30] and an evening concert.

'It was enjoyed by everybody but General Cox,' Ted Rule chronicles. 'The old man was furious because someone had entered his tent and purloined his supply of whisky.'[31] Cox is incandescent with rage and threatens holy hell to the perpetrators ... if he can just find them.

The only clue that they're out there is the band, 'in every conceivable state of undress',[32] suddenly striking up the tune to 'Hold Your Hand Out Naughty Boy' . . .

•

The Western Front is confirmed!

And they will be going within weeks.

And it is with precisely that in mind that the 14th Battalion must now engage in a far more specific training regime. They will have to learn to make attacks under the protection of a creeping barrage, a system whereby a rain of artillery shells moves just ahead of them, the wall of fire leaping forward 100 yards every two minutes. Ideally, it will pass over the front-line trenches of the 'Hun' – as the Germans are often referred to – just seconds before they rush in, not giving the defenders a chance to get up from their deep dugouts, gather themselves and their weapons. And then they will have to get to work with bullets, bayonets and these new 'Mills bombs' – advanced versions of the jam-tin bombs they had used in Gallipoli.

Many of their instructors are British veterans who have fought on the fabled Western Front and have been invalided to these posts.

'"You go and do your whack, and get knocked out, and see if you want to go back there," one of them says, with a faraway look in his eyes'[33] – but they are more than happy to pass on to the soldiers and officers what they have learnt, and then give them exams at the end of the week.

Such intense training is occasionally interspersed with the soldiers taking leave to Cairo – mostly to visit the bars and brothels in the 'Wazza', the city's red-light district, but Jacka has no interest. For one thing, he has kept faithful to his Rechabite pledge never to drink alcohol, and, for another, his best intention is to remain a virgin until he is married.

(Jacka's only involvement in the famous Battle of the Wazza, where a mass of drunken Diggers rioted and burnt some of the brothels to the ground had been to call some of the men to account. 'I've got to punish you, Fitz,' he had been obliged to tell his old mate Bill Fitzpatrick the next day. 'Cookhouse.'[34] Bill had to spend several days peeling potatoes, by way of penance. Let this be a lesson to you, Bill. Don't *ever* burn down brothels again! And he never did.)

Anyway, right now Jacka has his hands more than full consolidating his role as an officer. There are no problems with leading the men.

This is not to say he tries to be a friend to all. Far from it. Ted Rule knows that Jacka's tongue can be as sharp as any sabre when slackness is seen.[35] For his part, Fitzpatrick remembered Jacka's treatment more softly: 'Good soldier. Training. Good officer. Treated his men beautifully.'[36] Still another, Private Arthur Tulloh, will maintain, '[We] would have followed him anywhere.'[37] One thing that Tulloh particularly notices is that Jacka remains one of the men, preferring to spend his time with the soldiers than withdrawing like most other officers who have risen from the ranks.

Far more tricky for Jacka is dealing, as a junior officer, with his senior officers who – he can't help but feel – stray too close to the English model of officerdom which is, 'Do it, because I am your superior officer, *and* of a higher class than you,' rather than the Australian way which is, 'Do it, because this is the best way for all of us.'

It is for this reason that Tulloh would also say of Jacka that, straining the limits of staying this side of a court martial for insubordination, 'he wouldn't do anything that he didn't want to'.[38]

For senior Australian officers in Jacka's rough outer orbit, the best of the lot of them is still Monash; he is the canny commander who seems as loath to lose his men's lives as much as the men do themselves.

Jacka does not feel the same about Major Otto Carl Wilhelm Fuhrmann, the Commanding Officer of the 14th Battalion's B Company that he has been assigned to. The issue is not the fact that Fuhrmann is of German extraction – born in Melbourne to a carpenter father from Hamburg – for his loyalty to the British Empire has never been in question. No, it is his manner of speaking, his arrogance, the way he talks down to everyone beneath him, while talking up his own exploits – which, at Gallipoli, never seemed to be within a bull's roar of the front lines. Jacka's frustration is that the further he goes in this caper, the more he realises that he knows better than many of his senior officers how to lead men, how to get things done, just as he feels – and as he had demonstrated at Zeitoun – that he has a good grasp of tactics, and can more than hold his own on the administrative side of being an officer.

So why can't he rise further still?

•

The day has come at last.

Just under six months after leaving Gallipoli, the Australian soldiers of the 4th Division – by now burnt dark brown by the Egyptian sun – must follow the path forged 10 weeks ago by the 1st and 2nd Divisions, and march from their camp two miles east of the canal, across a swaying pontoon bridge to the railway station at Serapeum and are soon to haul their kit onto open, flat-top rail trucks.

Spirits are high, and as they march, they sing, to the tune of 'Waltzing Matilda', a newly favourite song:

> *Fighting the Kaiser, fighting the Kaiser*
> *Who'll come a fighting the Kaiser with me*
> *We'll drink up his beer and eat all his sausages*
> *Who'll come a fighting the Kaiser with me.*[39]

The short answer is, everyone, and their own movement at the station is nothing if not swift.

All aboooooard! Toot, toot!

Their packs and rifles are placed in a line right down the centre, and they are able to use those packs as a pillow, in two rows of 18 soldiers. No matter that it is as uncomfortable as kissing Great-Auntie Doris ... they are all soon asleep to the rocking rhythm of the railway.

Morning sees them coming into the port at Alexandria, where a mighty ship awaits, the 15,000-ton liner SS *Transylvania*, ready to take the 4th Brigade across the Mediterranean to France.

2 June 1916, upon the sunny Mediterranean, bound for Marseilles

To sail on the sea with only the slim chance of submarines to bother you is very near heaven for Gallipoli survivors like Albert Jacka. For submarines are problems for the navy to worry about. The mighty 4th

Brigade, of which the 14th Battalion is the proudest unit, is simply on a cruise to France – which is where French women are, and that is where the thoughts of those aboard remain.

But now that they have arrived must they really stay on board when, just beyond yonder gates at the dock, they can see bars, *women*, people, *bars* and WOMEN!?

Maybe not, but what about the sentries on duty at the gates?

Bugger the sentries.

If a dozen of us rush them all at once we will get through.

And a dozen of the hard-core hard men of the 4th Brigade do exactly that, even knocking off the sentries, only . . .

Only to suddenly be confronted by – oh Christ – an Australian officer with a pistol pointed straight at them.

Worse still, it is Captain 'Mad Harry' Murray. Not one of them doubt that he will pull the trigger if they take another step. And if there is a blackness more black than the black of a pistol muzzle pointed right at you from 10 yards away, they haven't seen it. Meekly, they head back to the ship.

At least in a few hours' time – and this time in an orderly fashion – the men of the 4th Brigade are able to march to the Marseille–Saint-Charles railway station, whereupon things quickly become a lot more cheery.

'*Bienvenue, les Australiens! Merci! Merci!*' Welcome, Australians! Thank you! Thank you! Beautiful young French women flock to them, throwing their arms around them and kissing them on both cheeks. Unfortunately so do the less attractive French men, and soon *les Australiens* beg for mercy from all this affection.

All aboard to safety on the train. That *is* a train, isn't it?

Well, some would call it a carriage.

'The thing that struck us most forcibly was the notices on the cattle trucks (as they are called in Victoria),' one Digger notes. 'Each one bore a notice stating that 6 *chevaux* or 40 *hommes* could be packed into the trucks. I think that 6 horses would have more comfort in them than 40 men.'[40]

Soon enough, whatever you want to call it, they are on their way.

'For 60 hours,' Rule would record, 'we forgot that we were on a deadly mission, and in imagination lived within the pages of Grimm's fairy tales. Mansions nestling into the folds of hills, and old castles perched on crags, overlooked the verdant valleys, while the beautiful River Rhône was never out of the picture in the early stages of the journey. The farms were the envy of us all. Everything was so peaceful that the existence of a state of war was almost incredible.'[41]

At every stop the soldiers are plied with 'coffee, vin and fruit' from the ever-grateful and warm-hearted French people, who, as one Digger records, 'made us feel that they and their beautiful country were worth fighting for'.[42]

But hang on, why are so many of the women wearing black dresses and shawls and . . . ?

Ah, the penny drops.

'Everyone you met on the station,' Private Harry Preston will recount, 'the women – were in dark dresses, because they'd had someone killed. We *parlez-voused* a little, but not much. You went into some of the places for a meal – you wanted bacon and eggs, or something – you couldn't tell them what you wanted: you'd cackle like a fowl. "Oh, *comprends, comprends*, oh yes. I'll cook for you."'[43]

At a brief stop at Lyon, the French crowd cry out, '*Vive l'Australie!*'[44]

This vision splendid of rivers, streams, green fields and endless avenues of trees continues all the way north, as the Diggers gaze with wonder at the vision splendid of the sunlit plains extended that look 'like, a succession of cinematographic views of Paradise'.[45]

The castles! The cathedrals! The gorgeous fields with thousands of poppies that dot them like drops of blood, and wild marguerites! Albert Jacka is as entranced as all of them, though, given his former job, inevitably finds his eyes drawn towards France's thick green forests which seem to grow mostly in the mountainous areas where farmlands have not taken over.

Paris passes in a blur as they steam towards Calais, and on arrival they see the new odd steel hats all the Tommies are wearing, called a 'battle bowler' by the troops. They're not exactly stylish, and very much roundhead instead of cavalier, but apparently these metal domes will spare your life if shrapnel heads towards them. The train ride slows to a crawl as parades of British troops now come aboard achingly slowly, and they are stopped time and time again to make way for more and more trains filled with munitions and men. If this is war by timetable; somebody has not been following it very well; it would be quicker to walk if it weren't for the howitzers.

Finally, morning comes along with a sign: 'Hazebrouck', it reads. This is where they get off, and kits and caboodles are clambered down and marched 10 miles to the village of Thiennes to their billets ... make that barns. But at least with clean hay! No luxury spared for our gallant boys.

As they prepare to bunk down, a sound hits them. And hits. And shakes and rumbles and tumbles and does not stop.

Guns. Big guns. Flashes of light break up this night, high rockets that shoot up and hang in the air; the Verey lights that signal to the artillery where next to pillory. It's the Western Front. They are sleeping next to the bloody Western Front. Sweet dreams, boys.

It will take a few days of moving about, marching and settling in, but by the middle of June they have arrived just outside the town of Armentières, just three miles from the Western Front, where they are put into billets. Many of them find themselves in farmers' barns, where they have to argue the toss with pigs, geese and chooks as to who the primary residents of said barn are – with the only saving grace being that it is not put to the vote, as it would be a 98 per cent win for the mice – but they make do.

For the moment the 4th Brigade is being held in reserve, assigned to stop any German breakthrough that might occur. In the meantime each battalion, including the 14th, sends working parties of 400 men 10 miles forward each day to work right behind the lines, hauling munitions forward, and bodies back.

A few days later, three platoons of the 14th are rotated into the front-line trenches to relieve the 19th Battalion. They can see the Western Front up close, take their turn at being pounded and – most terrifying/exciting – go out on night-time patrols into No Man's Land where they will try to get as close to the German lines as possible without being seen.

Now, to the veterans of Gallipoli, a lecture on warfare is like telling your grandmother how to suck eggs. She knows already. But right now, it is the newly arrived Diggers who don't know; here on the Western Front they must face a devilish new weapon previously unfaced: chemical warfare. *Gas.* You can dodge bullets by ducking your head, and escape shell shrapnel by diving into a previous shell-hole – but neither manoeuvre will save you against gas. When the cry of 'Gas!' goes up, you will go down in agony within 30 seconds if you don't *immediately* strap your gas mask on. Yes, you might live if the gas is not too thick, but even then you will have ruined lungs for the rest of your now much shorter life.

So let us drill. Put your cumbersome masks on, and walk through this poisonous cloud of gas created for your benefit. The Diggers look at each other. Are these bastards serious?

They are. And it is a direct order.

Reluctantly, they strap their ruddy respirators on, don their helmets, and charge through an invisible enemy; canaries in this giant coalmine of catastrophe.

Oh, and welcome to the Western Front. We've been expecting you, and so are the Huns.

Under the current plans, the British are about to launch their biggest stunt of the war to date, with the 4th Division to contribute key support immediately afterwards. General Godley has picked Monash's crack 4th Brigade for the job, and General Monash has picked the 14th Battalion to open the batting!

The man himself actually addresses his most potent unit, using stately and simple words to let them know how important their work is, how they are to fight for themselves and for Australia.

You must never underestimate just how strong we are, how well we had done at Gallipoli, and I have every confidence that you *will* do the same here. Always remember that, for every major raid you take, it is important that everyone knows what everyone else is doing, everyone must fulfil their own roles, and each of you must have *many* skills, so that if any of you go down, you can adjust and compensate. And rehearse, rehearse, rehearse every move you make!

As ever with Monash, he just has a way of speaking to the men which gives them focus on the job at hand, and confidence that it can be done.

All of which is wonderful.

But who from the 14th Battalion will, out in No Man's Land, lead the first serious raid being planned on the enemy trenches?

Surely, the honour will go to 2nd Lieutenant Albert Jacka VC, the indisputably finest and most famous soldier they have among them?

Actually, no.

While Monash is insistent that the raiders should all come from the one company to heighten cohesion, the bad news is that the pride of leading the actual on-ground assault will not belong to D Company, but . . . as decided upon by Colonel Charles Moreland Montague Dare himself . . . to A Company, and a group of raiding volunteers led by Captain Harold Boyd Wanliss.

Albert Jacka VC is more than a little annoyed – this far in, does he really have to still prove that he is good at this caper?

Despite this being his first action, Wanliss is already regarded, as Ted Rule will later characterise him, as 'energetic and careful, idolised by his men, their idea of what an Australian should be in character and ability – undoubtedly one of the grandest spirits we ever had in the AIF'.[46]

Jacka is not yet convinced.

Wanliss is an admittedly top-shelf officer – *and* a gentleman – superbly well-educated, not only from Ballarat but descended from one of the prime movers of the mighty Eureka Stockade. Devilishly handsome, with a dimpled chin and thick brown hair permanently set in an elegant sweep, he looks like a lawyer you might trust or a politician you would vote for; a statue of solid virtue alive in front of you. Only his impish grin betrays that he is not as relentlessly respectable as he seems.

After badly breaking his leg in Australia around the time of the outbreak of war, he had arrived late, as one of the reinforcements after the rest of the 14th Battalion had arrived back in Cairo from Gallipoli, and had been training with his men ever since.

Look, Jacka respects firm officers and hard-working soldiers who never take a backward step like Wanliss, but he has *no* battle experience.

It seems to many in the battalion that Dare has picked A Company and Wanliss, rather than D Company and Jacka, as a slight to the latter – whose fame and independent spirit has made him something of a maverick; an alternative voice to Dare's own in the battalion, and one that the men actually listen to?

Perhaps. But when Jacka dares to raise the issue with Dare he is firmly told to mind his own business, and that the Colonel will not have his orders questioned! All that Jacka can do for the moment is watch and wait, observing closely over the next fortnight as Wanliss and the group of five officers and 80 odd soldiers who will go on the raid to do their training. There is no doubt they are working hard, as each man is assigned specialist roles, and time and again they go out beyond the wire, becoming so accustomed to the terrain at night they can read it like the back of their land. Their training exercises include crossing a small stream before getting to grips, and pliers, with the wires.

'We were trained there for three weeks,' one of the raiders will recall, 'just like a football team. We were taken on runs, and given a cold bath every day, and extra food. And we rehearsed the whole show time after time; it's simply wonderful the way everything is arranged for, and the time worked out to seconds.'[47]

All identifying papers are removed and their faces and hands are completely blackened with burnt cork – as are their bayonets.

'Only about four men out of the 66 carry rifles and bayonets. Those who carry the bayonets have them painted black. The rest carry weapons according to their jobs, most of them carrying revolvers, bombs, and "knob-kerrys" . . . an entrenching tool handle with an iron cog-wheel on the end. The scouts have revolvers, bombs, wire-cutters, and a tomahawk.'[48]

Specialised 'bombers', who will hurl grenades great distances with formidable accuracy, will be issued with eight Mills bomb fragmentation grenades, which weigh 1 pound 11 ounces and can be thrown as far as 40 yards if a man is strong enough. Officers are given SOS rockets – which, when fired, will explode in three red blobs or the like – to call down artillery in case of trouble, ideally just in front of where the SOS is fired, on the heads of the Hun.

The scouts go out night after night into No Man's Land. They know that, come the stunt, they will have just three minutes from the barrage on the German lines ceasing to cross the ground and get through the wire – the last bit should only take 30 seconds, if the barrage has done most of the work – and to the enemy trenches, followed by five minutes of wreaking havoc, before getting out again!

Again and again and again they rehearse until it is like clockwork. All they need is for the big British stunt to take place, and then they will be going out on the next night.

Dawn, 1 July 1916, in the Valley of the Somme, fie the cannons' roar

It is to be the biggest battle in the history of the world. But talking about it in such terms is not the British or Australian way; it is just a 'stunt'. The biggest stunt in history, and it is hoped it will end the greatest war in history.

The artillery before the battle is expected, but its length and amount is like a flood through the air; it is incessant, unprecedented and brutal. If it is possible to break the Germans' desire for fighting, this will prove the point. An entire week of shelling! Surely any German commander must guess what is coming next? The French have lost 80,000 trying to hold Verdun; how many men will be coming now in attack? How many dead can the Allies afford? This month will tell.

At 0730 hours, the killing will begin in earnest. The British will leave their trenches and push across No Man's land. The place for attack is named the Somme. Right now it is just a valley in northern France, just as Gettysburg was once a field near a town in southern Pennsylvania, and Waterloo used to be an anonymous municipality in Belgium. The Somme is simply part of the German defences and it is about to be tested to the extreme. The Western Front will be broken here; the Allies will crack the wall of armaments and men and flood through. The entire German line will then be swamped and drowned in the aftershocks of this great blow.

The morning begins with the British soldiers hidden in the mist; hunkering in hollows and waiting for the order to reveal themselves. As the sun rises on the Somme, one million men will see each other. At 0625 the artillery fires to ensure this sight is concealed for as long as possible, it is 'hurricane fire' and the eye can barely comprehend the fury unleashed. Another tempest begins and four mines will be set off at 0728 at La Boisselle on the roads approaching Pozières. These mines are no small affairs, the two greatest are packed with 40,000 pounds and an unbelievable 60,000 pounds of explosives; they will destroy any soldier near and create a massive crater to defend in an instant.

No fewer than 120,000 British infantry will be the encore to that blast, spread across 16 miles, a thousand field and heavy guns at their backs to attack the enemy's rear. They will take the Albert–Bapaume road, the village of Thiepval to their left and the village of Pozières on the right. When that is done, the ruined windmill of Pozières Ridge will serve as a perfect observation point for the whole battle and the artillery can be relayed deadly and precise instructions. To the south of the Somme, 60,000 Frenchmen can't be wrong and they shall be along their six-mile front with six more divisions to back them.

Quite a stunt. *Ready?* It is 0727 and in just a few more seconds the end of the war will begin . . .

BOOOOOOOOMMMM! The mines explode with a blast so loud that it will rattle the windows in Kent, across the channel, 100 miles away! And we are a hell of a lot closer than that and we can barely stand in the shockwave as the ROOOOOOOOARRRRRRRRRRRRR begins and 16 miles of British men go over the top. The deaths start at once, some before a step is taken, some when they feel their foot tug upon a wire just yards out, but most by the hail of bullets that hit them as they run. ON! Those still living cannot be still, they run 'into the darkness of death, cheering each other with cries that could be heard above the roaring and the crashing of the battle'.[49]

CHARGE!

•

From atop a hill just north-east of the town of Albert on this morning, Charles Bean and the other war correspondents stand gathered at the spot to which they have been taken by the British press officers and watch carefully.

Less than a mile away, they can see a line of British infantrymen marching over the crest of a small rise and disappearing from view. As the war correspondents strain for their next sight of the British infantry, whole minutes pass until . . . until, for the Australians, it is a little like the verse from *The Man From Snowy River* . . .

> *Then they lost him for a moment, where two mountain gullies met*
> *In the ranges, but a final glimpse reveals*
> *On a dim and distant hillside the wild horses racing yet,*
> *With the man from Snowy River at their heels.*

For there they are again.

On a dim and distant hillside, midst shrouds of smoke and dust, the British soldiers are visible once more, marching to war. At least, some of them are. For, clearly, many have been struck down, and, as the newsmen continue to watch, many more are falling.

For the tragic truth is that the British artillery is too thinly spread across the front they are attacking, and little damage has been done to the German wire or machine guns. It means . . . massacre. Across the lines on this terrible day, serried ranks of British soldiers march straight towards their certain deaths, following their orders that all but guarantee such a result.

At Serre, a 720-man battalion of the East Lancashire Regiment, composed of Accrington Pals, loses no fewer than 584 killed, wounded or missing by 8 am. The Newfoundland Regiment starts the day with 780 healthy men, and finishes with only 110 neither killed nor wounded.

Also devastated is the British 2nd Division, which had been set the task of taking the village of Pozières and pushing beyond it to the windmill. They do not get within a cannon's roar of it. When they are relieved at 7 pm by the 12th Division, the headcount of survivors does not take long, for there are so few. From 9600 men who had attacked, the 2nd has lost 200 officers and 4908 other ranks, killed, wounded or missing.

All up, at the end of the first day's battle, 20,000 British soldiers lie dead in No Man's Land, with another 37,000 maimed. There has been no British breakthrough.

2 July 1916, Bois Grenier, trenchant trench raid

Finally, all is in place, for the 4th Brigade of the 4th Division – in the form of the 14th Battalion – to make their first raid on the Western Front.

Just before midnight on 2 July they engage in the real thing and slip through their own wire to disappear into the night, and get to the spot in No Man's Land where white luminescent tapes have been laid out.

Scarcely daring to breathe, they stare intently at the German wire, and parapets that lie just beyond it.

Sure enough, at *exactly* 11.35 pm, as planned, their own artillery opens up on the German wire and trenches directly in front of them, as the parapets they have been staring at intently become a mass of flame and billowing smoke. At the same time the shells from the trench mortars start to land on the wire, blowing big holes in it, but sending out such strong concussive blasts that a couple of Wanliss's men start bleeding from their noses.

Hold on!

This tornado fire is to be as intense as it is short, and after just three minutes, the last of the blasts on the German front line cease, and the previously flaming parapets go dark.

All ready?

Ready.

NOW!

Charging as one, with the dashing Wanliss in the lead, they get to the river, and wade across the icy-cold and fast-flowing waters with their munitions and weaponry held above their heads before they start scrambling up the far bank and through whatever gaps in the wire they can find.

Rehearsals on similar landscape nearby have shown that it will take 80 seconds to cross to the German line – and it is important that it take no longer, for they must hit the defenders before they can recover from the barrage and bring their machine guns to bear.

By now, and this is key, the tornado fire has moved back, as part of a strategy known as a 'box barrage', where, after the shelling has destroyed a section of the first line, it moves methodically down the two sides along support and communication trenches, before decimating the parallel section of the second line – thus isolating those soldiers in the first line, who should be easy pickings.

Alas, alas, they reach the enemy line, only to find that the barbed wire is 'hardly touched'.[50]

Christ!

'Imagine how we felt,' one of the scouts will recount, 'when we dashed up to the wire and found we had 60 yards of entanglements to go through hardly cut at all – the artillery had been firing just too far, and nearly all their shells had landed in Fritz's front trench, instead of in his wire.'[51]

Worse still, they have been spotted, and machine guns have already opened up on them as they go to ground and begin cutting the wire, crawling forward. In some places, where it is too slow, some of Wanliss's men make an extraordinary sacrifice to hasten proceedings.

'Hands, legs and faces of most of the party bear witness to the fierce struggle they had to get through the uncut wire, clothing being torn to pieces. Also trip wire gave a lot of trouble. Our scouts, and some of the wounded threw themselves on the wire, so as to form a bridge for the rest of the party to walk over them.'[52]

With calm confidence, Wanliss continues to give the orders for some of his men to cut through the wires while the others prepare to provide covering fire on the Germans, when they are inevitably discovered. And yes, one of the blizzard of bullets coming the Australians' way hits Wanliss – the bullet going through one cheek and out the other, taking a bit of tongue and a few upper teeth with it – and felling him. Nevertheless he is *still* in command, and rises once more to give orders rinsed with blood, as his troop continue to cut their way through the wire.

'There were four lots of barbed wire with an interval between them of about three to ten yards,' one of the soldiers will recount. 'The first three lots of wire were about 16 yards across and the last row was about 20 yards across and iron stanchions used to peg the wire in. The wire was very long barb and is a dirty brownish colour.'[53]

Finally they are through the wire, and now charge the German trenches. Two dozen of Wanliss's men enter the enemy trenches, which prove to have been heavily damaged by the Allied shelling. Wanliss, as it happens, is the first on the German parapet and about to jump down when another bullet hits him, this one entering his body under his right arm and stopping just short of his heart.

Still he rises, and continues to bark out orders, not to mention teeth.

'Tight parties led by Sgt. Garcia, of the right hand assaulting party,' one of the Right Bombing Party will record, 'methodically bombed a series of dugouts – at least three, probably five in all, crowded the enemy ... Several men confirm hearing screams and groans in these dugouts as bombs exploded. A conservative estimate is that 25 enemy were killed or wounded.'[54]

Mission accomplished, Wanliss now gives the order: 'Out!'

And yet, inevitably, some of their own are also hit, including Lieutenant Robert Julian, who has been leading the right-hand trench party – shot in the back, just as he is climbing back up over the parapet.

Bleeding badly, he is huddled up on the ground.

'I took him by the belt,' Wanliss will recount, 'and tried to carry him, but I had been hit myself and was too weak.'[55]

From the darkness comes a man who looks very much like Sergeant John Pearce – though it is hard to tell with their blackened faces – he tries to help, but soon enough both come to one inescapable conclusion by Lieutenant Julian's lack of protest.

'He is dead.'[56]

Another three dozen soldiers of Wanliss's troop are wounded, with nine missing. Despite his own wounds, Wanliss still does everything he can to help the retreat – no easy matter, as getting the wounded through the pressing wire under more enemy fire is problematic – until he takes a third bullet, this one in his left side.

He collapses and this time simply can't rise, though at least manages to fall into the stream, which offers some protection, and revives him enough to enable him to cross and crawl into a ditch filled with freezing flowing water.

Back at 4th Brigade HQ, Brigadier General Monash is desperate for information, but getting little.

'In spite of the most elaborate system of alternative lines,' he will note, 'both permanent and emergency, buried and overground, and with ladder wiring, every telephonic communication between my HQ and the fighting battalion was cut. The rockets supplied as supplementary signals failed to act. All intelligence had to be collected by runners and liaison officers who were new to the ground.'[57]

It is as well he knows nothing of the current fate of the raid leader, Captain Harold Wanliss, who now lies perilously close to dead in a ditch.

As it happens – *Hello, Bendigo!* – it is Stephen De Arango, now Sergeant, who had first covered himself in glory at Gallipoli in Jacka's VC action, who grabs Wanliss by the collar and drags him to the safety of their own trenches.

Scenes of great heroism take place as stretcher-bearers and others risk their lives, again and again, to bring the wounded to safety.

'While we were lying there I got one of the frights of my life,' one of the wounded will recount, 'a shell burst so close that the chap next to me and myself were buried with earth . . .'

They dig themselves out, only to find the Germans have brought searchlights and machine guns to bear, and their only way out is to crawl along a drain.

'I got along at first by digging in my fingers and pulling, while the chap lying behind me pushed my right foot.'

When this is too slow, the chap behind crawls over the top.

'I hung on to his braces and tried to keep my face up out of the mud as he dragged me through. When we got to the end of the drain a big sergeant of ours [Fred Anderson], was waiting there, and he picked me up and carried me right across to our trenches with the bullets snapping all round. As soon as he got me back over the parapet he went for more, and while I was waiting for the stretcher-bearers he brought in four more. He must have had a charmed life. I don't know how it is they did not get him. Australians will do for me, after the things I saw them do that night.'[58]

Once the Wanliss raiding party get back to the Australian trenches, the wounded, like the shivering Wanliss himself, are evacuated and the word spreads that, such has been the heroism he has displayed, he might even be recommended for a Victoria Cross. That would mean the 14th would boast *two* such heroes! Right now, Wanliss is so badly hurt he is beyond caring and will be sent all the way to England in the hope he can recover.

The following night the German response to the artillery is even more severe.

'I could see streaks of fire curving through the air as their trench-mortar bombs fell on our wire,' Ted Rule will recount. 'When they landed and burst the earth rocked, even 300 yards away.

'In the sector occupied by Jacka's men things must have been very lively. One of his Corporals, Charlie Smith, told me they had to lie in the bottom of the trench along with several dead men, but Jacka kept walking to and fro as cool as an iceberg. One of the company runners told us afterwards that Jacka came to the company headquarters where a man or two might be sheltering. He was not long in finding someone.

'"Hello, hello, what the devil are you doing here?" Jacka is heard to shout. "Come on, get out of here before I pull you out of it by the legs."

'"What's all the trouble about?"

'"Holy Moses," Jacka shouts, "is it you? You're a damned disgrace to the battalion."'[59]

It is at this point that another two shells explode nearby, killing off the rest of the exchange, at least so much as the rest of them can hear, and Jacka is soon back among them.

'We never knew to whom it was that he had spoken like that,' Rule will recount, 'but there were several malicious conjectures.'[60]

One of those conjectures, of course, centres around Major Fuhrmann, as it is the view of the battalion that when the shells are landing, and the bullets are flying, he is rarely found in the front lines – but nothing is said.

Things become further complicated when the Germans send out their own raiding party, which now sees Jacka and some of his own men getting involved to beat the beggars back, firing their .303s and hurling Mills bombs. A frenetic fire-fight takes place, and at least a dozen of the attackers make it all the way to the Australian parapet, with half-a-dozen jumping in, at which point the fight is with bayonets, before the surviving Germans are forced to retreat.

Seeing that some wounded Huns have been left behind in No Man's Land, Jacka jumps the parapet with a couple of men and hauls three of them back, with a view to having them interrogated by the 14th's Intelligence Officer, the man responsible for collecting and collating all information about terrain, enemy strength and movements.

Yes, the whole thing can barely be chalked up as a 'victory', but it is still an impressive performance all round, both from Wanliss and his men – and from Jacka and company.

But it intimidates some. For the following day, Sergeant Ted Rule is quietly approached by one of the most muted men in their mob, Private Harry Danman. He doesn't drink, doesn't swear, and has a way of speaking that is as refined as silverware that is actually *silver*. And he is young, not just on birth certificate, but in the sense that he has a face that looks completely unmarked by life. Some blokes in this company have faces like a dropped pie – Harry's is as blemish free as the day he was born. But now he has a problem.

'I don't seem to be able to adapt myself to these awful conditions like the rest,' he tells Rule. 'And when I think of how Lieutenant Jacka abused some of us for funking in those shelters last night, I feel thoroughly ashamed of myself. I could not help feeling afraid, but Lieutenant Jacka seemed afraid of nothing.'

Rule is more than happy to make Danman understand the truth of things.

'I've not the least doubt that Jacka was not afraid,' he tells him. Jacka is just like that. The point though is, he's pretty much a one-off. So, Harry?

'Don't think you're peculiar. I've not heard of anyone else going into raptures over last night's entertainment.'[61]

The exception is General John Monash, who is more than pleased with the results of the raid. His 4th Brigade has demonstrated its capacity, successfully pulling off a raid that has done real damage to the Germans and surely made them wonder where the next blow might fall. Yes, the British attack on the Somme Valley is already looking disastrous – as in a hurry of flurry, reports come in of shocking casualties – but at least the Australians have been able to strike a real blow, with minimum casualties overall, in no small part because they had done so many rehearsals they had been prepared for every contingency. Typically of Monash, he had been right in the front lines himself to oversee the raid, and personally commends the men on the success, noting it as 'worthy of the highest praise and reflecting the greatest credit on their offensive spirit'.[62]

And how had they done it?

Well, as Monash writes to his wife, in a letter that boasts of the first raid he has been in charge of, disposing of over 50 enemy: 'The design and preparation for these enterprises are the most extraordinary things it is possible to imagine . . . Success lies in a combination of the highest scientific preparation with the greatest gallantry. Our boys are splendid.'[63]

Alas, now the news breaks.

Monash has been so successful in nearly every venture he has embarked on that he is leaving them, being promoted to take over the AIF's 3rd Division, now being heavily trained in the south of England, and in need of his magic. He is to be replaced by Colonel Charles Brand.

When it comes to their new commander, Jacka is sceptical.

Brand's face is like the rest of him: tall, thin and worried. What remains of his white hair juts from either side of his distinguished pate, his watery blue eyes are the only colour that separate him from his uniform, even his moustache appears to be khaki. He may smile in private, but as far as anyone can see a grimace is the best that the public will get, along with eyebrows permanently raised in disappointment. In civilian life he was a teacher, and he carries with him the air that he would like to make you repeat a year, for your own good.

It is true that the 43-year-old Brand – a Boer War veteran – had been at Gallipoli, and had generally been thought to have done well in command of the 8th Battalion. But certainly not as well as *he* had thought he had done. For, only shortly after taking over as Brigade Commander, Colonel Brand addresses the men at Domart and boasts in passing that, 'I won my DSO before any of you were on Gallipoli.'[64]

For soldiers taking the measure of the new bloke, against the massive silhouette of the one just departed, it is disastrous. Monash would *never* have talked about himself in such a manner, let alone to belittle the soldiers of whom he is now in command!

'When the parade was over,' Rule notes in his diary, 'the Brig was just about the most unpopular man in France as far as our brigade was concerned.'[65]

Charles Bean will later characterise the speech as, 'an extraordinarily inept and egoistic oration'.[66]

For now, it is time to move once more.

As the Somme campaign goes on – essentially lurching from disaster to disaster, as many thousands of men are being killed for almost no gain in ground – the Australians will be called on to buttress defeat with their own efforts. This includes the 5th Division being thrown into the line at Fromelles, while all of the 1st, 2nd and Jacka's 4th Division are to attempt to do what the British have failed to do in three weeks of trying – crack the German line at Pozières.

Companyyyyy! Fall in!

To move from their current position at Domart to Naours, 10 miles to the south-east, takes the better part of a day, but at least it is through achingly beautiful countryside. Strangely, for men who have just arrived from Egypt, it is the sun that saps.

'Hard as we were,' Rule chronicles, 'we had men lying out all along the roads for miles, too exhausted to go farther.'[67]

Fer *Chrissakes*!

Making matters worse is when their Colonel and his adjutant take a wrong turn and they only discover the mistake when they are right near the top of a very steep, very long hill.

'Loaded as we were, we almost sweated blood over that hill (and it is still talked about by the old hands), and, when the Colonel turned us about and marched us down the hill again to hunt for the lost road, the camel's back fairly broke. If curses ever did men any harm, the lives of those two were ruined for ever.'[68]

Arriving outside the village of Naours in the late afternoon, at least they are able to move into very comfortable digs in the farms around.

This is to be, effectively, a training camp for the 4th Division before they are thrown into the line.

•

At the HQ of the AIF 5th Division, just near Fromelles, General Pompey Elliott, the Commanding Officer of the 5th Division's 15th Brigade, is ropable.

General McCay has just finished briefing the commanders of his three brigades on the British orders for attacking the nearby German line, and Elliott can barely believe his *ears*.

Caught between stupefaction and horror, he quickly surges towards anger instead. Try as he might, he can barely bring himself to believe that they are serious.

But they are.

As serious as premeditated murder.

He listens with rising fury as this ludicrous mishmash of ideas is fleshed out by McCay, in his insufferably pompous manner.

Clearly pleased that the 5th is at last to be blooded, McCay goes on. The men will be a yard apart, charging forward, with the two assaulting battalions from each brigade providing four waves of some 200 men at a time. The first two waves are to be ready in the front-line trenches three hours before, and the next two waves are to be ready to move forward, positioning themselves in the support lines 300 yards back.

As ordered by General Richard Haking, the Australian Corps' Commander for this stunt, the bombardment will go for seven hours, and the instant it lifts, the men must charge straight at the German guns.

The next waves will follow them out with an interval of 100 yards between.

The way McCay speaks about it, the plan is all fairly straightforward, and he sketches a scenario whereby few things can go wrong. But Elliott remains outraged. In front of his 15th Brigade, No Man's Land extends for *400 yards*. And his brigade has to cover *that* distance, against *entrenched* positions, with *untested* troops who have only *just* arrived? Straight at a German bunker called the Sugar-loaf, which fair bristles with machine guns, and all of this in broad *daylight*?

Most problematic of all, of course – for any fool can see it – is that the whole scheme lacks the supreme element in war . . .

Surprise.

For instead of coming at the Germans when and where they least expect it, this attack will give them three days' warning . . .

As McCay will not listen to his protestation, just a few hours later, Pompey Elliott's anger is so focused he realises he must do everything in his power to change the order and so has shanghaied Major Harry Howard from the British GHQ – where the orders have emanated from – to come and see for himself just how catastrophically things will turn out if the British orders are followed.

He steers him towards a spot known as VC Corner, just to the east of the Sugar-loaf.

Do you see, Major Howard?

To get to the Sugar-loaf, to even *begin* to attack it, his men will have to cover 400 yards of open ground, under fire from shot and shell, shattered by shrapnel, and fording a deep drainage ditch before, under heavy fire, getting to grips with rolls of barbed wire, the 10-foot-high parapet and the dozens of reinforced concrete shelters.

Surely this experienced British officer, who has the ear of none other than the supreme commander Field Marshal Haig himself, must realise that!

'Major,' Elliott now implores. 'I want you now to tell me as man to man, in view of the fact that you have had nearly two years' experience in this fighting as against my 10 days, whether this attack can succeed . . .'[69]

Major Howard is, frankly, a little stunned. This is *not* the way things are done in the British Army. One does not speak 'man to man'. One speaks by rank, and is sniffingly superior or cloyingly deferential, accordingly.

What to do? The Englishman pauses, and turns a deep shade of red. But then he gathers himself. 'Sir,' he says carefully to General Elliott, 'since you have put it to me in that way I must answer, but I expect the result to be a bloody holocaust.'[70]

Surprised by the frankness, the Australian officer urges him to go back to Haig and tell him so. Howard promises he will do exactly that.

Now settled into their digs at Naours, Colonel Brand soon has the 4th Brigade engaged in heavy training, heading off on long route marches, working in unison to charge at abandoned trenches, working out how Lewis gunners can best work in tandem with bombing platoons and so forth.

Jacka is in it with the best of them: exhorting, demanding, demonstrating how it is to be done. As they train, the rumble to their east is constant, night and day, as the disastrous British campaign on the Somme goes on, and the word spreads that their own 4th Division will soon be called on.

Late morning, 21 July 1916, Albert, fie, the battle is nigh

Captain Charles Bean has a crippling weariness about him that is not just lack of sleep. It is that even the sleep he has had has been haunted by nightmares of having witnessed the aftermath of the slaughter of the AIF's 5th Division at Fromelles. Just on 7000 Diggers had gone forward, following insane British orders – which had seen 5000 casualties and nearly 2000 killed, for not a single yard of trench taken.

Worse still, he has seen wounded Australians left dying as General McCay refused 'negotiations of any kind, and on any subject',[71] with the Germans. And so the wounded die in No Man's Land . . . on *principle*.

Despite it all, Bean is determined *not* to miss out on the Australian attack going in at Pozières and he has arrived at the HQ of the AIF's 1st Division's General, Sir Harold Walker, just in time for a meeting on the timing of the battle's start.

After being ordered on 18 July by the Commanding Officer of the Fifth Army Corps, General Sir Hubert Gough, to 'go into the line and attack Pozières tomorrow night!'[72] Walker and his Chief of Staff, Colonel Blamey, have been fighting a furious rear-guard action since.

So far, the British have expended 14 Divisions and lost 88,000 men, going straight at the most powerful of the German defences. They had taken the town of Pozières itself – or at least the shattered remnants of it – but are still to take the high point behind it, marked by a windmill.

Gough wants Australia's 1st Division to do just that, attacking straight at the German guns. Walker and Blamey had left the first meeting with Gough fuming, Walker writing candidly of the rancour in his diary that night: *Scrappy & unsatisfactory orders from [Gough] – Hope I shall not be rushed into an ill-prepared operation, but fear I shall!*[73]

It is for this reason that Bean finds Walker flustered. He is desperate to save his men of the 1st Division from total destruction. The best he can hope for is only substantial destruction.

As Walker and Blamey emerge from their tense meeting with Gough, they have news of agreement for Bean. The attack will go in at 12.30 on the night of 23 July, in the first moonless pitch of the midnight hour. The plan they have come up with is better than the British one, but defeat is still the only result they can see.

'Walker said to me,' Bean records in his diary, 'that the 1st Australian Division would be knocked out by this attack though most people think they will succeed.'[74]

Eager to see things for himself, the next morning Bean decides to walk with the rest of the traffic pushing to the north-east to get a look at the night's proposed battle site from a high spot just back from it. He is so close that stray shells fall in the near distance, and even behind him.

Is *that* Pozières?

Involuntarily, he lets out a gasp.

So pulverised is the whole area that you can just see the rough contours of the village's old layout – not by the shattered buildings, for they are indeed so shattered there is nothing of them left but brick-red powder, but by, as a soldier puts it, 'the shredded stumps and trunks of trees which once made the gardens or orchards or hedges behind the houses'.[75]

As for the Albert–Bapaume road – built right through the middle of Pozières by the Romans back when Caligula was no more than a toddler – you can discern its course because that is where many of the shredded stumps are aligned. Poplar and plane trees, planted a century earlier by order of Napoleon, used to stand silent sentinel on both sides of the thoroughfare as travellers made their way through.

Never were there travellers like these Germans, though. Merciless in attack all through Belgium and the north of France, they are also, clearly, implacable in defence. Visible at the base of the slope that lies before the village is Pozières Trench, behind which lies a mostly still standing copse of trees, with all their leaves blown off by the bombardments.

And there, high on the slopes on the upside of the village, Bean can see the second trench system, where stands a mound. This, he knows from his discussion with General Brudenell White, is the ruins of the windmill – the key objective of future Australian attacks, though tonight they're just going after the village. Ultimately, if they can get to the windmill, they will control the highest point on the entire Somme battlefield – which will be enormously significant from the point of view of both firing and directing artillery on the rest of the valley.

But will the Australians be capable of achieving that?

The one thing the men themselves know is that it is going to be tough – that much is evident from the thick carpet of corpses that lie all around their positions; soldiers who have tried to do what they are about to embark upon, but who will never return. Their bodies lie everywhere, as do their body parts.

Most of the Australians – the 1st Brigade on the left and the 3rd Brigade on the right – have been substantially in position since the wee hours of the night of 19/20 July, at which point it had been thought they would be attacking in the early hours of 21 July. The two subsequent delays have given them more time, yes, but the waiting has also been exhausting, the more so because the men's breathing is labouring through the gas masks they have been made to wear.

(By now, the men have seen up close the results among those not quick enough to whip their masks on when the attacks come: first coughing, wheezing, choking and suffocating before feeling like their lungs are filled with red-hot needles. They inexorably weaken as the toxicity seeps into their eyes, their nostrils and ears, their mouths, the pores of their exposed skin, then their vision goes fuzzy, a searing pain and a terrible itch spreads around their face. They turn every colour from blue to green to black, as their tongues hang out, their eyes turn glassy, and they cough up green froth. Actual death is a blessed relief.)

However, their hell on earth consists of more than just the stench, the fear of death and the difficulty breathing. There is also the matter of German shells falling among them, regularly killing and maiming dozens at a time. The only consolation is that, however badly they are copping it, the Germans appear to be copping it worse. The Australian artillery, which has been systematically bombarding German positions for the last three days – since two o'clock on the morning of 19 July – is now firing as never before on the trench system the Australians must soon attack.

'They are firing like mad & have got the range to a nicety,' Private Archie Barwick would record in his diary, with no little satisfaction.[76] 'The way they shell the wood in front of us is something terrific. All day long there are shells bursting in it from 3 in. to 12 [in.]. I can tell you the latter send the earth & stuff easily 300 ft high and go off with an ear-splitting roar. I have seen them uproot big trees, such is their power ... I reckon for every shell the Germans send over we send 20.'[77]

CHAPTER FIVE

THE VALLEY OF THE SOMME

As one writer to another Jacka was, between ourselves, a curious character. He was a great fighter, one of the most fearless in the AIF. He did not minimise his actions afterwards in talking of them – his nature was consistently expansive ... I think if you regard Jacka as a good fellow of a rather crude type you will probably arrive at the best estimate of him and his narrative.[1]

Extract from a private and confidential letter written by Charles Bean to 14th Battalion historian Newton Wanliss, 1923

Afternoon, 22 July 1916, Pozières, last things first, salute salutations

The time has come for the 1st Division to launch their principal attack on wresting Pozières from the Germans, a task which the British have been valiantly attempting to do for the last three weeks, at stupendous human cost.

No fewer than 18,000 men of the 1st Division are ready to go. It just needs the finishing touches put to the plan.

Late in the afternoon, senior officers of the 2nd and 4th Battalion of the 1st Division are consulting their maps, right by the appropriately named Dead Man's Road, in a spot where the shells landing all around are *slightly* less likely to kill them, by virtue of the remnant of a wall on one side, albeit 'amid dozens of corpses and moaning wounded, mainly German'.[2]

Their maps show just how close they are to breaching the key defensive line known as Old German 1 and the support line behind it, Old German 2 – OG1 and OG2 – even if, so far, every yard gained has come at a cost of half-a-dozen dead Diggers.

And yet their deliberations are suddenly interrupted by a runner eager to give them his message, which has come straight from General Gough himself. The runner's eyes dart left and right – spinning wildly – as he gives them the envelope, hoping against hope that there will be no message in reply so he can be gone again. For who wants to stay longer than he has to in this, the most heavily shelled spot in all Pozières?

On the front of the envelope is marked 'Urgent and Secret'. They open it quickly, knowing only too well that it will be of momentous import, likely affecting their whole plan of attack.

Oh.

Oh, dear.

```
A number of cases have lately occurred of men failing to
salute the army commander when he is passing in his car,
in spite of the fact that the car carries his flag upon the
bonnet. This practice must cease.
General Gough[3]
```

Early hours, 23 July 1916, Pozières, Tommy guns . . .

The Allied barrage has built to a climax, every gun firing, each one emitting clouds of choking smoke. Many of the Diggers of the 1st Division start to cough as the smoke gets thicker. Pressing themselves into the bosom of Mother Earth before the whistle blows, they can still see by the fading and flickering ethereal light thrown by the endless flares that the German machine-gun bullets seeking them out are now so low that 'we could see [them] cutting off the poppies almost against our heads'.[4]

One soldier is 'crying like a baby', pausing only between sobs to repeat, 'We will never get out of this . . . we will *never* get out of this.'[5]

And he might be right.

'The flashes of the guns, the bursting of shells, and the Verey lights, made the night like day,' one Digger will recall, 'and, as I lay flat to the ground as possible, I was expecting to stop one any time.'[6]

Lying out in *Niemandsland*, among his mates, a 19-year-old Lance Corporal from the AIF's 1st Battalion, Ben Champion, is doing his best not to piss his pants with fear, but . . .

'I couldn't stop urinating . . .' he would record in his diary. 'It seemed as if the earth opened up with a crash. The ground shook and trembled, and the concussion made our ears ring.'[7]

At last, it happens.

'Suddenly,' Lance Corporal Ben Champion will recount, 'there was a pause for a second, and then we saw the barrage smoke move forward . . .'[8]

The Australian barrage is lifting off Pozières Trench, and shifting to the orchards behind.

The whistle blows, and the Diggers of the AIF's 1st Division charge towards the German guns. She's *on*, mate!

Dawn, 28 July 1916, Warloy, spectres from the fog

Jacka and his men can hear them long before they see them.

It is that strangely rhythmic rumble of a mass of men, coming their way. Not quite marching in the morning mist, but something a little like it. Sure enough, little by little, the phantoms of the fog emerge from the east along the cobbled road. Second Lieutenant Albert Jacka and his men of the 14th Battalion have spent the night bivouacked near the town of Warloy, awaiting orders to go forward. They know that the first lot of men who they are to eventually relieve in the line will be coming this way, and so it is natural enough that, to a man, they now lean forward and gaze hard at the hundreds of men emerging in serried, if shattered, ranks from the swirl.

Jesus Christ.

It is indeed the 1st Division AIF coming back, having been relieved in their front lines by the 2nd Division, who had finished their move up the night before. But, geez . . . just look at 'em! Yes, Jacka and everyone in the 4th Divvie know that the 1st Divvie has been in the thick of a tough fight, but until now they'd had no idea just *how* tough.

'They looked like men who had been in hell,' Ted Rule will recount. 'Almost without exception each man looked drawn and haggard, and so dazed that they appeared to be walking in a dream, and their eyes looked glassy and starey. Quite a few were silly . . .'[9]

Er, *silly*?

Yes, knocked silly. Giggling, noisy and gadding about in a completely disconnected fashion from the crowd of their silent comrades. They are with the 1st Division AIF, but not truly *with* them. Shell-shocked, broken, they are simply being swept along in the tide. Marching in any fashion is completely beyond them, and they are just as likely to leave the line to pick a pleasing flower as to listen to the barked orders of a Sergeant. And this was *after* they'd been able to bathe in the village just back from the line and even grab a night's shut-eye.

Fer Chrissakes, how must they have looked when they were first pulled out?

And it's not just their appearance. The most devastating thing of all is the gaps in the ranks. About half of them are missing. Well over 5000 of them!

'Some companies seemed to have been nearly wiped out,' Rule observes. 'In all my experience I've never seen men so shaken up as these.'[10]

(Some, like the 2nd Battalion, have been indeed all but wiped out. Just a few days earlier, when they had gathered at Warloy, before heading to Pozières, they had been 985 soldiers strong. Now, they can muster just 125 men still standing on their own two feet.)

The last time the 4th Division had seen the 1st Divvie in bulk had been back in Egypt upon the 1st's departure, when the men of the 4th had been *so* envious that this fine body of their fellow Australians – fit, tanned, trained up and fully reinforced – had been picked to go to the Western Front first.

'Those who watched them will never forget it as long as they live,' Rule will recount. 'These men seem more like wraiths than soldiers, dazed shells of men, spent and fractured. Battalions have become companies, companies reduced to sections; decimation and decay on staggered parade.'

The obvious question begs, like a Cairo street urchin.

Is *this* to be our fate too? Is this what *we* will look like, once *we* have gone forward to relieve the 2nd Divvie? And which of *us* will be the ones now represented by the gaps in those ranks?

THE VALLEY OF THE SOMME • 125

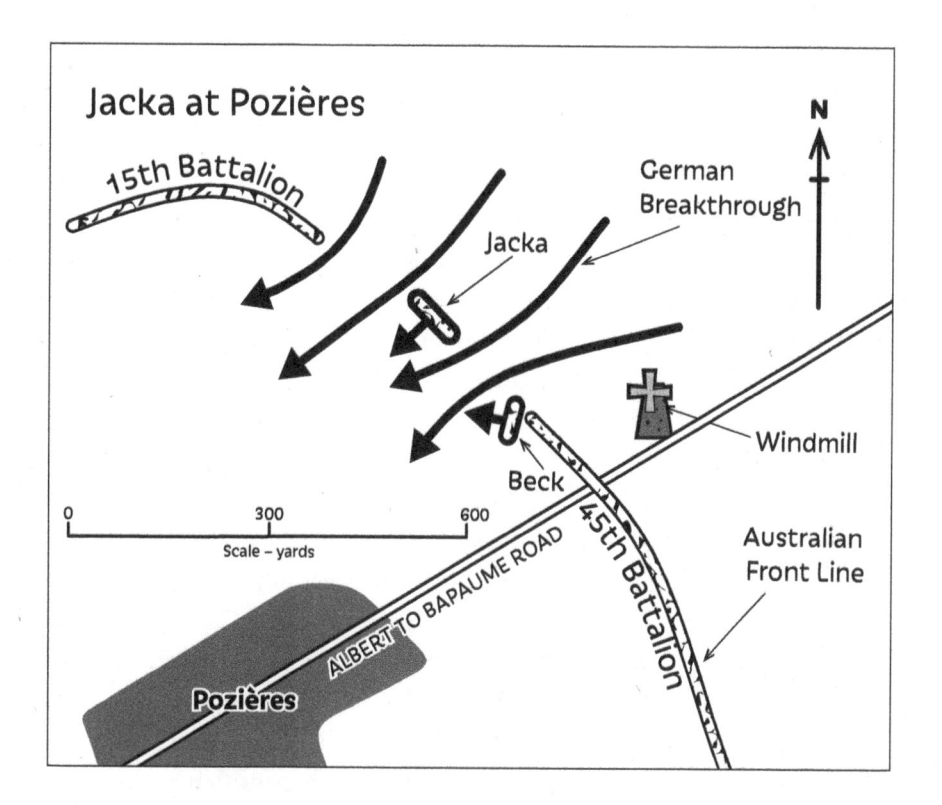

Jacka at Pozières

[Map showing 15th Battalion, Jacka, German Breakthrough, Beck, Windmill, 45th Battalion, Australian Front Line, Albert to Bapaume Road, Pozières. Scale – yards: 0, 300, 600. North arrow.]

Afternoon, 4 August 1916, Warloy, French Fanny in the night

Always it is like this.

While the 4th Division is billeted in the pleasant town of Warloy, out of the blue, the word has come through.

The time has come. Up stakes, pack up what you bothered to unpack, and give up your hopes of becoming better acquainted with local mademoiselles.

The division must now move forward to replace what is left of the shattered 2nd Division in the front lines at Pozières. In the case of the 14th Battalion – the last whole battalion of the 4th Divvie to move forward – they must take over the positions still held by the remnants of the 26th and 28th battalions.

When?

Tonight.

Saddle up. We move out at 9 pm, by order of company, at intervals of 10 minutes.

Which way?

That way, to the sound of the booming guns coming from the east.

Companyyyyyyyyy . . . forward . . . march!

As the word spreads around the village of Warloy that *les Australiens* are soon to be on the move, the villagers come out to wish them well, to thank them for their courage, their fortitude, their willingness to put their lives on the line for the cause that will save *La France*.

'*Allez, les Australiens!*'

'*Bravo!*'

'*Merci!*'

The Australians are gratified at such support, a spring in their march now – *Marchons! Marchons!* – buoyed by this genuine Gallic gratitude.

'It was good to see,' one of the Digger officers, Captain Robert Hayes, will chronicle, 'the faces beaming with cheery determination and note the firm step of our splendid boys.'[11]

They are 750 strong, a fine body of Australian men, embarking on an admittedly difficult mission, but filled with confidence they can get the job done.

Jacka's B Company is the second to leave, marching in the informal 'column of fours' formation with the men marching four abreast. Lugging their packs, which now contain just their essentials – an additional hundred rounds of ammunition was issued to each man, who now carried 220 rounds, two Mills bombs, and two days' iron rations, in addition to the 24 hours' ordinary rations – they move off, and keep going well into the night, the sound of the guns getting progressively louder, and their eastern horizon starting to pulsate ever more clearly. The more educated of them can tell how far they have to go by counting the seconds between a big flash of light and the boom reaching them.

Nearing midnight, exhausted, they have arrived at the wracked remnants of the French town of Albert, which they know is a mile back from the front lines, and four miles from Pozières. Wide-eyed by the wan light of the moon, the soldiers gaze at all the ruined buildings, the detritus in the streets. Clearly, this was once a prosperous town, but right now there is little left bar – strangely – the church. And at the top of the church they can see the famed statue of the Virgin Mary, leaning out over the street in what appears to be a supplicatory pose.

The statue has already been christened 'Fanny' by the previous Australian division, for her resemblance to the famed Australian swimmer Fanny Durack about to dive into the pool, but a more religious view is recorded by an Australian officer.

'You could readily imagine [of the Virgin Mary],' he writes, 'that she had purposely leaned down over the street to bless the thousands of soldiers who pass and re-pass day by day and going to and returning from the battle line . . .'[12]

Either way, local lore has it that when the Virgin falls into the street, the war will end,[13] which gives rise to the obvious solution that someone should knock her over now?

Maybe, Digger. For now, let us bivouac just outside the town and get some shut-eye, as we prepare for what is likely to be a big day ahead for the lucky ones, and eternal night for the rest.

•

When the 2nd Division arrived in the trenches of Pozières, all the men were more frantic than a Marseilles pox doctor. Well, it was one thing to take what's left of the German trenches; it's another now to dig them out while holding them against both the Hun's artillery barrage and the inevitable counter-attack. They occasionally discover German dugouts still mercifully intact. (Some of these, as Archie Barwick would attest, are stunning: 'Their dugouts here are easily 20 feet below the surface and fitted, in some cases, with beds and tables and pianos and even electric light . . . They thought they were there for good apparently.')[14]

The most urgent priority is to try to impose order on chaos, as Sergeants look for Lieutenants, who are in turn looking for their Captains. A pecking order established, the highest-ranking officer starts shouting orders over the cacophony of exploding shells and whining bullets. They set men to digging out the shattered trenches, while NCOs are sent to the left and right to make contact with the rest of the platoon or, perhaps, the enemy. Meanwhile, their own Lewis guns must be set up, sandbags filled, the wounded evacuated, prisoners escorted back under guard and notes scribbled to give to dashing messengers to report the position. Hurry! Hurry! *Hurry!*

The Australians know the Germans will counter-attack; they just don't know when. If there is time, they may even be able to bury some of their dead and gather in stray limbs for some kind of decent burial in a shell-hole – a commodity they don't lack, as new shell-holes are being created all the time, producing so many more dead bodies and stray limbs that it is hard to keep up.

The Germans, knowing the battle is in the balance, plaster these positions from midnight with such intensive shelling that it exacts a dreadful toll among those Australians not yet properly dug in, which are many. But enough Australians still hold on to these hard-won positions that there is some confidence they will see off any counter-attack. So good is the Australian position that, though they are not yet quite to the ruins of the windmill, they can see where the German artillery is coming from – flashes in the night reveal the location to be 1500 yards to their north-east, over by the town of Courcelette. As to Pozières itself, this one-time flower of France has been completely destroyed by the endless blizzard of shells that falls upon it, and is now 'nothing but a blackened waste amid which the scarred stumps of trees shorn of limbs reared themselves like so many scarecrows . . .'.

•

Attennnnnn-shun! Now, with just a short time to go before they will be hurled into the line, no less a personage than General Birdwood – the Commanding Officer of the I Anzac Corps – has arrived to inspect the 4th Division. Yes, Birdie is a man of many failings, but the Australians retain a rough affection for him.

Whatever else, at least he turns up occasionally like this, just as he had when they had first arrived on the Western Front, all those many years ago . . . back in . . . early June. The Birdwood inspection complete, the 4th Division, including the 14th Battalion, moves off. Within three hours, they are within coo-ee of the battle's roar.

'With the darkness,' Ted Rule would record, 'came "wind up" – our knowledge that we were going into hell . . . made us very uneasy.'[15]

The roar of artillery fire rolls over them, as does the distant sound of machine guns going nineteen to the dozen, even while the sky to the east pulses with angry flashes of light. And they are heading right into it.

'We moved out,' one soldier will recall, 'into where the roll and flash of guns and flares lit up the sky . . .'[16]

A shudder of horror moves through the men. Hell is just ahead, and their every step is taking them closer to it.

Well after dark, they get to Brickfields, outside Albert, just back from the front, where they are to bivouac for the night.

They try to sleep, though that constant *boom-BOOM-boom-BOOM* makes it hard. They're still two miles from the line and the ground is shaking *here*.

What must it be like in the middle of it?

•

As Charles Bean moves among the 2nd Division soldiers on this late afternoon of 4 August – at a time when the German shelling on the front lines at Pozières is singularly intense – even he is stunned at just how shattered and exhausted they are, the very reflection of the village territory they now possess.

'Pozières has been a terrible sight all day,' he notes in his diary, 'steaming with pink and chestnut and . . . smoke. One knew that the Brigades which went in last night were there today in that insatiable factory of ghastly wounds. The men are simply turned in there as into some ghastly giant mincing machine. They have to stay there while shell after huge shell descends with a shriek close beside them – each one an acute mental torture – each shrieking tearing crash bringing a promise to each man – instantaneous – I will tear you into ghastly wounds – I will rend your flesh and pulp an arm or a leg – fling you, half a gaping quivering man like these that you see smashed round you, one by one, to lie there rotting and blackening like all the things you saw by the awful roadside, or in that sickening dusty crater. Ten or twenty times a minute. Every man in the trench has that instant fear thrust tight upon his shoulders – I don't care how brave he is – with a crash that is physical pain and strain to withstand.'[17]

More than a few Diggers become homesick for Gallipoli.
Under attack like that, and Gough wants them to keep going?
It can't be done.
In the end, there is only so much that flesh and blood – and, more to the point, bloodied flesh – can bear. It is General Birdwood who steps in, insisting to Gough on the afternoon of 5 August that his 2nd Division must be pulled out immediately and their last remaining fresh division – the 4th Division, who have already been moved forward – sent in. It will be for them to take over the positions and secure them against all comers.

But, good . . . *God*, what a journey it is to get there.

'B Company in advance march,' the Official History of the 14th Battalion will recount, 'reached Pioneers trench and passed along it in single file; it was particularly long and uncomfortably narrow. Ghastly sights were witnessed on the journey. Scores of bodies had been partially buried in the soft earth and bloody hands and feet protruded at frequent intervals. Boxes of ammunition and rations lay scattered about where fatigue parties had been annihilated by artillery fire.'[18]

After 11 days in the line, the 2nd Division's original contingent of 11,000 infantry has been whittled down to just 3200 men still standing with rifle in hand.

The cost notwithstanding, it has been an extraordinary achievement, as even Sir Douglas Haig acknowledges in his diary that evening.

'The Australians gained all their objectives north of Pozières and beat off 3 counter-attacks. A fine piece of work.'[19]

1.40 pm, 5 August 1916, Albert, truth and Dare

This ain't '*La Marseillaise*', that beloved national anthem the French are prone to sing at all times, more often than not with tears in their eyes, particularly at the part of *Marchons! Marchons! . . . Aux armes, citoyens! Formez vos battalions.* No, in this instance, while the battalion of men approaching along the cobble-stoned paths of the French countryside are indeed, *marchons, marchons*, marching, marching, the song they are singing is in English, sung in a broad Australian accent, and is of a rather different calibre.

For as Albert falls behind in this late afternoon of 5 August it happens.

Jacka's mob are indeed belting out the 14th Battalion's song:

Way down upon the Swanee River,
Far, far away,
There's where my heart is turning ever,
There's where the old folks stay.
All up and down the whole creation
Sadly I roam,
Still longing for the old plantation,
And for the old folks at home ...

... when the words start to die away and the harbingers of horror are there before their eyes. Shell craters dot the countryside like angry boils on an otherwise beautiful face; broken farm equipment lies forlorn in the fields, once proud farm buildings are in ruins, and, yes, there are so many *dead bodies* lying around it is rather beside the point to bury them as there will clearly be so many more to come. Maybe you.

Before them lies a muddy wasteland of trenches, shell-holes, soldiers with thousand-yard stares and scattered human body parts strewn about like ... like ... well, like nothing they have ever seen before.

This is the Western Front in all its gory, all its sound and fury of endless artillery exchanges, *knock-knock-knock* of heavy machine guns and distant screams.

Which way? Which of the many lead-in trenches leads to the one, which leads to the other one, that leads to the one that they are ordered to take over?

Look, this is not like finding your way in Melbourne, when you're on Collins Street and want to get to Flinders Street. Back there, you *never* – GET DOWN! – had to ask directions while disembowelled men are screaming for their lives just yards away, as – GET DOWN AGAIN! – shells explode and shrapnel whistles and machine-gun bullets buzz all around.

But, ask they must, and who better than their 'old Brig' – Colonel Charles Brand – who happens to be passing by on horseback. If the Commanding Officer of their own brigade doesn't know, who would?

'What, lost in daylight?' Colonel Brand harrumphs. 'Don't know what you'll do in the dark.'[20]

Quite. They are finally saved when one of the 14th Battalion's own Majors comes back to guide them into the beginnings of Sausage Valley, 'a long, narrow valley, two or three hundred yards across',[21] dominated by heavily sheltered artillery batteries, lined up very nearly 'wheel to wheel' all along it, with yet more labyrinthine paths through it. The batteries keep firing, their crews covered in grim grime as they keep feeding shell after shell into their killing machines, which regularly erupt with shattering roars. Strangely, the battery crews barely blink with each explosion. This is their *world*. This is what they *do*. The only pause is when, every few minutes, they must throw water down the barrels of the guns to clean them, causing huge clouds of steam to rise, one Digger says, 'like an overheated car engine after a steep climb'.[22]

And now back at it.

The only things more red hot than the guns are the gunners themselves, all of them drenched like drowned rats in their own sweat and working in relays, to the point of collapse, to keep the barrage up right on the Huns' noggins.

By the time Jacka and B Company mob are nearing the head of the valley the newly arrived soldiers of 4th Division are 'a trifle deaf'.[23]

Here at the top of the valley, the 14th Battalion men again must wait in the heat of the day, getting what shade they can while watching the endless stream of wounded men, covered in blood, groaning, screaming, being carried back by the brave stretcher-bearers. It is not much of an advertisement for where the new men are going. But it is the awful truth of what they are likely facing themselves.

And yet not all of the sufferers are physically wounded, and not all need to be carried. 'One shell-shocked case . . . came along,' Sergeant Ted Rule would recall, 'the picture of terror, and trembling from head to foot. His legs trembled so much that they just about carried him, and that was all.'[24]

Further on, they experience even worse than that as the ground underfoot in the trenches seems strangely . . . spongy?

How could that be? It's not even muddy, so that can't be the answer. It takes a while but they finally understand.

The ground is spongy because of the many dead soldiers beneath their feet.

'In that hour,' one of the 4th Brigade soldiers, Private George Mitchell, who will memorably record the experience of approaching the Western Front for the first time, 'was born in me a fear that lasted throughout the whole winter. It was the dread of dying in the mud, going down in that stinking morass and, though dead, being conscious throughout the ages. Waves of fear at times threatened to overwhelm me, a little weakness, a little slackening of control at times and I might have gone over the borderline. In the light of the sun, on firm ground, I could laugh at fate. But where the churned mud half hid and half revealed bodies, where dead hands reached out of the morass, seeming to implore aid – there I had to hold tight.'[25]

So great is the grim reaper's harvest – 9000 casualties from the 2nd Division alone – it really does lead to a horror that before this war none of them could even have imagined.

'We could not even get the dead buried,' one Digger will recount, 'as no-one could live in the open. It was awful seeing the dead and wounded fellows lying everywhere. Germans and all were mixed up . . .'[26]

Jacka's mob get their orders; they are to be the next to the front. C Company will follow. March and don't think. But as they march, fragments of life lie around them – a child's doll, a sewing machine, a tambourine – all surviving among the rubble of a dead village. What chances do the Australians themselves have of emerging from the rubble of battle that rumbles ahead?

Outside the town of Albert they are allowed to rest and camp on a paddock for the night. The next day they approach Pozières and there is a sudden roar, like a freight train hurtling earthwards from the sky, and, no more than half a stone's throw from Jacka's B Company, a German shell lands, showering a dozen soldiers in mud and human body parts.

There is no need for Albert Jacka to look at the map with which all NCOs have been issued. If we are being showered with shells, and all we can see is a muddy hell, strewn with bodies and the holes those shells leave . . . this must be it.

Onwards!

They are purposefully arriving on site just before dusk, when *they* can see what they are doing from up close, but the Germans will struggle to see them from a distance. And then, if the Germans want to counter-attack, it will be *them* trying to move in the pitch dark while we will be firing from a position of strength.

One thing they can see, amazingly enough, are the German shells.

Percy Bland hears a BOOM in the distance and he knows, right now, what is about to happen. Only a second of silence and WHRRRRRRRRRRRRRRR they can see the shell fly over their heads, it shoots past and they watch death in the air now, that blackness is traced in the sky, a funeral on its way and, watch it now, the blackened metal drops and they see it drop just half a mile away. BAM!

Some of their comrades are surely dead, but they live, and they wait and watch for the next shell, and the next.

Jacka now leads 5 Platoon into muddy wilderness, to the rough position they have been assigned, at the most southerly point of the 14th Battalion in OG1. And yet, while there is a communication sap that leads in the general direction of the front line they must hold, it is hell on earth to get there.

'At 8 pm,' Private Frank Miller will chronicle their experience to his family, 'we reached our trenches after two hours crawling through sap that were stinking with dead bodies . . . we passed one chap lying on a stretcher in a shell-hole. He had been there two days . . .'[27]

The reality is that they have not gone 200 yards before what had been the sap disappears as they come to a series of shell-holes that have so obliterated the former front line and the saps leading up to it that no actual trenches are in existence. The best that can be done is to line up in a rough line among the shell-holes that align with where the front-line trenches of OG1 used to be.

How to get into them?

The way Jacka does. You wait until just after a flurry of shells have exploded, then make a mad dash across open ground until you can dive into a shell-hole, and form up from there.

Needless to say, such shell-holes as they choose are littered with the limbs, torsos, severed heads and extremities of the previous occupants

– some of which have been arranged as part of the parapet – and the stench of rotting bodies, leavened only by the smell of burnt cordite, could peel paint.

And the rent on this place is what, you say?

We will have to pay for it in blood, and sometimes with our lives, by the hour?

That much is obvious.

But it has to be done, and the 44 men of Jacka's 5 Platoon soon find themselves in, as Jacka himself will describe it, 'a number of shell-holes, joined by a little digging',[28] stretched out across some 50 yards. Yes, on the one hand shell-holes are not as ideal to defend from as formal trenches, with built-in dugouts.

'But this is where the advantage of utilising shell-holes comes in,'[29] Jacka will note. For the reason the trenches have been wiped out is because the German artillery had already 'registered' on them, meaning they had been able to bring a blizzard of shells right on them. As the shell-holes are more scattered, it is not so easy to concentrate fire. One digging Digger will later note that, despite the sense they are in a landscape that would do Armageddon proud, Jacka 'seemed strangely suited to such grim surroundings'.[30]

Jacka and his men keep digging, the best they can, positioned at the most forward bulge of the entire line at Pozières, a place called the Elbow, on the maps.

'I had to start digging defences,' one of his men, Private William Bourne, will recount. 'We had to throw three dead Australians out of the trench.'[31]

It is the very spot that is most threatening to the Germans as it is foremost, but also means the Hun will be able to attack it from three sides when the time comes – shortly – to neutralise it.

Unbeknownst to Jacka and his men, from the German side of the line a constant train of carts loaded with shells is moving forward and being stockpiled, ready to feed the big guns that had been moved forward earlier in the morning.

Jacka and his men dig in, trying to lift the parapet with everything they have available – yes, including bits and pieces of Diggers.

Over to the west of Jacka's 5 Platoon, Lieutenant Henry Dobbie's 6 Platoon is doing the same, while 150 yards behind them Lieutenant Frank Appleton's 8 Platoon is digging in, acting as reserve.

Well back from them all, Major Otto Fuhrmann has found a capacious dugout to establish the B Company HQ.

Just over to their right and joining them on the Elbow, another 4th Brigade unit, the 48th Battalion's C Company, is dug in and has already been there for a day. Their Commanding Officer, Lieutenant Colonel Ray Leane – a 38-year-old Gallipoli veteran from Adelaide known as 'Bull' by his men for a certain undeniable resemblance to that powerful animal – now feels it more strongly than ever. He is sure a German counter-attack is just hours away. And Leane is not the only one expecting the Hun to soon be upon them.

•

By the time the men of the 14th Battalion's C Company, with Sergeant Ted Rule in the lead, get close to their allotted position in relief of the 2nd Division's 28th Battalion, even Rule himself is spooked ... and something more.

'I was more than terrified,' Rule would recall. 'I had never before been so horrified in my life. The shelling, and the dead lying in all sorts of attitudes, were enough to send new men mad.'[32]

There is no time for either reverence or revulsion. Needs must – *forward*.

The men push on some 400 yards and come to 28th Battalion HQ, situated in an old Hun dugout, and pause for a moment, awaiting orders.

Scurrying along the trench, coming the other way, is a just-relieved 28th Battalion officer, hurrying to get the hell out.

'What,' Sergeant Rule asks, solicitous of the need for his own soldiers to have the same, 'have the men of your unit done with the blanket and waterproof that each one carried in?'

'You will be damned lucky,' the officer tosses back over his shoulder in reply, his voice getting more distant by the word, 'if you'll ever use a blanket again.'[33]

This, frankly, seems like a fair point under the circumstances, and all the more so because, as Rule feels, even if you did live through it, you probably still wouldn't be able to get any sleep. On the strength of this, he throws his blanket off his back and leaves it there, marching off. Now that specific orders have emerged, telling C Company which trench they are to take over – a support line with its left end on Pozières cemetery – they quickly crowd into it, such as it is.

'I've never seen men so closely packed in a trench,' Rule will recount. 'It was not a bit of wonder that men were being killed like rabbits. Every shell that got into the trench simply cleaned it out, and it was easy to see how one shell could smash up a dozen men.'[34]

The most important thing now is to secure the trenches that have been so hard won by their comrades of the 2nd Division. That means digging out once again all those trenches that have collapsed and throwing out all detritus that is cluttering up the floors, which most certainly includes dead bodies but also shattered rifles, scattered letters, a smattering of personal effects, empty boxes of ammunition and half-emptied Maconochie – meat and veg – tins. Of course, all over the Pozières slopes, others of their battalion and the wider 4th Division are doing the same – digging in, trying to maximise their chances of getting through the night.

Some 400 yards forward of Rule's men, Jacka and 5 Platoon are now fully dug in their adjoined shell-holes on the ridge crest and . . .

And what now?

Lance Corporal Sidney Jorgensen, commanding a Lewis gun section of eight Diggers, arrives with his Lewis gun. In all the chaos, he has not been able to find his own platoon, which is useful.

'Can you stay with us,' Jacka asks, 'as our guns have not come up?'[35]

Jorgensen agrees and has soon set his gun up, firing off a few bursts to make sure it is still okay after being knocked around while coming up. Then a nearby shell-burst sends a cutting bit of shrapnel straight into his breast. Jorgensen is hit, badly. Dragged away by his fellow Diggers, the Lance Corporal is bandaged up, the best they can, in the faint hope he might survive.

•

Still not satisfied that he has all his men in the best defensive position, Sergeant Ted Rule leaves half of them in the first position they have settled and orders the other half to follow him. But now here is the Commanding Officer of the 28th Battalion, the last officer of his unit to depart.

'What should I do?' Rule asks him simply.

'Get up to the front line and help your mates,' the Lieutenant Colonel calls back over his shoulder as he departs, 'you'll be attacked tonight.'[36]

Good luck, God bless and quite probably goodbye.

Into the darkness now, up this next hill, over that dead body; the going is grim in two senses. Rule falls over in the pitch black and when he gets up it is to find his hands are covered in blood. It is not his own, he has tripped onto a fresh corpse. There is no time to be disgusted; the shells falling behind you are warning enough to hurry. New dead will be coming soon if you don't hurry. Up ahead at least there is a flickering light, something to head for and hope that a friend will be there. Rule is taking no chances and goes first with his pistol drawn, only to find two flickering candles and two flickering Australians; these poor soldiers are officers, but they looked dazed and lost as they gaze up at the intruder.

'Sir,' says Sergeant Rule to the senior officer. 'I have about 40 men up on top. We have no orders, neither have we an officer. What shall I do with them?'

The officers stare with the glazed eyes of exhaustion, horror and fear. The candles sputter. Outside, the dull, muffled thud of landing shells and the distant chatter of machine-gun fire are a constant. Will they *never* answer?

Finally, the senior officer responds. 'How are your men standing it, Sergeant?'

'They are feeling the strain of it a little, sir.'

There is a long pause.

'All right, Sergeant,' the officer finally speaks, not with military authority but in the tired voice of a father who realises he is too old and weak to do anything more for his son. 'Take your men along the trench and attach them to the company lying in support.'[37]

In other words: go away. They do so in an orderly fashion and, the night and Sod's Law being what they are, they find themselves back exactly where they started. It is the end of the support trench which finishes where Pozières cemetery begins. How very handy.

Even though well back from the front line, these support trenches are being shelled through the night as never before. All the men can do is huddle at the bottom of the trench, shoulder to shoulder, knee to knee, and pray that every succeeding, screeching shell doesn't land on them. Time and again that happens to nearby bays, and they all must scramble along to help the poor bastards who have been buried alive.

'Willing hands would quickly get to work and dig them out. To be buried alive by the earth showered over him by a shell-burst is just about all a man can stand, and retain his reason. We tried to be cheerful, but the jokes were very feeble.'[38]

But, for the moment at least, Sergeant Rule's bay stays intact.

Beyond the artillery, all are aware that their most severe test may well be yet to come. What was it the Commanding Officer of the 28th Battalion had said as he left?

'You'll be attacked tonight.'[39]

CHAPTER SIX

ATTACK!

[Jacka's] fighting spirit and independent nature constantly brought him into conflict with those in higher authority. For some reason unknown to me, men who did not know him in action were sometimes under the impression that he fought without brains, like a mad bull in a crockery shop. Nothing could be further from the truth. Fate seemed to lead him to where desperate situations required desperate remedies, and stories of his audacity will be handed on to generations of Australians.[1]

Captain Ted Rule

The man who has never been frightened has never been to France.[2]

A frequent saying of Albert Jacka at the Western Front

6 August 1916, Pozières Ridge, warfare for trenches

At nine o'clock, suddenly, it starts. There is a boom in the distance, followed by a whistling, and the worst happens. Shells start landing all around, perfectly ranged. *Dig, Digger, DIG!*

Instead of the artillery fire being spasmodic, and distant, it is constant, and right on their noggins!

Again and again and again, the German shells land on the Australian front lines, sometimes killing the Diggers outright, at other times ...

DIG, Digger!

The artillery continues, the thudding blows drowning out all communication as the night continues and the trenches are dug apace, the incentive of survival making every Digger a veritable digging machine. The screaming shells from the 12-inch howitzers, the little 'whizbangs' that shoot their death spray with a screaming fall, split the air with sulphur. If this isn't hell, then it's only because the Devil is lazy in comparison. The ground around them spits with shards of shell, shatters and dissolves as the shock of the artillery fire causes fissures through anything stable. It is beyond belief, except they can see and feel it.

'The very earth, lacerated and torn, rocked and dissolved under the weight and force of the metal blown into it. Both the earth and the heavens seemed rent by this concentrated effort of man's fury.'[3]

Every shell that lands within 50 yards of their position throws out tons of mud, which frequently completely engulfs the Australians' none-too-shallow graves. You're just firing your rifle, trying to shelter when suddenly there is an explosion so close it near shatters your ears, and now the blackness closes, burying you in mud, crushed by a truly terrible weight, and you struggle and fight for life, for light, for air, knowing your time on earth has come to an end or ...

Or there is a slight easing of the pressure, and a scrabbling, and your desperate mates suddenly drag you from your grave and you're alive, you're alive, and can *breathe*, and can see, and . . . and must get back to your post, knowing exactly the same thing might be about to happen again, and you will either be buried once more, or it will be your turn to dig your mates out. Some can be saved – including Lance Corporal Jorgensen with the bandaged chest. Time and again Jorgensen is buried, only to be hauled from the mud by his ankles, or whatever other bit of him they can grab.

'I had to lie in the trench all night,' Jorgensen will recount, 'as shells one after another kept bursting just in front, a few feet away, and the concussion would nearly tear my chest open, and half bury me.'[4]

For the moment at least, he lives to be buried again. Others don't, as the ranks thin through the night and the shells keep landing, and the initial platoon of 44 men keeps diminishing with men killed, wounded and missing.

God Almighty!

In the midst of what has become 'a heaving volcano',[5] 2nd Lieutenant Albert Jacka somehow remains calm, despite mud and death surrounding him through the night as the barrage goes on.

And just as the darkest hour is before the dawn, so too in wartime is it often the noisiest as, presaging an attack scheduled for first light, the enemy unleashes everything they have.

Hurricane fire!

•

A little over 500 yards forward of the German lines, Albert Jacka stirs in his OG1 shell-hole. His sixth sense alerts him that something may be up, and now he climbs to the top of the shell-hole to look out onto No Man's Land. His eyes of blue look straight through the gloom. But in the semi-darkness of dawn, there is absolutely nothing apparent – apart from three shells a minute, landing within 50 yards of him. *Nearly* absolutely nothing. Still uneasy, however, Jacka slides back down into the shell-hole, remarking only to his men that things are 'just the same'.[6]

Or are they? It seems unlikely that a barrage of this intensity does not presage trouble. He stays alert, on principle.

•

In his own dugout, 400 yards back from Jacka, Sergeant Ted Rule has a sudden presentiment similar to Jacka's. Is there something of a diminution in the number of shells landing on this support line? Is the shelling moving further back, perhaps putting down a 'curtain' behind them to cut off whatever supporting troops might try to rush forward as the Germans attack?

When Sergeant Rule mentions his fears to the officer nearby, Lieutenant Stanley Thompson, the Lieutenant laughs lightly and tells him to sit down again.

But Rule is not so easily persuaded. 'I'm getting my rifle and bombs ready, anyhow.'[7]

•

For those in the front lines to the right of Jacka, it happens in an instant. From seemingly out of nowhere, waves of Germans are suddenly upon them, surging forward, throwing grenades and firing from the hip. Some pause to jump into such Australian trenches as there are, others keep racing on.

'Figures flit before us, right and left of us,' runs one German account, 'huge bursts of fire – bullets fly everywhere – a machine gun rattles away.'[8]

Right by the windmill, the first of the two waves of Germans – totalling some 1600 soldiers – attacks on a 1200-yard front, helped by a mist clinging to the hollows there that hides their advance. In a mad moment, German soldiers from the 63rd Regiment, aided by sections of machine-gunners, *flammenwerfers* and pioneers, have broken through in the centre, on a 300-yard front at the Elbow.

The Germans quickly pour through the gap.

•

A few hundred yards to the west of the initial breakthrough Albert Jacka and his men are still unaware that a crisis is upon them, even as two German soldiers arrive above their shell-hole.

With the sun still not risen, the Germans can see no more than a black hole, with no signs of life, but, just to be sure, one of the soldiers takes from his belt a *stielhandgranate*, stick hand grenade, pulls the cord and, after four seconds, throws it down into the hole. Most of Jacka's men are still dazed, almost slumbering after their long night from hell, and don't hear the grenade rattling off the rubble. But Jacka himself is wide awake and hears it clearly, managing to dive behind what cover there is in terms of mounds at the bottom of the hole before it explodes.[9]

In the midst of the roar, blinding spray of mud and subsequent screams of more dying men, it is Jacka and Private Billy Williams who respond most quickly. Jacka is already taking his Colt .45 pistol in hand, and jumping over the wounded, scrambling up the muddy slope to the lip of the hole with Williams by his side.

There! Near the top, through the smoke, it is Williams who sees them first, and alerts Jacka. They can both dimly perceive what must be the two Huns who have dropped the grenade, now walking down the slope towards Pozières, with *hundreds* of other Huns.

Jacka is calm, cold and calculating. A deathly stillness has come over him. The Germans have broken through the entire line and are now pushing towards the actual village. But what now? They are circling around, behind the position of the 48th which is holding the line to the right of the 14th.

Something must be done. He is the man to do it, but he will need help. Below in his shell-hole the groans and screams go on. He and the other half-dozen survivors must help where they can, but most urgent now is to gather whatever coughing, spluttering soldiers he can – those who are still capable of fighting on – and strike back at the Germans who have broken through.

Follow me. There are seven of them left, who, on his signal, climb with him, up to the parapet of their shell-hole to get the lie of the land.

In the meantime, Jacka sends back one runner with a message – heading on a circuitous route to evade the Germans – reporting his position, the need for support in terms of soldiers coming forward and an artillery barrage to start on the direction the Germans have come from, on the other side of Pozières Ridge, to prevent reinforcements coming. The Germans who have broken through must be isolated.

Go! GO!

Ride boldly, lad, and never fear the spills.

•

It all happens so fast. One moment the men of Lieutenant Lionel Carter's B Company of the 48th Battalion are peering into the luminescence of dawn, expecting the German attack to come from the north, when suddenly marauding German soldiers are coming at them from the west!

Shocked, stunned, afraid for his own life and that of his men, Lieutenant Carter – a Methodist clergyman from Western Australia – takes a decision as instant as it is regrettable.

'Drop your weapons!'

There is a moment's confusion. Many of these Diggers of the 48th Battalion still have a lot of fight left in them, and want to go on with it, taking to the Germans with pistols, bayonets and their bare hands.

But Lieutenant Carter has given them a direct order. Enough of the men instantly obey, throwing down their rifles that the others – even those desperate to fight on – have no choice. Orders are barked, and while the bulk of the marauders start to dig in to hold the new line, another 85 of them are dispatched to lead their 45 Australian prisoners back to lines, to ultimately be sent back to Germany to work for the rest of the war.

•

Jacka and his men, still on the lip of their shell-hole, have been watching closely.

He would later remark that, 'the Germans passed right over us . . . the Germans went over without seeing us'.[10]

'When they went past the trench they took a turn about half left,' Jacka will recount, 'and they appeared to have surrounded a number of the 48th Battalion and taken them prisoners.'[11]

Things are grim and getting grimmer.

He and his men have a choice.

Fight and perhaps die, or meekly surrender.

For Jacka it is no choice at all.

'It did not seem any good being taken prisoner without putting up a fight,'[12] he will note. But, most crucially, do his men feel the same?

'This is no good, boys,'[13] he notes as his first observation.

Agreed.

'If we stay here, they are bound to capture us,' he goes on. 'And I would sooner be dead than a prisoner. The supports cannot be long in coming for us, let's go for them.'[14]

Let's go for them.

It is not really an order, more along the lines of a strong suggestion, in the Australian fashion.

'Will you join me, in attacking them?'[15] asks Jacka.

You mean, will we join you in charging straight at a bunch of armed Germans who outnumber us something like ten to one?

On the one hand these Victorians are a bunch of likely lads, grizzled veterans who are always ready for a scrap. On the other hand, before the war had started they were very *unlikely* lads to find themselves in this position: Clarence Taylor had been a hairdresser; Frank Miller, a coppersmith; Horace Carroll, a brick-layer; while Jack Finlay, Billy Williams and William Bourne had all been simple labourers.

But right now, they are willing alright, and that is all that counts.

No-one says anything, but there are no protests and each man gives that all but imperceptible nod of the head – not even a quarter-of-an-inch, with the eyes right on you – which says, 'We're with you, cobber.'

For one thing, it is not just anyone asking them. This is *Jacka VC*. None of them can reach his level, but they can at least bloody well support him.

'He was our officer,' Miller will later note his admiration, 'and a better or a gamer man never lived.'[16]

For now, Jacka orders them to lie doggo, until it is time to let the dog see the rabbit.

Just one thing.

'Fix bayonets,' Jacka tells them grimly.

Across the gaggle of goggle-eyed soldiers bayonets are quickly clicked on to the lug of their rifles.

'The fellows behaved like bricks,' Jacka will chronicle. 'Not one of them needed asking twice. Their dash and willingness made all the rest possible. They fixed bayonets, and I got a rifle with a bayonet on it [from one of the dead men].'[17]

Wait for my word. That word, when the time comes, will be 'Charge!'

'Don't move,'[18] he says.

We need Fritz close before springing on him.

Jacka, with his eyes just above the parapet like a crocodile in a swamp observing its prey, watches carefully, even as his men steel themselves, waiting for his command.

•

Back at the 14th Battalion HQ, Major Otto Fuhrmann is suddenly confronted by a breathless runner, come from Jacka's 5 Platoon.

The Germans have broken through. Jacka and half-a-dozen survivors are still in their original positions, but they need immediate help.

Fuhrmann quickly sends out orders of his own, for the platoons he has in reserve to get to Jacka.

•

Still the crocodile watches as the Germans get closer.
100 yards . . .
In Jacka's right hand he has his .303 with fixed bayonet.
70 yards . . .
In his holster he has his Mills bomb.
50 yards . . .
And when that is all done, if it comes to it, he has his fists.
30 yards . . .
NOW.
'Charge!'[19]

At the head of his men, Jacka fires from the hip with his .303 as he goes, straight into the mass of Germans leading the Australian prisoners. Two immediately go down, as a series of Teutonic cries ring out – *'Ich bin erschossen!' 'Stoppen Sie!' 'Die Gefangenen kontrollieren!'* – before still more fall.

A visceral howl arises from Jacka and his men as they burst forth, firing, yelling with a primal passion, a bursting bloodlust from these hounds of hell let loose and now on the hunt, knowing they must kill or be killed. Running side by side, so their own shots don't risk hitting each other, they keep firing, and running.

For the Germans it is all happening so fast!

After the success of their attack, the Germans had just been leading their prizes back, when suddenly up from the ground in front of them, like demons, arise half-a-dozen more Australian soldiers, coming straight at them, and *firing* right into them.

All around them their fellow soldiers and officers continue to fall, as confusion reigns.

In the meantime, Fuhrmann's orders have got through and Lieutenant Henry Dobbie and his 6 Platoon of the 14th start moving towards Jacka, as does 2nd Lieutenant Frank Appleton's 8 Platoon.

Some 100 yards back, Lieutenant David Dunworth of the 15th Battalion sees what is happening and rushes forward with a platoon, as does Lieutenant Oswald Law of the 48th, who comes forward with two platoons. One of them is physically led, if not commanded, by Sergeant Frank Beck, who now throws caution to the wind and runs in a dead *sprint* to Jacka's aid.

(Yes, Beck's family had begged him before leaving Australia to take no unnecessary risks, but what can he do? This is life or death.)

Further back still, in a former German dugout well back from the current front lines, Private Northcote from B Company 14th Battalion – whom Jacka had dug out from the mud in the middle of the night and had been evacuated – is suddenly aware of activity all around him.

'A lot of our machine-gunners were in there,' he will recount, 'and when the word came shortly after daybreak that there was some business doing, they went up those stairs just as though they were off to meet their best girls.'[20]

From all directions thus, exactly as Jacka had been counting on, his fellow Australians are rushing to support him and his men.

Still they keep charging, firing from the hip, though now three of his men – Jack Finlay, Frank Miller and Billy Williams – go down, knocked into a trench by a German bomb.

Jacka, now a little out in front and still firing as he goes, is the first to be right on top of the Huns, a blur of movement – thrusting, parrying, stabbing and cutting them down.

Supported by his four still-standing comrades, they are soon together with . . . the Australian prisoners, who now join in the fight, and grab what weapons they can from fallen or stunned Germans.

All around them, as the Official History of the 14th would record, 'Germans were mixed up with our men like players in rival football teams during a match.'[21]

Jacka's men quickly engage in activities that would have sent them from such a football field straight to the cells on charges of murder, before focusing on the next development.

Yes, the Germans outnumber the Australians, meaning the men born beneath the Southern Cross are quickly encircled, but even then there is an unexpected advantage for, as one account will note, 'it prevented the further loosing of rifles at that short range. There was more bayonet-work and hand-to-hand struggles in that ring of enemies.'[22]

Sometimes the Australians show mercy, but more often . . . they show steel, ruthlessly applying Guiding Rule Number 8 of the *British Army Manual*: 'Four to six inches' penetration is sufficient to incapacitate and allow for a quick withdrawal, whereas if a bayonet is driven home too far it is often impossible to withdraw it. In such cases a round should be fired to break up the obstruction.'[23]

And none is more devastating with the bayonet than Jacka.

'He was young and not of the splendid physique of most of the Australians,' a fellow soldier notes, 'but he was greased lightning with the bayonet.'[24]

He is genuinely blinding in his speed, cutting an actual swathe through the enemy soldiers. As Jacka keeps forging his way ahead, he suddenly sees the tops of four German soldiers in a shell-hole *aiming their rifles at him*.

There is no time to react. As the first bullet hits, Jacka goes down, but he still manages to leap up again. Again, he is hit, and again he leaps up.

'I do not even remember feeling the two bullets striking me. They, and the other shots by which the men with me were wounded, must have been fired when we were actually struggling hand-to-hand with the Germans . . .'[25]

By the time Jacka is right upon them, the four shocked Germans – how can this *schweinhund* still be *alive*? – throw down their rifles and put up their hands.

Jacka, still mightily aggrieved at the indignity of having the grenade thrown into his dugout and losing so many of his mates, not to mention being shot himself, shoots three of them through the head and bayonets the fourth.

'I had to do it,' he explains later. 'They would have killed me the moment I turned my back.'[26]

And now another shot from just behind. Jacka whirls around to see an enormous German soldier, who must be all of 18 stone – keep the change – bearing the stunned expression of one who has realised he has just missed out on shooting the Devil himself. The Hun is coming right at him, bayonet poised . . .

Back down at Tramway Trench with those of the 14th Battalion in reserve, Sergeant Ted Rule is slipping a magazine of cartridges into his rifle when a dishevelled and panicky Australian soldier comes running along, yelling out, 'Jacka is killed and the Huns have got the ridge!'[27]

Rule's Commanding Officer, Lieutenant Thompson, will not hear of it.

'That man's gone off his head,' he says.

But, of course, alarmed, Rule looks to the ridge and quickly sees the carnage playing out.

From 500 yards away, the mesmerised Sergeant Rule now gazes at this most extraordinary spectacle on the ridge ahead, in this first gloomy glimmer of dawn: men running along the crest. Swiftly bringing his binoculars to bear, Rule can see the wild melee breaking out.

'Some were shooting point-blank at others face to face with them. Others were fighting with the bayonet, this being one of the few occasions when bayonets were really crossed. Others were on their knees in front of standing figures, praying for their lives, and several were bayoneting Huns. It was one of the queerest sights I've ever seen ... Each Aussie seemed to be having a war all on his own.'[28]

It is wild.

'A sensational and desperate, furious fight occurred,' the Official History of the 14th will record of this cataclysmic clash in the first light of dawn, 'the odds against the Australians' counter-attack being at least twenty to one.'[29]

For, despite the advantage of surprise, and the fact that the liberated prisoners of the 48th are now joining in, the sheer numbers of the Germans mean they are getting on top, until . . .

Until, here comes the cavalry!

'At this critical moment,' Jacka will recount, 'the shout of the supports rang clear and loud.'[30]

From one direction arrives Sergeant Frank Beck on the fly, with a couple of dozen men from the 48th Battalion. From another, Lieutenant David Dunworth with a platoon from the 15th, even as Lieutenants Dobbie and Appleton from the 14th charge forth with their own men.

With the last bit of strength he has in him, Jacka dodges the bayonet thrust of the enormous German who has come at him, and kills him with one thrust of his own bayonet, right through the heart.

The German drops, and Jacka – now spent – drops on top of him; his worst two wounds being a bullet through the back of the neck, and another through the left shoulder.

He is more fortunate than others.

For now a German bullet comes, and Sergeant Beck's head explodes. Lieutenant Dobbie of 6 Platoon also goes down, mortally wounded. Of Jacka's original hellhounds, Privates Clarence Taylor and Horace Carroll are also killed.

Even as the battle continues all around, a stretcher-bearer gets to Jacka and begins to patch his seven wounds, dodging the bullets the best he can.

In the end, it is the Australians who get on top and – aided by the fact that Jacka's requested barrage to prevent German support getting through now begins, isolating the men they are attacking – the final result is an extraordinary victory for the Australians.

'Already a number of the Germans had their hands up, and their prisoners (our 48th) were helping us. It was all confused after that. Some of them ran and were shot down by rifle shots; machine guns accounted for others, and we took 47 prisoners on the spot.'[31]

Jacka and *all* of his seven-from-heaven marauders are casualties, with two killed.

Of the survivors, Jacka will note, 'each is amazed to examine the others, because they have not been wounded once, but twice, some three times . . . while others who suffered one slight shot fell'.[32]

Bless them all!

'Every man in that platoon was a hero,' Jacka will record, 'every inch of him.'[33]

For now, however, Jacka himself is in a particularly bad way.

'Both shots were fired almost at point-blank range, and both bullets missed the spinal column by a mere trifle.'[34]

The one that has hit him in the back has left a hole that you could just about put your fist in. The first stretcher-bearer to him stuffs in some scrunched bandages to try to stem the flow.

•

In the shell-hole that Jack Finlay, Frank Miller and Billy Williams had been blown into, Finlay and Miller gather themselves at much the same time – amazed that they are still alive. Miller starts to bandage up some of the wounds of other Australians in the hole who are worse off than him, while Finlay decides to have a look-see over the top of the parapet.

There is the roar of a machine gun and poor Jack falls back into the trench, dead, with most of his head blown off.

'And so died,' Miller will write to Jack's father, 'as game a little gentleman as ever lived. God rest his soul ... May the Lord in his mercy soften your sorrow, but you will be proud of such a fine manly son and if ever I return to sunny Australia I will come and see you both. It is two years since I saw my dear old mother.'[35]

•

Back at the shell-hole Jacka and his men had originally departed from, Lance Corporal Sidney Jorgensen is still in a bad way, now made worse by receding Germans who have spotted him in the growing daylight as they beat their retreat.

'They came to me with their fixed bayonets and bombs, and shook them in my face, but some of them were decent chaps, and pointed to my wounds, and left me alone.'[36]

It is as well, for no sooner have they done so than Australians of the vengeful 48th Battalion sweep through and, spying the Germans, throw Mills bombs which wound or kill most of them. Some of the wounded fall upon Jorgensen.

'But my mate,' Jorgensen will recount, 'who was also badly wounded, helped me from under the dirt and Huns. I then helped to bandage him up. I then started off for the dressing station, but had to stay in a crater hole all day instead, as the shell fire was too severe for our brave stretcher-bearers to get to us ...'[37]

•

And now here is Ted Rule, pushing forward, and first passing the 80 German prisoners being led back to Australian lines.

Yes, their German captives are now prisoners, but at least they are no longer fighting barking-mad Australians, led by one iron lunatic who just won't lie, sigh and die, no matter how often they shoot, stab or bomb him. 'They were certainly the most joyful looking lot of Huns I'd ever seen,' Rule notes. 'They looked as if they were all off to a wedding . . .'[38]

For they are at least still alive, and have every chance now of surviving this war.

But Rule pushes on, until he comes to the first of the stretcher-bearers – marked by the red cross on his upper sleeves – making his way back to the Regimental Aid Post, bearing the worst of the wounded.

'Who've you got there?' Rule calls out to the first man.

'I don't know who *I've* got,' the fellow replies, 'but the bravest man in the Aussie Army is on that stretcher just ahead. It's Bert Jacka, and I wouldn't give a Gyppo piastre for him, he is knocked about dreadfully.'[39]

The word quickly spreads around the entire battalion: Albert Jacka! He's done it *again*! With just half-a-dozen blokes, he's taken on all but a full company of Germans, charged straight at 'em, personally killed more than a dozen of them, and liberated no fewer than 50 Diggers who had previously been captured!

But . . . he and his whole platoon have been cut up very badly. Of his original complement of 52 soldiers, only four of them are still standing with no wounds at all, while Jacka himself is one of the worst hit.

They reckon that with no fewer than seven wounds, including at least three bullets in him, it is a wonder that he is still alive at all. But he surely hasn't got long.

Within minutes the word has come to Bert's brother Bill, who had been holding the fort just over from Bert's own outpost, and he quickly follows the path of the stretcher-bearers all the way down to the Advanced First Aid Post at Sausage Gully – where it does not take long for him to find his brother. For despite the abundance of men missing arms and legs, there is a particular flurry in one corner where the Army doctors are doing everything possible to save Australia's hero to beat them all – or at least stabilise him enough so he can be rushed away to receive medical care at a better equipped medical facility.

Bill catches sight of his brother's face and is profoundly shocked. It is not just that blood is all over it, but just how blood-*less* those parts of his face that are visible are.

'I'd never seen anybody look so terrible in my life,' Bill Jacka will recount. 'He'd been shot through the nose, in fact it looked as though he'd been shot everywhere, his face . . . a lump of lard . . . and I thought "By Jove, you've had it Albert, I won't see you again."'[40]

(Much later, Bill will ask Albert why he had done what he had done and taken such extraordinary risks.

'I was a VC,' his brother will explain. 'What else could I do?'[41]

When you've won the VC, there is a certain standard one must reach, every time.)

The accounts of the number of his wounds will vary, though two particularly bad bullet wounds are certain, as are wounds to his head and back from being splashed by the exploding bomb.

What is certain, is as reported: *'Jacka and his gallant seven had suffered severely in the struggle . . . Each wound represented a miraculous escape from death. Every man was wounded in two or three places, and each owed an escape from death to some fluke equally outrageous.'*[42]

In short order, Albert Jacka is placed in an ambulance, and rushed away; Bill Jacka gazing momentarily mournfully after it, before rushing back to his own section of trench which must continue to be defended.

As it happens, the work of Albert Jacka and his men has already achieved a great deal in retrieving the whole situation.

'The position,' the Official History of the 14th records, 'was now as follows: The first German waves, arriving under cover of darkness, had entered the Australian lines, and though a portion of it had been smashed by Jacka's violent attack, other portions were still scattered about our front. The succeeding waves, received by a hot fire, had been mostly destroyed or driven back, whilst their reserves, cut up by our artillery barrage, was unable to follow up the success of the first waves.'[43]

As the morning wears on, it is clear that the thrust of the Germans across the line at Pozières has been definitively blunted . . . allowing

Bill time to reflect on whether or not his beloved elder brother is even still alive.

At least, he knows, with these new motorised ambulances, it won't take Albert long to get to serious medical care.

Back at Pozières, Lieutenant Colonel Ray 'Bull' Leane is just going through the first of the casualty reports with his brother, Major Benjamin Leane.

'War is <u>hell</u>!!!' the younger brother notes in his diary. 'We have had 48 hours of the most frightful time I ever wish to experience. Of the 900 odd men we took into the trenches at Pozières, we have tonight out less than 200. The remainder are all either killed or wounded. Gallipoli was a paradise to it. Pozières is a veritable charnel house. God! The sights one sees. How any of us are alive seems a miracle . . . I have seen men trembling in every limb, weeping like babies, cowering at every explosion . . .'[44]

•

Even before noon Jacka is being settled into the '4th Australian Field Hospital', a rather glorified name for dozens of beds set up in a village school not far back from the front line. Jacka keeps coughing – in a manner which makes you think he must surely cough up his very lungs.

A few bunks along from Jacka, the shattered Lieutenant Lionel Carter of B Company of the 48th Battalion writes a grave letter to his Commanding Officer, Lieutenant Colonel Ray Leane.

'I wish to make it quite clear the fact that I was responsible for the surrender.

'Now that I think of it calmly I am ashamed and feel I deserve every censure which you and our Brigadier can give me . . . I feel very sorry for having brought this disgrace to the finest battalion in the AIF and to its best company.'[45]

Carter is relieved of command and given a paper-shuffling job instead.

•

Others continue to shine. Just a few days after Pozières has been secured and the 4th Brigade is now moving on Mouquet Farm, 1000 yards to the west, Major Percy Black has the honour of successfully leading an attack as the newly installed Commanding Officer of the 16th Battalion's B Company, where they happily capture a large section of German trench. True, the furious Hun then unleashes the hounds of hell upon them by sending down a horrific barrage on their old digs.

As it happens, one shell lands on Black, burying him, but mercifully leaving his moustachioed melon above ground. And who should discover him in the early evening when the 13th Battalion comes forward to relieve the 16th?

Well, it is none other than his brother from another mother, Captain Harry Murray.

'I had a flask of whisky which was strictly for wounded men,' Murray will recount. 'I considered he had qualified and offered him a spot, and seldom have I seen a spot enjoyed so much.'

Several deep swigs later, Black can speak.

'Harry, I've always said you were the right man at the right time, and you are living up to your reputation.'[46]

Another officer might have taken a break after such an ordeal, but two nights later Black is back in the front lines with his men.

As night falls and the German barrage on their trenches is at its most intense, he walks along and regularly asks young soldiers, things like, 'Got a match, lad?'[47]

Yes, he could easily use his own matches to light his pipe, but the questions are calculated on the reckoning that, despite the endless shelling, the shattering roars, the regular destruction of whole parts of the trench, 'things couldn't be so bad after all, if the Major was only concerned about little things like that'.[48]

Truly?

Things are very bad. And Black is far from sure if his B Company can hold on. He sends back for more Lewis guns to replace the ones that have been destroyed and the soldier sent forth with the first of those guns will leave an account of struggling into the living graveyard with the vile stench of death to find Black sitting on a mound of earth in the trench 'calmly puffing his pipe, looking like a man who has dismounted after a long ride and sought the shelter of a shady tree to rest'.

Grateful for the Lewis gun, Black still must ask as he takes it from the private, 'Where are the others?'

'They're at back of me.'

'Will they be long? It won't do for you chaps to delay your return. Want to be clear away from here by daylight.'[49]

The soldier is stunned.

This is an officer who truly cares. Yes, he wants more Lewis guns, but he also wants to make sure that whoever brings them doesn't get caught in the barrage of dawn.

'I had heard a lot about Black,' the soldier will recount. 'His name had become synonymous with all that a soldier should be in the days of Gallipoli . . . He had a magnetic personality . . . You instinctively say to yourself, "I'd follow that man through hell!" And you mean it. There was an undercurrent of power about him, a purpose in the quiet, unassuming voice and the square chin. He seemed to me a typical bushman . . .'[50]

So impressed is the soldier that he lights a pipe of his own and sits companionably beside Captain Murray as they chat of many things – of home, of the war, of the men they have lost – until the first rays of the sun show the devastation of the detritus around them, the dead bodies, collapsed walls, scattered shell cases.

'Better be tootling, lad,' Black says, as the first German shell of the day lands nearby with an explosion to shake the dead.

'I rose to my feet . . . I looked back several times as I walked swiftly across the uneven ground. He had not moved . . . I felt a different man altogether on the road home. A braver man. I had gained something – a trust I have never lost. I had met one of the gods.'[51]

•

Is he about to meet God?

More than once, Albert Jacka is convinced, in his haze of hell, that heaven must be close. And yet, once he is stabilised, he is placed in another motorised ambulance which gets him to Calais, where the HMS *Dieppe* takes him across the Channel. Within just three days of his action, Jacka is being superbly cared for at the 3rd London General Hospital in Wandsworth, South London, which before the war had been the Royal Victoria Patriotic School.

•

It is time for the 13th Battalion to pull back from Mouquet Farm, all because they have been too successful in pushing forward, leaving the battalions on either side behind, thus exposing their own flanks to German attacks.

Alas, with each staged withdrawal, organised by Captain Murray, the Germans press harder still, with withering fire cutting into their sides, and a wave of stormtroopers at their heels.

'In those hectic moments I had experienced many a cold shiver,' Murray will recount, 'as I thought of the bayonets of the [*enemy*], because it seemed to me, as I ran, that I was almost within reach of those lethal, shining blades.'[52]

An explosion now, in front. From behind, a German stormtrooper has hurled a grenade that has taken down one of Murray's soldiers and killed him by . . .

No, wait!

Just as Murray is about to hurdle over his bloody form, there is movement. He's ALIVE!

Everything hangs suspended.

Somehow, despite everything he has faced to this point, Murray is now – mentally and emotionally at least – 'in the hardest battle of my life'.

Every instinct in him, bar two, is to keep running.

But there is duty, and there is mateship.

It is his *duty* to help the fallen man if he can, and he must also help a *mate*.

Murray stops, grabs the fallen man, and lifts him up onto his back, even as grenades from the pursuers keep landing. He runs the best he can, blood running down his back, his lungs bursting and his legs wobbling, but he keeps going. He is still 200 yards from their own newly established lines and relative safety, when he sees them.

It is the 13th's specialist bombing platoon, coming towards them, led by his mate, Lieutenant Bob Henderson, himself risen from the ranks. Bobby hasn't seen them yet, and is calling for him, knowing Mad Harry will be here somewhere.

'Here I am, Bob! Have you any bombs?'

'Any bloody amount,' Henderson replies, before turning to his men, and snapping an order. 'Throwers to the front!'[53]

In an instant, the hunters become the hunted. Each of Henderson's men has 30 grenades, and a blizzard of them are soon descending among the stormtroopers, who must beat their own retreat in turn. Mad Harry gets back to the lines with his man, and collapses.

•

Among the survivors of the 14th Battalion, and soon enough the survivors of the 4th Brigade, Jacka's feat is already more than mere legend, it is iconic.

All but single-handedly – at least in the sense that, without him, it would not have happened – he has turned what would have been a shocking defeat into a singular triumph. So many of the survivors have a story to tell!

'That Lieutenant Jacka's a daring devil,' Private Northcote, a Shepparton man and fellow patient at Wandsworth, tells a journalist from the Melbourne *Herald*. 'He'd go through anything. I reckon I owe him a lot of gratitude. He's in this very hospital now, and I don't suppose he knows there's a man in here that he got out of a nasty fix.'[54]

Do tell?

'There was another chap with me in a shell-hole ... We heard a shell coming over. It must have come behind us and blown [up] ... I was flung up and then pinned down by some timber and stuff. The other chap – his name was Hollywood – I don't know what became of him, but I know he was hurt too. Well, Lieutenant Jacka had seen that shell come over, just as he was out with another chap on some other bit of business. They came across and gave us a hand, and I got my wounds fixed up temporarily. I thought at the time I had two, but when they got me cleaned up later on they found I had seven. I heard that Jacka got knocked himself the following morning in a bit of a German counter-charge. They reckon he'll get another bar to his VC for what he did then. Well, I know he deserves it. There's no doubt about that man's pluck. He has a marvellous influence over the men of our battalion. We're extra proud of Lieutenant Jacka.'[55]

Indeed, surely, such feats can only result in him being awarded a *second* Victoria Cross – or as the protocol runs, a 'VC with bar', the bar signifying the second VC?

That is not only the view of Jacka's comrades in the 14th Battalion, but also the press. One story will be carried in the Sydney *Sun*, and in papers around the country.

JACKA'S 'SECOND V.C.'
ODDS OF TWENTY TO ONE

> A THRILLING EXPLOIT. Lieutenant Jacka, V.C., of the 14th Battalion of Australian Infantry, is an outstanding example of one of the human facts established by the Great War. He lives to prove that a man who has performed one amazingly brave and skilful feat of arms is extremely likely to repeat the performance.

An account of what Jacka and his men had accomplished follows, before the article finishes.

> The net result was that not one man of Lieut. Jacka's platoon was on the effective list seven hours after they took possession of the trench. But they had held the fort against 20 times as many Germans, killing or capturing them all.
>
> And that was how Jacka V.C. added the second bar to the little copper cross he had won at Gallipoli.[56]

For its part, the *Sydney Morning Herald* goes big on the story:

JACKA, V.C.
FURTHER HEROISM

> *GALLANTRY AT POZIÈRES* LONDON, Aug. 14 Corporal Jacka, V.C., has earned further honours, and is now in a hospital in London, suffering from eight separate wounds. His comrades are full of admiration for him, and declare that he deserves another Victoria Cross.[57]

Strongest of all, however, is *The Age*.

LANCE-CORPORAL JACKA, V.C.
AUSTRALIA'S IDOL

> The man figuring most prominently in the public mind in Australia yesterday was not Mr. Hughes, the recently returned Prime Minister, but Lance-Corporal Albert Jacka, V.C., the young Victorian soldier who, after winning the Victoria Cross for conspicuous gallantry and heroism on the Gallipoli Peninsula, has again sprung into the front rank of fame by reason of a most remarkable display of daring and resourcefulness, performed this time on the battlefield in France . . . The public all the world over dearly loves a hero, and Jacka was undoubtedly Australia's idol yesterday. To-day he may be superseded, but he has had his hour; in fact a second hour, of national worship, and the memory of his deeds will live for ever in the annals of Australian history.[58]

Much later, the Official History of the 14th Battalion will be equally certain as to what is deserved.

'It was a marvellous piece of work, bold in conception, brilliant and heroic in execution, smashing and demoralising to the enemy, and fruitful in its results – a splendid piece of bluff carried to a successful and glorious conclusion by a handful of men who had already endured a nerve-racking bombardment of several hours. The records of the AIF teem with successful exploits in the face of great odds, but they do not contain anything which surpasses (if anything quite equals) the work of Jacka and his seven on Pozières Ridge.'[59]

Which is as may be.

But at this time, Ted Rule, for one, is not so sure if, despite the extraordinary nature of what Bert has achieved, he will get the VC after all, no matter that, 'he certainly deserved it'.[60] Part of the problem might be that to be awarded the most coveted medal, the feat had to be witnessed by a superior officer, and Jacka's superior officers, Lieutenant Colonel Dare and Major Fuhrmann, had been bunkered down some 300 yards back from the front line.

For it is while visiting that deep bunker – a former German command post – after the battle that Rule happens to spy the draft citation that Lieutenant Colonel Dare and his adjutant have prepared to pass on to

Brand for his official recommendation for a bravery award for Jacka: *'For conspicuous gallantry. He led his platoon against a large number of the enemy who had counter-attacked the battalion on his right. The enemy were driven back, some prisoners they had taken were recovered and 50 of the enemy captured. He was himself wounded in this attack.'*[61]

Sorry, *what*?

Rule is stunned.

'Conspicuous gallantry'? That's *it*?

Conspicuous gallantry had merely been the first station along a ten-station journey, with the last one being, as Charles Bean will characterise it, 'the most dramatic and effective act of individual audacity in the history of the AIF'.[62]

Rule is appalled at the proposed recommendation's understatement. Jacka didn't just lead 'his platoon against a large number of the enemy'! He led seven men against 80. And they WON! It wasn't just 'some prisoners' that were liberated. It was all of them. He was merely 'wounded in the attack'? How 'bout two bullets put in him, and five other wounds?

Rule smells a rat.

It is as if Dare doesn't *want* Jacka to receive another VC, as it would make him even more difficult to control than now.

'It struck me,' he will note in his diary that evening, 'that resolution [to get Bert a VC] was lacking very much in the two of them.'[63]

Unbeknownst to Rule, Otto Fuhrmann will even claim to Charles Bean that the man most responsible for cutting Jacka loose at the Germans was – well, he has to say it – himself, Otto Fuhrmann.

'When Jacka saw the Germans attacking he reported to [myself, who] sent Appleton up with the reserve platoon of B Coy . . . As soon as Appleton's platoon arrived the three platoons went into No Man's Land and counter-attacked to the right front.'[64]

Fuhrmann will even claim to an officer by the name of Lock – who will tell Bean of his words – that 'Germans coming up over OG1 were in five waves. [The] 48th bolted back before them. [I] sent up a platoon at once under Jacka who was with him.'[65]

That is simply not true, but who is to know in the top echelons of the military? It is Fuhrmann, the Commanding Officer of B Company, who must make the initial report to Lieutenant Colonel Dare, who will then make the recommendations to Brigadier General Charles Brand. As the recommendation moves up the chain of command, each officer has to agree and sign the form. At any level along the way any one of them might stop it, upgrade or downgrade it. In the case of Jacka's VC at Gallipoli, it had come from Monash's determined questioning of surviving eyewitnesses, and he had guided it through. In this case there is no such questioning, despite the many soldiers who witnessed the deed – including a rough 50 who were spared being German prisoners because of it.

That Jacka has done enough to be awarded the Victoria Cross for a second time is not in question for anyone even remotely familiar with what he has done – notwithstanding the fact that in the seven-decade history of the award only one soldier had received the award twice.

Just what would he be like with *two* VCs?

For the moment, such military machinations can look after themselves, as, after a couple of operations, Jacka continues his convalescence in London.

•

Finally, Pozières is secured.

It is the only high point in five weeks of disaster; a triumph tripled by its very isolation. It is secure enough for the 14th to be finally withdrawn, relief coming from the 49th. On the morning of 13 August, the 14th have the luxury of retreating to rest at last. As they make their way back, they pass an English artillery officer who is gazing into the distance by virtue of his field glasses.

'Can you see any Huns?' one of Ted Rule's mates asks.

'No,' the English officer replies thoughtfully. 'I think you bastards have killed them all.'[66]

More to the point is how many of their own mates have been killed. The three Australian divisions had been in the line for six weeks, and in that time had not only unleashed 19 attacks at the German strongholds, but also beaten back nine major German counter-attacks.

The final 'butcher's bill', as it is known, is 23,000 Australian casualties, of which nearly 7000 have been killed outright – making the place about as lethal as Gallipoli, but that was a nine-month campaign. When those numbers are put together with what had happened at Fromelles, in just over six weeks the Australians in France had suffered 28,500 casualties for nearly 9000 soldiers killed. All up, half of the men in every infantry battalion that had arrived in France earlier in the year had by now been killed or wounded.

Christ Almighty. And despite their collective sacrifice, their heroism, it is barely acknowledged by their Imperial overlords.

In August 1916, Bean writes in his diary, 'G.H.Q. acts with funny motives; it was thought at one time that the Canadians were getting too much kudos and a hint was given to close down on them . . . G.H.Q. has apparently chosen this time to insist that too much appreciation shall not be given to the Australians. It is a miserably foolish decision when my country is fighting the greatest battle in its history and the hardest battle the British army has ever fought. Still, it appears to be deliberate . . . I can't help thinking it is another instance of jealousy. They put us in to fight the brunt of this battle and the AIF has done it – broken itself and broken the kernel of the fight opposite to it.'[67]

CHAPTER SEVEN

GLITTERING PRIZES

We are a rag time army,
A funny lot are we,
We cannot shoot, we don't salute,
A bloody rag time lot are we.[1]

14th Battalion marching song

There were few of us who escaped [Jacka's] displeasure at some time or another. His candid tongue left welts in men's memories, but war was a man's game and strong stimulants were needed.[2]

Captain Ted Rule on Jacka

August 1916, London, rank treatment
Albert Jacka, though ailing, is in reasonably good spirits, if sometimes a little jumpy, and with troubles sleeping as in the silent watch of the night the phantoms stalk.

One thing that helps lift his spirits is his long overdue promotion to the rank of Lieutenant.

'I have got my other star since I saw you,' he writes happily to a friend, early in his convalescence. 'It was in the list of promotions dated the 17 Aug. Needless to say it was rather a pleasant surprise.'[3]

Just how much higher can he go in this war?

Jacka is not sure, only certain that he wants to keep going, convinced that the higher the rank he achieves, the more influence he will be able to have on the fate of the 14th, to win as many battles as possible, while saving the lives of his own men.

His brother Bill, who had also been wounded on the Western Front and is also recuperating in London, albeit in a different hospital, comes to visit and tells him of just how legendary his exploit had become among the Australian forces and how 'the news spread like wildfire'.[4]

You'll *hafta* get another VC, Bert!

Late August 1916, Melbourne, a prescription for conscription

There is no way around it. Due to the devastation of the Australian forces at Pozières, the British Government sends a cable to the Australian Government of Billy Hughes to gravely inform them that, 'owing to heavy casualties recently suffered by the Australian Divisions in France, it will be necessary to draw on the 3rd Division for reinforcements'.[5]

The only way to stop the break-up of that cherished Australian Division, the cable says, is for Australia to provide a 'special draft of 20,000 infantry, in addition to normal monthly reinforcements',[6] and that thereafter for the next three months, they will be needing – dot three, carry one, subtract four – 16,500 soldiers per month.

Billy Hughes is adamant. If that is what the British Government wants, then that is what they will get, and after days of discussion with his colleagues he is able to force it through the caucus, enabling him to cable the British Army Council: 'I will send a special draft of 20,000 infantry immediately, as transport comes to hand, and thereafter 16,500 per month.'[7]

There is, of course, only one way that Hughes can fulfil that commitment, and on 30 August 1916, he announces it. In just two months, on 28 October, a referendum will be held on whether or not the nation should introduce conscription so it could provide the manpower the British Empire needs, allowing the government to force all able-bodied men over 21 to wear a uniform and fight for their country, whether they wanted to or not. The question to be put is relatively straightforward, if cleverly phrased . . .

Are you in favour of the government having in this grave emergency the same compulsory powers over citizens in regard to requiring their Military Service for the term of this war outside the Commonwealth as it now has in regard to Military Service within the Commonwealth?[8]

In snarling halves, the nation now divided up on that very question. And though there are myriad exceptions, in broad brush-strokes the

Protestant middle class is in favour of conscription being introduced, while the Catholic working class, and particularly those of Irish extraction, are against it.

Billy Hughes is apoplectic in response to all those who speak against conscription, starting with Cardinal Mannix, and builds a case that the referendum is no less than a fight for the heart and soul of Australia, and something more besides. For Australia itself, the whole continent, is *in peril!* No matter that 20 years before Hughes had argued in the NSW Parliament that 'Australia needs no armies at all, because it is 10,000 miles from danger.'[9] Now, time after time, he sounds the same general theme: 'Germany has long coveted this grand and rich continent, more than 14 times as large as Germany, and if she wins, she would certainly claim Australia as an important part of her spoils. For this reason, the ramparts of our native land are in fact in the Allied trenches in France. If Britain falls, in Australia there will not be warfare, but massacre. We would be like sheep before the butcher.'[10]

What say you, Jacka VC?

It is a question much of Australia wants answered.

Quietly, privately, Jacka's first reckoning is that he is against conscription, on the grounds that there is nothing more dangerous in the trenches than a soldier who simply does not want to be there and does not have his heart in the fight. But on deep reflection decides he is ... for conscription. It does not seem fair that blokes here are bearing this burden alone, while fully capable blokes at home are doing nothing. Yes, his father, he knows – a staunch Labor man – would be dead-set against it, and would be saying so loudly. But Albert – while not relishing the stoush with his father that must come, is his own man, and is for it.

Excellent. His superior officers make an approach. We want you to come home and sing its praises – to attend rallies, and say to the country, 'We *need* this.'

Will you come?

We can have you on a fast ship and you can be home right at the time the campaign for conscription is at its height, just before the vote is taken.

What, not go back to the mud, blood and gore of the trenches on the Western Front, and instead return home immediately as a feted hero who has done his bit?

Jacka is appalled.

He will not have a bar of such malarkey and says so. He is a man of trenches and No Man's Land, not of soap-boxes and pavilions. Why should his opinion count more than any other bloke? Because he won the VC? What of it? Tens of thousands of Diggers have gone through exactly the same privations, taken much the same risks, and are pretty much as lucky to be alive as him.

None of it sits right with Jacka, and he insists he will return to the Western Front and rejoin the 14th Battalion when he recovers, *if* he can recover.

'My place,' he tells the authorities, 'is with my battalion. If you want me to get back to Australia, you will have to get me back in chains.'[11]

•

Sorry, what?

Sergeant Ted Rule is stunned.

Returning to France himself after recovering from a battlefield wound in England, he picks up a copy of an English newspaper, *The Daily Sketch*, that is floating around and can't believe it.

Albert Jacka. Dead!

Lt. Jacka, the Australian who won the VC in Gallipoli and was subsequently – after capturing 46 Germans – wounded in the Great Advance, has just died.[12]

Devastated, he turns to one of his mates to express his dismay, only for the other soldier to burst out laughing.

'I can see that you don't know the sequel to Bert's death,' he says.

'What do you mean?'

'Well, Bert has been killed in a way. But what has finished him has been the kind attentions of all the old ladies in England – and not only the old ladies by any means; some very attractive girls found their way to his bedside.'[13]

The report of his death was due to a response he had given to an orderly who had told him there were yet more females wanting to see him: 'Oh. Tell 'em I'm dead.'[14]

'Bert's far from dead, don't worry,' his mate says. 'We'll have him back with us yet.'[15]

Back in England, however, Bert is *very* annoyed – and all the more so when it takes several cables to calm his mother in Wedderburn, who had been advised of the false report.

He had never said any such thing to any orderly!

'It was rather the limit advertising a man's death from wounds,' he writes to a friend. 'I have no idea how they got hold of such an idea. I went under an operation the afternoon before that appeared in the paper so I came to the conclusion somebody must have seen me in the throes of an anaesthetic and thought I was dead.'[16]

A couple of weeks later, a particular visit lifts his spirits.

Why, it is General Cox himself, the Commanding Officer of the 4th Division, and, as an excited Jacka will write to Lieutenant Colonel Jack Corrigan, another Digger wounded at Pozières and now recovering in Scotland, 'he told me that I have the D.S.O. and that it would be officially published next week'.[17]

The Distinguished Service Order is usually 'awarded for meritorious or distinguished service by officers of the armed forces during wartime, typically in actual combat, serving under fire, and usually awarded to those above the rank of captain',[18] and, though not a VC, it would be really something.

When Cox brings his wife and daughter into the ward he repeats the news.

'He said to his wife that I had now won the DSO too, so I am beginning to think I must be getting something alright. I tell you, Jack, I earned a DSO right enough. If I get it, I will look sideways at Dare and some of his mob.'[19]

Oh, and one more thing.

Tomorrow, he is 'going down to Windsor Castle to be decorated [with my Gallipoli VC] and I am staying to luncheon. A man will be amongst some class then, won't he?'[20]

And so he is, when, on 29 September 1916, in his best dress uniform, a still ailing Albert Jacka is presented – in the company of other Australian military men being honoured – to the King of England. You can see Bert, there. He is remarkably skinny, almost gaunt, and must wear an eyepatch to cover a still ghastly wound right by his eye.

Now, remember.

When you are presented to the King, or His Majesty himself greets you – for you are *not* to say a word to him, unless directly addressed – you bow your head as a mark of respect.

You will address him as 'Your Majesty' the first time, and after that, 'Sir'. If he is accompanied by Her Majesty, the same first rule applies but when you address her as 'Ma'am' thereafter, make sure it rhymes with 'jam'.

Under no circumstances are you to touch either of them.

With the grandeur of centuries past resounding through it, a trumpet sounds. The battle of etiquette has commenced and there is a flurry of flouncy activity at one end of this 'Grand Reception Room', which is very grand indeed; the bits that aren't marble are either dukes, duchesses or constables. Through the door now comes the King's Body Guard of the Yeomen of the Guard, looking as though they have stepped out of Gilbert & Sullivan by way of the Tower of London, and for any still confused about who is about to arrive, the band strikes up 'God Save the King'.

And now here is the King himself, George V, smiling, nodding vaguely at officials and even saying hello to some of them.

The Australians stand to rigid attention as, one by one, each man has his name called out and must march to His Majesty, salute, and again stand to attention with head bowed, as King George V, by the Grace of God, of the United Kingdom of Great Britain and Ireland and of the British Dominions beyond the Seas, King, Defender of the Faith, Emperor of India, pins the medal each man has been awarded above their left chest pocket.

Jacka is last.

'Lieutenant Albert Jacka VC . . .'

'Congratulations,' His Majesty murmurs to him. 'Your feat was remarkable. I am astonished you have been fighting for two years, and I hope you will live long to enjoy this high distinction.'[21]

As is the protocol, the King now shakes Jacka's hand, before Jacka takes two marching steps back, to snap off another salute.

Thank you, Your Highness.

As for the Victoria Cross itself, it is a small Maltese Cross, famously cast in bronze from cannon that had been captured way back in the Crimean War in the mid-1850s.

Afterwards, Jacka and his fellow medal recipients are invited to stay for lunch in St George's Hall, where – almost more formidable than facing the Germans on the Western Front – they are presented with a bewildering array of silverware and must carefully observe which implements those to the manner born are using, before picking their own up. For the others – Jacka still does not drink – it all might be easier if they could have a beer to settle themselves down, but the palace is as dry as the Nullarbor for the duration of this war, on the direct orders of His Majesty.

•

While the trip to Windsor Castle is a rare excursion out of the hospital for Bert Jacka, another of his comrades from the 14th Battalion, also recovering from his wounds at the hospital, decides to venture further afield. Private Arthur Tulloh has found the address of one of his heroes, the great English poet and Nobel Laureate, Rudyard Kipling – living in an ancient mansion, constructed in 1634, down in the quaint village of Burwash, in East Sussex. So let's go, mate, and knock on the door of the man who has written the immortal words:

> *If you can fill the unforgiving minute*
> *With sixty seconds' worth of distance run,*
> *Yours is the Earth and everything that's in it,*
> *And – which is more – you'll be a Man, my son!*[22]

No, it is not something a common English soldier would do, but they are Australians and don't care for class differences. And Kipling is a man whose poems have buttressed the whole idea of the British Empire, of going to war, of showing the Hun what is what, who is who, and how. On this sunny afternoon, after a long journey, Tulloh and his mate arrive at the mansion and knock on the door. It is opened by a maid who, before they can even state their business, gives them such short shrift it goes no higher than their British bootstraps.

'Away with you bloody tramps, we don't want anyone like you here!'[23]

This is the treatment accorded to soldiers of His Majesty, by the greatest cheerleader of the Empire?

Disgusted, Tulloh and his mate are just turning to go when a head appears from an upstairs window. It is the bespectacled, bewhiskered Rudyard Kipling himself.

'Bring the gentlemen up . . .'[24]

In short order the said maid, still glowering, is obliged to serve Kipling, Tulloh, and his mate, tea and scones, as he questions the soldiers closely about Gallipoli, trench warfare, the conditions, the Turks, the Germans, the guns. Just the year before, Kipling had finagled to get his beloved son, John, into the British Army at the age of 18, despite his poor eyesight, only to lose him in an insane charge at the Battle of Loos.

These days, he is not so gung-ho, Gunga Din, on the war and will soon write the words, in his 'Epitaphs of the War' that sum up his feelings:

If any question why we died,
Tell them, because our fathers lied.

In fact, he has already written the three words that will be the most repeated after this war, in remembrance of those who have fallen, for decades to come,

Lord God of Hosts, be with us yet,
Lest we forget – lest we forget!

Arthur Tulloh and his mate take their leave, feeling privileged to have been in the great man's presence.

•

On 14 November 1916, the news comes through.

For Albert Jacka's daring derring-do, done at Pozières – at a level of insane courage never before witnessed – he does not receive a second

Victoria Cross, nor even a DSO but instead the third tier award ... the Military Cross.

It is gazetted: *2nd Lieutenant. Albert Jacka, V.C., Infantry. For conspicuous gallantry. He led his platoon against a large number of the enemy, who had counter-attacked the battalion on his right. The enemy were driven back, some prisoners they had taken were recovered, and 50 of the enemy captured. He was himself wounded in this attack.*[25]

As an echo of Tennyson's 'Charge of the Light Brigade' ... was there a man dismayed? Yes, many. Among them is Charles Bean, who will later note that, 'no action ever performed in the AIF quite so thoroughly deserved the higher award [VC]'.[26]

Why, then, is Jacka so denied? One officer will later assert 'the weight of jealousy against Jacka, whether it came from inside or outside his battalion, was sufficient to deprive him of a Bar to his V.C.'.[27]

Yet another soldier, 'Euripides', the pen name of one who fought beside him, will state it most starkly: 'The reason that Jacka did not get the Bar [to the VC] was, and I am sorry to say it, perhaps that he had not the social pull ... Jacka might have done better had he been more tractable. He had a habit of always hitting out straight from the shoulder and that is not always politic when senior officers get to hear about it. I think it was realised that Jacka, the higher the rank he obtained, would cause more trouble to some of his superior officers. They were satisfied that if he took it into his head [that] a job had to be done a certain way, it would be useless to tell him to do it another way.'[28]

Exactly what has happened will never be confirmed, only that within the files the recommendation from Dare that Jacka receive at least a DSO is sent to 4th Brigade level – commanded by Brand – where those letters are crossed out, ~~D.S.O.~~ with M.C. scrawled underneath. (In a whodunnit murder mystery, it would not be the butler, but Brand wotdunnit.)

Jacka himself makes no public complaint. Quietly, he is disappointed, feeling, as he will later tell the 14th Battalion historian, that his Pozières counter-attack was 'the greatest of all his personal exploits and rates it six times as high as his V.C. performance [at Gallipoli]'.[29]

Beyond that, five other soldiers have received a VC for their actions at Pozières, but not him. As one shrewd observer notes, 'If a higher standard than the Pozières Ridge work [by Jacka] had been set before the VC could be won, it is fairly obvious that not a soldier would have received the VC in the Great War.'[30]

The main thing now for Jacka is to recover, so he can get back to the front lines with the 14th.

But will he be capable of doing so?

Perhaps, he ponders, it is time to change tack completely and . . . join the Royal Flying Corps as a pilot! In France, he watched the acrobatics of the Albatrosses and Sopwith Pups with wonder, and often wondered how he would go . . .

So why not now?

He could be completely his own man, not dependent on the whims of senior officers.

As later recounted by Ted Rule, 'he actually took lessons and flew a plane after two hours' training . . .'.[31]

On the other hand?

On the other hand, what of his mates in the 14th? What about returning to do what he knows he does best, fighting in the trenches?

'He said the game did not appeal to him,' Rule records, 'he wished to rejoin the 14th'.[32]

The idea of joining the RFC falls away, while his determination to return to the Western Front rises.

What he most needs now is more rest. A few weeks after meeting the King, Jacka is moved to Perham Downs in Wiltshire, which serves as both a training camp for newly recruited soldiers, and a place for wounded soldiers like him to recuperate before heading back to their units. Alas, as the time for returning gets closer, Jacka has another problem and it is getting worse.

(Say it quietly, for fear he will jump.)

For you see, it's his nerves. After nigh on 18 months of being under fire, of hearing shots whizzing past your ear, not to mention into your torso, of having shells explode all around you, of being spattered with the blood of your mates, of killing other men in cold blood . . . Jacka is not coping. It's not just that anything that reminds him of the war makes him jump, it's pretty much that anything, no matter how trivial, reminds him of the war.

'The iron will was so badly shaken,' a sergeant at Perham Downs will record, 'that the noise of a box-lid hurriedly closed would set up a physical shaking that would continue for hours at a stretch. [Afterwards], he was incapable of signing his name to an order or memo.'[33]

The sound of a motorcar back-firing sees him hurl himself to the ground and shiver for minutes afterwards. He has trouble containing his emotions even when nothing is happening.

A slammed door means he must stop speaking, and sometimes cannot resume for minutes.

To try to overcome his nerves, Jacka makes his way to local firing ranges to fire a rifle, but, again, is reduced to a quivering wreck.

In sum, given his traumatic experience, Jacka has gone from the fog of war to the fug of war. Is *anything* worth it, when so many people have died, and will die, almost certainly including him? How could he escape it? He has been so lucky to this point, surviving against all odds while all around him good men have been cut down, so what on earth could make him think he could escape his fate?

He must find another way to test his nerves . . .

There is a roar in the distance.

It is a motorcyclist, on a British 'one-lunger' Rudge Multi TT 500cc, hurtling along the country lanes around Perham Downs, his wheels angrily spitting out loose gravel as he leans into every corner, before lifting, straightening, changing gears, turning the accelerator to go even faster into the next corner. As Albert Jacka VC roars along, his heart races, his breaths come in gasps as the rush of wind tears at his face, all while he grips the handlebars harder, goes faster still, and leaves appalled hikers in his wake, staring open-mouthed at this noisy larrikin making this dreadful noise that destroys the bucolic peace. Jacka doesn't care, and aims to always stay just 1 mph slower than an accident until inevitably . . .

He is 1 mph *faster* than an accident.

'On two occasions this lack of nervous control led to severe motor-cycle smashes on a level road,'[34] Ted Rule will recount.

Mercifully, it is the bike that takes most of the damage and Jacka loses little more than skin.

It is at least some sign that his courage has not wavered. It is only a question of whether that courage will hold up in battle.

Are there any soldiers like Jacka? There is at least one staying here at Perham Downs – a West Australian, Private Martin O'Meara VC of the 16th Battalion. Where did you get yours? Pozières! Jacka dips his lid, as . . . they were hard to win at Pozières in his opinion. A mate of Jacka's, Lieutenant Frank Wadge, has told him (and the brass) of just what O'Meara did to deserve it. He went in to No Man's Land, not once, not twice, but at least 20 times to bring in wounded Diggers who were lying, dying, out there. This was not done in a calm saunter with a kind enemy refraining from fire; oh no, the Hun machine-gunners and snipers had their shots by the hundreds and missed! Out he went again! Now there is bravery and there is madness, and the difference between the two is motivation. When you are in the fever of action, if you are lucky, if you are one in a thousand, something overtakes you and you find yourself acting against all sense of preservation for yourself and only for your fellows. If you die in a second, you are forgotten; if you live and keep performing the miracle, they give you a VC. Pleased to meet you, Marty. Shaking hand shakes shaking hand, and the two recuperating heroes talk as the ordinary men they know they are.

The two have much in common, beyond their staggering bravery and VCs. Both are teetotallers and while in civilian life Jacka had cut down trees, O'Meara is a sleeper-cutter in Collie, Western Australia, turning the logs into useable foundations for railway lines. And, despite the horrors they have known, both are eager to get back to the Western Front and their battalions.

'I would sooner be back with the boys in the trenches than anywhere else,'[35] O'Meara had told the press, and Jacka feels the same.

Very quietly, just between them?

Both are having trouble sleeping and are having ever more shocking memories bubbling to the surface. It is not that they have been knocked 'silly', like blokes who had had too many shells landing too close, but both know something is not right.

By now Jacka is certain that he will go back, while equally convinced that one of the first bullets to come his way will have his number on it.

•

In Wedderburn, Nathaniel Jacka is ropable!
For this, *this*, has just appeared in *The Argus*.

LIEUTENANT JACKA ON CONSCRIPTION
WHICH WAY WOULD HE VOTE.
ADVISES ALL TO VOTE 'YES.'

On Tuesday night last, at a meeting of 'Antis' at the Melbourne town hall, it was reported that Mr. N. Jacka, father of my pal Lieutenant Albert Jacka, V.C., said these words:

'My sons would scoff at the word conscription.' I do not like to have to contradict Mr. Jacka, but in view of the fact that I have a letter in front of me from our V.C. hero, I feel in honour bound to tell the public that Lieutenant Jacka, V.C., is absolutely in favour of conscription.

'Do what you can, Reg, to urge all your friends to vote "Yes". All the boys over here will send their "Yes" votes. I don't think any decent man will vote "No".'

Reg. W. Turnbull

Linda Cottage, Wedderburn, Victoria, October [36]

Well, Nathaniel Jacka will not stand for it. On the basis of his own views and the fame of his son, Jacka Snr has become a regular speaker at anti-conscription rallies in Melbourne, where, alongside the likes of a rising unionist by the name of John Curtin, he has thundered that conscription will trap Australians 'under the iron heel of Prussianism, and under the mailed fist of capitalism',[37] and he feels it with every fibre of his being. With a hand trembling with rage, he writes his own letter to *The Australian Worker*, which is quickly published.

LIEUTENANT JACKA, V.C., AND CONSCRIPTION, SWORN DECLARATION BY HIS FATHER.

SONS' LETTERS AGAINST CONSCRIPTION. WHO IS 'REG. W. TURNBULL, OF WEDDERBURN?'

A damn good question! Mr Jacka Snr has never heard of the fellow. And Wedderburn is not exactly London, everybody knows everybody! Turnbull is an impostor and Mr Jacka is so furious he swears a formal declaration that:

> *'I, NATHANIEL JACKA, of Wedderburn, in the State of Victoria, laborer, solemnly and sincerely declare as follows:*
>
> *'. . . I have received several letters from my sons, Lieutenant Albert Jacka, V.C., and Lieutenant William Jacka, who are in France . . . Never in any letter have any of my sons supported conscription, and in my belief they are all still opposed to it.*

As a matter of fact, Mr Jacka swears his boys are enjoying their war and tell their father: *'we have plenty of fun'*.

As for this so called 'Reg Turnbull'?

'The only Turnbull in Wedderburn is Walter Turnbull, a butcher, who is childless.'[38]

Take that!

Nathaniel Jacka has the satisfaction of seeing the referendum narrowly defeated. Whether or not Reg Turnbull voted will remain a mystery . . .

•

In France, even in his absence, the legend of Albert Jacka VC continues to grow. From Armentières to Pozières to Etaples, wherever they go, the mighty 14th Battalion start to hear themselves referred to with one particularly resonant phrase.

'Hang on, aren't you blokes Jacka's mob?'

'There goes Jacka's mob.'

'Look, Bluey. We are being joined by the 14th. That's Jacka's mob.'

Jacka's mob. They so love it, being so intimately associated with the most famous Australian there is in this war, that they start referring to themselves in the same manner.

Who are we?

Why, we are Jacka's mob!

Alas, when Jacka himself might return to them, or even if he *will* return to them, they know not.

•

Say . . .

Who, one of the new officers of the 14th Battalion asks, on this freezing day of mid-December as the winter closes in, is that 'retiring-looking chap sitting on a valise?'[39]

Yes, that one over in the corner.

Sergeant Ted Rule looks.

It is Albert Jacka VC!

Look, Jacka was never the noisy one in the room, or in the trenches. There has always been a certain diffidence to him. But this Bert Jacka who has just returned to them is different from the one who had left them, after being wounded at Pozières.

Welcome back, Bert!

Thanks.

There is now a remoteness to him, a sense that he perpetually has something on his mind, and it is something heavy – and probably bloody – at that.

And they are right.

For now that Jacka is back on the Western Front, with that constant thunderous rumbling in the distance, that eternal pulsing light of explosions, he is very quietly suffering.

'Little though we dreamed it,' Rule will recount, 'our hero, too, went through the valley of the shadow . . .'[40]

But it is there, alright. He is in the valley, and the shadow of death is always present, stalking him, forever darkening his soul.

Just how will he go when once again under fire?

Whether he is well enough mentally and emotionally remains to be seen. He is much stronger than he was before, but he also knows the only way to find out will be to go out under fire and test himself.

At least, from the moment of arriving back with the 14th Battalion, who are now billeted in that muddy mess of a town that is Ribemont, beside the river Ancre, fourteen miles north-east of Amiens, there is good news for Jacka.

For after Brigadier General Brand had held Lieutenant Colonel Dare responsible for trusting a 4th Brigade battle plan to a private who had subsequently been captured by the Germans, with the plan now compromised, Dare is . . . *gorn*, headed for desk duties in England.

And it gets better still. Though Dare had originally been replaced by Major Fuhrmann, he too is soon replaced.

The 14th is now in the charge of an interesting cove who is quite a different kettle of fish from his predecessor.

The Official History of the 14th Battalion will describe Colonel John Henry Peck as 'perhaps the ablest man who commanded a battalion of the AIF in France',[41] and to Jacka he certainly feels like that from the first.

As opposed to the way Dare had gone about things, Peck – who has devoted his life to the Australian Army – doesn't give you tasks because he has seniority over you and you will be put on a charge if you don't do them. He asks you to do things because he has thought them through, has widely consulted, and has such confidence it is the right thing to do, he feels it would be good for everyone if you could give him the benefit of the doubt . . . even if you have one or two. Somehow, he manages to pull off the strange combination of being tough, smart, funny and firm all at once, while still being totally in command – and kind.

The men respond in kind.

A career officer, Peck hails from Sydney, and had served well at Gallipoli – always a marker for the men as to whether an officer was automatically worthy of respect. He had landed on the peninsula as a Lieutenant with the 3rd Brigade as adjutant, and had left as a Brigade Major, the Chief of Staff of that same 3rd Brigade.

Among his skills is the capacity to have the men relax and feel united with each other when the times are sunny, the better to make them act as a single sharp spear when the times are grim.

'He held an inspection [at Ribemont] one day,' Ted Rule will recount, 'and it was the funniest inspection I've ever seen. In his cheery, witty way he had everyone rocking with laughter, yet when he wanted the men to do any particular movement, they would move as one man.

As time went on our regard for him grew . . . until we just about worshipped him.'[42]

In response to the question of what he thinks of the new commander, Jacka offers three words.

'He'll do me,'[43] he says.

It is enough. Always a man of few words, those three words are all that need to be said, and Peck returns Jacka's admiration in kind, quickly recommending that Jacka VC be promoted to the rank of Captain, while also exploring the possibilities of soon making him the 14th Battalion's Intelligence Officer, responsible for reconnoitring, observing and reporting.

Perfect!

(Confidentially, Peck is of the view that Jacka, despite his reputation, is troubled, and making him Intelligence Officer will keep him back from the worst of the actions in the front lines until he is stronger.)

As the snow falls and they lie shivering in their billets – with nothing between them and the bare ground bar their waterproof, and annoyed because 'You couldn't afford a blanket underneath because you wanted it on top'[44] – what is that strange sound they hear after dark every evening, and again just before dawn, like the constant roaring of motors?

•

And now, something strange on the German side of the Western Front. For, unbeknownst to the Allies, a new rule is imposed. Beyond normal traffic, there is to be no major movement of men or the machinery of war until after the sun has gone down. Everything is to appear sleepy, inactive. But after the sun goes down? Well, together with the normal night-time sounds of dogs barking in the distance, owls hooting, cows mooing . . . there is now the endless rumble of trucks moving back and forth, followed by the ceaseless tramp of feet.

They are labour battalions, busy with construction. Quietly – because right now secrecy is important – the *Deutsches Heer*, the German Army, is more active at night than during the day. The only giveaway is the trucks that are bringing the worker battalions forward after dark, and taking them away before dawn. With 450 soldier-workers going hard, it takes six hours to build 250 yards of a zig-zagging trench, two and a half feet wide by six feet deep. To add the extras – barbed wire, duckboards, sandbags and dugouts for sleeping, stores, first aid posts, communications equipment and HQ posts – is about the same amount of time again. The saps and communication trenches leading to the back areas, allowing the movement of men and *materiel* back and forth? Another 450 men going for six hours.

But it must be done.

After their catastrophic losses at Verdun, and the Somme, the Germans simply cannot defend the long line and so must reduce their perimeter by contracting their whole line. It is with this in mind that 'the Hindenburg Line' – named for Field Marshal Hindenburg – is being constructed over 90 miles long, and up to 30 miles back from the original line. The contraction sees a shortened front to defend, requiring fewer troops, but that is not all.

Because of careful design and clever positioning – like a links golf course, complete with bunkers – it has been built along contours where the natural defences of gullies, rivers and hills make it nigh on unconquerable as the landscape itself has been conscripted to help the German soldiers. Further, bristling with machine-gun posts, pillboxes – the Germans call them '*Mannschafts Eisenbeton Unterstände*' (reinforced concrete shelters) – and superbly engineered trenches that are impregnable to all but direct hits of artillery, it is no less than the strongest defensive line ever built in the history of warfare.

'The wire entanglement of the Hindenburg Line was known to be the most formidable ever constructed,' Charles Bean will note, after it is discovered, 'aeroplane photographs showed its broad belts, three deep, the last of them 50 yards out from the first trench, and a single strong belt before the second trench. The front wire was in many places triangular, so that machine guns could fire along its edges, and an attack would split and lose direction. The wire alone – not to speak of the two well-dug trenches 150 or 200 yards apart, would require protracted bombardment.'[45]

•

Ah, Ribemont. While each town has its own eccentrics, and every camp has its characters, in the life of the 14th Battalion there has never been an eccentric character quite like Incinerator Kate. The colourfully attired Frenchwoman is around 50 years old, filthy in both language and body. She can outswear a British battalion without trying, you can smell her from 50 yards *upwind*, and she is devotedly and permanently drunk. She is the scourge of officers, the humiliator of higher-ups and the sweetheart of the enlisted, who delight in seeing her scandalise their betters. They most particularly love it when she stands on a corner and smartly salutes the troops marching past – as if she is herself a grand officer – before racing from corner to corner around the town, doing the same.

Everywhere they look, there is Incinerator Kate!

It is all they can do not to weep with laughter.

'She was a little old woman half dotty, very stout, old clothes falling off her, a face as ugly and red as a turkey cock, about five inches of hair which she always tied in a ball on the top of her head. Her boots were old ones worn by the soldiers at one time or another. She made her living poking around the soldiers' camps collecting old socks, bottles etc.'[46]

Her real name? It is *Mademoiselle* Katherine Janton, and don't you forget it. But this name is only used for arrest and despairing official complaints. To every soldier she is known as 'Incinerator Kate'. Kate dresses in their discarded uniforms, rescuing scraps of clothing and food and anything from the incinerator, and eating, wearing or selling whatever she can scavenge. The selling is done so she can begin buying and consuming alcohol. It is a Sisyphean process because Kate can never have too much to drink, so always needs more rubbish to sell.

Kate will be sober approximately three days after she is dead. The fumes are so strong from her at all times that it is a wonder Kate can stand so close to an incinerator without bursting into flames. It is amazing that she can stand at all, given, firstly, that she is always wearing boots five sizes too big, and secondly, that she is rolling drunk. Her legs are as bare as her *derriere* will be on one famous occasion. For as it happens, the grand home where Colonel Peck is billeted also has Kate and one day he is *most* annoyed when he returns to find her in his bedroom.

'Look here,' the Colonel promptly says to his batman, 'it's bad enough to live in the house, but I won't have "Incinerator" in my bedroom.'

'Yes, sir,' replies the British batman, whereupon, seeing Kate passing by, he calls out: "Ere, Kate, you keep out of my boss's room see . . . ?'[47]

Incinerator Kate will not be spoken to in that manner, and the next time Colonel Peck leaves the house, she gathers up his things, puts them in her ubiquitous wheelbarrow and deposits them clear at the other end of the town.

There is hell to pay. But before Kate can be found to be severely remonstrated with, there is a Regimental Parade, where the entire 14th Battalion must turn out with their uniforms cleanly pressed, and their boots polished, while the ramrod straight Peck takes the salute.

But what now, as the band strikes up the Regimental March and the troops begin the march-past?

'A roar of laughter broke from a thousand throats on the square. For Kate, moving quickly ahead of the officer of the guard, swept in front of the saluting point. Before the command "Eyes left" was given, she executed her characteristic *"Pas de Quatre"*, thumbed her nose at the Colonel, then exposed to view to the strain of "The Girl I Left Behind Me" that part of her anatomy, not protected against the winter winds, on which it is considered dishonourable to be wounded.'[48]

Oh, how they laugh.

It is legendary stuff, and a form of free entertainment that will never pall. You can stuff the Folies Bergère, they have Incinerator Kate.

•

By late January the 14th Battalion is assigned to move into the reserve line of the Western Front, near the village of Flers, two miles from Pozières, to take over from the 26th and the 28th Battalions, who have earned a rest.

The opportunity is too good for Jacka to miss. It is what he has been waiting for. If they are in the reserve line, it can only be a matter of time before they are moved into the front line, and as one of the leading officers of the 14th Battalion it is his *job* to go out into No Man's Land in the night to gather information on the landscape and German defences, so he can properly guide the 14th on future 'stunts'.

He will take with him two newly appointed officers, Lieutenant Ernie Edmonds and Lieutenant Herb Anderson, to show them the ropes. They move out after darkness falls on 23 January 1917, the air, as ever, is filled with the crackle of sporadic rifle and machine-gun fire, just as the throbbing light of shell explosions is nothing if not consistent, as are the Verey lights, lazily arcing up and flaring before . . . . . . ebbing away.

But at least none of them is very close.

Via a labyrinthine pathway through their own rolls of barbed wire, across the ravaged muddy ground filled with shell-holes and the detritus of war, Albert Jacka and his two officer companions are now out in No Man's Land.

And now he hears it.

It is the distinctive whistling of the 5.9 shells, those German monsters that blow holes in trenches at least 20 yards wide and kill everyone standing within 50 yards. The whistling roar, like a train hurtling past, gets louder. It's going to be close!

Jacka steels himself, while the other two stare wide-eyed – scared, but too inexperienced to know just how close this is going to be.

Get down!

The shells land in quick succession a little more than a stone's throw away, with massive explosions.

Picking himself back up, Jacka smiles.

'They say a man is never the same after he has been wounded.' He grins, with infinite relief. 'I'm damned if I notice the difference.'[49]

He is going to be alright. Bring on the war, once more.

His self-assurance will be confirmed a short time later, when he actually goes into the front lines around Flers to test himself under fire. Again, all his deathly calm has returned, despite bullets buzzing all around.

'I didn't flinch,'[50] he will recount to Rule.

•

Gawd help us all. It is the pompous Brand and his regulation khaki moustache once more. Dare might have gone, making the world a better place – even on the Western Front – but Brand remains in charge of the 4th Brigade. Will this infernal officer leave them alone?

On this day, Jacka happens to be with his platoon, knee-deep in mud, when the Brigadier comes by. It is not certain that he has specifically sought Jacka out, but whatever his intent, his remarks seem to be offered in the belief that they will infinitely please the battalion's VC winner.

'I have great news for you, boys,' he announces. 'I have just received from division a report that the French attacked last night and captured many thousand prisoners.'[51]

Silence.

This is your great news?

We Australians seem to always be hearing how the French have accomplished great things, only to find that, more often than not, we are the ones who are steered towards accomplishing what our Gallic comrades have actually failed to do.

They stare back at him.

The subsequent silence is crashed by a Digger, who asks: 'Do you think we are winning, sir?'[52]

'Of course I do – am I not telling you what the French did last night?'

'Well,' the Digger replies, looking all about him at the acres of mud, the lack of dugouts and cubby-holes, 'if we're winning, God help the bloody Germans.'[53]

It is a story that Jacka will repeat, with unaccustomed gales of laughter, for many moons to come.

Fortunately, whatever Jacka's continuing antipathy for Charles Brand, his rapport with Peck continues to grow, in no small part because Peck realises that when it comes to front-line activity, Jacka knows a whole lot more than he does, and so *listens* to him, even taking notes on some occasions.

'Under the virile leadership of its new and capable chief [Lieutenant Colonel Peck],' the Battalion's Official History notes, 'the 14th attained the high-water mark of discipline, efficiency, reputation and contentment.'[54]

They continue to train daily for the trials to come, their efforts including long route marches, musketry and bayonet practice, and how to both read signals from the front and pass them on. There is yet another storm brewing, and they must be ready for it.

•

The French call them *estaminets* – based on the word '*staminet*', meaning 'cowshed'. Before *la guerre*, they held cattle and produced . . . bullshit, among other things. These days, more often than not they hold soldiers and produce . . . much the same thing! For many of the impoverished French farmers near the Western Front have found the best way to turn a profit from the rich guests they are billeting in their barns, the Australians earning a colossal six shillings (150 francs) daily, is to serve them expensive grog. It only needs a few tables and chairs, a few comely *femmes* from the village as waitresses, and a cosy kind of bar is formed. On the drinks menu is piping-hot tea from Madame, watery beer, and most particularly *vin blanc* – inevitably referred to by the Diggers as 'Point Blank'.[55]

And while business is always good, it explodes around the time of '*les* stunts', as anxious soldiers contemplate their possible fates and not blowing their pay becomes rather beside the point – while afterwards, survivors gather in huddled groups, talking over what has happened.

Some *estaminets* boast dancing girls, and some go further still, with bedrooms upstairs, with one soldier recording, 'We were drinking *vin blanc* in the *estaminet* and it was absolutely crowded. There were five women in there, and it was five francs – just 2½ pence! – to go up the stairs and into the bedrooms with them. The stairs leading up to the bedrooms were full; there was a man on every step, waiting his turn to go in with a woman.'[56]

On this evening, the two Australian officers sitting at the corner table, with no interest in either grog or women, are none other than the lieutenants Jacka and Wanliss.

Wanliss, like Jacka, is a life-long teetotaller and equally of the view that the only woman he wishes to sleep with will be the wife he suspects he has not yet met. Jacka still holds something of a torch for sweet Elsie Raff, the Wedderburn reverend's daughter.

For all that, both Australian officers like being around their men outside the trenches, and as the men like to be in the *estaminets*, that is where the two officers often meet. Jacka's resentment at Wanliss's selection ahead of him to lead the first raid of the 14th Battalion on the Western Front has long since disappeared, so well did Wanliss do, displaying such bravery. What is more, Wanliss has now recovered enough from his wounds to be able to return to the 14th and take up a new position as Peck's adjutant, essentially his secretary, doing all the paperwork for their commander. As much as he will miss the front-line action, it will give him more time to recover and expose him to the higher echelons of command. He is already one marked out for promotion.

On occasion, the two are joined by two other officers, Captain Harry Murray and Major Percy Black, a twosome so often together that seeing one without the other seems like a mistake. The short one is Black, who looks like a stockman from a Banjo Paterson poem caught in the wrong century by mistake, but he'll be damned if he is going to be the one to change. The big bloke is 'Mad Harry' Murray, his handsome hawkish face centred with a small red-brown moustache; his thick mop of hair seems to be standing at attention at all times, and the dimple on his chin is deep enough to strike a match in.

Each is always eager to tell of the other's prowess, but Black is particularly proud of Murray lately and reckons he is in line for the Victoria Cross itself for his work in leading a death-defying charge at Stormy Trench in February.

Murray doesn't talk about it much himself, but is the exemplar of true bravery being the capacity to follow through *despite* being scared.

'I fought many a hard battle ... between duty and funk,' Murray will later note. 'Cowardice was practically the same thing as self-preservation, it was the first law of nature, and while some men may be so constituted that they require no artificial stimuli I cannot make such a claim.'[57]

So yes, Harry and Percy, pull up some chairs and let us talk into the night: of home, of the war, of just what lies ahead ...

CHAPTER EIGHT

RECOVER, RETURN, REVENGE

> *Many people have the impression that Jacka went berserk in action. That is wrong. He was the direct opposite – cool, deliberate and calculating – always fighting to win, not merely by sheer bulldog tactics, but by out-generalling the opposition, and saving the lives of those whom he commanded.*[1]
>
> Captain 'Mad Harry' Murray, 13th Battalion

Mid-March 1917, Ribemont, Captain courageous

So highly does Colonel Peck regard Jacka that he reserves for himself the pleasure of personally giving the Victorian the good news. He has been formally promoted, and is now *Captain* Albert Jacka VC. (It has taken quite a while, and the theory that some of his superior officers are reluctant for him to continue his rise persists.)

Well, we will all see how Captain Jacka behaves now. To begin with he is thrilled, at least in a very Bert Jacka kind of way – if you look closely, you can see that both ends of his mouth are slightly turned up, in what just might be a smile.

Just how far could he take this? Could he become a Major, even a Lieutenant Colonel? How many VCs does it take to be a full Colonel, in charge of the whole 14th Battalion?

Jacka aches for exactly that, to form up his own battle plans, to stop the useless slaughter of Australian lives, to win this war as quickly as possible and get home. It is all so obvious to him that it is madness to keep pursuing the current British 'tactics' of sending masses of men straight at Turkish and German guns, but they keep doing it, keep giving orders for Australians to do the same, and the result is tens of thousands of dead men who needn't have died!

Further recognising Jacka's nascent intelligence and capacity to grow as a man, Peck places the forestry worker front and centre of the evening lectures he has organised for the battalion. While the carefully coiffed Harold Wanliss gives a lecture on Napoleon's military campaigns – one of which came through these very parts – and another officer lectures on the current state of the war, it is Albert Jacka who lectures on forestry, boxing and bicycling, as under Peck's tutelage the 24-year-old's confidence in public speaking, and expressing himself clearly, grows. Almost as if back at school, he learns how to write such lectures, structuring them so they are coherent, and finishing with solid conclusions.

Jacka also chairs the discussion on '*Australian problems. The rainless area*'.[2] Lack of rain is no problem here, a drought might go a good way to clearing up the trench foot and the murk that lurks at the bottom of every pack. What is clear is that there is a fair bit of this war to go, and that the 14th Battalion will remain in the prow of the action. Right now, they are based at Ribemont, part of General Sir Hubert Gough's Fifth Army of 14 Divisions, and the coming plan to break through the Hindenburg Line. To their north-west is the Third Army, to their south is the First Army, each threatening the German line.

Early April 1917, approaching the Western Front, all eyes on the prize

They are a magnificent body of men, marching east, through the glorious French countryside. After six months of reinforcing their ranks with reinstoushments, following the disaster of Pozières, and training them, the 14th Battalion is again ready for action and has been assigned to take over from the 51st Battalion in the French village of Noreuil. Then they will be rotating into manning the Allied forward defences before the Hindenburg Line around the fortified village of Bullecourt.

Oh, the sheer beauty of this place! The magnificence of their farms, their meadows, their villages!

Out in Western Victoria, where many of the 14th Battalion soldiers are from, it can be 100 miles across the dust-bowl from settlement to settlement. But as they approach this part of the Western Front for their next assignment in hell, this part of the world looks a lot like ... heaven.

The fields are green, the trees are verdant, the people are friendly – '*Allez les Australiens, et MERCI!*' – there seems to be a small pretty village or a large gorgeous village every five miles or so, while French women of much the same description are even more frequently seen on the cobbled paths, in the fields and on the streets.

If you are going to put your life on the line to defend a place, it doesn't hurt that it looks like heaven on earth, even if the rumble to their east getting louder is a sure sign that hell is just next door, about where you can see the puffs of flak filling the skies, near the observation balloons and . . .

And what is *that*?

Suddenly, from the eastern skies, half-a-dozen planes appear, most of which are painted in different hues of blue and green, but one of which is . . . red! A cheer goes up. It can be none other than the legendary German ace, Manfred von Richthofen, better known as the Red Baron, for the fact that his Albatross is always glaring red . . . and for the fact that he is a baron. This pilot *wants* the pilots of the Royal Flying Corps to come at him, to take him on, as he fancies his chances. And as one who, it is said, has already personally downed no fewer than 50 planes, he's probably right.

Albert Jacka and the soldiers of the 14th Battalion, stop, entranced. This is a moment they know is history in the making, to see the Red Baron in action, throwing his plane about with expert, effortless ease, as he fires, swivels and swerves, skives and dives, climbs and cavorts. On this occasion there are no planes from the Royal Flying Corps willing to take him on, so he finds another target: yonder observation balloons! Yes, the Allied soldiers and artillery crews below are putting up fearful fire to protect those balloons, the puffs of flak exploding all around him, but the Red Baron doesn't care. Coming in low, his Albatross keeps twisting and turning, always just beyond reach of where the defenders had presumed he would be just seconds before, and as his machine guns start clattering, suddenly two of the observation balloons burst into flame and start plummeting to the farmland below!

The Red Baron and his circus make good their escape, and despite themselves, the men of the 14th roar in delight.

'The little red-bellied machine flew very low in the performance of its work,' Newton Wanliss will chronicle, 'and hundreds of our rifles and machine guns were turned on it. Though the focus of a tremendous fusillade, it escaped to the accompaniment of loud Australian cheers, the admiration and sporting instincts of our men overcoming all political animosity.'[3]

They have seen an exhibition by the master at his best.

Early April 1917, Noreuil, timing is everything

After a brief stint well behind the lines to work on a light railway, Sergeant Ted Rule is now pressing forward to return to the 14th Battalion in their current position at Noreuil, soon falling in with another soldier also returning after a stay in hospital. As they approach the front lines the two run into one of the 4th Brigade's better-known officers, Lieutenant William Shirtley, who is glad of their return.

'You are,' he says, 'just in time for the biggest battle that has ever been fought.'[4]

•

General Sir Hubert Gough, the Commanding Officer of the Fifth Army, is an odd one.

On the one hand, he is a stickler for military formality: as he had so remarkably demonstrated before the Battle of Pozières, when his chief concern had been the lack of Australian soldiers saluting him.

On the other hand ...

Well, on the other hand he is a real 'thruster', someone who Field Marshal Haig can count on to take it to the enemy, come what may, to not be weighed down by casualty lists, to not waste time with any wringing of hands. And right now, belying his hang-dog appearance – and though the heavy bags beneath Gough's eyes reveal his growing exhaustion – he is still *desperate* for his forces to unleash an all-out attack on the Hindenburg Line and crack it wide open. And he does not mean *soon*, or *when we have everything in place*, he wants it to be NOW.

Right now, Haig wants Gough to thrust at Bullecourt, and that is precisely what he intends to do – with the Australian 4th and 12th Brigades both at the pointy end of his spear.

The only thing holding him back for the moment is seeing how the coming Third Army attack scheduled for the early hours of 9 April at Arras – ten miles to the north-west – will go. If the Third can make a breakthrough, then he is inclined to push his own forces forward – despite the Fifth Army's lack of sufficient artillery and knowledge of just how strong the German forces are.

For, sometimes in war, you just have to go with instinct, and Gough is certain the Germans opposite are no more than a 'rear-guard force', that the blighters are actually retreating *en masse*, and there is no more than a skeleton crew still manning the Hindenburg Line in front of his Fifth Army Corps. Now ten miles north-west of Bullecourt at Arras, Allenby's Third Army is set to push east towards their general objective of Cambrai. Gough's plan is an audacious flanking assault to assist the Third Army.

Between now and then, he is eager that all preparations be made to get ready to attack, and his forces are so advised. Beyond everything else, Field Marshal Sir Douglas Haig is following the situation very closely, and has already positioned the 5000 mounted members of the 4th Cavalry Division – he insists that men on horseback have a place in modern warfare – close, in the hope that if the Fifth Army can punch a hole in the Hindenburg Line, they can burst through and sow havoc.

•

That flitting figure gingerly stepping into No Man's Land from the 14th Battalion's front line, just before midnight on 7 April?

It is the 14th Battalion's newly appointed Intelligence Officer, Captain Albert Jacka VC, moving out over the first part of the muddy landscape of No Man's Land like a big cat, noiselessly padding forward in a half-crouch, with a patrol of three soldiers in his wake. Their task is to work out just what lies between their own lines and that of the Germans, some 1000 yards away. Observers in Allied planes have come back with some photos, but in territory as fiercely defended as this, it is difficult for them to fly low enough to get real or useful detail, for fear of a single Mauser bullet in their petrol tank bringing them down.

True, there are things happening – occasional booms of artillery and chattering machine guns, mixed with the odd lazy flare throwing dim illumination – that would strike terror in the heart of normal souls. But for veterans of these parts like Jacka and his three companions it's not *too* far from . . . all quiet on the Western Front.

The key part of their mission is to find out if a sunken road about 300 yards marked on the maps left to them by the 51st Battalion is occupied by the Germans or not. Such roads – deep imprints on many French farms caused by centuries of carts rolling along the same track – are enormously valuable as ready-made trenches, and it seems obvious the German troops will have taken over such a strategically important position. If it is, well, it will be bad luck for them, and for whoever they manage to shoot before they are shot.

If it is not, and there really is a coming thrust to be made on the line at Bullecourt as Jacka has been told, it will be a precious bit of real estate to take over, and the men of the 4th Brigade – the 13th 14th, 15th and 16th Battalions – will make it their first position to gain and hold in the battle to come. To get there, Jacka and his men must first climb up and over the railway embankment that runs parallel to the Hindenburg Line, about three quarters of a mile back, before getting on their bellies and slithering forward from here like big snakes. Ahead, there appears to be not the tiniest sound, glint of helmet in the moonlight, nor even a whiff of cigarette smoke – all things that usually give away the presence of a mass of soldiers, no matter how strict the regulations.

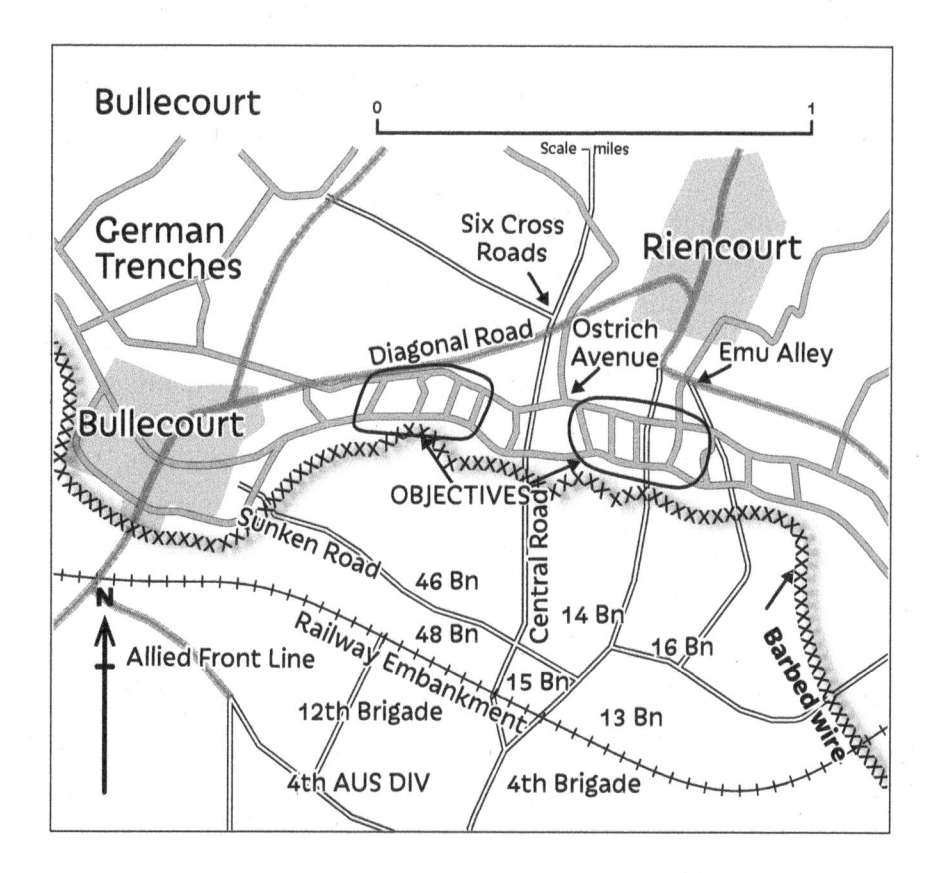

As ever in such situations, Jacka crawls a few yards forward, then for a minute freezes – sometimes literally – to listen for any noise, before moving forward a few yards more, and repeat. It is slow going, but there might be an enemy patrol out doing exactly the same thing.

As Jacka continues to crawl closer, his hands always roam for any obstacles ahead that might cause noise, before moving his knees forward in kind. At every moment, he braces himself for a German cry of challenge – *Achtung! Achtung!* – but there is nothing. By 2 am they are staring over the lip of the sunken road, which in turn runs parallel to the Hindenburg Line, some 300 yards further on.

Jacka can barely believe it. For the Germans to have abandoned such a strong defensive position seems extraordinary. But the key thing right now is to claim it as quickly as possible. It will bring a company of the 14th Battalion 300 yards closer to their target, without loss. And if they can secrete themselves there without the Germans being aware of their presence, ideally the Germans' defensive artillery barrage can fall on Australian trenches behind them that will be substantially empty.

Returning to his lines, Jacka quickly arranges to see the highest man in the 14th Battalion pecking order.

Lieutenant Colonel Peck does not hesitate, and gives his orders accordingly. As soon as dusk falls this evening, a company of the 14th moves forward and by 9 pm on the night of 8 April they are in possession of the sunken road. In an environment where every yard of turf has to be paid for with gallons of blood – at Pozières, a 1000-yard advance had cost nearly 7000 lives – Jacka's initiative has saved his battalion and brigade incalculable losses.

•

It all happens so quickly.

In the early hours of 9 April, Easter Monday, the Third Army Corps launches a successful attack on Arras.

Following a creeping barrage of artillery, with an intensity the likes of which had never before been mustered by the British in this war, no fewer than 154,000 British soldiers attack the German lines. They are assisted by 48 Mark II tanks – a step up from Mark I, but still without armour, meaning they can be easily pierced by German shells – and even though most of them break down, or get lost, or indeed get blown apart, both the Germans' first and second lines are taken. It is the greatest one day advance of the British Army since trench warfare began. It remains to be seen if the Allies can also push through the Germans' subsequent defences, but for the moment the news is more than enough for General Gough.

His conviction that the German forces opposite him at Bullecourt are little more than a facade is bolstered by three English soldiers who had escaped from the Germans and report that the enemy's ranks are thin. On the strength of it, Gough sends out a message to his strongest units, including that of Albert Jacka.

AWM 14th Infantry Battalion Appendix No 5
9/4/17 SECRET Fourth Australian Infantry Brigade Order No. 74
On a date to be notified hereafter the enemy will be driven from the Hindenburg Line.[5]

Be ready. We are going to attack, and soon.

But the happy circumstance to beat them all comes in the early afternoon of this day. It is a visit at the Fifth Army HQ's ruined (if once glorious) chateau at Bihucourt from Lieutenant Colonel John Hardress Lloyd of the Tank Corps, accompanied by Major William Watson. They have arrived to advise that they have command of the dozen tanks that have just been assigned to the Fifth Army, and they and the tanks are . . .

Reporting for duty, Suh!

And right off the bat – and despite some of the obvious failings of the tanks during the attack on Arras – the Lieutenant Colonel waxes lyrical about what his tanks are capable of doing.

'We want to break the Hindenburg Line with tanks, General,'[6] he says.

Not only that, they have a plan of how to do it. As a matter of fact, it is young Watson – who is in direct charge of the tanks on the field – who has developed it.

Indeed he has!

Watson, a history graduate from Oxford, has put a whole three months into training with tanks at the Tankodrome at Blangy-sur-Ternoise – mostly with mock-up tanks, but still, he can't see his idea adopted quickly enough.

(Wait, what? 'Mock-up tanks'? Well, they were large wooden frames covered by a canvas screen and, if you tilted your head and squinted your eyes just right, they looked rather like tanks. They had neither tracks, nor wheels. Each tank was carried by the crew who were supposed to be pretending to be in it. So, they were really a mockery of mock-up tanks, but at least they were something. The thought occurs that this was rather like planning cavalry movements based on research done with a pantomime horse . . . Very well. Carry on.)

Watson has already heard that the Fifth Army's artillery is sparse as they have lent much of it to the Third Army for the attack on Arras, and beyond that Field Marshal Haig had put out an edict the week before that 'the roads are not to be ruined by hurrying up guns and ammunition'.[7]

So here's the thing, General Gough.

We take them by surprise!

We don't precede an attack with an artillery barrage, which we don't have in any case. We just roll the tanks forward to crush the wire – not firing at all until they are through and right on the trenches, so as to keep the element of surprise – and put the soldiers in behind. Further, we don't spread the tanks over a wide front, but concentrate them over 1000 yards.

'[I foresee] an attack in which my tanks, concentrated on a narrow front of a thousand yards and supported as strongly as possible by all the infantry and guns available, should steal up to the Hindenburg Line without a barrage.'[8]

That is, there would be no barrage below the usual cheerio exchanges between the big guns overnight. At Zero Hour the Allied guns would bombard the flanks to prevent support rushing in, but the trenches being attacked would be spared from artillery, so that the tanks could quell them without being troubled by their own fire.

The key will be to make the breakthrough in the Hindenburg Line, get the tanks and soldiers through and sow havoc from there! Once the German trenches are secured, then you bring down whatever barrage you can muster to thwart German attempts to stem the breach.

Like it?

Gough loves it!

He immediately tells Hardress Lloyd and Watson he wants them to launch the tank attack in the early hours of *tomorrow morning*, with Zero Hour on the line at Bullecourt set at say . . . 4.30 am? Yes, that's it, 4.30 am.

Major Watson, for one, is stunned. It is one thing to entertain the idea – and quite another to put lives on the line by actually launching it in less than 18 hours!

Yes, sir. In short order the two tank officers are racing away to visit Anzac Corps HQ to tell the Australians what is expected of them.

Driving at breakneck speed, Hardress Lloyd and Watson race to the chateau nearby where the I Anzac Corps has its HQ and they are quickly ushered into the presence of General Sir William Birdwood, now the Commanding Officer of I Anzac Corps in France, and his Chief-of-Staff, Brigadier General Cyril Brudenell White.

The hasty plan is even more hastily explained, focusing on the use of the new super-weapon, the tanks.

The Fifth Army Corps has just received a dozen of them, and we are throwing them into battle in the early hours of tomorrow morning! We will be doing so with your soldiers of the 4th Brigade coming in behind!

Sorry, *what*?

There is a stir around the table.

Both General Birdwood and General Brudenell White are very unhappy. For one thing, why is it all so rushed?

Usually before a stunt, there is time to plan, to spot and work out how to exploit enemy weaknesses, to endlessly rehearse their own moves. But they are told that General Gough wants this full-blown attack to go in the following night! And so does Field Marshal Haig – who remains particularly keen on the Fifth Army making a breakthrough in the line so he can unleash the cavalry unit he has on standby, and finally prove, once and for all, that cavalry still have a place in this war.

Generals Birdwood and White exchange careful looks. This makes no sense.

Beyond everything else, the part of the Hindenburg Line that Gough wants them to attack is a strong indent in that very line, meaning they will be pushing into a massive cul-de-sac and taking fire from three sides!

•

Preliminary orders have come through foreshadowing the objectives to be taken by the 4th Brigade in driving the enemy from the Hindenburg Line.

So simple, on paper. The tanks go forward, crush the wire, flash their green discs (essentially small green lights) and the men come forward to claim the trenches – almost as if there are no Germans there to stop them. But there *are* Germans there to stop them! In *force*. Albert Jacka VC has seen them! And it seems highly likely that the Germans will have some plans of their own, and some weaponry, to stop them.

The 14th Battalion, meantime, will just have to rough it out in the freezing conditions, not giving away any clue that they are there. Jacka is not the only one who is unhappy. When Peck takes it higher up the chain of command, he is told that each link in that chain is equally unhappy, but that counts for nowt when the next link along, General Gough, Commander of the Fifth Army, is insistent that it is done *as he commands*, in no small part because that is what is ordered by the immoveable anchor at the end of the chain, the British supremo, Field Marshal Haig.

This is going to happen, whether the Australians like it or not.

Jacka is appalled.

He knows that the No Man's Land they have been ordered to cross is as flat as a billiard table, with *no* cover. Once you cross the railway embankment, and then the sunken road, it is all flat farm land without even hedges to obscure the view of the German gunners.

Colonel Peck could not agree more, but the Fifth Army is convinced that there are very few Germans actually there – those soldiers that Jacka has seen are no more than a rear-guard – and should crumble quickly. General Gough believes that as the first stage of the attack on Arras had gone so well, advancing over three miles and capturing over 8000 Germans, the Germans must have thinned the line at Bullecourt to try to compensate. They may even have abandoned the line here, and pulled back to another line they can hold. It would be good to get a little more confirmation of the paucity of the German defences.

On that subject, Peck has just received an order from the Commanding Officer of the 4th Brigade, Brigadier General Charles Brand, which he has clearly dashed off.

> *9/4/17 5 pm*
>
> *Dear Peck,*
> *I hope Jacka and Bradley will be able to find out something about the HINDENBURG LINE tonight. Be sure the information gets*

back to Bde Hd Qtrs as soon as possible . . . Suppose it is rather too much to expect a couple of strong patrols to occupy the line in case no or few Bosch.[9]

Sorry, what?

'No or few Bosch'?

Peck is sure of it: Brand is not listening. There's not 'no or few Bosch' there. There're hundreds and likely thousands of the brutes! Jacka has already seen how strong they are with his own eyes. That is the intelligence he has provided as Intelligence Officer, and it is being completely ignored.

Evening, 9 April 1917, Bullecourt, tanks but no tanks

With the fall of darkness – pitch-black as it happens, with a cold and miserable sleet of snow falling – the overall tank commander, Major Watson, walks down the Bapaume Road and arrives at the small canvas huts of Australia's 4th Division HQ, to present his credentials to Major General William Holmes. Watson is worried. It is not the usual way of things for different arms of attack to be meeting for the first time less than 12 hours before Zero Hour. Battles can and will be a moveable feast, often the left hand does not know what the right is doing, but they have at least met!

But these are tanks. *Nothing* is usual, because this has never happened before. Nevertheless, a brief discussion ensues with the equally alarmed divisional staff to ensure all is in order, before he is offered a bunk to get some kip. The main thing, he is told, is that his tanks arrive with plenty of time to spare. The tanks will arrive, Watson assures them, but he lies down for a charade of slumber; his nerves beating his tiredness in an uneasy gallop.

For the truth, and he knows it, is that these new tanks are a little touch and go at the best of times. They are 28 tons of steel, and their six-cylinder petrol engine, which is right in the cabin with the eight-man tank crew – of whom two are drivers, with two others controlling the gear changes for each track – generates just 105 horsepower, meaning there are fewer than four horses to pull each ton! Going downhill, and on the flat on even ground, they can usually manage it, at about 2 mph, without breaking down. On difficult terrain, and heading up a slope – particularly a muddy one, which clogs up their tracks and make the tanks even heavier – it is a fairly frequent occurrence that the horses give up the ghost and the tank engines either blow up, or are just not strong enough to keep the tank moving.

•

As the night wears on, a malaise of unease settles upon commanders at all levels. In desperation, at 11.15 pm, in an effort to avert disaster, General Birdwood puts in a call to Gough's chief-of-staff, imploring him to try to persuade the commander to call it off. *'We have had too little time to prepare, the German wire is too strong, and just a few machine guns could tear us apart. We don't even know if the Hindenburg Line further north at Arras is broken! At least give us another 24 hours to prepare, by which time we will also know the situation of the Third Army at Arras?'*

And yet, *still* Birdwood can't bear it, and 45 minutes later his own Chief-of-Staff, General Brudenell White, calls Gough's HQ again. He has in his hands Jacka's patrol report. The Hindenburg Line is strongly held, and now more information has come to hand revealing that the attack at Arras by the 21st Division and the right of the Third Army ... has been driven back. This 'materially changed the situation and made a haphazard attack hard to justify'.[10]

As Charles Bean will record, 'Gough replied through his chief-of-staff that he was not prepared to alter his decision, since the failure of the Third Army's right only increased the need for action by the Fifth Army.'[11]

For his own part, Brigadier General Charles Brand is equally desperate to restore some sanity to the orders, and calls 4th Division HQ to see if, instead of the artillery going on only on either flank of their attack, it might go – you know – right on the noggins of the defenders? Such artillery might, beyond killing off defenders, disguise the noise of the approaching tanks.

No, he is told in turn.

General Gough has been insistent on this, too.

The General believes that some orders he has sent out to the machine-gun companies to fire when *they* can hear the sound of the tanks will disguise their approach. And besides that, with so little artillery to spare, General Gough wants what artillery they do have to go on either side so as to isolate the defenders from support. This has also been the specific request of the tank commander – who wants there to be no chance of Allied artillery shells dropping short and hitting his tanks.

•

Nervous men gnash their teeth. Angry men grind them.

In this meeting of notably 'despondent'[12] Brigadier General Charles Brand at his 4th Brigade HQ at Noreuil, with the commanders of the 13th, 14th, 15th and 16th Battalions respectively – together with some of their senior officers – all of them are both gnashing *and* grinding. This plan to attack Bullecourt in the early hours of the following morning is not only dangerous for their men, it is borderline insane.

In the words of one of those officers, Captain Donald MacDermid of the 14th Battalion, 'the whole thing looked like it had been conceived in a hurry and had to be rushed through before the originator of the scheme had time to change his mind . . .'.[13]

Captain David Dunworth of the 15th Battalion feels the same.

'Then and only then we learned that the orders had been altered,' he will recount. 'The barrage had been dispensed with and tanks substituted. This news came as a thunderclap. Now we were to cancel all instructions and rush out fresh ones. No chance to get the men together. The 4th [Brigade] had every confidence in its ability to follow a barrage . . . But tanks we knew nothing of. We had never seen one in action. In vile humours we rejoined our unit.'[14]

And yet, despite this view being held among the highest echelons of the Australian forces, somehow, all of the 4th Brigade, with the 46th and 48th Battalions of the 12th Brigade, with the 47th Battalion in reserve – must charge on to their nearly certain destruction. Because they are orders. *British* orders. From on high.

Shortly afterwards at the 14th Battalion HQ, Colonel Peck and his adjutant Captain Harold Wanliss break the news to their own men.

If you can believe it, General Gough's Fifth Army has ordered us to attack the German line at Bullecourt just before dawn on *the morrow*, 10 April 1917!

But, here's the thing. And now it's definite. This time they will be supported by *tanks*.

Tanks?

These new-fangled machines they've heard about, that seem to be steel boxes on tractors, with guns attached?

Yes, tanks.

And Gough is so confident of their capacity that he has ordered the 4th Brigade to make their charge without an artillery barrage to soften up defences first!

No artillery barrage?

Heading straight at German guns, with nothing forcing the enemy to keep his square-head down, and we are reliant on the tanks to do all the heavy lifting?

That's the plan.

Impregnable, the Mark I and Mark II tanks will surge forth, and simply drive over the barbed wire and German trenches, forging a path for the Australian infantry to follow. Once they have crushed the wire and done the job, they can signal back for the infantry to follow by displaying their 'green discs'.

The 4th Brigade – like the 12th Brigade attacking to their left – will be assigned 12 tanks in all. With just one look at the broad brush-strokes of the plan, however, the 14th's Intelligence Officer, Captain Albert Jacka VC, is beyond alarmed.

This is more *madness*.

For one thing, tanks are so newly on the scene that they have only once, at Flers in September 1916, worked successfully in tandem with infantry – with only mixed results, at best. (Of the 49 tanks assigned, only 18 even made it to the starting line.) For another, what happens when the tanks are inevitably hit by German shells? Will they keep going, or be knocked out? If the latter – or they break down while advancing through this mud-mess – won't that leave the 14th Battalion stranded at the impenetrable barbed wire he has seen for himself and reported on, and completely at the mercy of the German machine-gunners? And how can we Australians successfully work with tanks, when we have never even seen one?

But, let's just say the tanks *do* make it through. What little Jacka does know of tanks is that they are slow – less than the walking pace of a man. The very nature of attacking the enemy line is to *chaaaaarge*, go at full tilt, right at 'em. But if they do that close to the German line with tanks, they will immediately outstrip the tanks, and find themselves between the Hun and the Mark IIs! *Nothing* about this makes sense, and he isn't even up to the worst part yet.

For why on earth would they try to do this with no artillery barrage on the heads of the defending Germans? Yes, there is the element of surprise – but, seriously, what are the chances that lumbering, roaring, tanks will surprise the German line?

Sending soldiers forward straight at the German line, bristling with guns and glinting with rolls of barbed wire, *without* a rain of shells coming down upon them? And all because you are relying on untested tanks to do the job?

It seems to Jacka, like *murderous* madness and he says so to his superior officer.

Colonel Peck takes his point, but has no choice. Orders. He is also sorry to inform Jacka that the tanks themselves won't even be at Noreuil, itself one and a half miles south of Bullecourt, until just before the battle, as they will have to be transported from where they now lie camouflaged in a quarry at Mory, nearly four miles away, and will only arrive on site just bare hours before the men go over the top.

At 16th Battalion HQ, a similar mood prevails. At the conclusion of the meeting, Major Percy Black, commanding B Company of the 16th Battalion, turns to his Commanding Officer, Lieutenant Colonel Drake-Brockman, and remarks, 'Well, goodbye Colonel. I mayn't come back, but we'll get the Hindenburg Line.'[15]

(It is, yes, Black humour. And very 'Percy', who is highly regarded and has picked up a DSO for his work at Mouquet Farm. 'They tell me it is about a record for the Australian Army,' he had written to his mother of his rapid promotion. 'I have been given preference over a lot of officers who were senior to me, but they don't seem to mind.' And don't worry, Mother. Yes, things are dangerous, but it 'is up to me to do my best for the sake of our name'.[16])

Get the Hindenburg Line you say, Percy? Drake-Brockman has little doubt his men will do precisely that. Major Black, particularly, is outstanding in the field, and if anyone can do it, he can. But at what cost? Drake-Brockman is so concerned he dares make his own protest to higher authority, only to be told he and his 16th Battalion 'must do as they are told'.[17]

Very well, deep sigh, onwards.

Theirs, not to reason why . . .

Early hours, 10 April 1917, Noreuil, once more unto the breach . . .

It's time.

Just hours before, the 14th Battalion had been told there was a stunt on tonight at Bullecourt, and they must pack their kit with rations, rifles and Mills bombs, sharpen their bayonets and prepare themselves for battle.

There is no talk of tanks, as that information has been withheld from them, just as it has been from all bar their Commanding Officer.

As Intelligence Officer, Captain Albert Jacka has already gone well ahead, but the rest begin their march forward after dark, heading down the cobbled lanes moving east, as a light snow begins to fall, and their every breath blows out steamy plumes in the cold air.

Onwards, they go, 'neath the incurious moon with a seeming swirl of fireflies at their feet, the result of their hobnailed boots striking sparks from the cobblestones. And listen now, lean closer, as the metallic beat of those hobnails and horseshoes on cobblestones comes ever closer, together with the shouts of the Sergeants and Corporals along the column keeping the men in time, and on time.

Now and then a soldier starts up a marching song, which flares like a lit match in the darkness, flourishes for a short time before slowly fading away, replaced once more by the rattles of gear and swooshing legs and slowly . . . silence once more, as they disappear in the night.

Onwards along the roads, onwards into the night.

•

Both Captain Harold Wanliss and Captain Albert Jacka have been frantically busy in the leadup to the attack.

'The battalion staff were working at concert pitch over the final preparations,' a soldier documents, 'and Captain Wanliss's cheery smile of optimism was infectious. Captain Jacka had taken over the duties of I.O. and everything was completed to the smallest detail with a thoroughness that could not be surpassed. Everyone welcomed the instruction to move forward to the jumping-off place in a sunken road about 800 yards from the Hindenburg wire . . .'[18]

Just before they go, however, it is Jacka himself who must start the fray before it has even begun. It is his role as Intelligence Officer to slither, run and crawl right to the edge of the German wire, and ideally to the trenches beyond, to work out just what it is that they will face on the morrow. No Man's Land is Jacka's Land. To his fellows he appears nerveless, but that is not the case. It is simply that Jacka's jangle of nerves, that shimmer of shell shock that haunts him in everyday life, disappears when he is in the thick of it. Only then is he truly cool and collected; a diamond created by pressure. Jacka knows the more he can see, the more Allies might live when the sun comes up, and the more Germans will die. One of his hopes is that, because 'shooting of our artillery was very accurate yesterday evening' and 'the heavy and field guns playing well onto wire all along our front',[19] he will find most of the wire between them and the German trenches destroyed. But there is only one way to find out.

So now in the company of Lieutenant Henry Bradley and Lieutenant Frank Wadge – the latter is the Intelligence Officer for the 16th Battalion – they head out. Jacka sets the pace, and it is slow, as they crawl ever closer, over the mud, through the mud, under the bloody mud at times, grasping the grass, snaking their way, wide-eyed and watchful, until they approach the first line of German wire.

Dammit, it has held, after all! Yes, it is 'smashed by shell fire in places' but just in places. For the most part it is 'generally unbroken',[20] which is not what the Generals want to hear. In some places the 'front line wire [is] about 20 feet through, and some of it as thick as your finger'.[21]

The previous artillery fire was not enough, the running tomorrow will be rough. Alright, pause now, it is time to go past the wire, this is the end of No Man's Land and the beginning of madness. Jacka will go solo here; leaving the other two gratefully behind for this most dangerous part. Should he buy it; they must return with what they already know. Jacka finds the twisting narrow path that goes through the wire, and begins crawling forward, alone.

But he is not alone, for as he gets close to the other side, and as he will tell Ted Rule, 'I saw for myself the density of machine guns and men in their trenches.'[22] It is stacked and packed, a tinderbox that the tanks will explode. To think that some of their senior officers had been insisting that the Germans had abandoned the Hindenburg Line and it was theirs for the taking!

Far from it.

For, make no mistake . . .

'The garrison was holding it in strength and was very wide awake.'[23]

And, good God! Now a German patrol of nearly a dozen men is walking towards him, and there is nothing for Jacka to do but roll himself under the wire, lie completely still, stop breathing, and pray. In his right hand, he clutches his pistol, ready to spring into action at their first cry of alarm. For the moment, though, nothing. The quiet guttural chatter of the Germans sounds like drumbeats to Jacka's ears, closer and closer, still he is, and pray he does, as they . . . amble by . . . and past. Thank Christ!

As Jacka retraces his path, he is, of necessity, able to get a good look at just how impenetrable this wire is, as he will record in his intelligence brief for this battle that should not be:

'Wire before the front line is very massive and of an average depth of between 30 and 50 yards. This is supported on heavy wooden stakes, few iron pickets being in use . . . Wire between front and support lines is thin, only about 5 yards wide, and supported on ordinary corkscrew stakes. This was found almost untouched by our gun fire, but generally was negotiable.'[24]

Negotiations continuing, Jacka gets through and can see that the second line of barbed wire ahead is also completely intact. There are endless rolls of vicious barbed wire, and a mass of men running up against it would have no chance of penetrating it before being cut to pieces by machine guns. The only hope now would be for the barrage to specifically target this line and blow it to pieces. Which would lose surprise as the Germans would know it's a prelude to an assault. Now that he is closer to the trenches, he can certainly hear movement, and it sounds like there are a *lot* of German soldiers.

Jacka has seen and heard enough, and crawls back through the wire to rejoin Bradley and Wadge, his head spinning with the likely consequences of what he has seen. The crestfallen Lieutenants are the first to hear the bad news. Jacka also reports his encounter with the patrol.

'How they failed to see me was a puzzle,' Jacka whispers. 'They almost trod on me'.[25]

But what would you have done if they had trodden on you? Weren't you frightened?

'Oh no,' murmurs Jacka. 'I was quite calm because I knew what to do.'

Oh, yes? And what would that be?

'I was watching them, and if they had discovered me, I was going to get in among them and shoot the lot before they knew what had happened.'

Right. Good to know.

'I would have got away easily enough.'[26]

Yes, he bloody would have. Bradley and Wadge, who are not immortal, imagine their very different fates. But out here, now, the shell-shocked Jacka, the man who shook for an hour when a drawer closed too quickly in a military hospital, has vanished.

As a matter of fact, he is now *so* confident that when one of his companions notes just how quiet the Germans are, and lightly wonders if there really can be *that* many of them, Jacka decides to *prove* it to him. Taking off his helmet, he starts bashing the wire with it, the jarring sound cleaving the night.

Everyone down!

There is an immediate and furious fusillade of fire from German lines so strong that his companions are shocked.

'How many do you think there are [*now*]?' Jacka asks, once it has died down.

'A million,' the gurgled answer comes back.

'Don't exaggerate,' says Jacka, 'I want to make a report. I don't think there is half that number.'[27]

But let's get back now, boys, for we have a disaster to avert!

The three head back, more rapid in retreat, calling their password as they go through their own wire, whereupon Jacka heads to the 14th Battalion HQ, where he is immediately in deep consultation with the always available Colonel Peck, only to be suddenly joined also by Brigadier General Brand.

Jacka does not hold back, and tells the two senior officers straight out.

If the 4th Brigade goes ahead with this attack, as things stand, it will be 'pure murder'.[28]

True, it is not in the normal way of things for a Captain to speak in this manner to officers so high above him in rank. But Jacka is not just any Captain, and his power goes far beyond his rank. This is the man the Australian Government have been putting on recruitment posters, the emblem of the Australian Imperial Force.

And so Brand listens and Peck rocks back and forth, musing as Jacka unrolls each daunting detail. To Jacka the situation is as plain as the nose on your face: the attack as presently envisaged is doomed to catastrophic failure. You wanted intelligence; well, now you have it, and you must use your own *and stop this attack*.

Lieutenants Bradley and Wadge have already passed on Jacka's warnings to the 16th Battalion, whose own intelligence report notes that: '... *they got out as far as the enemy's wire and found that it was badly smashed in some places, but in others it was still intact. They also reported that the garrison of the HINDENBURG Line was very strong and that there were also no signs of probable evacuation.*

They reported that there was considerable enemy movement in front of his own line in the shape of strong patrols. They advised that it was useless to attack the HINDENBURG Line without Artillery support and until the wire was thoroughly cut.'[29]

•

It will only be possible to brief most of the men about the tanks while they are already gathered in their staging point at the sunken road, and on the railway embankment just two hours before Zero Hour.

As they shake with cold and nerves, the adjutant of the 14th Battalion, Captain Harold Wanliss, has briefly emerged from Battalion HQ to walk the line, checking with good cheer that every man has what he needs, that all is in place. The men know he is not just doing his duty, he is performing a great kindness; calming the men with questions he already knows the answers to; checking what is already clearly there, adding normality to the terror of this moment. It is the silence in the chill that gives away despondency: chatter means that spirits are alive; quiet means they are thinking of death. *Have you a water bottle? Is your rifle clean, so it will not jam? Are your socks dry?* The mundane will quell the pain of worry; and Wanliss wanders back and forth, soothing with each step.

•

Where are we?

The commanders in the tanks are lost; and yet the men they are searching for are not miles away, but mere feet – some of whom are in danger of being crushed. An officer is supposed to lead each tank on foot, and presumably they are, but a blizzard has swept upon the downs and visibility is now down to near zero as Zero Hour approaches.

And so they must proceed *very* cautiously, lest you run over your 'guide' or crash into the tank in front. The blizzard buries landmarks in sudden blankets of white, and lamps that should shine instead flicker so dimly they would lose out to a glow-worm in a brightness competition.

The men inside the tanks would be in a cold sweat if they could get cool enough; the steamy stink of petrol surrounds them, their nerves increasing as their speed slows. They are *crawling* along now. Bloody hell, they are supposed to be leading this battle and they are losing the race to even start? What happens if there is a blizzard during the battle? The Germans are not going to allow a rain delay.

In his tank, Captain Wilfred Wyatt checks his route again and again, each post ticked off in his head, each one leading closer to the valley from Vaulx-Vraucourt to Noreuil, and when they reach there it will be just two miles to their first position. But when will they get there?

Late. Very late.

•

Out in the field and up with the most forward of the 14th Battalion men securely established in the sunken road by 2.30 am, Albert Jacka's outrage has only doubled, but now with added stupefaction.

It is simply staggering that an attack completely reliant on tanks being in place to quell German defences should have been ordered, and yet no tanks are yet visible, an hour before it is to begin – and *still* the order to attack is in place.

The result could only be slaughter on a massive scale. And he has no hesitation in telling the men what to expect: 'the wire entanglements are not very well cut and that the enemy appear to be fairly strong'.[30]

Finally, Jacka can bear it no more and hurries once more back to Brigade HQ at Noreuil to find General Brand.

You must call off the attack, or at the very least delay it.

Brand, knowing the tanks are still at Mory, around four miles from the starting line, reluctantly agrees to a 30-minute delay.

Brand would have allowed even more of a delay, but . . .

'More than half an hour's grace would have disclosed to the enemy our intentions for at 5 a.m. day was breaking.'[31]

As it stands, darkness is their only protection. If the tanks do not arrive, this will be the blackest farce any have seen on a battlefield; and it will be the last thing that too many men will ever see.

•

Jacka, Lieutenant Bradley and the others of their patrol follow their orders to lay out the starting-line tape – luminescent, white and waiting.

Zero Hour will make it the start of a sprint to death; whether for the enemy or themselves is for fate to decide.

It does not take long for the 14th Battalion's tape to be readied just 300 yards beyond the sunken road, still some 700 yards before the first band of the German wire. The supporting battalions behind the railway embankment will have over 1200 yards of hard slog to get there.

Jacka and his men are just about to complete their task when they see them. It is a German officer and orderly coming their way. It looks as if they are 'checking the boundary fences', making sure nothing untoward is happening out in No Man's Land on this night.

Jacka holds his breath. If they keep coming, they will discover the tape, in which case he will have no choice but to kill or capture them. It would be catastrophic if they were to report back that, as a tape is down, an attack is imminent.

Drawing his pistol, and circling around behind them like a panther hunting its prey, Jacka waits until they are nearly right upon the tapes before stepping forward and with his pistol pointing directly at the officer's head, just five yards away, shouts 'Halt!'[32] a word he knows has the same meaning in German. The officer has a cane, the orderly a rifle – but both refuse to hold up their hands.

Jacka pulls the trigger.

(*Click.*)

The pistol has jammed!

And so, bugger it.

Jacka steps forward and roughly collars them, banging the officer on his bonce with the jammed gun – now both the cane and rifle dropped.

'Get moving!'[33]

It's not what he says, it's the way he says it.

They understand. Come with Jacka, or die where you stand.

When Jacka starts driving them back towards the Australian line, a large German patrol is heard, which sees the officer – a Lieutenant from the III/124th Württemberg Infantry Regiment – hang back, clearly thinking of making a run for it. Again, Jacka steps forward with the pistol, and gives the officer a conk on the head. One shout, and they will start this battle right now . . .

At this instant a large flare rises from the Australian line, momentarily illuminating the area where the German patrol stands. The patrol turns and moves rapidly to escape the light and the threat of becoming Australian target practice. That is one set of Germans dealt with, now for the two in hand. Jacka hands them over to a Digger, with orders to take them back. As for Jacka, he is headed back to the starting line, ready to guide the tanks forward, once they arrive.

If they arrive.

•

Back at 14th Battalion HQ, Colonel Peck is being confronted by a very angry and newly captured German Lieutenant, who is fiercely complaining of the rough treatment he has received at the hands of his captor, an Australian Captain of the 14th Battalion. Why, he struck me! On my *Kopf*, head! With . . . and why are these men grinning? Despite the grimness of the whole situation, with Zero Hour now looming, Peck laughs and puts the German straight. You obviously don't know just who it was who captured you, but let Peck tell you one thing: 'You are a bloody lucky man to be alive.'[34]

They should all be so bloody lucky before this day is through.

Once the officer settles down, he is much more co-operative and even gives enough valuable information that Colonel Peck is able to write a note to an underling: 'Tell the Vickers gun officer that the captured officer states the Hun reserve total 6 companies in between Riencourt and Bullecourt.'[35] Once the breakthrough is achieved, this will allow the Commanding Officer of the machine-gun section to most effectively aim his machine-gun barrage to prevent supports coming forward.

•

Oh, God!

One by one, all of Major Watson's tanks are heading straight for the cliff, and before his very eyes tumble into the sea!

. . .

. . .

Oh.

No. It was just a nightmare. A very strong one, but a nightmare nevertheless. He remembers now. He has had a kip at the Australian 4th Divisional HQ, and they are relying on his 12 tanks for the attack. Rousing himself, Major Watson gets up and looks out the door of the hut.

A full-blown gale is now blowing, and what had just been sleet is now mixed with snow. It is freezing. He tries to check with his section commander, but there is no news of where his tanks are.

Bloody hell!

It is like seeing a mass death notice before it has happened, and noticing the names of all your friends.

His unit had only just taken possession of these tanks some weeks before, and he knows from experience just how many mechanical things could go wrong with them. If there is many a slip twixt cup and lip there are even more between the front and the brunt for a tank, a tank doesn't cross the finish line when it arrives at the front line, that is just the starting point, a point that seems to recede as sweaty minutes tick by.

By 1 am there is still nothing, which is a real worry. His orders had been for the commander of the tank unit to telephone him the moment the machines arrived in the village of Noreuil – and even then it will take them 90 minutes to get from there to their jumping-off point. The minutes tick by, the tension rises. By 2 am, it seems everyone is at him.

Where are the tanks?

Why are they late?

When will they be here?

Phone calls are made. Watson is able to establish that no-one at the 4th Brigade Headquarters at Noreuil has seen tanks, or even heard them, but they have sent out soldiers to look for them. What is even more troubling is that the weather at Noreuil is even worse than here, with a powerful gale and heavy snow making visibility very poor indeed.

By half-past two, Major Watson is beyond anxious.

'The attack was set for dawn,' he will note. 'The infantry had already gone forward to the railway embankment, from which they would "jump off". In daylight they could neither remain at the embankment nor retire over exposed ground without heavy shelling.'[36]

How the hell do you lose a set of tanks? Very easily, it seems. The question now is how to find them . . .

•

Major Watson is staring to the east through the window of the chateau being used as the 4th Division HQ and can just see the first glimmers of dawn when he hears the telephone ring.

The Australian staff officer picks it up, has a brief conversation and then hands the receiver to Watson with a smile of relief.

'It's one of your men,' he says. What once was lost, now is found crackling down the line. Taking the receiver, Watson can hear the tired voice of his section commander, Captain Wyatt.

'We are two miles short of Noreuil in the valley,' he says, his voice straining to be heard through the static. 'We have been wandering on the downs in a heavy snowstorm. We never quite lost our way, but it was almost impossible to keep the tanks together. I will send in a report. The men are dead tired.'

'How long will it take to get to the starting point?' asks an anxious Watson.

'An hour and a half at least,' Wyatt replies, his voice cracking with fatigue.

'Stand by for orders.'

Major Watson must do some quick assessment.

'It is one and a quarter hours before Zero, the Australians are out on the railway embankment and dawn is breaking.'

His men are fatigued, his tanks have been running all night and will not be able to get to the starting line before . . . before it is too late. There is less than zero chance of making Zero Hour, which marks this as a catastrophe in the making. Watson immediately goes to see General Holmes to explain the position.

'What will happen to your tanks,' Holmes asks, 'if I put back Zero another hour and we attack in daylight?'

'My tanks will be useless. They will be hit before they reach the German trenches – particularly against a background of snow.'

Holmes glances at his watch: 3.15 am. He glances through the window to note that, even now, dawn is taking hold. And the tanks are not even to Noreuil!

'It can't be helped.' Holmes finally sighs. 'We must postpone the show. I think there is just time to get the boys back.'[37]

Brigadier General Brand communicates to the 4th Brigade shortly afterwards.

The stunt is off. Disposition as yesterday. Move.[38]

•

Shivering in the snow, straining their ears for the sound of approaching tanks, the men of the 14th and 16th Battalions are confused. Zero Hour had originally been 4.30 am, moved back to 5 am, and by now the tanks were meant to be well past them and crushing wire. But there has been nothing? Stone-cold, *really* cold, motherless nothing!

And now the word comes from breathless runners, sent out by the 14th Battalion's adjutant, Captain Harold Wanliss: *Get back to Noreuil. The stunt is off.*[39]

Thank Christ. They are off too, and the German sentries on duty on the Hindenburg Line are stunned to see hundreds of black figures rise up in No Man's Land and start walking *away* from them!

Quickly, the Germans send up rockets calling in an artillery barrage beyond the railway embankment and the back areas, but for the most part the soldiers falling back are gone before the shells land.

Not that the soldiers falling back escape casualties, however. They are particularly exposed when going over a rise near the railway embankment, and some men go down. A notable exception is out on the left where the receding 48th Battalion is hit amidships by a single devastating shell with 21 killed or wounded.

As it happens, the Commanding Officer of the 48th Battalion, Colonel Ray Leane, sees a man hit so badly he has been decapitated and nearly cut in two.

'Poor fellow,' Leane comments to his accompanying staff officer, 'I wonder who he is.'[40]

(Only a few hours later, Lieutenant Colonel Leane will discover that it was his brother, Major Ben Leane.)

Out to the far left, the British 62nd Division has not been informed of the Australian cancellation, and at the time have three patrols of the 185th Brigade, right on the wire when, at 4.55 am, they are hit by murderous fire. They withdraw, suffering 162 casualties.

'. . . but, just when all felt the Brigade doomed to annihilation, snow commenced to fall heavily, the kindest snow we ever experienced'.[41]

For the rest, 'It was like after a football match at the MCG to see all the troops going back in broad daylight over the open country,' one of the soldiers will note. 'This of course, the Hun saw.'[42]

(For Percy Bland it feels less like being part of a football crowd, and more 'like a stray lot of goats walking over No Man's Land'.[43])

In any case, the true value of what the Germans see lies in the intelligence. 'Tommy' is preparing to attack around Bullecourt. Very well, let him come back.

Wir werden warten. We will be waiting.

•

Shivering and pissed off, the troops of the 14th Battalion and the wider 4th Brigade head back to Noreuil.

'Cold, cramped and stiff,' the Official History of the 14th Battalion will chronicle, 'feeling the reaction after being keyed up for hours to a concert pitch of expectation, all started back to their starting point at the Noreuil Valley . . . The bungling that had resulted in this grotesque fiasco was evident to everyone and confidence in the higher leadership was badly shaken.'[44]

Some of the men coming back with Jacka learn a lesson they'll never forget. For even as they can hear a steady pop of bullets coming from behind, Jacka maintains a steady pace.

'Don't hurry,' Ted Rule insists. 'There's no need; it's no good rushing. You only rush *into* something.'[45]

What? Yes, for Jacka it's like walking in the rain without an umbrella; if you run you'll just get wet faster. Besides which, if you move fast, you are more likely to catch the eye of a sniper looking for a moving target. Slow and steady will win the race for survival. Hold your nerve, hold your pace. If your number is up, it's up.

Jacka's ease is infectious on the field if you can bear the initial strain. And so they stroll back, a walk to remember.

Once they get to their tents, things are only a little better, however. For those tents have been pitched in the mud, and the rain is pounding.

'Oh, the water was just flowing through the bottom of the tents. You couldn't even sit down in it.'[46]

And there is no food waiting for them. Their last meal had been 15 hours before, they have been up for a fight all night, and no-one has thought to provide food!

'Didn't [Jacka] go crook!'[47]

A cook is rustled up, and he in turns rustles up some food, only for . . .

Well, only for – *incommmming!* – a stray shell to land nearby, resulting in a piece of shrapnel killing the cook outright. Shocked, Private Percy Bland and a couple of others bury the cook more or less where he drops, only for – *incommmming!* – a second shell to come looking for the stray, and finding it.

'Within an hour he was blown up,' Bland will recount, 'a shell had landed right on his grave and he was blown up again. That's what Bullecourt was.'[48]

For the 48th Battalion and 15th Battalion it takes much longer to get any respite, as they are billeted seven miles further on.

Lance Corporal George Mitchell, one of the Lewis gunners for the 48th Battalion, will long recall something he learns over the breakfast of croissants they wolf down. Apparently, there had been some appointment with some tanks that had been meant to come but not turned up, and that is why the stunt had been cancelled!

Tanks?

It is the first he and his mates had heard of it.

Studio portrait of Captain Albert Jacka VC MC and Bar. (AWM A02868)

Recruitment poster showing Lieutenant Albert Jacka in uniform, 1915.
(State Library of Victoria)

Albert Jacka
in camp at
Gallipoli, around
August 1915.
(AWM P02141.003)

Dug-out life, Anzac Gully,
Gallipoli. (Mitchell Library, State
Library of New South Wales)

Third line of trenches, Gallipoli, 1915. (State Library of New South Wales)

Dressing station during battle. (State Library of New South Wales)

The aftermath, Polygon Wood. (State Library of New South Wales)

General Sir William Riddell Birdwood (*right*) shaking hands with Captain Jacka VC MC and Bar (*left*), after presenting him with a bar to his MC for bravery during the first attack on Bullecourt, near the Hindenburg Line. (AWM E00438)

Jacka's notes from the 1920s, when he gave lectures for both commanding officers and enlisted men on subjects including the maintenance of small arms, trench warfare and more generally on 'the Great War'. (AWM 2018.785.10)

The funerals of General Sir John Monash and Albert Jacka VC took place within a few months of each other. Here, the front page of *The Sun News-Pictorial* shows the crowds lining the streets for Monash's ceremony in October 1931. (National Library of Australia)

The Sun News-Pictorial front page showing Jacka's funeral in January 1932. The eight pallbearers were fellow VCs and many of the diggers in the crowds at St Kilda Cemetery wore their war decorations. (National Library of Australia)

The funeral march for Captain Albert Jacka VC in Melbourne, 1932. *Clockwise from top left*: gun carriage team, three horses and two riders; gun carriage and coffin, stationary; eight senior officers marching; armed soldiers marching in formation, bayonets fixed; large group of marching men in civilian clothes, holding their hats against their hearts; the gun carriage and coffin moving away. (Bendigo Military Museum)

CHAPTER NINE

BULLECOURT BLUNDERS

It was not Jacka's martial spirit that was most striking. It was the wonderful combination of that dashing vitality with a nature that was gentle, and even sentimental. He had a schoolboy sense of honour such as fades shockingly in most of us, even before our school days are past. He regarded his commission as a sacred trust. His men were his children. They could approach him at any leisure moment, and he would hear them out to the last. Many of our toughest officers were admired all their time in the front line, and well hated out of the line. Bert Jacka was admired in the line, and regarded with affection in billets.[1]

'G', described by *The Land* as 'a close friend of Capt. Jacka during the Great War'

10 April 1917, before Bullecourt, Huns on the run
Schnell! SCHNELL!

On the German side of the line on the morning of 10 April, there is great movement. After what had been spotted just before dawn, it is obvious that a major attack is imminent. It does not seem likely that the Allies would dare attack in exactly the same place that they had abandoned on the previous night, but something is surely brewing in this area, and it must be strengthened immediately. (So much for the theory of a surprise attack. The only surprise now, and it is shocked astonishment, is that the British commanders could still think there was any secrecy left about their intentions. Now this same desperate attack is to be repeated? Without the protection of shellfire to shock any German troops waiting for their prey to appear?)

Throughout the day there is a movement forward to the front lines of German soldiers. With this oncoming tide come mass munitions and machine guns, as the 27th Württemberg Division does all possible to bolster its defences, given the scare of the previous night. Most importantly, more rolls of barbed wire are installed where previous barrages had broken their thorned forebears to pieces.

Meantime, back around Noreuil, the soldiers of the 4th Brigade who had been expecting to attack the night before are just awaking from having snatched a few hours' sleep, when they at last see them.

Tanks!

Growling their way forward in the daylight, regularly coughing up front and belching out back with black bursts of smoke, they are huge lumbering beasts, which bring to mind the famous line by the Duke of Wellington in Spain before the Peninsular campaign against the French in 1809, when surveying his troops: 'I don't know what effect these men will have upon the enemy, but, by God, they frighten me.'

The tanks do indeed sound and look terrifying. War winners, they say. Perhaps. Battle winners? Today? Men's lives depend on it.

•

Again, this time just before noon, the senior officers of I Anzac Corps are gathered at the Fifth Army HQ at Albert, 20 miles south-west of Bullecourt, to meet with General Gough. Again all talk is of the attack at Bullecourt that Gough wants to finally go ahead tonight. It is insane, and it is time to tell Gough that, politely perhaps or roughly if need be; but let it be known, clearly, Generals Birdwood and White want it called off.

General Gough is insistent that it go ahead.

Why, that very morning, General Allenby of the Third Army had sent out a cable to his own corps: *Third Army pursuing beaten enemy: risks must be taken; isolated detachments must not delay general progress.*[2]

That may be, sir, but it is *madness* to attack at exactly the same spot after having already given the Germans fair warning of our intent. The entire attack was predicated on surprise, and that surprise has now gone.

No, gentlemen, that is a *risk*. And Gough is prepared for you to take it.

Very well, beyond that, after the failed attack last night the men are exhausted, and the fact that the tanks couldn't even get to the rendezvous point on time is surely a fair indication of their failings.

No, the answer comes back. General Gough is still insistent. He is vastly experienced in these matters and knows that in similar situations, 'at least 75 per cent of them would reach the enemy's trenches'.[3] Besides all that, Field Marshal Haig also wants it.

The attack must go in, as ordered.

Can we really expect success tonight, relying on those same tanks to be there, and be effective, when there has been no time for even the most basic rehearsal?

And now, just as the immoveable rock of Gough's mind is being swayed by the irresistible force of the irrefutable logic of his desperate officers, another voice is heard. *The* voice. Yes, Gough must urgently excuse himself so as to take a phone call from the Chief of Staff to Commander-in-Chief Field Marshal Douglas Haig.

At least it doesn't take long.

But when Gough returns, only minutes later, it is to gravely inform them that Haig has made clear that he regarded the attack at Bullecourt as 'a very urgent and important matter and that he set great store by it'.[4] He has specifically 'directed that the attack should be made'.[5]

Gough is now powerless to prevent it. For he, too, must follow orders. The matter is settled, from on high.

Brudenell White, for one, is sick at heart.

'I felt that no further opposition was open to us . . .'[6]

•

It is as before.

Only this time the soldiers of the 4th Brigade, including the 14th Battalion, are completely exhausted after their previous sleepless night and supremely restless day. But again – when the orders come through at 6.30 pm that they are to resume the attack of the night before – they must pack up their troubles in their old kitbag, leave Noreuil and march towards Bullecourt where, if you can believe it, Digger, we are to have another crack at them, from exactly the same spot. It is not *déjà vu,* more like *bugger you,* but they must march grumpily over familiar ground once more. Orders are orders. Those higher up must surely know more than we do.

In fact, their immediate superior officers feel every bit as grim about it as they do.

With typical humour, Colonel Peck tries to lift his officers' morale, saying to them before they depart for the jumping-off point, 'Off you go, out to die, so I can get a decoration!'[7]

As to Albert Jacka, he is flat out like a lizard drinking, doing everything possible to ensure that, despite the shocking cards that the 14th Battalion has been dealt, they can be played with a maximum of cohesion. The afternoon has been spent just as the morning had been, going from officer to officer, giving them fine detail of what to expect as they go forward, and what is expected of them.

For all that, Captain Harry Murray VC – for his Victoria Cross for his actions at Stormy Trench has been confirmed just the previous month – with his men of the 13th Battalion's A Company at Noreuil, and about to move forward, is firm in his view.

'I was hoping that the plan would be abandoned because it seemed to be a most desperate gamble by means of a frontal attack, unsupported by artillery fire.'[8]

If it is not, all they can do is follow orders, follow the 16th in, leapfrog them into the village of Riencourt, 'dig into the rear of the village and mop it up, as would also the 50th Battalion supporting the 14th and shoot the Germans at our leisure. Great was the risk and glorious the prize.'[9]

But, surely, common sense will prevail and the stunt will be cancelled again?

•

Back in the day, and certainly in these parts, all roads did indeed lead to Rome. (Many of the ancient roads are still in use, having been originally constructed by the Romans themselves.)

But tonight, as midnight beckons, they all lead to Bullecourt – with the only problem being that there is simply too much traffic to cope.

From Noreuil come the 14th and 16th Battalions; from Favreuil, the 15th and the 13th Battalions.

It has been a restless day.

The men keep moving, even as cars and trucks of various descriptions try to push their way through. Not tonight, cobber, we are not in the mood. They march moodily as one; the machines will have to wait their turn.

•

With a staff officer in tow, Major Watson of 11 Company, D Battalion of the Heavy Branch Machine Gun Corps is again pushing forward to the front in the early evening, only to find the going too slow with mud, slush and so many marching Australians again moving into position – together with dozens of rumbling trucks – that they park their car and walk the last few miles.

At last, in the valley just above Noreuil, they find what they have been looking for: their dozen tanks 'hidden against the bank at the side of the road, shrouded in their tarpaulins'.[10]

His men are stacking ammunition, tinkering with the engines, and about to have their evening meal before the battle ahead. One tank has the engine ticking over quietly and it is so cold that some men are warming themselves by holding their hands close to the exhaust. They are far past exhausted themselves, but it is time to begin.

Gather round, men. It is time for your final briefing from Major Watson before you go into action.

As one, the officers of each tank's eight-man crew huddle tightly around him, though it is so dark they appear to Watson to be little more than 'ghosts'. He more hears them than actually sees them, and makes his apologies for what had happened the day and night before.

General Gough had been so keen on pushing their schedule the day before that he had felt obliged to see if it could be done, and the fact that it was not manageable had been a sad disappointment to them all. Nevertheless, it is all booked in for tonight, with one key difference. Tonight, when you get to the wire there is no need for you to fuss about sending a green signal back to the troops to follow. It has been decided by General Gough that the troops will go to the wire, irrespective of what happens with your tanks. The fact that this is hardly a vote of confidence is lost on none of them, nor is the shock of the next news. The tanks are to leave the starting line at 4.30 am, and the infantry is to follow at 4.45. If you are delayed with the tanks, the soldiers have been ordered to advance anyway!

'This meant,' Charles Bean will note, 'that the infantry, or part of it, might have to attack the Hindenburg Line in spite of a breakdown of some of the tanks . . .'[11]

How are they to fire and function if their own men are just ahead?

An excellent question, and if anyone has an answer they are welcome to tell it to their commander. Watson listens patiently.

'One or two of them naturally complained of changes made at such a late hour. They did not see how they could study their orders, their maps, and their photographs in the hour and a half that remained to them before it was time for the tanks to start. So, again, I set out carefully and in detail the exact task of each tank.'[12]

A few nervous questions are asked, led by the section commander, Captain Wyatt, and Major Watson answers each calmly in turn. A final salute and his officers go to their tanks, while their commander heads to Brigade Headquarters. There is still time for someone to change their mind, and Watson will be there if it happens. (Not that he himself has doubts. When asked by Brigadier General Robertson if the tanks might be vulnerable in battle, Watson replies, 'Only a direct hit by a heavy gun could put a tank out of action. Such a thing is impossible.'[13]

That's settled then . . .)

•

It is 1 am, and Ted Rule watches the mortars pelt gas bombs into Bullecourt. The Germans fire immediately in response, not back at them, but flares into the air: the very Verey lights that will show the path of these gas clouds and where safety might lie. The Australians can now see their own bombs bursting clearly, despite the night, but can't see how many Huns in that village can avoid getting caught in that fog of death, descending and spreading where the wind takes it next. One whiff of waft and you will go down, struggling to breathe. George Mitchell is another who notices with interest the 'gas wave billowing over the German lines. Showers of sparks rose out of the gas cloud as enemy countering shells fell.'[14]

Again, it is strangely beautiful, for such an appalling thing. Men are *dying* in the middle of that cloud. Well, ideally, anyway.

Clearly, the Germans are not happy about it, as they fire a couple of 9-inch shells just near where the 14th Battalion is positioned – on the reckoning that is from where the gas shells are coming.

'One landed on two trench-motor crews, blotted them right out; between 30 and 40 men were killed or wounded. The other almost robbed us of Jacka.'[15]

Luckily, Jacka is only blown off his feet; the man standing next to him, assistant intelligence office Lieutenant McKinley, is fatally wounded.

As the gas clouds grow, the tanks, which around three o'clock have at last arrived, begin to join the line. Rule watches each one *chug-chug-chug* forward in a muffled roll, slow and silent as a tank can be, towards where C Company lies now, near a railway embankment. As each tank stops, their crew emerge to breathe properly, and do such things as checking the tracks, tightening nuts and so forth. Rule strolls over to mix with the tank crews and keeps hearing the same question: 'I wonder if the Huns heard us coming in?'[16]

Rule doesn't think it likely, but there is one thing that he noticed, tiny sparks coming out from their exhaust pipes, those strange little lights attract his eye, and if they caught his attention then surely the Germans might . . . but there is no call to be negative about what must be done. Rule tells the men they can't have been seen or heard; it is what all want to hear.

C Company lines up now, ready to make for the tape. Captain Alf 'Lofty' Williamson – a football star for both the Carlton and Melbourne Football Clubs before the war, and recently promoted to the rank of Captain, despite being only 23 years old – is everywhere at once, giving orders, settling the men, getting everyone ready for the battle to come.

What a man he is, what a soldier, what an officer.

'He stood six feet in his socks,' one of his mates would recall, 'and was as handsome as a Greek god. He was the men's ideal of what a man should be, and to know him was to love him.'[17]

Another will recall, '[Lofty] was the finest man [who] ever stood in shoe leather. The men were ready to follow him anywhere.'[18]

Beyond everything else, it is his attitude of complete defiance that inspires, telling everyone that, no matter what happens, 'he would not be taken a prisoner unless both his arms were broken'.[19]

Captain 'Lofty' now approaches Sergeant Ted Rule, and tells him, 'You are to take charge of the bomb dump, see that the ammunition is sent up to me during the op.'[20]

Once they get through the wire it is going to be important to have plenty of bombs ready to go, to hurl forward into the German trenches before they charge.

Nearby, Bert Jacka has a face like thunder. And it is not because he so easily could have been killed just minutes before. It is because he is certain of what is going to happen to the 14th, and while he has done everything he can to stop it, he is powerless as they move towards their fate.

All he can do now is to follow orders, so once again he heads out into No Man's Land to find the tape he had laid the night before. Despite the snow, it does not take long and once he pulls it up and walks along the luminescent tape springs to the surface once more – the starting line for destruction apparent to all who will come forward.

As the exhausted men struggle forward to take up their positions, Jacka, his face pale in the moonlight, softly tells them to 'fix bayonets but on no account fire . . .'.[21]

He can't say it, but the truth is that their only hope is to get *en masse* to the wire, undetected.

Out to the left, with the 48th positioned just behind the 46th, 200 yards in front of the railway embankment, Lance Corporal George Mitchell lies shivering in the snow. His Lewis gun rests on its bipod, 'snout raised as if snuffling the battle'.[22]

As the snow falls, the moon gradually goes behind a cloud, and his fellow soldiers of the 48th become a bunch of white blobs, all of them shivering and waiting for the order to advance.

'Away on the left, artillery pounded heavily, but ahead and behind us might have been dead polar regions for all the sign of life we could see or hear. A light rocketed up, perilously close. Four Maxims commenced to jabber fiercely and strings of bullets hissed overhead ... Lady Death was ready to take the stage.'[23]

Unfortunately, she is about to play to a packed house, with a stacked deck. And the Lady is not for turning.

•

The men of the 4th Brigade keep moving, marching towards Bullecourt in rough formation over the stark snow-blown landscape, as the railway embankment comes into view in the soft moonlight. In short order, Jacka's mob, with the 16th Battalion, are up and over the embankment and march forward in single file with 10 yards distance between platoons, to again take up their position in the sunken road, while the 13th and 15th Battalions remain behind the embankment ready to move forward when the time comes for the second advance.

For now, all must settle down, shivering, as they await the whistle of Zero Hour, due at 4.30 am.

Intelligence Officer Albert Jacka is with them, noting each development as it comes, or fails to.

'*2.15 a.m. – Battalion started to move out into position in Sunken Road ...*'.[24]

But where are the bloody tanks?

Good question.

According to the hastily formed-up plans, the tanks are meant to be at the embankment by 3 am, ready to move forward to cross the sunken road, and be at the starting tape, well before 4.30 am, which is Zero Hour. But not only are they not there, there's still no bloody sign of them! Are we to go through the same debacle as last night? All dressed up, with no tanks to go, no tanks to anyone?

But hark.

What's that?

It can only be one thing.

'Presently,' one of the 14th Battalion officers will recount, 'we hear a noise like an express train and see a couple of tanks coming up, gaily emitting thousands of sparks giving away their position ...'[25]

Yes, *sparks*. It looks like some massive Catherine wheels are coming their way! So much for sneaking up.

Still, at the sight and sound of these tanks approaching, the 4th Brigade's machine-gun companies on the left of the advance do as ordered. Three machine guns out on the left of the Australian advance open fire, hoping to disguise the noise, joined shortly thereafter by eight machine guns on the right. There is also a little artillery falling on both flanks.

(Does it successfully shield the sound of the tanks approaching? *Nein.*)

At last, Jacka can see the first tank clearly: a dark blob slowly heading their way over the white snowy landscape. He walks down towards the roaring beast, which slowly, oh so slowly, makes its way towards him in turn, its engines roaring, its tracks making an extraordinary *flap-flap-flap* like the padding webbed feet of a gigantic metallic duck. There is a mad menace about these machines, and it is not menace in a good way, or even a directed way, like they are dangerous to the enemy alone. They feel dangerous to *everyone.*

Slowly, oh so slowly, they come forward.

A flock of sheep, a pride of lions and a . . . . . . trundle of tanks.

By 3.20 am, Jacka at least has three tanks at the rendezvous point and is trying to lead them across the snow-covered ground to their designated jumping-off point, which lies just on the other side of the sunken road. Each tank coming forward has a distance of some 100 yards from their nearest on either side, so it is no easy matter to guide them.

One thing that shocks Jacka is just how slow they are. There is so much stopping and starting that they are going only a third of the speed of a man's walking pace at best, no more than 30 yards a minute. The German bullets and shells are going to travel at exactly the same speed as usual, however . . .

•

In the forward ranks of the 123rd and 124th Württembergers, in the trenches next to Bullecourt that the Australians are due to attack, there is sudden pause.

Was ist das?

It is, over the distant roar of artillery fire now falling on Bullecourt itself, the sound of engines. *Ja,* it is only faint, but it is clear.

It can only be the new British *Superwaffe*, superweapon, the iron monsters the British call 'tanks', and the Germans call '*Panzerkampfwagen*', armoured fighting vehicles, or '*Panzers*' for short.

Tanks!

HQs are so informed, along with artillery and front-line soldiers.

'*Der Tommy ist am angreifen!*' Tommy is attacking!

•

Stop!

For the perpetually calm Captain Jacka, it has admittedly been a bit hairy, standing 20 yards in front of this roaring beast lurching up the slope, and waving his arms, but . . .

But on the other hand, the thing is moving so slowly that if it had not stopped, he would have had at *least* 30 seconds to jump out of the way. He might even have been able to have a quick cup of tea.

Finally though, it lurches to a halt, and from out of an impossibly small side-hatch, a tank officer emerges.

Captain Wilfred Wyatt, 11 Company, D Battalion, Heavy Machine Gun Corps.

Jacka presents his own credentials.

Captain Albert Jacka, Intelligence Officer, 14th Battalion.

He tells the Englishman that he will guide them to the starting line, which will firstly involve following this particular track over here to get to the only level crossing in these parts that will get you to the other side of the railway embankment. Then I will follow you along the path that will get you to the best part to cross the sunken road, before we get to the soldiers on the starting line and . . .

And, yes?

The Englishman is confused.

Soldiers?

Yes, our soldiers are waiting some 200 yards up ahead, and your tanks are to join them by 3.30 am.

Again, the English tank officer reacts as if that is all news to him.

'The tank crews seemed to know little or nothing of an attack by infantry,' Jacka will note in his intelligence report, 'and nothing whatever about the particular operation they were to participate in.'

Jacka informs them, the best he can, what the plan is, and when they need to *be at the wire!* The tank commander, however, replies in plummy tones that while he appreciates the plan, 'The tanks cannot traverse No Man's Land in the time allotted.'[26]

He and the crews of the other tanks will do their best, but can make no promises.

Make no promises? *Hundreds of lives are depending on it!*

The problem to Jacka is immediately obvious.

If the tanks start off at 4.30 am as planned, the three remaining tanks won't be able to cross the 700 yards to the wire in the time allotted, and the soldiers will get there ahead of them.

Quickly, Jacka races back to Colonel Peck – whose HQ is always as close to his men as possible – requesting that the tanks leave the starting line at 4.15 am instead, so as to get to the wire before the soldiers. Peck agrees, and the request is passed up the line to 4th Division HQ, before their answer comes back: all battalions must 'Stick to the programme'.[27]

Now, while it is one thing for Jacka to guide the tanks – there are now five of them – up and over the embankment, it is quite another for them to be able to follow. Inside the belly of the beasts, the horsepower of the roaring engine has a hard time pulling the 28 tons on the flat, let alone up and over a rise to the level crossing that Jacka is trying to get them over, and even steering to that crossing is not easy, as it relies on altering the speed of each track. Not one man-jack of the crew is experienced in tanks, for how could they be when the machines have only been operational for eight months, and the men's training has been no more than a few months?

Honestly, for Jacka, it is like trying to herd massive drunken cats, each with a mind of its own.

'The organisation seemed to be bad,' Jacka will recount, 'and no-one appeared to be in direct command of the show. This was shown by the fact – that the tanks wandered aimlessly about in every direction, thereby drawing enemy fire on us, and on the trenches.'[28]

All is chaos.

With gritted teeth, Ted Rule watches as one tank heads straight towards the edge of where he knows a bomb dump is!

Rule runs out right in front of the tank to stop it; he dances, he jumps, he screams and he has 'visions of bombs, tank, and men mingled in one grand explosion'.[29] Finally, Rule is noticed but the damn officer inside the tank only directs it to change course by a few feet. Rule runs to be clear of the blast and watches as the tank ... squashes a couple of boxes of bombs into the earth and rolls over them. Thank God. A wooden case and a bit of mud has just saved them all from Kingdom come. Rule had thought this was going to be a dull night for him, but his pulse is racing faster than any man in the battalion that is disappearing in the distance.

Captain Fred Stanton – once Private Stanton, back at Gallipoli, who had boasted to his family of being 'great pals' with Jacka VC – appears now with an odd question: 'Have you seen any of my company? Evidently, I've lost some of them.'[30]

No, Rule explains, he is the only one here. Ah. Stanton leaves him to it and heads to the action.

•

The 14th Battalion is going in at the prow of the 4th Brigade, secreted in the sunken road with the 16th Battalion by their side – each divided into four waves – while the 15th and 13th Battalions will form up behind the railway embankment and be ready to move as the second advance.

To the left of the 4th Brigade, the 12th Brigade – boasting the 46th and 48th Battalions – will attack the line just to the right of Bullecourt.

Further to the left, the British 62nd Division will be attacking right to the fringes of Bullecourt itself. In all, no fewer than 13,000 soldiers are set to attack the German line next to the French town, and hopefully overwhelm it.

By 3.30 am all of the men are in position, ready to go when Zero Hour comes. Some of the men know about the mechanical help that is due to arrive. Many don't. When most of the senior officers themselves had not had it confirmed until midnight, there simply had not been time to properly brief the ranks of the tanks.

Any questions?

Yes, as a matter of fact, Lieutenant William Pentland from the 46th Battalion has one. It's about the 'green disc to be shown on the side of the tanks', in fact a small green light.

'How, exactly, are we to see a green disc a quarter of a mile away in the dark?'[31]

Is it too late to eat carrots? For God's sake, that green disc is to indicate that the tank is firing. Well, wouldn't the fact that the tank is firing also indicate this? Again, battles on paper make much more sense when they are left there. When theory meets reality, that's when it gets messy. Question time is over, action is to begin.

•

Albert Jacka is beside himself with rage.

Worse than herding cats, this is closer to trying to herd blind elephants.

One of the tanks has tried to get over the embankment without using the level crossing, only to slide off and partially turn over. It now can't move, one track turning uselessly in the air, the other not powerful enough to budge it either way. Another has broken down. Still another refuses to follow Jacka to the shallow part of the sunken road that he has selected for them to get across, and has also got stuck.

'It seems probable,' Charles Bean will note, 'that the subaltern in the tank, realising that he was late, attempted a short cut to save time.'[32]

Jacka is nigh struck dumb with fury. They are Zero Hour minus 60, and the men of the 14th about to charge at German defences are again facing chaos! Part of the problem is that none of the tank commanders is subject to Australian orders.

To make matters worse, Jacka discovers that the officer commanding the No. 2 tank has not even synchronised his watch – his time reading 5 minutes behind that of the infantry.

Well, the hell with it. Jacka effectively takes charge himself, barking orders to the tank commanders on what they must do, and how they must do it – commanding that they follow him. No, he doesn't draw his gun on them, but there is something about this Australian officer in the moonlight, as the light snow falls, which commends one to doing your best not to anger him, what?

Walking back and forth along the line of the chugging monsters, keenly aware that their black forms on the white snow will make them perfect artillery targets for the Germans once they zero in after Zero Hour, Jacka walks in front and guides the surviving tanks into position.

•

Major Watson, at Noreuil, now having travelled to Brigade HQ – situated, mercifully, in the very deep cellar of a factory that is still standing – waits, and again the anxiety is killing him. Yes, at least this time, he knows his tanks have started from much closer, and were not journeying from afar before even beginning to make their way to the starting line. But even with that, there are problems, as the continuing reports coming back to him show.

The snow is now thick on the ground, with some ice, and the tanks are making heavy weather of getting through, but for the moment there is nothing that can be done about that. While some piping-hot tea is served, and various officers fuss about, Brigadier General Brand heads off for a kip.

Which is alright for some.

For Watson, word comes back that one of the tanks has got stuck while trying to climb out of the sunken road, and is now out of action. Watson heads out to verify the report and is at least relieved to find that, while there was truth that it had got stuck, it has only been delayed and is now moving forward. The bad news, however, is that the night is freezing but clear. These are shocking conditions for the troops lying out there waiting for the tanks, but when the tanks do arrive, the German artillery spotters should have little trouble in seeing them.

Watson returns to Brigade HQ to find more activity than before, as more officers and orderlies are turning up from their own rest, as Zero Hour gets closer. Reports are now coming in that the Germans have increased their shelling overnight, including at Noreuil, which is where the tanks had been based. More worrying still are solid reports that the railway embankments and surrounds have also been shelled, indicating the Germans must suspect that they would be mad enough to attack again on this night, but nothing is certain.

And now he receives the most important message, even if it will later prove to be totally false.

All tanks are in position.[33]

•

It has been ridiculously difficult, but by 4.17 am Jacka has indeed got all three surviving tanks – three have been lost to mechanical problems and getting bogged – to the starting line. One tank has been placed in front of the 16th Battalion, while two are in front of the 14th.

The Australian soldiers and the British tank crews, who have momentarily emerged from their roaring hotboxes to get air – look at each other warily. There is just 10 minutes to go, and having never met or even seen each other before – they will now be fighting for each other's lives. The tanks are to depart at Zero Hour of 4.30 am and – come hell or high water, by hook or by crook, baby and bathwater, pell and mell, quick and sticks – all the troops are to follow at 4.45 am sharp.

If the troops pass the tanks, so be it. I repeat: the attack is going in. There is at least some time now for some last-minute cigarettes before the balloon goes up.

Albert Jacka's smoke is coming from his ears.

This is madness. Absolute madness.

What are they *thinking*?

•

For the artillery corps of the 123rd and 124th Württembergers, the reports are expected. For, once again . . .

'*Der Tommy ist am angreifen!*' Tommy is attacking!

Their big guns are already in position, with their shells loaded and primed.

'*Fünf . . . vier . . . drei . . . zwei . . . eins . . . FEUER!*'

Fire!

'*Feuer!*' '*Feuer!*' '*Feuer!*'

•

Waiting, waiting, waiting.

In the bowels of the basement HQ at Noreuil, Major Watson is extremely worried.

'I was desperately anxious that the tanks should prove an overwhelming success. It was impossible not to imagine what might happen to the infantry if the tanks were knocked out early in the battle.'[34]

And now all eyes are glued to their watches as the minutes tick down to Zero Hour.

And suddenly it happens.

In the distance they hear 'a whistling and rustling' followed by 'a succession of little thumps, like a dog that hits the floor when it scratches itself'.[35]

The Battle of Bullecourt has begun. Watson glances at his watch. It is a little earlier than expected. It is still Zero Hour minus seven, just 4.23 am, but one way or another, it's on. The Germans clearly know that an attack is forming, and are laying out their version of a *willkommen* mat.

Strangely, at the 4th Brigade HQ, it causes a release of tension. For whatever else, the wait is over, and the wheel of fate is actively turning. Fate is just that, it doesn't vary from moment to moment. Where it will stop is beyond their control, so they may as well light up their pipes and cigarettes.

Alas, even before they have blown out their matches, there is 'a reverberating crash overhead'.[36]

If you were a betting man, you'd reckon the Germans know exactly what is happening and how to stop it, and as well as plastering the area right before their own lines, are now sending shells onto the Divisional HQ!

•

For the men of the 14th Battalion, it is – *incommmmming!* – horrifying. German shells are starting to land all around and on them, and they still have not reached Zero Hour.

Clearly, the Germans have heard the tanks, and know they are there, even if they can't see them, yet. In the field, the soldiers of the

14th hug the snow they are lying in ever tighter, to try to escape the shrapnel as, over the shattering roar, the screams and groans of the unlucky ones fill the night.

What to do?

Start the tanks now?

No.

'Stick with the program.'

The troops of the 4th Brigade stare balefully at these mechanical monsters. Are *these* the things they are relying on? They seem so lumbering, so slow, so *lacking* in menace.

Zero Hour minus five . . .

Zero Hour minus one . . .

Zero Hour.

With a roar, the three tanks in front of Jacka waddle forward, with the troops knowing they must follow in 15 minutes, *whatever happens*.

And they must proceed without Jacka. As Intelligence Officer, his job is to hold back, to be the forward eyes and ears of what is happening and send messages back to Battalion HQ. He must be close enough to observe, staying with the last wave for the moment, but never close enough to be hit.

It is as well, for what happens now. For no sooner has one of the tanks set off than it suddenly opens fire on flitting figures in front – only to find they are Australian soldiers, carrying trench mortar bombs forward. Three of the Diggers are killed, and three precious trench mortar bombs lost.

Sitting in the bellies of their beasts, the British crews of the tanks are hot, deafened and practically choking as they try to make their way up the slope. In terms of the landscape around, most of them are blind, too, though the drivers can at least see a little through the small slit. They are hoping to get close enough to first crush the German wire and then bring their two six-pounder guns and Hotchkiss machine guns to bear. To steer, the captain of each crew must first bash a heavy spanner on the steel wall in front of him to get the attention of the driver, and then use prearranged hand-signals to veer left or right, depending on what he sees.

And now their tanks start being buffeted by the massive concussion coming from shells landing close, even as a relentless *ping-ping-ping* of bullets hitting steel can be heard over the roaring engines.

They keep moving towards the wire, which is just now becoming visible some 200 yards ahead – which of course means the tanks themselves are visible to the German artillery.

The Commanding Officers of each Company of the 14th Battalion – Lieutenant William Wadsworth, Captain Fred Stanton, Captain Alf 'Lofty' Williamson and Captain Bob Orr – check their watches. Zero Hour minus six for the infantry and . . .

And *what now?*

At 4.40 am the Germans suddenly send up flares lighting the entire battlefield, including the tanks, which are still going – and in 10 minutes have covered no more than 300 yards, and have still not got to the wire. It means the soldiers of the 14th and 16th will be advancing as easy targets.

'As one looked around in the breaking dawn with the ground snow white,' one of the soldiers will recount, 'he saw thousands of men calmly moving forward in perfect formation with here and there a man falling as a bullet struck home.'[37]

Onwards.

•

For the Germans in the Hindenburg Line, things are becoming clear.

4.45 motor engines sounds are louder, evidently approaching.[38]

Bring *more* artillery to bear!

•

At the conflagration in front of them – as the German flares illuminate this fresh hell, with shells landing all around the tanks – those soldiers in the front ranks, lying in the snow, look at each other.

Jesus Christ Almighty.

Are we really meant to be walking into that, to try to penetrate a wire that is still substantially intact, with no guarantee that the tanks will even get there to crush it?

Yes.

Zero Hour minus one . . .

'Word was passed along, "One minute to go,"' one 14th Battalion Sergeant will recount. 'Mates gripped hands, a murmured, "Good luck old man," a momentary tightening of the muscles, and then the order to advance.'[39]

Zero Hour.

The whistle blows. The men of the 4th Brigade rise and stiffly move forward, following the tanks towards the wire, with the soldiers of the 14th Battalion on the left, and the 16th Battalion on the right.

On the basis of Jacka's report, 14th Battalion HQ duly notes:

4.49 All infantry gone. [40]

As shocking machine-gun fire soon starts cutting them down – as cries ring out, and urgent shouts to 'Stay low!' – many of them are gone to God. (It is not the screaming ones who alarm, because as the veterans among them know, a 'badly hit man never yells'.)[41]

But things are torrid, and no mistake.

'The Hun commenced to put up lights,' Ted Rule documents, 'and during one lot that lit up the place like day, I saw a sight that I'll never forget. Advancing along the side of the spur as if they were on parade, with their rifles held at the high port, was a line of our boys. There were gaps, and in one or two places big spaces. With such intense machine-gun fire, there was no need to inquire what was happening.'[42]

It is something like mass murder.

Out to the far left, because of confusion with the 12th Brigade orders, the likes of George Mitchell and others in the 48th Battalion are not even close to moving off. Their own tanks have not yet arrived, and their officers still believe their orders are to only move off 15 minutes after their tanks, so there will be no concerted attack between the two brigades.

As to Britain's 62nd Division, they are to attack the line to the left of Bullecourt, thus drawing half of the fire from the defenders of Bullecourt, but so far there is no sign of any such attack going on.

Captain Harry Murray of the 13th Battalion's A Company will never forget it.

'We swung along a bit faster, the men keeping a wonderful line. The whole front was now in an illuminated panorama of swift stabbing lights with a blended roar of rifles and machine guns sounding like the cackle of a bushfire, fanned by the wind and racing through a field of ripe wheat.'

Oh, but there is worse, for . . .

'Like wheat stalks, our men were collapsing before it, punctuating this sustained and furious roar with thunderous crashes of exploding shells hardly needed however, in the face of more imminent danger.'[43]

•

And now, the 124th Württemberg Regiment can actually *see* the tanks themselves, followed by five lines of infantry and denser columns in the rear approaching.[44]

The paths they are pursuing, their positions on the map, and the part of the Hindenburg Line they are heading to are all noted, and both the machine-gun sections and the artillery advised so they can adjust their fire accordingly.

•

The men of the 14th Battalion and the 16th Battalion trudge forward, noting with growing unease just how quickly they are catching up to the tanks. At the head of their troops are the company leaders, Captains Fred Stanton, Lofty Williamson and Bob Orr.

'Stanton and Williamson,' one Digger will recall, 'were my two favourite officers. You could *talk* to them, you know, sit down and talk to them.'[45]

Like Diggers, only they are officers.

As Albert Jacka watches them depart, he is beset by an even more extreme anxiety. He can hear the familiar staccato bursts of the German Mausers and . . . oh, *Christ* . . . the rapid, menacing *knock-knock-knock-knock* sound of German machine guns, getting ever heavier.

Knock-knock-knock-knock.

Who's there? Who's . . . *there?*

The Hun, in terrible force.

Is his 14th Battalion, and the 4th Brigade, about to be wiped out? In the original plans, there were meant to be six tanks each, for the 4th and 12th Brigades.

The way things have turned out, however, there will be just three in front of the 4th Brigade, and an indeterminate number in front of the 12th Brigade – as they have not turned up yet and are certainly nowhere near the starting line, just meandering in that general direction from behind the embankment.

Suddenly, up front, there is the familiar sound of what the troops refer to as a 'whizz-bang', a particular German shell so called because of the distinctive whizzing sound it makes before it explodes. Everyone tenses . . . . only for it to land right by Captain Bob Orr, so closely that it is very much him who explodes and he is, effectively, killed many times over.

Aghast, but resolute, his men keep trudging.

Out to the right, also moving forward, at the head of the 16th Battalion's B Company is Major Percy Black.

The best they can, the tanks in front of the 4th Brigade keep making their way forward.

'We saw the tanks over on the right,' George Mitchell of the 12th Brigade's 48th Battalion will recount, 'big black blurs outlined sharply against the snow. They lined up and moved forward slowly. They would stop, move on, then stop again. Their exhausts flared red in the night. Their droning noise aroused the German lines.'[46]

At least with shells now falling all around the tanks in front of the 4th Brigade, there is no further need to go quietly, and the tank drivers open their throttles to surge forward, as fast as 3 mph.

The engines of the tanks are roaring, their whole structure vibrates with the strain, not to mention the machine-gun bullets hitting their side, as each driver attempts to get his 28 tons of machinery where it's meant to go, right at the German wire. In the lead tank it is already hell on earth – courtesy of the roaring engine and cramped space that is suffocatingly hot, choked with acrid engine fumes, incredibly noisy and insufferably smoky – when it happens.

The first tank encounters a 'hurricane of hail' as German bullets and shrapnel hit its half-inch of steel protection, and unleash small splinters of metal inside the tank's interior that ricochet around, causing devastating wounds as they rip into fragile flesh.

Desperately, though bleeding from the face from the splinters that have hit, the driver pulls hard on the driving handles on each side of his knees to alter the speed of both tracks and make the tank veer away, but it is too late. The next shell hits amidships, and even as more splinters fly around the cabin, the tank stops, with ruptured tracks and a huge hole in the side, while the usual tank fumes of petrol and cordite now have an overlay of that curiously sickly stench that is fresh hot blood.

Out! Out! Out!

Within a minute, the most able of the survivors have come out of the side-hatch of the tank, dragging their bleeding comrades with them.

And now, another tank stops, though it does not appear to be hit...

To the sheer astonishment of many of the 14th Battalion, and none more than Jacka himself, it seems like this tank has not even waited to be hit, and the crew are simply abandoning ship.

You *miserable* bastards!

Despite his own orders to stay safe, Jacka runs forward to remonstrate with them, to ask them to get back in the tank and keep moving towards the wire that the 14th Battalion is counting on the tanks crushing.

Get back in, and go!

But nothing will convince them – and in the military hierarchy, Jacka has no actual authority to order them to go forward.

The Australian is incandescent with anger.

Too tough for you with half an inch of iron protection, but we infantry are meant to go at the wire alone and unassisted?

It defies belief. (Though to be fair, as 'Mad Harry' Murray notes when it comes to the tank crews, 'they were manned by mechanics instead of soldiers'.[47])

It leaves just one tank going forward for the 4th Brigade, of the six machines that were originally meant to be there.

To the right of the 14th, the tanks are also going awry, and Captain Daniel Aarons of the 16th Battalion will recount what happens when they inevitably pass the tanks and suddenly find themselves at risk of being shot from behind from one of the fiercely meandering monoliths!

'The tank, during its approach to Fritz's line, had changed direction obliquely and it was I personally who ran up to the tank and directed the operator to change direction. The tank was firing at various times and it was firing across our line of approach that made it necessary for me to communicate with the operators of the tank.'[48]

Out to the far left, meantime, the two tanks left standing for the 12th Brigade finally arrive at 5 am.

'The tanks slid smoothly past me in the darkness,' Lance Corporal George Mitchell of the 48th Battalion will recount, 'each like a patient animal, led by his officer, who flashed directions with an electric lamp. The stench of petrol in the air, a gentle crackling as they found their way through the wire, the sweet purr of the engine changing to a roar when they climbed easily on to the road – and then, as they followed the white tape into the night, the noise of their engines died away, and I could hear only the sinister *flap-flap* of the tracks, and see only points of light on the hillside . . .'[49]

Not all the animals, however, are so patient . . .

Out to Mitchell's front, where the 46th Battalion is preparing to be the closing force of this attack, another tank is heading some 30 yards to the right of a group of Diggers under the command of Lieutenant William Pentland – a coach-builder from Port Melbourne – when it suddenly stops and . . . swivels. And now it . . .

OPENS FIRE!

The Diggers dive for whatever cover they can find, shouting angrily to 'STOP FIRING, WE ARE AUSTRALIANS!'

Lying prone in the mud, the outraged Lieutenant William Pentland glares at the tank, only to see 'a little green light blinking in and out of the side of it. The signal for us to advance, needless to say we didn't obey the signal.'[50]

It will take some time to sort out, but the tank commander had been convinced he was facing Germans and given the order to fire. The tank proceeds for another 30 yards before stopping.

A small shutter opens. The face of the tank commander appears.

'*Who* are you?' an aggrieved voice asks in plummy English tones.

'WE ARE *AUSTRALIANS!*'[51] Pentland roars back.

Oh. The tank commander gets out.

'I am sorry for having fired on you,' he says. 'Where is the German line?'[52]

Pentland, himself on the aggrieved side of things, points to the enormous band of barbed wire up ahead, just visible in the Verey lights, and the tank commander gets back in through the impossibly small hatch – just two by two feet – and the tank waddles off in that general direction.

•

Up ahead of the 4th Brigade's 14th and 16th Battalions, all is exploding shells, a scything lattice of machine-gun bullets, burning tanks, and a mass of barbed wire that looks like a sea of steel thorns.

But it is the guns doing the most damage.

'They opened up,' Alwin Dalitz, the Sergeant Major of D Company 14th Battalion will recount, 'with what appeared to me to be 50 machine guns.'[53]

There is only one thing that can be done.

Run.

Towards the guns.

The men of the 14th and 16th are running hard now, as bullets whizz past and comrades fall beside them. The only thing that keeps you alive in the face of the whirring shards of shrapnel is your mate copping it beside you.

After ascending a slight rise, and now fast approaching their objective, the wire is exactly as Jacka had detailed in his intelligence report: it is waist high, in a thick band that goes for nearly as far as you could throw a Mills bomb, and filled with razor-sharp barbs that could not only kill a brown dog, but disembowel him on the way through. And it looks pretty bloody *intact*, with few if any discernible paths through.

Worse, now that the desperate Germans can see – to their amazement – that their enemy have made it even this far, they are bringing all their fire to bear, and Australian after Australian goes down, cut to pieces. Their bodies start to pile up both before and on the wire, in the latter case sometimes used as a stepping stone for others to get deeper into the wire. The air is filled with the relentless *thud-thud-thud* of the Hun machine guns, their bullets throwing up sparks from the wire, and the sound of maimed men crying for help. Things are grim, with the only hope being to keep to the shelter of the one tank that is still moving forward.

Out on the far left of the advance, half of a platoon – 15 men – coming in the next wave are blown apart by a single shell falling among them.

To Jacka, watching closely from behind – where he has been ordered to stay – it seems clear that their only hope is to forget the remaining tank and rush the wire themselves. If he was leading that is exactly what he would do, but he must follow orders and simply watch, his rage rising at what is happening to his battalion.

For the 16th Battalion out on the right, the blizzard of death is even worse, as they are also taking fire from their right flank, as the German soldiers defending the village of Quéant bring their own firepower to bear.

'When the troops got very close,' Captain Daniel Aarons of the 16th Battalion will later write to Bean, 'if not almost up to Fritz's wire, they opened with countless machine guns and shrapnel and literally mowed down our troops by the hundred. The wire was uncut, in fact is almost impassable. It was so thick that it was almost possible to walk along the wire.'[54]

Finally, Major Percy Black has had enough. Though now in his proper position at the rear of his battalion it is so obvious that they must pierce the wire or perish, he shouts to his men, 'Come on, boys, bugger the tanks!'[55]

With a roar, he and his men rush forward and look for ways through the wire.

The front-line soldiers of the 14th Battalion are soon doing the same, even as chattering German machine guns continue to reap their terrible harvest.

'The Hun could be seen,' one soldier will recount, 'standing shoulder to shoulder and waist high over their parapet.'[56]

It is a turkey shoot for them, in scenes reminiscent of the attack in Gallipoli where Jacka had won the VC, except this time it is the Diggers who are the turkeys being shot. The survivors try to hack at the wire, either with their bayonets or – for those very few who are so equipped

– wire-cutters. A few particularly brave ones try to 'clod-hop' their way through, placing their boots on each strand to quell it, and carefully stepping forward, the problem being they must remain upright to do so, and most are cut down, inevitably getting caught in the barbed wire as they fall and being difficult to extract because of it. At least those who are clearly killed can have their bodies used by the next ones to come as paths to get further into the wire.

Screams fill the shattered night . . .

CHAPTER TEN

'COME ON, BOYS!'

Bullecourt, more than any other battle, shook the confidence of Australian soldiers in the capacity of the British command.[1]

Charles Bean

Wee hours, 11 April 1917, Bullecourt, tanks for nothing
Finally, out to the far left, with the 12th Brigade – and a good 30 minutes after the 4th Brigade had gone on in – it is time. With their two tanks having departed for the wire just after 5 am, at 5.16 am the whistle blows.

At last, for George Mitchell and his company men of the 48th Battalion the word comes from the sergeant.

'Prepare to advance.'

Mitchell gets up, stiffly, completely frozen. It is half an hour after all the other soldiers to their right have started to move, due to confusion with the 12th Brigade orders.

'Advance!'

Slowly, they begin to move forward, climbing up and over the embankment.

'Down a steep bank I slid. The gun broke the sling, and plunged its nose into the dirt. Precious seconds were wasted while I slung it on my shoulder. My team ahead called on me to hurry.'[2]

If only someone had said the same to the tank crews.

For within a minute the men of the 48th have gone well past the tanks and are right in the thick of it.

'A tornado of thunder and flame fell upon us,' George Mitchell will recount, 'beyond anything I had known or imagined. Close as trees in an orchard were the trees of flame. The blast of one shell would send me forward, while another would halt me with a wave of driven air. A headless man fell at my feet, as I rolled over him a sheet of flame fanned over the blinding light. A score of men just in front melted into bloody fragments as a big calibre shell landed. The air was dense with bullets, and thick with the blood-chilling stink of explosives. The plain was carpeted with bodies, mostly lying still but some crawling laggingly for cover. A man cannoned into me and fell leaving a bloody patch on my shoulder. But there was no sound of human voice in all that storm.'[3]

Their tanks?

One of them simply turns around, still unhit, and, as one soldier will recount, 'was making its getaway when a shell burst in its side. I saw the crew flop out one at a time and run for dear life. Several were burning fiercely.'[4]

The horror! The *stench* of burning human flesh. And it all means the wire in front of the 48th remains entirely intact.

A little later one tank does come forward, and the tank commander emerges to ask Colonel Ray Leane what he needs done.

Leane barks orders, or at least requests.

'Move to the left flank of the 48th, and clear the Germans from the sunken road there. Also suppress the German machine gun you will see firing on the left flank of my men, from Bullecourt.'[5]

'Easily done!'[6] says the tank officer, before climbing back in and heading off. Suddenly, however, after going just 400 yards, firing as it goes, the tank unaccountably does a laboured U-turn and comes back, whereupon it is hit by a shell and damaged near the railway.

The tank can still operate, in extremis. But it is not just that it has left the battle, which enrages Colonel Leane. It is that the tank is now a magnet for artillery fire, and shell are landing all around HQ!

The entire 'panic-stricken' crew now emerges, to be confronted by Lieutenant Colonel Leane – who has lost his brother in this debacle, just the day before – and asks what the hell they are doing and why are they leaving their tank?

The crew commander replies.

'We have had a direct hit, and one man has been slightly wounded by the door blowing in. The tank is still all right and can be driven.'

'Can you try?'[7]

The short answer is no, and in any case his terrified crew has already disappeared. In the full light after dawn, the immobile tank continues to provide perfect target practice for the German artillery, and it is inevitably completely destroyed.

Right up front and well away from this, the men of the 48th keep moving forward.

'Big shells smashed among us. Our platoon commander, Caldwell, got it first. Others staggered back looking like snow men save where the blood showed black.'[8]

One part of the problem is that, to the left of the 12th Brigade, the British are not also attacking, as is part of the plan, and are holding back.

Under no pressure from the 62nd Division, and untroubled by the gas attack, the German defender can bring so much firepower to bear that, as noted by the 12th Brigade's Commanding Officer James Robertson, 'a fly could ... have hardly got across'.[9]

For his part, Lieutenant Colonel Ray Leane will note in the 16th Battalion diary as a reason the operation is now in dire peril: *'The tanks not carrying out their work. Failure of the British to attack left of Bullecourt.'*[10]

•

Both the 14th and 16th Battalions are being completely cut to pieces, with anyone above the wire immediately targeted by myriad guns and blown apart. If you kept below the wire you were alright.

'If you held your hand up it would have been chopped off,' one of the Diggers would recall. 'And to hear the screaming – oh God, I've cried since. Often.'[11]

While many of their dead and wounded lie suspended on the wires, the survivors are still straining mightily to get through, led by Major Percy Black. All the while constant fire keeps cutting into them.

It does not take long for succeeding waves to understand the carnage up ahead.

Leading his men of the 13th Battalion's A Company forward, Captain Harry Murray can sees his best friend Percy Black and his men of the

16th being torn apart, even as he and his own men get hit by a storm of machine-gun fire themselves.

'Suddenly the ground around in front, under our feet, leaped to feverish life, spattered, whipped, and churned by swathes of machine-gun bullets.'[12]

With his own experience of machine guns coming to the fore, Murray realises, by the shifting arc of fire, that the Germans are searching for them, blindly, throwing out a wide net rather than zeroing in.

'Get down till it passes!'[13] Murray roars to his soldiers above the angry chatter, as they all throw themselves to ground. It is while so prone that Murray gets a grasp of just what *terrible* shape the 16th is in, as the men are taking fire from three sides. A lesser man and officer would have stayed put, but Murray is made of sterner stuff, as his primary instinct – to fight not falter – takes over.

'Come on, men,' he shouts, 'the 16th are getting hell!'[14]

As one they charge forward, Murray guiding the point of attack – 'Get to the right, boys!'[15] – arriving at much the same time as the 16th Battalion's one surviving tank, which now actually reaches the wire and is indeed able to suppress much of it.

'[The tank had] showers of sparks flying off her,' Murray will recount, 'as rifle and machine-gun bullets lashed her piteously ... Surely, an ant would not emerge alive from such an inferno?'[16]

But they don't call him 'Mad Harry' for nothing.

Despite his views on the dim survival prospects of even an ant, Murray now goes forward himself, and struggles with wire that is 'too high to straddle and so crossed and intertwisted that it formed an eight-foot mesh netting ... of which the enemy fire converging from all points sang a ceaseless death song'.[17]

He essays to squeeze past on the left, only to be caught between the tanks and the wire and is obliged to fall back once more. Perhaps though, the right side might be better going?

Pushing that way now alongside the roaring tank, Murray has no sooner got halfway past it than he sees a German machine-gun nest no more than 10 yards away, manned by three brave German soldiers who have remained at their post, and are 'maintaining continuous fire on the leading companies of the advancing 13th'.[18] The dead soldiers of the 16th lying suspended on the wire are testament to the previous work of these gunners, and they are still exacting a terrible toll. But not for long.

After lobbing a grenade their way, Captain Murray quickly shoots them for good measure. There will be no more fire from that Maxim.

True, a German bullet now creases the back of his neck and Murray drops to the ground, knowing he is 'done'.[19]

But no. Though there is some blood seeping down his back, to Murray's amazement everything still works and he is able to rise again and keep pushing forward with his progressively thinner force, as all three platoon commanders have been cut down, and of his original company of 150 soldiers, only 40 remain.

The sole tank, alas, which has done the good work of crushing the wire suddenly comes under heavy fire from Riencourt, behind those Australian soldiers who have just broken through, and after two direct hits is left as a smoking hulk.

They are on their own.

•

It takes every ounce of strength Jacka has in him *not* to rush forward. On the one hand he knows his place is right at the front, with the men of the 14th Battalion. On the other hand, he is under very strict orders. The job of the Intelligence Officer is to be HQ's eyes and ears, a link between the front and the back. If he goes forward and is killed, the link is broken in the chain of the command. So he knows he must stay back. And he also knows that things are bad – just not *how* bad.

•

To the right, against all odds, the valiant Major Percy Black and his men of the 16th Battalion's B Company have got through the wire, and equally charged into the first German trench. Just as Black had promised Lieutenant Colonel Drake-Brockman only the morning before, they have reached their designated target!

'When we reached the last line of barbed wire we were able to use our Mills bombs,' one Digger will recount. 'This kept the Hun down while our first wave – what was left of them – rushed out and captured the impregnable Hindenburg Line.'[20]

They are in the German trenches! It is bitter, take-no-prisoners fighting, and the Australians are quick to avenge themselves for all the men they have lost.

'Fighting in the trenches was very severe,' one Digger will recount, 'bayonets and bombs being freely used,' and freely dodged by the Huns, buoyed by the sight of German reinforcements racing to them now. The Australians beat back the first Hun counter-attack 'but our ammunition was almost done and some of the men were fighting with shovels . . .'.[21]

With the trench secured, Black gives his runner a progress message to run back to 16th Battalion HQ – *First Objective gained and pushing onto Second*[22] – as they move on to the second band of wire that lies before the second German trench. As ever, Black is leading his men when suddenly, in a completely unnatural motion, he flings his arms skywards, before sinking – dead before he hits the ground.

It is a devastating blow to his men, but one that puts them in a mood of particular savagery, as they are now through, and hit the German trenches as a rolling ball of battle-violence – rifles firing, bayonets slashing and bombs flashing up and down the earthen alleyways. The 16th are soon joined by Harry Murray's men of the 13th.

Within a minute, the Bullecourt trenches are overwhelmed by these wild colonials as the night is filled with cries of '*Nein, kamerad, nein, NEI . . !*'

The Australians fight with a savagery borne of at last being able to get to grips with those who have exacted such a toll on the 4th Brigade, while the Germans are stunned that, despite everything – their machine guns, artillery and seemingly impenetrable wire – these demons have still made it across No Man's Land. It is enough to take the fight out of any man, and many Germans do indeed surrender.

But what a price the Germans exact.

Just to the left of the slain Black, the men under Captain Fred Stanton have taken the first trench.

Sergeant Blackburn is told by a medic what he has already seen. His corporal, Ken Miller, is shot in three places: the neck, the chest and the leg. He is heading to one place, the Great Beyond, very soon; he might have half an hour at best. Miller is faring better than Ken Buchman, who was shot dead as he reached the top of the trench. And where the hell is Bill Nicholls? He was hit in the thigh, fell back and has vanished, hopefully into enemy hands and still alive. The maths is alarming; they have been fighting less than 30 minutes, and by Blackburn's current tally, half of the section is dead or done for! At this rate, none will last the hour. Forward it is then.

Trying to expand their patch, Blackburn leads his crew along the trenches only to come face to face with 'a mob of Huns. We went back a few yards for bombs. After bombing for three quarters of an hour and gaining 20 yards we decided to barricade the trench and hold the position.'[23]

Amid the cacophony of catastrophe all around, others are now pushing on to the second trench, having just got through the band of wire that protects it, when a German machine gun opens up on them.

Taking matters into his own hands, Captain Fred Stanton of B Company shouts, 'Come on, boys, show these blighters that we're Australians!'[24] and takes five men with him as they outflank the trench of the gunner, while still getting close enough to hurl bombs. They have just succeeded in their task when, as Jacka will recount to Stanton's cousin, John, '[Poor Fred] paid dearly for his great gallantry. He was shot almost through the heart, the bullet entering his left breast and passing through him. Death was instantaneous. Fred's conduct throughout the fight was most gallant and all ranks are loud in their praise of his noble work. We can ill afford to lose such a brilliant officer as your brother.'[25]

(Jacka had always liked Fred a great deal personally, but has had an extra soft spot for the fact that, just like him, he had risen to the rank of Captain from Private and had demonstrated just how good officers from the lower ranks could be.)

Harry Murray and his men of the 13th are quick to keep pushing forward, ready to leapfrog the 16th at the second trench.

'The thought of our mates [drove us on],' Murray will recount. 'No time to waste.'[26]

Not even when . . .

Oh, God, *no* . . . he sees him.

It is the 'bravest man in the AIF',[27] and his best mate . . . Percy Black. Dead.

'I saw his body within 15 minutes of his being hit. He was shot through the head . . . I had not the time to even take his personal effects.'[28]

Vale, Percy. They had manned the same machine gun on that first day at Gallipoli and fought many battles since. But Murray is the man still standing and his only chance of so remaining is to keep going.

Onwards!

Take the second trench!

The saying is easy, the doing is hard. In the smoke, the screams, the endless shells exploding, the barbed wire looking truly 'dreadful with dead men strung on it like clothes pegs',[29] 2nd Lieutenant Henry Eibel of the 15th Battalion turns to the soldier beside him as they beat off attack after attack from German bombing raids and, after retrieving papers from his pocket and handing them over, says quietly, 'Give these to Captain Dunworth and tell him I'm finished.'

'But,' says the soldier, 'you're not dead.'

'No,' Eibel replies, 'but I will be by that time.'[30]

He is killed a short time later.

Others, like Private William Evans of the 12th Brigade, are taken prisoner. But in all the chaos, as one Hun soldier leads him along the trench at the point of a bayonet, an opportunity presents itself. For when they meet another German soldier coming the other way, Evans' guard stops momentarily as the two start barking at each other in that curious language of theirs, before they pause to jump on the fire-step and fire at some Diggers. It is in this circumstance that Evans notes a dead Digger at his feet. If he has a Mills bomb in his pocket where they are usually carried . . . well . . . come in spinner!

Kneeling as if he is tying his shoelaces, Evans quickly rummages through his dead comrade's pocket. There it is!

Taking out the pin, Evans places it between the legs of the two Germans and – 5 . . . 4 . . . 3 . . . 2 . . . 1 – scarpers around the corner just in time. Behind him he hears the explosion and screams, taking the opportunity to jump out of the trench and race back to his own lines.

•

What now? Over on the left, Lieutenant William Pentland, still trying to organise his fighting force of the 46th after the disruption caused by the wild tank, is suddenly confronted by a British soldier, dressed in the same uniform as the recently departed tank commander.

With a streaked face and wild bloodshot eyes, the soldier tells him he had indeed been part of the crew of that tank, but, 'We have been hit and I believe I am the only survivor.'

'We are going forward in a few minutes,' Pentland tells him. 'You can come with us.'

'I will come as far as our tank,' the crew member tells him, 'and set fire to it.'[31]

Damn the tanks! The soldiers meant to follow them must rush past each of the lumbering liabilities, as the tanks have either been destroyed by the enemy or puttered and petered out of their own accord. It will be a cold day in hell before any Australian soldier will trust the buggers, or forget how many lives they have squandered this bloody day and night.

•

Finally, Captain 'Mad Harry' Murray and his surviving men from A Company of 13th Battalion are through to the second trench! Charging like wild things at the German trenches, there is no mercy. Using cricket-ball throwing skills learnt on the playing fields of Melbourne centuries ago, they hurl their bombs straight at the German gunners, and the Lewis gunners quickly follow up with sprays of their own, further quelling what had previously been strong German resistance.

Even now, many of the Hun refuse to surrender and the results are as brutal as they are bloody, as Murray and his men seek to make the section of the OG2 trench they have won secure from counter-attack. (Despite the extremity of the situation, many of the Australians cannot help but notice how well constructed the trenches are, deep and wide, with massive traverses and myriad reinforced dugouts that look more than capable of withstanding even direct artillery hits.)

All is chaos, with the battalions hopelessly mixed up.

'But,' Harry Murray notes, 'it was in just one of these situations that the Australians were in their element. Our system of discipline permitted the rank and file to give full expression to their individuality in times of intense crisis. Every man was a potential officer. German discipline, on the other hand, tended to make machines of men ... Hastily organising our defences, we began to draw each unit together.'[32]

Chaos, confusion and catastrophe are still coming at them hard.

'The action now resembled a bushfire which has been partly beaten out. The main blade has been broken up into smaller detached fires, all heavily attacked by groups of firefighters. German bombing parties counter attacking force from the right, sustaining a swift and bloody repulse from the 16th. With sufficient numbers and grenades, I feel sure we could have driven them out of all the trenches.'[33]

Alas, they have neither number nor the bulk grenades they need. But at least they have a chunk of OG2!

•

Across the line now, and despite their devastating losses, both the 14th and 16th Battalions have secured a foothold in the Hindenburg Line, against all odds.

'In the trenches,' Captain Robert Hayes will recount, 'a fierce hand to hand fight is speedily decided in our favour.'[34]

Once this line is secured, the next part of the plan is to secure the second line before establishing their own line further in, a big call given how diminished their numbers are, but the first of the 4th Brigade soldiers at least set off to do precisely that.

On! Faster! Further! Only a minute later, while actually through the second band wire and leading the charge to take the second trench, Captain Lofty Williamson also takes a burst of machine-gun fire, and his body slumps on the lip of the trench, blood pouring out of him – though he stubbornly refuses to die.

The best he can, the champion of the Carlton Football Club crawls to a shell-hole, and takes out his pistol.

Only two days earlier, Lofty had been heard to say that he would not be captured while he had will to resist.

Well, though bleeding badly, neither arm is broken. When one of the other soldiers offers to take him back for medical help, he refuses, and orders the soldier to keep going forward to help the others.

With his revolver in hand, he makes a vow: 'I won't be taken easily.'[35]

•

At 14th Battalion HQ, positioned just on the lee side of the railway embankment from the battle, near the Regimental Aid Post, Colonel Peck's chosen adjutant, Captain Harold Wanliss, is beside himself with anxiety.

At 7.21 am, a message comes through from Colonel Drake-Brockman of the 16th, originating from Captain Jacka, to the effect *'tanks were a failure and casualties heavy'*.[36]

What more is happening out there?

What might he be able to do to help?

Shouldn't he be with his men?

'I'm going to ask you once again, Colonel, to let me go,' Wanliss says. 'We've a good idea now of what's happened, and I can't be any use here. I feel I ought to be up there doing what I can to help the fellows. God knows what has happened to Jacka and the rest of them, and I can't stand the suspense.'

But Colonel Peck will not *hear* of it.

'Look here, Wanliss, do you think it's an easy matter for me to stay here glued to this damned dugout, simply waiting for news?'

'All the more reason why I should be out there sending you information.'

'Wanliss, listen to me,' Peck replies with near theatrical exasperation. 'You've been a soldier long enough to know that it's sometimes harder to stick this waiting than it is to fight. Your idea is to leave me all alone with my responsibilities.'

'Well, Colonel, if you put it that way, I'll not ask again.'[37]

Colonel Peck is more than a little relieved.

(In truth, he doesn't need Wanliss particularly but has an ulterior motive in keeping him here. So outstanding a man does Peck find the Ballarat officer to be that he has become convinced he is dealing with a future Australian Prime Minister or the like, so long as he can survive this war. Peck intends to do everything he can to protect him, without actually telling him so.)

•

For the best part of an hour back at Divisional HQ, there have been no reports worthy of the name, but now they start to come back in, from wounded men and goggle-eyed runners alike.

'Heavy casualties before the German wire was reached . . .'

'Enemy barrage came down, hot and strong, a few minutes after zero . . .'

'Fighting hard in the Hindenburg trenches, but few tanks to be seen . . .'

'The enemy are still holding on to certain portions of the line . . .'

'The fighting is very severe . . .'

'Heavy counter-attacks from the sunken road . . .'[38]

Little is solid, and much is still confusion.

The messenger from one company wants a protective barrage put down in front of them. But another messenger, from another company, seems to make clear that such a barrage would land on the second company.

A battalion on the prow is in real trouble and asks that reinforcements be sent forth from the reserve battalion.

And they are running low on bombs! Send some forward, urgently!

Captain Wadsworth, 9.07 am: '*Ammunition is wanted extremely badly, also men.*'[39]

(Also, some sanity would be handy.)

•

The tanks are under attack. By Bert Jacka. 'Why don't you go forward?' he yells 'Help clear that communication trench!'

'We don't have an officer!' yells back the head emerging from the tank. 'So we can't.'

Yes, you can!

But they won't.

Jacka spots one tank crew heading past him . . . without a tank. What happened? 'Why have you left your tank?'

'It caught fire,'[40] one man answers.

It caught fire? As in artillery? No, as in it burst into flames. Oh for God's sake. And now Jacka notices that they are carrying two bags: one contains 'enamelware and the other food'. War is no picnic, but these former tank dwellers are perfectly prepared to have one. Unbelievable.

Stories will circulate afterwards that Jacka has to be restrained from shooting them.

•

All eyes turn to the Brigadier, to take command of the emerging situation. To a certain extent, he does, but it is hard to know exactly what to do until they know what was always going to be the most important factor in this battle – the fate of the tanks. As with everything else, the fog of war is impenetrable.

'One report states that no tanks have been seen, another that a tank helped to clear up a machine-gun post, a third that a tank is burning.'[41]

Finally, however, one of Major Watson's tank commanders, Lieutenant Richards, bursts in, clearly almost broken with exhaustion, emotion and, very likely, enough narrow escapes from exploding shells to fill out his dancing-with-death nightmares for decades to come.

'Practically *all* the tanks have been knocked out, sir!'[42] he reports.

Bloody hell!

Disaster. Everything Watson had ever feared.

Before replying, he glances around the cellar.

'These Australians had been told to rely on tanks. Without tanks many casualties were certain and victory was improbable. Their hopes were shattered as well as mine, if this report were true. [But] each man went on with his job.'[43]

•

To the far left, with the 12th Brigade, George Mitchell is one of those who have survived against all odds to this point, and is close to being able to get to the trenches himself.

'Carefully,' he will recount, 'I picked my way through the wire and the limp forms that dangled over it. Sometimes I was hooked up. The deep front line was manned by our 46th men. I walked alongside a sap toward the second line. On top of the sap lay a man on his back, who was swinging both arms to and fro in a strange restless action. Caution whispered into my ear to get into the sap 'ere I shared his fate in the bullet-lashed zone.'[44]

For *still*, the British 62nd Division to their left have made no move, which will see the Commanding Officer of the 48th, Lieutenant Colonel Ray Leane later writing to Charles Bean that the 'Battle of Bullecourt was ill-conceived and badly prepared for. The English who were to attack Bullecourt never advanced. Therefore, we were placed in an impossible situation.'[45]

11 April 1917, 4th Brigade HQ, fiasco fallout

Disaster is all around. The dead and wounded Australians are strewn all over the battlefield, with brave stretcher-bearers trying to reach the latter through an ongoing lattice of death. When it comes to the things that were meant to protect them from this very fate – the tanks – as Bean chronicles, 'before 7 o'clock, their carcasses could be seen motionless, and in most cases burning, all over the battlefield'.[46] And the crew of those tanks, too, have been devastated. There had been 102 men in the crews of the 12 tanks that started out, and of them no fewer than 52 have been killed or wounded or are now missing.

Just after 7 am, Jacka himself, in cold fury, bursts through the doors of General Brand's 4th Brigade HQ, and tells of the debacle he has seen.[47]

Yes, the soldiers up front have made it into the German trenches, but with so few soldiers left it is going to be touch and go as to whether they can hold them. Three of the four battalion commanders have been killed.

At 9 o'clock, another runner gets through, this one from the 13th Battalion's Captain Murray – the highest-ranking officer among those who have taken the trenches, and taken command of all survivors of 4th Brigade in the trenches.

'We hold first objective and part of second. Have established block on right of both objectives . . . There are six tanks at a standstill . . . Quite impossible to attack village. A Company 13th badly cut about by machine-gun fire in wire, some of all other 13th companies here O.K. We will require as many rifle and hand grenades as you can possibly send, also small arms ammunition. Most of Lewis machine guns are OK. Have four Vickers guns. Fear Major Black killed. Several officers killed and wounded... Have plenty men. Have about 30 prisoners of 124 Regt. Will send them over at dusk. Look out for S.O.S. signals. Send white flares (as many as possible).'[48]

He finishes with a message that will become famous in the circles of the Australian Imperial Force.

'With artillery support we can keep the position till the cows come home.

'H. Murray. A Coy.'[49]

Murray further tries to get that artillery support by sending up SOS artillery flares, urgently requesting a barrage to be dropped on their Teutonic killers, some 200 yards beyond the second Hindenburg trench.

Alas, in possession of a report that some of the troops and tanks have been seen well to the other side of the Hindenburg Line, the Artillery Group commander, Lieutenant Colonel Reginald Rabett, takes pause. Our own troops are already through Riencourt, and heading to Hendecourt. If we put shells there, we will be putting them on our own people. Brand insists that these reports are wrong and that the barrage must come down.

But that is not enough, as will be noted by the official historian of the 14th Battalion.

'Its observation officers and others seem to have been obsessed with the same optimism that possessed Gough. Messages from the front (from men who were actually in the firing line) were treated with contempt, and S.O.S. signals frequently sent up either not noticed or disregarded.'[50]

No fewer than 18 such S.O.S. signals are sent skywards before 8 am, and yet they are *all* ignored, despite Murray's and Brand's growing outrage. In the end, it is Lieutenant General Birdwood who must resolve the dispute and he comes down on the side of the Artillery Group Commander. There will be no barrage.

Yet another false report that British troops have been seen in Bullecourt itself leads to Lieutenant General Sir Robert Fanshawe ordering the 62nd Division, who are yet to attack, to simply advance into the town to join them – only for the leading elements to be cut to pieces because the German defenders still hold Bullecourt, unchallenged.

•

Captain Murray, come quickly!

Something extraordinary is happening.

Out on the far right of the trench they have taken, a sole soldier – the only survivor of his platoon – is doing precisely what he had been told to do before the battle had begun. He is furiously filling in this part of the trench so that Field Marshal Haig's cavalry will be able to charge across without trouble.

Scarcely daring to believe it, Murray heads along the trench, and sure enough . . .

'There he was, on top, quite oblivious to the danger, a splendid target for enemy fire, picking and shovelling industriously and filling the trench.'

The sheer bravery is staggering.

'What are you doing, lad?' Murray demands.

The soldier stops, stands up, and tells him.

'I have orders from my Colonel to fill in the trench.'

'Get down at once. Don't fill that trench. We want it, and you will be killed if you stay there.'

The lad grins uncertainly, hesitates for just a second or two, and finally prepares to obey when, to Murray's horror . . .

'Sickening for me, a thud of a rifle bullet told me he had been squarely hit. He sounded a long shuddering "Ahhhhh!", and toppled over never speaking again.'[51]

As long as he lives, Murray will never forget the incident.

Right now, it looks like a cross between the cows indeed coming home, and Gough's chickens coming home to roost. Something, anyway. But without artillery support – 'the serried rows of steel monsters, waiting to be used',[52] – it is becoming clear that they will not be able to hold these hard-won German trenches much longer as the Hun counter-attack commences in earnest.

For now the Germans are starting to attack them from both sides, from those parts of the trench they still hold to the east and west, while also coming closer from their own reserves in the back area. It means that the fire on the Australians from both shot and shell is intensifying, and there seems no prospect of relief unless they can indeed get artillery support.

For the grenades that each man had carried forward are rapidly running out, and the second and third waves that had gone forward are inexorably being forced back. All while the German bombardment on their positions is horrifying.

'Fritz lobbed a shell amongst them,' one of Jacka's surviving men, Private Dunphy, will recount. 'One man was blown up about 40 or 50 feet high. His head was off. His body came down shoulders first. This made an impression on my mind . . .'[53]

If the 4th Brigade don't get their own artillery support, they will be finished.

It is with this in mind that, huddled in a bloody trench, surrounded by dead Germans and Australians, Captain Murray holds a quick meeting with Captain Daniel Aarons of the 16th Battalion, Lieutenant Jack Kerr and Captain Horace Hummerston. They have sent runners back for the last three hours, but as they have still had no artillery support it means they either did not get through, or those at HQ have ignored the pleas for reasons best known to themselves. Murray's best estimate is that he and his men can only hold on until noon if they don't get the coverage. What to do, as the shells keep landing and the bullets overhead keep whining?

With great bravery, Captain Aarons offers to go himself.

'It was about a 100 to 1 chance of getting through,' Aarons will recount, 'but I took the chance. Kerr helped me get out of the trench into a shell-hole and, by a little strategy and care, the runner who accompanied me and myself leapt from one hole to another and I do not recollect being in the air for more than a fraction of a second – ping, ping all around.'[54]

After three minutes, to his amazement, Aarons finds himself still alive, and close enough to a slightly elevated roadway that he is able to get on the lee-side of, and keep wriggling further away.

It is for this reason that the figure who bursts in on Brigadier General Brand at 4th Brigade HQ to identify himself as Captain Aarons of the 16th Battalion, suh, is covered from head to toe in mud.

'Things are very serious.'[55]

We need artillery, and we need it now, Sir! Whatever reports you have had of us advancing beyond the second trench are false. We can only just hold on right now.

'Our flanks are only being held by bombing, and we are running out.'[56]

Time is of the essence!

'Both flanks are being bombed back, supply Small Arms Ammunition and bombs almost expended and only 25 per cent of personnel left. Proposed to fall back to line of shell-holes out in front, out of bomb range and hang on there until night.'[57]

Another option is briefly canvassed.

'We can fall back to first trench, and hold on overnight.'[58]

This would at least give some time to allow reserves to be rushed forward. But what is needed right now is artillery fire on German positions!

Where to from here? Will they now get the support they need, with more men rushed forward to hold the trenches that have been so hard-won, or will they be pulled out? It is against the possibility of the former option, rushing forward, that Albert Jacka stays as close to the front lines as he dares, with such men from the 14th as he can gather, in the hope that they can go forward.

In the meantime, Brigadier General Brand advises that if Murray and his men can just hold on – no, seriously – 'pressure would be relieved by 62nd Division [attacking] from TONIGHT'.[59]

Lasting until *tonight*?

If they last till noon they will be doing well.

'Our gunners were standing by, lanyards in hand, praying for orders to send over a protective curtain of shrapnel and high explosives ... but orders were orders, and so the guns retained their silent immobility.'[60]

At 11.30 am at Battalion HQ, a breathless runner arrives from the front and reports forlornly that the supply of bombs and small arms ammunition is absolutely used up, as a result the brigade on the left, having lost around 80 per cent of its strength, is retiring.

•

At his HQ in Albert, General Gough, the architect of the whole attack, the thruster to beat them all, is very pleased.

He has his own reports that Bullecourt has been taken, and now gives orders for the 4th Cavalry Division under Major General Alfred Kennedy – 5000 men on horseback, armed with swords and rifles – to go through the breach and 'push on towards Fontaine les Croisilles and Chérisy'.[61]

(And they try. They really try. Alas, they are still three quarters of a mile away from Bullecourt when German machine-gun fire attacks them, and they suffer 20 casualties. The report of the breakthrough had been . . . horse-shit.)

•

In the midst of the carnage, Captain Murray and his men are indeed holding on – just. With shells landing all around, the constant hammering of German machine guns spraying the top of the trenches so heavily that it is clear that any Australian who rises will have his head blown off, and Hun bombing parties attacking from both ends . . . things are grim.

Without artillery support, Murray comes to the bitter conclusion that they can only last for an hour or two at best and he rejects entirely the message saying they must last until the 62nd Division attacks tonight. Firstly, they cannot, and secondly, even if they could, no-one has any confidence the 62nd Division will ever attack.

Murray himself is as busy as a bartender on payday, projecting confidence, barking orders, making sure that wounded men are being looked after and ensuring that such ammunition and bombs that they do have are in the hands of those beating the bastards back!

But how long can they hold on?

'Oh, for that barrage! How sweet it would [be] to listen to the sudden opening of a full throated "iron chorus".'[62]

But now a breathless runner arrives back from the 16th Battalion HQ with the message: there will be no barrage.

Murray knows it.

His men know it.

It is no less than a death sentence for most of them.

'What now?'[63] his men ask.

It is a good question and it is being asked across the line.

'Men who had all along been buoyed up by the expectation of support, looked serious.'[64]

What now?

Well, the answer is ever more obvious to all.

When the Company Quartermaster Sergeant, Les Guppy, of the 14th Battalion, comes back to his platoon from thwarting a German bombing raid, it is to find some of the survivors of his platoon attempting to hoist a white flag on the pointy end of a .303. He rushes forward to pull it down, as scared as he is.

'Well, Sergeant,' one of them asks plaintively, 'what are we to do?'[65]

'I don't know,' Guppy replies over the sounds of the bombs coming still closer, 'but it seems we should either follow the others in attempting to escape or remain to be captured.'[66]

From either end of the section of trench they hold, the sound of the German bombing parties comes closer and closer as they clean the Australians out from bay after bay. Guppy and his men decide to make a run for it, which is as well, for at much the same time, when Captain Murray spots a white flag going up from another shattered group of Diggers, he orders it *shot* down. But yes, the time has come to make a decision.

'Well, boys,' he tells his men, 'we'll have to get back as we've run completely out of ammunition and Fritz has been heavily reinforced.'[67]

What do you blokes want to do?

'There are two things now – capture or go into *that*.'[68]

All look . . .

That is the open ground between them and their own lines, now being sprayed with bullets from 15 German machine guns and 4000 rifles.

'It was like expecting to run for hundreds of yards through a violent thunderstorm without being struck by any raindrops.'[69]

All those who want to surrender should be allowed to do so.

But, one thing.

'All infantry,' Captain Murray says, 'must hand over all their ammunition, bar 10 rounds, to the Lewis guns.'[70]

For it is the mighty Lewis gunners – 10 of them – who will provide the covering fire they need to get back, before trying to scarper themselves.

For Murray, and most others, there is no question of surrendering. So again, let the devil take the hindmost and . . . come in, spinner! They would rather risk death than face years as German POWs.

The call goes out from one of his officers with a smashed arm: 'Every man for himself!'[71]

Murray must first pause to tear up his message pad and code signal book and tread them into the mud, before bracing himself.

'Now we turned for the last and most hopeless fight of the day; completely surrounded as we were, it looked as if it could only end one way . . .'[72]

Ready?

Now!

'Gritting their teeth, our boys plunged into the bloodbath, some only getting a few feet before being shot down.'[73]

For, how could they not be?

As the Germans now close to within 10 yards at either end of the trench they hold, Murray and several of his men vault out of the trench and start sprinting back through 'the fiery lane of blood and death'.[74] Bullets smack into the ground all around them, and higher still, around their heads, 'buzzing like a swarm of enraged bees'.[75]

And more Diggers still go down.

Eager to finish them, a posse of brave Germans break cover and charge after them, only for . . . the Lord to work in mysterious ways!

For in all the dust, haze, smoke and confusion, the pursuing Germans are mistaken by some of their own gunners for fleeing Diggers, and they consequently 'opened a murderous fire upon them, completely relieving pressure on us and thus giving us time to get over the wire'.[76]

At least most of the Diggers.

As to Murray, he is just getting through the wire when it suddenly feels like the Lord has turned, and this time slashed a massive whip across his back!

In fact, it is yet another bullet creasing his body, just breaking the skin for the shallowest of all possible wounds. Truly, much more troubling than the bullet is the sheer mental, physical and emotional exhaustion that hits him, just as safety is at hand.

'I ... could only go a few yards at a time, the terrain, not having been cut up by shellfire, offered little cover.'[77]

Spying one crater with no shelter beyond it, with his last ounce of strength, Murray and a couple of companions fall into it to catch their breath. Above, suddenly, the roar of an approaching train ...

This is going to be close.

Brace!

The shell lands 20 yards away, creating a splendid crater! It is more cover and, again, they break their own to stagger towards it and jump in.

As he lands, good news, he burns his hand on a red-hot shell-fragment.

'[The burn] acted as a tonic, bucking me up a little bit.'[78]

For, oh yes.

'Every man has reached such a stage of physical and nervous exhaustion after hours of desperate fighting, a little thing will revive him, the mind becomes extraordinarily clear and works at great speed, all feeling of fear being absent, lying down I began to think "Would this cursed war never end?" we couldn't last forever.'[79]

But we can last for now! At least some of us can.

Looking out, he can see many of his men being mown down and reflects, 'This isn't war; it's murder.'[80]

He cannot stand it.

'Some of those men helped me get my VC,' he says, 'and I must help them now.'[81]

With which, Murray charges out again and again and drags as many of the wounded as he can to safety in the shell-hole.

Finally, with one last mad dash, near carrying one of the wounded, Mad Harry is able to make it back to his own lines – against all odds, completely intact, bar the crease on his back, the burn on his hand and ... about a hundred of his men. For yes, just 50 of his Diggers from the original 166 of A Company are still standing.

Percy Bland takes one look at the scene and his brain cannot take in the breadth of the tragedy: 'Everything is such a mess. Such a bloody mess.'[82] Later on, those who write official accounts can give the scene an order and dignity it does not have now; and never will for the men who survive it. Look now, as grievously wounded men are choking on their own blood, while others are vainly trying to hold their slashed stomachs together by placing both bloody hands over the wounds. Everywhere, Diggers are groaning, crying and shrieking, all while the call goes up for stretcher-bearers over here! STRETCHER-BEARER!

Back in the hard-won German trenches, Sergeant Blackburn's platoon of Lewis gunners have remained behind for five minutes to cover the retreat, and are now ready.

'The locks were then taken out of the guns and we ran for our lives. Every man was a hero a dozen times over. I took 30 men in and came out with five.'[83]

There are men who get no chance to run.

'There were lots who never heard the [retreat order],' Ted Rule records in his journal, 'and fought on until surrounded by Huns who came in on them from rear and sides. Those who tried to break away were killed like flies. Numbers leapt out and lay in shell-holes until darkness set in, but those who lay doggo too close to the German lines were collected by Hun patrols.'[84]

•

Jacka is watching a minor miracle, a tank is actually reaching its target! Yes, one of them is actually at the Hindenburg Line and is firing into the German defences beyond and . . . a direct hit. From Riencourt. And another. And one more ends the life of the tank and the men in it. There has never been a target as slow and fat and tempting for artillery as a tank and the flaming wreck Jacka watches is the final nail in the coffin of his confidence. Tanks may win a battle one day, but today is not that day. He rushes another report back to Brand; but even as he does, Jacka is infuriated to see tanks dawdling – there is no other word for it; they are deliberately not headed towards the battle. They are wandering back and forth like they are patrolling the jumping-off point; their destination is their start! Jacka ask Brand for more artillery defence; there will be none from the tanks. The best they can do is draw fire.

•

Out to the far left of where the 4th Brigade has retired from, the 12th Brigade has come to the same conclusion that retreat is the only option and is also in the process of retiring from the trenches they have won at such cost.

The 48th Battalion is the last to move back, under both heavy machine-gun fire and shocking attention from snipers.

And now the cry goes up from one of the few surviving officers.

'Back to the front line!'[85]

Effortlessly, Mitchell swings his Lewis gun up onto his right shoulder – despite the fact it weighs no less than 28 pounds – and prepares to depart.

'A dead sergeant still lay massive on the parapet. Other dead lay limp on the trench floor. The wounded sprawled or sat with backs to the parapet, watching us with anxious eyes.'

One badly wounded man gurgles out a question to Mitchell.

'You are not going to leave us?'[86]

Mitchell can neither answer him, nor even meet his eyes. They *must* leave them, and hope that the Germans will look after them. The alternative is to stay here and be killed or imprisoned. With his gun over his shoulder, he joins the rest of the men, moving down the sap away from the very trench hundreds of Australian lives have been given to capture.

At least it is now, in the general retreat, that Mitchell and his Lewis gun are able to come into their own. To this point, it has been hard to get a bead on the flitting Germans in front without shooting his own men. But no such problem presents itself now, so Mitchell sets up his gun on its bipod, and positions himself just before the top of the rise that lies just next to the old starting line. It will allow him to get some protection for himself, while still getting the muzzle of his gun over the rise to fire on all those Germans who would dare to pursue the retreating Australians.

All up, Mitchell will cover himself in such glory, acting as an almost single-handed rear-guard for the 48th that he will be awarded the Distinguished Conduct Medal, 'For conspicuous gallantry and devotion to duty. He handled his machine gun with great skill throughout the operations, and was largely responsible for driving off a strong enemy counter-attack.'[87]

•

Though back behind his own lines, Captain Harry Murray is still not safe, as he tries to gather his shattered forces. Over there, sitting on an ammunition box, is one of his best officers, Lieutenant Tom Morgan, his head between his hands. Only minutes before he had been with his best mate, Lieutenant 'Bluey' Shirtley, when a shell had come and completely blown Bluey to pieces, his body taking the shrapnel that otherwise would have hit Tom.

And now, out of nowhere, another German shell lands, this time hitting Tom hard.

'When we picked him up, there was a slight smile in his strong lips. He might have been shaking hands with Bluey over on the other side just then. Tom was always smiling and took the game as he found it. Both he, and Bluey, were officers that it would be hard to replace, cheerful, bright and ready for anything under all circumstances.'[88]

And now they are dead.

As more shells land, the likelihood that they are about to be ripped apart themselves increases. But . . .

'What did it matter? What did anything matter? It was surely coming to us some time or other.'[89]

All that Harry wants to do now is lie down and sleep, maybe forever. Recognising it, and with no whip of God handy to fire a bullet across his back, or even a piece of hot shrapnel to hold to act as a tonic, his Commanding Officer of the 13th, Lieutenant Colonel James Durrant, hands him a flask of whisky and Murray takes several nips.

'As a rule, little spirits affected me, but . . . it had no more effect than water.'[90]

Beyond sheer fatigue he is filled with a strange mix of relief, admiration and anger.

'Every man who followed his officer through those shrieking fields of fire was a hero. The whole battle was as hopeless as the Charge of the Light Brigade at Balaclava, and the effort was sustained far beyond the limits usually assigned to human endurance, clinging automatically to the discipline of the AIF.'[91]

The relief of those who have made it is palpable, strongly tempered by the fact that they have had to leave so many wounded behind.

How to get them?

It proves difficult.

For one thing, the German soldiers are now swarming, capturing those incapable of even crawling away, and others caught in the wire and hiding in shell-holes.

One of the last is Sergeant Les Guppy, who had found himself under such withering fire in his own escape that he had jumped into a hole intending to stay there until dark.

Alas . . .

'At 4 pm a strong party of Germans with stretcher-bearers came upon me and took me prisoner.'[92]

Another who is caught is none other than the former Carlton player, Captain Lofty Williamson. When the Germans come for him, and it is clear they intend to take him prisoner, Lofty has one reply.

'Not on your bloody life will I be prisoner,'[93] says he, firing at one of his would-be German captors, who shoots back and Lofty is hit once more, ab . . .

> *Abide with me; fast falls the eventide;*
> *The darkness deepens; Lord, with me abide;*
> *When other helpers fail and comforts flee,*
> *Help of the helpless, oh, abide with me . . .*

Lofty dies.

Those of the 4th and 12th Brigades who have survived and are still capable of walking must now make their way back to their own digs, a difficult process for battered, shattered men, many of whom have not slept for 36 hours, and some of whom are wounded. Some are so exhausted they can no longer carry their rifles, and drag them, holding them by the sling and trailing the butts through the mud.

Their knees wobble, and they stagger on in a near dream-like state, though more nightmare in reality: the screams, the beheadings, the disembowelled Diggers. The snow has gone, and a heavy rain soaks them all to the bone.

•

Scarcely recovered, Captain Harry Murray is present when the four Colonels of the 4th Brigade meet with General Brand in his advanced HQ, now that it is all over.

'Weary to death as I was, I flinched at their expression, laden with bitter condemnation of those responsible for the ghastly blunder. Behind those burning eyes and stern set lips, one could sense the damn backfloods of denunciation which might break forth at any moment, but no word issued from these iron men.'

Gough had done this to them, and Holmes, and Brand who had not been strong enough to stop the insanity!

'The high command had blundered, and men had to pay the price, that was all. Had I been responsible, I would have soon gone through another Bullecourt than to face those men. Although their lips were sealed, they seem to epitomise in their stern silence all the tragic terror and heroic futility of Bullecourt.'[94]

For they feel exactly as Murray feels.

'Bitter grief and stern indignation at the recollection of their men, torn, dismembered and blown to shreds on that fatal barrier, then the hand-to-hand fighting, the temporary advantage and finally, the grim hanging on and waiting for the barrage and munitions that never came.'[95]

Bastards!

Harry Murray walks away, one thought foremost, the incident that 'stood out cameo-like in its clarity, the figure of that youth desperately making a passage for the cavalry that could not come'.

A pointless death?

'Well it was a quick death, and though it might weaken a man to see his comrades fall, there are worse things than that, far worse.'

And surely it can't be for nothing? Look at the big picture; the small ones are too depressing to gaze at for any length. Come on, Harry, buck up!

'All at once I felt fresh strength flow into my veins, we were going to win, Bullecourt was only an incident.'[96]

•

Was it only a bit over 24 hours ago that they had been coming forward to Bullecourt, 800 strong?

Now, there are just under 260 of them left capable of making it back under their own steam. Jacka leads the survivors of the 14th Battalion, but it is not easy in the dark, and the now pouring rain, to find their way all the way back to their new base at Beaugnetre.

In all of their exhausted agony, their shattered morale, at least they've been told that an English cavalry officer has been assigned to guide them, though so far there is no sign until . . .

Out of the darkness a figure gallops up, and yells at them with peremptory superiority, 'Halt! Halt!'[97]

Exhausted, most of the 14th are happy to do exactly that.

But happy does not describe the attitude of the already infuriated Albert Jacka, particularly when this same figure asks, with exactly the same tone: 'Who are you? Who are you?'

Jacka explodes. In the last 24 hours he has seen his battalion betrayed and near destroyed, by *precisely* this kind of 'superior' Pommy officer, suffering the colonials to do as they are bidden and not be respected in their own right. No, this Pommy had had nothing to do with the orders given, but he'll do.

Grabbing the bridle of the horse so there can be no escape, Jacka begins.

'Who are *we*? *Who are we?* YOU were supposed to [meet us hours ago]. You and your bloody horse.'[98]

He continues to berate the nominally superior cavalry officer until his fury is spent and then – 'I've never seen Jacka so upset in my life,' Percy Bland will comment[99] – and only then, does he let them go. But his rage does not abate.

'I *told* all the heads that it was pure murder to attempt the operation,' he says to one soldier. And we can all see what bloody happened!

The soldier is on Jacka's side.

'Jacka's ideas about military affairs,' the soldier will note, 'are well worth careful consideration.'[100] The sleet turns to freezing snow once more. They trudge five more miles to rest. A restless day of bitter reflection lies ahead, before they must march for Bapaume.

For Jacka, despite the devastation, there is one dreadful upside: it has shown the senior officers, the Generals who have ordered this, for the dreadful, callous fools that they are.

'He told me,' Ted Rule will later relate, 'that he couldn't help feeling a sort of satisfaction at seeing it pan out as it did, though for the men's sake he was very sorry.'[101]

They keep moving into the night.

'There has seldom been a more melancholy march,' the Official History of the 14th Battalion will document. 'It was snowing all the time; officers and men had had two successive nights without sleep; and had just survived a bloody and disastrous battle. Everyone was absolutely exhausted . . .'[102]

At last, nearing dawn, the 14th arrives in the town of Beaugnetre.

'The tramp out that night was a heart-breaker,' Rule will note. 'We were robbed of almost every ounce of energy by the thick mud that we had to get over, even before reaching the road.'[103]

Finally arriving, it is to find that their quartermaster has laid on hot tea, sandwiches, and one more crucial thing.

'For those who wanted rum,' Rule chronicles, 'there was plenty. In the AIF the rule was, no rum before a fight; the rum was given afterwards when the boys were deadbeat. But this feast looms as one of the best I ever had. Standing out in the open and with a couple of old lanterns to drive away the blackness of the night, we fairly gorged ourselves like beasts. It was just on 24 hours since anyone had had a hot meal.'[104]

Finally full, and sated, the survivors head a little down the road to a flat spot where they are at last able to safely collapse into the sleep of the dead and the dead exhausted.

It all just seems so extraordinary.

Only last evening they had been intact as a battalion, walking down cobbled lanes. Then the barbed wire, the bullets, the shrapnel, the broken tanks, the screams, the death, the retreat.

'It all came and went,' one of the Sergeants will later note, 'as a mad dream does.'[105]

•

It is the way of these things.

No formal truce is arranged. No white flags are waved.

But although there had been firing on Australian stretcher-bearers early in the afternoon, by the time the afternoon is ebbing towards dusk, the Hun's mood has changed. As the snow starts to fall, the Australian stretcher-bearers – bravely heading out into the field to retrieve their wounded – can't help but notice they are *not* being fired on. Soon enough, some of the German soldiers even come out and help them.

Both sides understand the horror of what has happened, and that one side, the Australians, has lost so comprehensively that right now they present no threat. So why not help? There is little common language, but the Germans even lead some of the stretcher-bearers to shell-holes where badly wounded Diggers can be found – some of them wrapped in German blankets to keep them alive in the freezing conditions until the stretcher-bearers can get there. Some of the Germans have even taken the rifles of the badly wounded and jammed them bayonet first into the ground by their shell-holes to mark where the wounded can be found.

'The German officers came out with them at dusk,' the 14th Battalion's Sergeant Boland will recount, 'and gave our stretcher-bearers all the severely wounded and took all the men with minor wounds back into their own lines.'[106]

After all, the most severely wounded prisoners would severely drain German medical resources, so it is better that the Australians have them back.

Tomorrow, we fight again. But for now, we are all soldiers sick of this horror, trying to help each other.

Danke schön.

•

As always, it is the saddest scene after all battles. The rain has poured down, and the men have pitched tents in the mud, but now each company must conduct a formal roll call, where the Company Sergeant

Major reads out the names in alphabetical order and marks off the names of those who respond.

In this case, the endless silences after each name are an agony.

Captain Orr . . . (*Silence.*)

Captain Stanton . . . (*Silence.*)

Captain Williamson . . . (*Silence.*)

There is a pause, and finally comes a shattered voice from the back. 'Gone.'

'The morning's muster,' Captain Robert E. Hayes will chronicle, 'was a sad one for there were scarcely enough men left to form a company . . .'[107]

Corporal Short . . . (*Silence.*)

Private Wilson . . . (*Silence.*)

Sometimes, a quiet voice will tell the Sergeant that he had seen such-and-such killed. Or another will say that Wilson had taken a bullet to the abdomen, but the stretcher-bearers had got him.

But there is something else, too. Sometime after a particular name is met with silence there is a wailing, as his mates realise that he is gone, one of their own, uselessly slaughtered in this whole fucking useless battle.

'It is the saddest thing I've ever stood in,' Percy Bland thinks. 'All the brains of the battalion are gone. Only the stragglers left I'd say.' He is one such straggler on this cold miserable morning. And now he hears a sound he has never heard on a parade. Weeping.

'It's the first time I've ever seen crying among my cobbers.' He manages to hold back his own tears, but not the gloom that falls over all who remain. This remnant, this wreck, is the 14th.[108]

CHAPTER ELEVEN

THE AFTERMATH

Your breath first kindled the dead coal of wars
Between this chastised kingdom and myself
And brought in matter that should feed this fire;
And now 'tis far too huge to be blown out
With that same weak wind which enkindled it.[1]

Shakespeare, *King John*

He was always a chap that saw more of his men than the officers, and that was the trouble, we always thought that Bert Jacka should've had three VCs instead of a Military Medal and Victoria Cross, however, as the Gods willed it, that's what he got, but [he was a] very fine bloke, and would do anything for you.[2]

Private Arthur Tulloh

April 1917, Bapaume, lest we forget

The 3000 fine Australian soldiers of the 4th Brigade are no more. Of those men, no fewer than 2339 are casualties, of which at least 1000 are now POWs.

The 14th Battalion, in the prow of the attack, has been all but wiped out, having lost just over 600 officers and men as casualties from around 755 starters. The 16th Battalion had gone in with 23 officers and 870 men, and emerged with just three officers and 87 men.[3]

And for what?

Look, there is no doubt their achievement, as that of the entire 4th and 12th Brigades had been phenomenal.

As documented by the 14th Battalion history, they've just been through 'the most disastrous, the most bloody, yet perhaps the most glorious day in the history of the 4th Brigade ... after two sleepless nights, four Australian battalions with only rifles and hand bombs to defend themselves advanced nearly three-quarters of a mile over completely open country under hellish frontal and enfilade fire, forced their way through wire entanglement, seized the famous Hindenburg Line, and, though cut off from reinforcements or assistance of any kind, held it without artillery support for seven hours, repelling innumerable counter-attacks from a far more numerous enemy, backed up by powerful artillery.'[4]

But all for what?

Not only is the Hindenburg Line as formidable as it was, but Bullecourt itself has not been captured. Hell, not even a single yard of enemy trench has been secured for the Allies.

The achievement is not in doubt.

'Bullecourt,' the 14th Battalion history insists, 'will ever remain an imperishable monument to the heroism, the fortitude and the unflinching hardihood, of the Australian race.'[5]

But the betrayal and bungling is equally beyond question.

Inevitably, the bitterness among the Australians towards the British GHQ after the catastrophe of Bullecourt is palpable. General Gough had been told it would be a disaster, and it was obvious to all that it would be exactly that! And yet hundreds, nay *thousands*, of good men had gone to their graves because Gough had insisted.

For his part, Bean will have no doubt where ultimate responsibility for the debacle of Bullecourt must lie: 'The blame for this action must rest with the man who planned it, and that is Gough.'[6]

Some of the heaviest criticism will come from General John Monash, who will write: 'Our men are being put into the hottest fighting and are being sacrificed in hair-brained ventures, like Bullecourt . . .'[7]

For General Monash it is *criminally* negligent, or worse, just criminal, to have launched a major battle on little more than 12 hours' notice. For the life of him he cannot understand, for the lives of others, how anyone could have ordered it, and continued with the orders even when it was obvious that hundreds of men, if not thousands, were about to die uselessly. As for those who survive, there are more Australians taken prisoner by the Germans in this action than any other battle in this war so far. It is a debacle, a disaster and a disgrace.

And yet, no-one is more ropable than Jacka himself. The sheer waste of so many good men is what makes him furious.

Captain 'Mad Harry' Murray entirely agrees and, noting it as Gough's 'worst stunt', blames him for executing a plan relying on 'the use of unproven tanks, an infantry assault without artillery ... and under-estimating the enemy'.[8]

Strangely, from higher up the chain of command – from those who have been most responsible for this whole devastating debacle – there is no such misery. Despite Gough's obvious culpability, Field Marshal Sir Douglas Haig will refer to him as 'one of my best officers'.[9]

For he is a thruster, don't you know? Some thrusts work, some don't. There is no use crying over spilt milk, or thousands of lost or maimed lives.

But enough. For now, the survivors are formed up and marched to Bapaume.

'All that was left of our battalion was here now,' Ted Rule documents, 'and as the little handful marched by, Brigadier General Brand and the C.O., Colonel Peck, were sobbing like little schoolgirls, the tears running down their faces. The pick of our battalion was gone ...'[10]

Peck, particularly, is inconsolable, his shaking voice telling Ted Rule, 'God, to think that the last words I ever said to them were "Off you go, out to die, so I can get a decoration!"'[11]

For nearly two dozen of his officers, that final joke became terribly true.

That night, in the village of Ribemont, Jacka and Ted attend a concert at the local school (although 'concert' is being kind, it is in fact a 'sing-song' as an amused Rule notes). The lighting for the concert is innovative: a candle plugged in the inkwell at each school desk. Afterwards, the singers depart but Jacka stays behind with Ted, and begins to talk and talk; the rage running out of him. Ted has never seen him like this, he goes on 'talking until the candle fat ran down the desks and the light went out'. In the darkness, Jacka's bitter verdict is rendered: 'Not only do I demand efficiency from those below me, I expect it from my superiors.'[12]

Enough table talk, Jacka is going to do something about this; something that will matter.

Aware of the outrage, General Birdwood turns up a couple of days after the massacre to try to mollify these men of the Southern Cross, these ragged remnants of the once mighty 4th Brigade, in this gathering of the men of the 13th, 14th, 15th and 16th Battalions.

In his stentorian tones, his words ringing out over the shattered force, Birdwood reports himself, 'satisfied that the effect upon the whole situation by the Anzac attack has been of great assistance',[13] even if, Charles Bean will recount, 'everyone was aware that the 4th Australian Division had been employed in an experiment of extreme rashness, persisted in by the army commander after repeated warnings, and that the experiment had failed with shocking loss'.[14]

Perhaps everyone but Birdy?

For Birdwood goes on, wishing to read a message from the Fifth Army Commander, General Gough, apparently based on the report he had himself received from the Senior Tanks Commander, maintaining the tanks and their crews had accomplished everything asked of them.

'What was accomplished upon the occasion in question by the 4th Australian Brigade was the most wonderful feat of arms in the history of the war. [I also want] to congratulate the Tanks Corps upon their success.'[15]

There is a rumbling in the ranks, re the tanks, the fucking tanks.

He said that. He really said that!

'The tanks!' Percy Bland will state his disgusted views, and those of his mates. 'They weren't worth two bob. I mean, they didn't ... I don't think they fired a shot.'[16]

And nor did they crush the bloody wire, like they were meant to!

Jacka is only one of many who are stunned, and worse, by the words. Birdwood's speech is completely off the mark.

'We were in no mood for "eyewash",'[17] noted one of the 14th's veteran officers, Captain Robert Hayes.

But Birdy goes on.

'These [losses] have not been in vain.'[18]

There is a rumbling, as the dam walls start to break.

'Officers, hard-faced, hard-swearing men broke down,' George Mitchell will recount.[19]

After all, how could Birdwood spout such nonsense?

How could *anyone* possibly think the tanks had done anything remotely connected with success?

(The answer, it will later emerge, is because all Gough and the like have to go on is the report from the Senior Tanks Commander affirming that the tanks had completed their mission, just as required, and all is in order. And why wouldn't Watson think so, when he had personally received a congratulatory message from General Gough: 'The Army Commander is very pleased with the gallantry and skill displayed by your company in the attack today, and the fact that the objectives were subsequently lost does not detract from the success of the tanks.'[20])

'Boys,' Birdwood goes on, as his eyes dart warily around, 'I can assure you that no-one regrets this disaster that has befallen your brigade more than I do.'[21]

Well, they can think of a few. The spirits of their dead comrades. The parents, brothers, sisters, wives and children of their dead comrades. And us. But do go on, sir, we await your next platitude.

'I can assure you that none of your own officers had anything to do with the arrangements for the stunt . . .'[22]

Oh. Not even he is going to try to defend Gough?

But for right now, men, you must believe me.

'We did our utmost to have the stunt put off until more suitable arrangements could be made.'[23]

He won't actually *say* that General Gough is the one who must be held responsible, but . . .

'It was plain to me,' Rule will recount, 'that he shrank from being contaminated by the bloody fiasco.'[24]

What is not plain to them is that Birdwood himself is order-bound to defend a decision he hated: 'I am afraid it was impossible to tell them what I really felt,'[25] he tells General Holmes. If the men knew how their commanders despaired, how would any have the morale to fight?

General Brand, who is also there, takes the opportunity to apologise for what has happened.

None of it mollifies the likes of Albert Jacka or Ted Rule, the latter of whom records that, 'From a man-in-the-rank's point of view I think Gough should have been relieved of his command of the Fifth Army, and then publicly hung and burnt.'[26]

Charles Bean, if not going that far in his later assessment, regards General Gough as the worst culprit in the entire exercise.

'With almost boyish eagerness to deliver a death blow, the army commander broke ... rules recognised even by platoon commanders. When, despite impetuous efforts, he was unable to bring forward his artillery and ammunition in time to cut the wire, he adopted, on the spur of the moment, a scheme devised by an inexperienced officer of an experimental arm [the tanks], and called the attack on again for the following morning.

'Finally, after the tanks on the first trial had confirmed the worst fear of his subordinates, he insisted on repeating the identical operation the next day. Within two hours of the attack being delivered, every one of his impetuous predictions [sic] were being paid for by the crushing of the magnificent force which had been given to him to handle.'[27]

Finally, for his part, Captain William Watson will accept no responsibility at all.

Yes, he will concede that, 'The first battle of Bullecourt was a minor disaster. Our attack was a failure, in which the three brigades of infantry engaged lost very heavily indeed; and the officers and men lost seasoned Australian troops who had fought at Gallipoli, [who] could never be replaced. The Australians, in the bitterness of their losses, looked for scapegoats and found them in my tanks, but my tanks were not to blame ...

'If the snow had not made clear targets of the tanks, the tanks by themselves might have driven the enemy out of their trenches in the centre of the attack.'[28]

•

For all the criticism of those who had planned this catastrophe, no-one was in any doubt that if not for men like Albert Jacka it would have been so much worse. He had found the sunken road, patrolled the wire, guided the tanks, and liaised with Battalion Headquarters.

Some think he will be awarded a bar to his VC for his efforts, while others think a DSO more likely.

For the moment, as they make their way back to their billets in the town of Mametz, it is ... deeply unsettling from the first. For as they straggle their way down the main street once more, the villagers who had been expecting to see old friends again only have to see their shattered force before they start to weep. Even the invincible Incinerator Kate is seen to cry.

Jacka would if he could. Either way, right now he finds himself with a notable task.

For there have been lessons learnt from the bloody Battle of Bullecourt, the first of which is that if tanks and infantry are going to operate in tandem, the tanks *cannot* be under independent command, and sending soldiers and tanks forth without artillery support is – what was that phrase again, Jacka? – 'pure murder'.

But while it is one thing for such lessons to have been learnt bitterly by the men, it is quite another for those on high to have to be promulgated by those with promotion. This brutal folly must be understood by the higher powers so there is no repetition of such mechanised murderous madness. Those who had been at the coal-face of the battle are in no doubt just how big the blunder had been. 'I have often wondered,' Captain Harry Murray will note, 'whether those responsible merely sent the tanks as an encouraging gesture, relying upon the fighting qualities of the AIF to do the rest.'[29]

Well, it is appalling, and must be called out.

As Intelligence Officer it falls to Albert Jacka to write a report on the tanks. The clear protocol in such matters is to frame your language in such a manner that whatever criticisms there might be are referred to obliquely – lest it be seen as a junior officer being insubordinate to senior officers by criticising them. But Jacka is jack of it. He decides to go for broke, and go to town while he is there, and say what needs to be said about the tanks, their officers, and the whole wrong-headed idea of using them in the first place. He wants to set down how they should be used if they are used again.

He was there. He saw it up close. He was appalled. He *is* appalled. He can see what needs to be done and is happy to write it all down – using some of the writing skills he has recently picked up, attending Officer's School and preparing lectures.

His thoughts don't merely spill out onto the page, he *brands* them there in a tone of barely controlled righteous fury. When Jacka kept a diary at Gallipoli, even winning the VC was deemed worthy of no more than a sentence or so. But this is different. This was a rolling slaughter that must not be repeated and he is the man to put a stop to it. Each dithering disaster of the whole murderous affair is laid out in prose and skewered in type.

When Jacka hands his report to Colonel Peck and Colonel Drake-Brockman, entitled 'Special Report on the Tank Operation in Attack Nights of 10/11 April', they are taken aback by both its vicious accuracy and the fact it pulls no punches on account of rank – making clear where responsibility for the catastrophe lies: with superior officers.

> *The tank co-operation in the attack made on the Hindenburg Line on the night of the 10–11th of April, 1917, was useless or worse than useless . . .*
>
> *Tanks were late in arriving at rendezvous, which meant they were late in getting to the jumping off place. In fact, only three reached the latter place at all.*
>
> *Of the six tanks allotted to the brigade, five reached the rendezvous; one being out of action before that place was reached. Of the five: One, disregarding guidance tried to cross a deep, sunken road, and in consequence could not get out again. A second one was out of action through engine trouble before jumping off place was reached, leaving three only to co-operate in the attack.*
>
> *The tank crews seemed to know little or nothing of an attack by infantry, or nothing whatever about the particular operation they were to participate in. For instance: In the case of No 2 tank, the tank commander had not even synchronised his watch, his time being 5 minutes behind time as given to the infantry. Further: Tank crews did not even know the direction of the enemy. This is verified by the fact that they opened fire on our own troops, thereby causing us many casualties. One tank opened fire on our men at jumping off place, killing four and wounding others.*
>
> *The organisation seemed to be bad and no-one appeared to be in direct command of the show. This was shown by the fact*

that tanks wandered aimlessly about in every direction, thereby drawing enemy fire on us and all our trenches.

One tank only reached the objective and did good work, but was almost immediately put out of action by direct hits from a gun in Riencourt. Commanders and crews of other tanks seem to make no effort to reach their objectives and although [some] tanks were in no way damaged, even after the attack was well underway and tanks could have given great assistance in helping to connect up between US and the brigade on our left, they made no effort to go forward and wandered back, moving along the front of our jumping off place and finally pulling up alongside one of our dressing stations. Other tanks which had made no effort to get up their objectives were found in various places on fire, although they had not been hit by shells.

One crew in particular, asked why they had vacated their tank, stated that it caught fire but gave no reason for same. This same crew returned carrying two sandbags, one containing enamelware and the other food. Personal safety and comfort seemed to be their sole ambition.

Another crew was asked why they did not go forward to help clear a communication trench. They replied, 'They had no officer so could not do so'. This showed a great lack of initiative and that the whole affair, so far as this tank was concerned, to be the responsibility of one man, and that man gone; the tank could do no more though undamaged.

One tank returned almost to Reserve Battalion Headquarters, pulled up right on the skyline and in full view of Bullecourt, thereby making a splendid aiming mark and drawing severe enemy gunfire which made the route very dangerous for troops.

The whole outfit showed rank inefficiency and [in] some cases tank crews seemed to lack British tenacity and pluck, and that determination to go forward at all costs, which is naturally looked for in Britishers.[30]

It ends with not just a punch, but a body blow to any delusional senior commander who still sees some light at the end of the tanked tunnel they are digging: *'In my opinion, manned by the bravest of crews and placed directly under the Infantry Officers concerned in operation, they would be of great help but they should NEVER be relied upon as the sole arm of support in an attack by Infantry. Further, when tanks are being got into position, we think it's absolutely necessary that heavy barrage be put up by our guns to deaden the sound of the TANKS.*

In our case not a shot was fired when TANKS were taking up their position, and so the whole operation was given away to the enemy. SGD. A, JACKA. CAPT. FAD.[31]

In short? The whole tank exercise has been a tragic farce, made worse by the insistence of the Fifth Army's General Gough that his suicidal orders be followed. And it is not just Gough who stands accused. The report makes the very serious charge that the British tank crews had been guilty of nothing less than cowardice – a very grave charge, which, if accepted, will see court martials.

It is strong stuff. Far too strong for Jacka's military career to survive. Even when on his best behaviour the man borders on insubordination, but this is *explosive*. And so, Peck and Drake-Brockman decide to take the bullets for him. Jacka's scathing intelligence report on the lack of intelligence of High Command will be sent to higher commanders, but with Peck's and Drake-Brockman's names on it. Jacka's entire report is retyped (and reset, his whacking CAPITALS for words like NEVER becoming placid lowercase, and 'my opinion' replaced by 'our opinion') and sent on, personally signed with a flourish by the commanders of the 14th and 16th Battalions of the AIF.

The reaction is swift.

General Holmes, the General Officer Commanding the 4th Division, wishes to see both officers, on the double!

Do you realise what you have done?

What you are asserting?

The consequences?

In no uncertain terms, Holmes tells them.

'This is the strongest thing in the way of a military report that I have ever seen. I want you to consider most carefully whether it should go forward or not. Can you substantiate everything that is in it, because if you cannot it may mean very serious consequences to you officers who signed it?'[32]

Neither Peck nor Drake-Brockman waver.

They insist that it be sent. It is a matter of honour.

A thousand men have died because of these infernal tanks and the appalling way in which they were applied. Thousands more will die if things are not rectified. Attacking in this manner, with no rehearsal, no co-ordination between tanks and infantry, and no-one properly in charge is insane. The report must be sent. And yes, we can back it up.

And what is more?

'We did not think it fair to hide ourselves behind the skirts of our Intelligence Officers when such serious allegations are being made,' Lieutenant Colonel Drake-Brockman would later recount of their attitude. 'We demanded that an inquiry should be held into the whole thing.'[33]

Holmes reluctantly agrees and, not surprisingly, the report indeed explodes like a bomb through intelligence, outraging many of the brass.

The rumours reverberate immediately, and General Pompey Elliott will later insist that, after General Birdwood discovered who the actual author of the report was, Birdwood sent for Jacka and told him, 'You must destroy all your notes of this occurrence. You will destroy every copy of your report sent to [Australian Imperial Force's Administrative Headquarters] Horseferry Road, so that every trace of the incident will disappear.'[34]

Word has it that Gough himself orders that the report 'should not enter the record'.[35]

Whatever the intent might have been of senior officers, numerous copies of the report will circulate. For many others take a shine to its frank rebuke and sharp 'suggestions'.

Even General Holmes will finally decide that the report is correct and pen his own, with a similar theme.

'The reasons for our failure to hold the line were in my opinion: Owing to the tanks giving no assistance whatever to the Infantry, the latter had to advance under heavy machine gun fire across open ground and clamber over wire which was in many places quite undamaged.

This caused heavy casualties and the troops, when they reached their objectives, were in considerable confusion and very reduced in numbers.'[36]

One man in particular, the Commanding Officer of the AIF's 3rd Division, General John Monash, reads the report so often he can practically recite it. That maestro of battle has long been musing how to fit the tank into his orchestra of attack, and the answers are all clearly set out in this report of ... Peck and Drake-Brockman, you say? It adds a new coda that beats insistently into his thoughts for future battles. The tank could win this war if used properly – and it could also lose it if they keep using it like they did at Bullecourt. Things will change, and this intelligence report will be the blueprint for battle in the future.

As for Jacka, he is not told by Peck or Drake-Brockman that his name has been removed from the most important document he has written in his life. They know that Jacka would not let them do it, he would insist on taking the fight up himself.

When rumblings are heard that an intelligence report of Bullecourt is causing ruptures, Jacka concludes that his hopes of promotion are on hold permanently. Well, it is something he knew before he wrote the thing. It has been said, it has been heard, so publish and be damned.

•

By the time of the second Anzac Day, the 14th Battalion has moved back to their favoured town of Ribemont, where the intent is for them to remain for many weeks and perhaps months, to recover, integrate their reinforcements, and train.

For the survivors of Bullecourt it is precious time to try to recover, and Albert Jacka is keen that their daily lives also have joy in them, which is why on the second Anzac Day he organises a sports day to be held, straight after the morning's church parade – a time when Diggers can compete against each other in a variety of sports, from sprints, to three-legged races, to tug of war, to myriad other events.

As it happens, Ted Rule is chatting to Bert Jacka when – lo and behold! – 'the crowd split in two, and Incinerator Kate come flying through it'. She is pushing a wheelbarrow filled with wood at great speed and she is pursued by, hang on . . . *Incinerator Kate*, holding a piece of wood? What the hell is going on?

'Faster and faster went the wheelbarrow, but the firewood gained steadily on it.' Now, the first Incinerator Kate slips over, her dress goes up, revealing khaki breeches! One of the Diggers has frocked up perfectly as the Incinerator, only to be discovered and chased by the *real* Incinerator, who thunders in with her plank of wood to beat her doppelganger's *derriere*. The Fake Kate catches a hiding to remember as 'she' rushes to escape from the wild windmill of plank spanking revenge that is the Real Kate. The two Kates race around the troops as they witness a one-sided battle and beating the likes of which they will never see again. Bert Jacka roars with delight at the surreal spectacle.

'I thought,' Rule will note of Jacka's reaction, 'he would never recover from his laughter.'[37]

You have to make your own fun in this man's army, even if it means becoming a woman.

As it happens, on this very day, Rule has something to celebrate. He and his friend Lloyd Gill have been commissioned as 2nd Lieutenants, a good effort in rising from the ranks just like Jacka, and it is Jacka himself who invites them to the Officers' Mess now.

'You and [2nd Lieutenant Lloyd] Gill come over and have tea with us,' he tells Rule.

As good as his word, when Rule and Gill arrive at the Officers' Mess – a village school they have taken over for the duration of their stay – they are warmly welcomed by Jacka, who, unaccustomed as he is, even makes a speech.

'This is the first time we have had the pleasure of entertaining you newlyweds, and I wish to welcome you to the brotherhood,' he says. 'In being chosen by Colonel Peck to fill the places of those who have gone out, you have been given a great responsibility. It's a great battalion; let us see to it that we make it greater. That's all I have to say. Spread yourselves and make yourselves at home.'

There is a warm round of applause from their fellow officers, before one of them chips in.

'That's right, spread yourselves but don't make yourselves at home with the skipper's girl. That's all *I* have to say.'[38]

At this point Jacka laughs and lightly throws a haversack at the wag's head, and there is general merriment all round. The skipper's girl is actually the school-mistress of the village, a petite beauty who has obviously taken a huge shine to the man she refers to as '*Al-berrrr Jjjjjack-errrr*', who she has been thrilled to accommodate in her home with several other officers. She is indeed the heart-throb of the officer corps, but she has only eyes for Alberrrrr. A different kind of man might have taken every chance of sharing her amorous affections in the wee hours . . .

'But Jacka was in love with his company. Not many of us looked forward to fighting, but we all knew Jacka's ambition. He was longing for the day when he could lead D Company into battle.'[39]

If that day comes, it will no longer be as part of General Birdwood's I Anzac Corps as, at the end of April, in an enormous divisional parade at Mametz, the 4th Division does a march-past – *eyessss . . . rightttt!* – General Birdwood, and formally takes their leave of I Anzac Corps to join II Anzac Corps instead. They will be under the overall command of General Alexander Godley and be operating in the big push on the Western Front up at the Belgian town of Messines, not far from the town of Passchendaele.

They have, at least, been promised rest.

And yet, further upset comes with the news that they are also to lose Colonel Peck as commander of the 14th Battalion, as the 3rd Division Commander General John Monash had now tapped him to join his HQ staff, leaving a vacancy as Commander of the 14th Battalion.

'Regret at his departure was universal,'[40] the Official History of the 14th Battalion will note, and it is all the more so when his temporary replacement is announced as, wait for it . . . Major Otto Fuhrmann. For Albert Jacka, if it is not the final straw, it runs it close. He had had no problem following the commands of Colonel Peck, as he had recognised his qualities and his care of the 14th. Whatever crazy stunts they had been sent on, Peck had at least tried to limit the damage.

But being commanded by Major Fuhrmann, even for a short time? Jacka can barely bear it.

Given his experience with him at Pozières, particularly – where in his view Fuhrmann had gone missing – Jacka frankly *knows* he would be able to do a better job than Fuhrmann. (For his part, and whisper it quietly, well out of earshot of Bert, Ted Rule has his own verdict of why Jacka is not promoted. 'I often wonder to what heights Jacka would have climbed had he possessed the amiable disposition of either Harry Murray or Percy Black. I think Jacka belonged to an age when it was possible for the individual to challenge with a club the right of leadership in the tribe.' Different clubs are in use today, and in these genteel realms Jacka, as the British would say, is 'unclubbable'. He is a man apart but in this Great War that means 'his peculiar talents were a hindrance rather than a help in climbing to the higher ranks'.[41])

Mid-May 1917, Mametz, bullied and beaten

Jacka follows the news, day by day, the best he can. Everyone at the 14th Battalion does, particularly those who have survived the first, failed attack on Bullecourt.

For early in May another attack on Bullecourt has gone in, using the 1st, 2nd and 5th Australian Divisions, *this time* with the benefit of artillery to break up the wire – huge artillery, in fact, courtesy of both the First and Third Armies each contributing 12 batteries of heavy artillery to bolster what the Fifth Army already had – the way it should have been done in the first place.

The Australian 2nd Division and the British 62nd Division – at last, they've made their move! – had attacked at 3.45 am on 3 May 1917 and fought bitterly to hold on to the breaches they had made in the German line. The 5th Australian Division had been thrown in to support them and, after bitter fighting going for nearly a fortnight, the Germans had finally withdrawn from what was now merely the smoking ruins of what once had been Bullecourt. The strategic importance of the village? Just about nothing, bar pushing the line back by about 1500 yards. The overall AIF casualties totalled 7482 from the three Australian Divisions, with about 2200 killed.

The extraordinary thing?

Despite the fact that since the beginning of the Somme offensive – which was meant to change everything, and bring the Germans to their knees – no fewer than 140,000 British lives have been lost, and the contours of the Western Front are substantially unchanged. Just as eight months of the Gallipoli campaign and 32,000 lives lost had seen little overall change in the ground held – only 800 acres, keep the change – so too, here.

Albert Jacka is ropable. There *must* be a better way of doing this! And he is not the only one.

'War of attrition!' George Mitchell, notes. 'To us it was the last word in ineptitude. The higher command seemed to say, "We will give you three dead British for two dead Germans."'[42]

The dead can appear among them at any time; there is no rhyme or reason to it, as Ted Rule knows. Take this day, as recorded in his diary: 'Lieutenant Ernie Hill was given charge of my boys and was put on to carry rations to the front line. Half-way up, and out in the open where there was no trench, a shell lobbed right into the centre of them and laid out eight, besides splashing the rations all over the place.'[43]

The rations are retrieved and eaten. The men are dead and buried.

•

Despite Jacka's disappointment at the elevation of Fuhrmann, at least in his own case, as a comfortable Captain, he has the pleasure of relinquishing his position as 14th Battalion Intelligence Officer and for the first time taking over command of an entire large unit – and no less than the very one he had made famous, D Company.

Back to action – and his command is well received. Jacka VC is back with us!

Others, mostly senior officers, are a little more dubious, on the reckoning that such a superb front-line soldier as Jacka would be out of his element on the training turf and parade ground – unable to understand why his soldiers could not do what he could do.

And yet the opposite proves to be the case.

'Everyone knows that Jacka was a front-line soldier of the highest grade, but it must not be thought that he stopped there,' one Digger will chronicle. 'He was a sound administrator, a keen disciplinarian so long as discipline was tempered with common sense, and he handled a parade like an Aldershot sergeant major.'[44]

Day after day, Jacka works his men hard on long route marches, bayonet drill, marching in fours, gas drill and the like. A friendly rivalry arises between him and A Company's dashing Captain Harold Wanliss, B Company's Captain Reg Jones, and C Company's Don MacDermid as to whose company was finest and best prepared for the battles to come, and despite them all still grieving the losses at Bullecourt, Jacka and Wanliss, particularly, prove to be key figures in restoring the 14th Battalion to vigour as reinforcements continue to flood in.

'They had more influence on the battalion than you realise,' one of their Diggers will later note. 'It was not only in the line that their men strove to look well in their skippers' eyes but when we were out it was just as noticeable. When Jacka had us, Kiwi [Polish] was always much more evident than when any of the second-raters had us ... On parade every man seemed to do his best to look and act like a soldier. I sometimes dodged parade, just for the pleasure of watching the company drill under Jacka. To my mind they used to look as well as the Guard mounted at Buckingham Palace and yet the same men under another officer could look very rag-time.'[45]

Paraaaade, leeeft turn!

By the riiiight, quick march!

'Captain Jacka VC had D Coy,' a Sergeant John Malseed will later chronicle to the 14th Battalion's official historian, 'and it was wonderful to see the influence he had on the men. They fell in and drilled and marched like Guards when he was on parade and later when we went into the line it was the same; every man seemed out to do his best.'[46]

Ted Rule would note just how much Jacka's men adored him.

'His bravery is known far and wide – it was a by-word far beyond the AIF – but his good fellowship is not. His praise was never lavishly bestowed, but his men treasured it more than medals.'[47]

D Company is now more than a fierce fighting unit, it is a family.

Late May 1917, Messines Ridge, hello, I must be going

Another month, another battle.

In mid-May, Jacka's mob leaves Ribemont, with that scuttling mess that signals a departure is on hand, and camps, women and other non-carriable items are abandoned in unseemly haste. (It is always the same; the strange tug of a temporary home. These sudden stays embed you in the lives of the French, and they seem surprised that you are about to leave! So soon? Yes, and it does not need a Sassoon to capture the sweet sorrow of new friends departing for good; it is written on every man's face. So they make their sullen march to the station and wait for the whistle that will signal the next chapter of their lives.)

They chug to Bailleul, all down and march to the farming village of Doulieu just ten miles from the German front lines at Messines. The *thump* in the distance, the tiny tremor that flicks into a quake when the Hun shells score a concentrated blast, that is the sound they will wake and sleep to now. When will they see the front again?

Three weeks, Jacka is told and the grim word is passed on. Three? *Oui*. It is a bloody liberty – they are still trying to recover from the devastation of Bullecourt – but they are promised an extensive rest after this one battle. And, given that Monash is planning this battle, they know it will be entirely different.

Instead of a battle plan formed up on a few hours' notice as had happened at bloody Bullecourt, everything will be done carefully.

All soldiers are to familiarise themselves with the geography of the area they are to attack, to understand the landmarks, where the farms are, the sources of fresh water, and where the Regimental Aid Posts will be when the battle begins. Courtesy of reconnaissance flights, captured German soldiers and scouting expeditions, the position and strength of all the Hun defences from artillery batteries to ammunition dumps to barbed wire belts to trench configurations and the positions of reserve battalions are not only understood but formed up into scale models so that everyone from platoon commanders up can have a clear idea of the battlefield they are embarking on dominating.

Ready now?

No, not ready. This time, the painstaking preparation includes placing 19 mines containing 455 tons of explosive directly under the defending Germans – with the newly formed 1st Australian Tunnelling Company doing much of the honours, for many months.

The evening before Messines, General Charles Harington gives a briefing to the press.

'Gentlemen,' he says, 'we may not make history tomorrow, but we shall certainly change the geography.'[48]

Early June 1917, Post-Bullecourt, Major pain

There are commanders who fit a battalion straight away, then there are the square pegs that have to be hammered into round holes, and *then* there is Major Eliazar Margolin, a Russian-born man pegged into the 14th by Brand with no give either way – though Brand will later claim that Margolin had been given temporary command of the 14th at General Birdwood's insistence. Ted Rule notes that Major Margolin, who has come to them direct from the 16th Battalion, speaks English that is so broken that every sentence can cut you. Oh, but there is one English sentence he has down absolutely perfectly: 'The 16th Battalion always do this . . .'[49]

The 14th don't give a damn what the 16th always do, but it is clear Major Margolin is pining for his old command and regretting his new one more each day every. Or 'each and every day' as people used to English might say. One sunny afternoon, the 14th are at a slouching rest when who should march by but Margolin's beloved 16th. At their head is the 16th marching band, and even the most loyal member of the 14th must admit they are bloody good. Major Margolin beams with pride until a voice from the 14th cries out: 'Give us your band and we'll give you back your bloody Russian.'[50]

No go. They are stuck with him.

'After Peck's virile leadership,' one officer will note, 'this cracked up the 14th altogether and nearly broke Captain Wanliss's heart as he had to hold the battalion together . . .'[51]

Major Margolin tries to be organised and set an example in the dugouts. (After all, the 16th Battalion always do this.) For instance, why scramble about when an attack is occurring? Be prepared. The BAB codebook is required to receive messages from HQ, so Major Margolin has it neatly hung on a string, directly in front of his nose in his dugout.

Unfortunately, when shelling starts, he tends to become forgetful. An urgent message arrives from HQ, coded, that requires a quick answer. Well, to do that the BAB is required so Margolin hurls himself about the dugout searching for it! Where the hell can it be? The men don't understand what he is about and his words give them little clue: 'De Bab, De Bab, de bloody Bab!' De what? The penny drops, and Margolin is led back to where de BAB is hanging and waiting. The 14th is resolute: De sooner de bloody Margolin is gone de bloody better.

•

For now, they must prepare for the battle ahead, and it is here where Jacka is at his best. While other officers look at the scale models of the Messines trenches and defences that have been made, Jacka spends *hours* actively studying them.

For though blessed with an intuitive understanding of military matters, Jacka has also come to appreciate that knowledge is power, and that knowing where the enemy guns are positioned, their likely lines of fire, and their avenues of advance and retreat makes you stronger. Not content with just impressions, Jacka takes detailed notes, a practice he had first begun at Gallipoli and continued since.

Frankly, Jacka's mob are not quite ready for this battle, having only fought a major battle two months before, but orders are orders and these orders are to attack Messines Ridge in Belgium, a place with crucial high ground dominance over the Belgian town of Ypres.

The 14th Battalion's 4th Brigade is part of a massive force, the II Anzac Corps including the New Zealand Division, the AIF's 4th Division, and the British 25th Division.

Battle of Messines

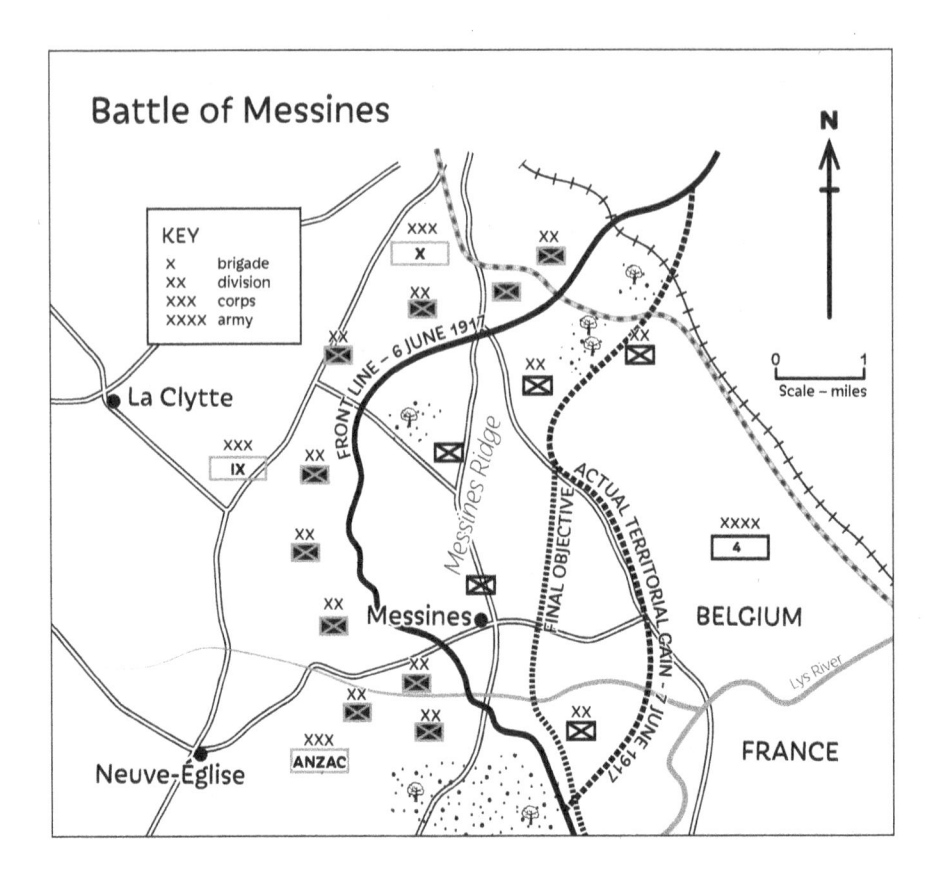

[Map of the Battle of Messines showing front line 6 June 1917, final objective, actual territorial gain 7 June 1917, with locations including La Clytte, Neuve-Église, Messines, Messines Ridge, Lys River, and the Belgium/France border. Key: x brigade, xx division, xxx corps, xxxx army.]

In all, 100,000 men are lined up to attack across a front of eight miles of the German lines. Jacka's mob are on the hard right of the line, positioned in the second wave to go in after the New Zealanders.

As a heavy artillery barrage opens up on those lines, they are waiting for just one thing, and it happens at 3.10 am. For it is at precisely that time that the 19 powerful mines directly under the German trenches – no less than a million pounds of explosive in all, placed there by assiduous tunnelling over many months – explode with a massive roar.

'The giant explosions ripped the earth, bursting through the darkness with a deep crimson hue which lit the sky for miles around and then slowly faded like a setting sun.'[52]

British war correspondent Philip Gibbs will describe it as 'the most diabolical splendour I have ever seen'.[53]

Across the entire line German soldiers are hurled skywards in fiery conflagrations, and the Allied troops rush forth.

By now promoted in rank, Lieutenant George Mitchell of the 48th Battalion notes that while the German forces in front were shattered, those to the side were intact, angry and accurate.

'Most of the fire came from the flank of the attack making the Australian front probably the hottest part of the line. Almost hourly it seemed that new guns, heavy and of light velocity were joining the fray. The peculiar snarling note of their shells seemed to dominate the land.'[54]

Jacka's mob are held in reserve for two days before, with B Company, under the command of Captain Reg Jones, they move forward to relieve the AIF's 50th Battalion.

'With darkness came our relief,' one soldier will record. 'Captain Jacka V.C. coldly efficient, came up with a bunch of men and took over from us.'[55]

With the Germans now substantially broken in this part of the Western Front, the next challenge is to hold on to the trenches that have been won – the green line on their maps the Diggers had been told to take, and defend.

But Jacka thinks they might be able to do better. When the sun comes up, it feels like the ground ahead has – dare he think it? – a skeleton crew of Germans, at best, defending it. There is only one way to find out. That afternoon he and Captain Reg Jones decide to reconnoitre, and despite heavy fire from their flanks, they make dashes from cover to cover in the sun-dappled landscape, eager to see if there are German outposts in the areas right in front of them. Towards evening the two captains each detail a patrol of 12 men who advance several hundred yards before returning to the unit.

For the moment there appears to be little German presence ahead, and the opportunity is too good to miss. After brief fights that secure Jacka a German field gun and machine gun, while Jones captures three machine guns, they bring their men forward and start to dig in, establishing a strong line of outposts.

'Jones' and Jacka's activities,' the 14th Battalion History will note, 'resulted in an advance of the battalion nearly half a mile into hostile territory, the work of these two intrepid and able officers typical of Australian commissioned officers' work at the very best.'[56]

In a war where, at places like Pozières, every yard gained had been bought with a dozen lives, the opportunity to get 750 yards for free is like manna from heaven. With their own men dug in, Jacka and Jones alert flanking British units to move forward in turn and establish two particularly strong defensive posts on two farms – DeConinck and Delporto – that have heavy stone buildings, just like grandfather used to make. If the Germans counter-attack, these will be the English troops' own pillboxes. Captain Reg Jones and his men use another farmhouse for the same purpose. By the time they are relieved, 48 hours after moving forward, Monash's plan in this area has succeeded beyond his wildest dreams.

'When we came out of the line at Messines,' one of the soldiers will recount, '[Captain Jacka] addressed the company and told them he was proud of them. The company was no less proud of their gallant skipper.'[57]

Yes, it is tragic to have lost five men killed and 45 wounded, but it would have been so much worse, and their achievements so much less, if not for such leadership.

(Both men have done brilliantly, and are nearly as daring as Captain Murray of the 13th Battalion, who, word has it, went so far forward on a scouting mission that he got to the River Lys – two miles from Messines – and even swam it to examine German defences on the far bank!)

Meanwhile, as Jacka settles back into the 14th Battalion's support lines, he soon finds himself on the topside of a trench that his Diggers have dug *particularly* deep in the hope of surviving, and he gazes down upon them with some benevolence.

They are good men, this latest lot, if still very young and wet behind the ears.

The men, in turn, look back at him with shock.

What is he *doing* up there?

If he's *lucky*, he will have only his arse shot off! And by the increasing amount of German fire in their area it feels highly likely that he will be unlucky.

One of the new recruits, big Bill Dawe bears it for as long as he can before he simply can't bear it any more.

'It's much safer down here, sir,' he offers to Jacka.

Translation: For *fuck's sake*, get down!

'Don't worry,' Jacka replies evenly, 'if they're going to get you, they'll get you wherever you are.'[58]

Just an instant later a withering burst of German machine-gun fire scudders along the top of the trench, only narrowly missing the 14th Battalion's hero. Dawe cannot help himself. In a split second he has reached up, placed his arms around Jacka's legs and pulled him down to safety!

True, it is undignified, and yes, both the Western Front and Gallipoli are littered with graves of other men who have tried sudden moves on Albert Jacka VC. But Dawe had operated from nothing other than protective instinct and can only speak honestly.

'We can't afford to lose you, sir,' he says, as Jacka picks himself up from the bottom of the trench.[59]

For a couple of seconds, things seem to hang in the balance and it is not out of the question that Dawe will receive an uppercut for his trouble, but Jacka seems to recognise both that the young man's intent had been pure, and that his life may indeed have been saved. For with a curt nod, he wanders off, leaving the open-mouthed Dawe behind him.

Had he really just done that? Dared to force Albert Jacka VC to do something that he had not wanted to do?

And he is not the only one who cannot quite believe it. 'You shouldn't have manhandled the skipper like that,' the corporal remonstrates.

But the more Dawe thinks about it, the more the young fellow is convinced he need make no apology. 'I'd give my life for that man as easily as I'd give you a cigarette.'[60]

Understood. As will be recorded in the Official History of the 14th Battalion, 'The unit's work had been not only clean, crisp and efficient, but of a distinctly high order. The Corps Commander sent a congratulatory message.'[61]

One who is impressed, in spite of himself, is the CO of the 14th Battalion, Major Margolin, who – despite having fallen into a shell-hole in the battle and so badly twisting his knee he can barely walk, and will shortly be placed on the invalid list – writes a citation recommending that Jacka receive a medal for his work: '*He had a patrol out into hostile area, successfully drove back several snipers who were harassing our lines, seized a Machine Gun and occupied DeConinck Farm and returned to his main line. This he improved and after arranging co-operation with the British forces on left he established a strong line of outposts and occupied 600 yards in front of "green line". He sent back most lucid and comprehensive information and throughout displayed his usual coolness and judgement.'*[62]

Appropriately, as they had done it together, Margolin writes much the same citation for Captain Reg Jones.

The two captains and their men have done well.

Not all battalions have. The 37th Battalion, under Colonel Walter Smith, has been so ordinary that the 3rd Division's commander, General John Monash, will take particular aim at him, noting, 'I am of the opinion that under the stress of the fighting, he personally lost control and grasp,'[63] and on the strength of that assessment, Smith is removed from command and given an administrative role in the back areas.

June 1917, Bailleul, knockout justice

Trouble in the ranks.

Not bad trouble, just drunken trouble which, nevertheless, risks turning into double-trouble if it is not dealt with quickly. After returning from one of the *estaminets* – French for piss-poor pub – one of the 14th Battalion's Diggers is so full of ink he is in the mood for a stink and really does not care who with. Shouting, carrying on, he throws wild punches at anyone who gets within range. One of the few who ignores it is Jacka. No matter that he is a teetotaller, he understands that sometimes the men need to let off steam in this way, to a point, and trusts that one of the junior officers, if not the Digger's own mates, will quickly sort it out. Certainly, it is against regulations to behave like this, but that is neither here nor there.

'Providing that men were good soldiers in the line, he turned a blind eye to their failings when out of it.'[64]

On this occasion, however, the remonstrances of others do nothing to quiet the fellow and it is now to the point – with much shouting, and a mob of Diggers gathering – that Jacka himself must reluctantly get involved.

'What's all this about?' Captain Jacka asks, as he wades through the parting mob, like Moses through the Red Sea.

The drunken Digger stands before him, unburdening himself of various grievances, most of which he appeared to have spied at the bottom of several bottles of wine.

'Well, Nugget,' Jacka replies evenly, 'you can have what you like. Either come up before me in the morning, or else take me on now for a few rounds.'[65]

Take *Jacka* VC on?

Actually take a few swings at the most famous soldier in the Australian Army?

He'd really rather not.

And yet?

And yet when the mob guffaws at his obvious reluctance, that bloody well *does it*. If Jacka is up for a belting, for a hiding just like father used to make, then Nugget is the man to give him one, oh, yes, he is. And youse blokes may as well be witness to it.

Great!

'Come on now, make a ring,' Jacka says, and in no time at all it is done, with a 12-foot circle drawn on the rich French soil with a line going right through the middle. The usual rules apply. They will go at it, bare knuckle, for three-minute rounds until one either goes down for 10 seconds, or refuses to come out at the bell, or yells 'Uncle!' Oh, how the men roar!

Yes, in the absence of a bell, a verbal *ding-ding* to commence the ding-dong will have to do. As the men press close, emitting a guttural roar that comes not just from them but from ages past, the two begin to shape up and the fists begin to fly. Nugget might be big, and drunk, but he is fast and strong, and if just one of his wild haymakers connects, Bert will find himself in the middle of next week. But Bert is faster, and nimble, and has no trouble swaying out of the way of most of Nugget's furious flurries, before crashing in with his own body blows to the wild man's ribs. But enough. One blow on Nugget's chin throws him back on his heels.

'Oh, no,' murmurs the mob. This is not going to go for as long as they would like.

Another doubles Nugget over.

'Oh, no . . .'

A final one straightens him up again.

'Whack, whack, whack,' runs Ted Rule's report on the bout.

It is over.

Nugget is not sure if he is Arthur or Martha, and right now can only be sure that Bob is not his uncle. But he is certain he does not want to go on with it.

'Off you go and have a sleep,' Jacka says gently, pointing to the billets. 'You'll get all the fighting you want in the near future.'

Nugget staggers off, leaving Jacka's diarist, Rule, to sagely note: 'Of course, it is not every officer that could do this sort of thing – perhaps there was not another that could fight with one of his men and preserve his dignity. But Jacka was . . . well, just Jacka.'[66]

Now if you are going into the ring with Jacka, you had better put some effort in and punch him properly. This was something his own batman discovered when he wandered into camp late one night, half soused and fully pissed, and unwisely picked a fight with his boss: put your hands up and let's settle it. Jacka belts him and is extremely disappointed with his easy victory.

'You drunken bounder!' yells Jacka. 'I'm goin' to crim you for this. If you had put up a decent fight, I'd have let you off.'[67]

Remember to hit your officer harder in the future.

(Not for nothing will Charles Bean later comment with regard to Jacka's approach, '. . . some of his methods could not have been adopted generally in the AIF without disaster. For example, his way of punching his men, on occasions, instead of "criming" them, may have worked well enough in Jacka's case but it would have wrecked any army in which it was generally attempted.'[68]

18 June 1917, Western Front, double-crossed

The news breaks. While some had thought another Victoria Cross would be appropriate for Jacka's actions at Bullecourt back in April – finding the sunken road, spotting the wire and enemy disposition, capturing the officer, guiding the tanks and submitting cogent reports throughout the battle – he is at least to receive a Bar to his Military Cross.

The citation reads: '*Capt. Albert Jacka, V.C., M.C., Infantry. For conspicuous gallantry and devotion to duty. He carried out a daring reconnaissance of the enemy's position and obtained most valuable information. Later, he rendered invaluable assistance in guiding troops to their assembly positions . . .*'[69]

Ted Rule is bitterly disappointed, 'Most of us considered that it should have been a bar to his V.C.'[70]

Much later Brigadier Charles Brand will insist that he had put Jacka forward for a VC but had been ignored, 'because VCs are rarely awarded when enterprises fail'.[71]

For his part in the battle, Harry Murray – who was immediately made a temporary Major in the wake of Messines – received a bar to his DSO, though in his case, too, many argued that a bar to his VC would have been more appropriate. Murray will later note, 'Birdwood personally told me it would have been a bar to my VC had we won the battle.'[72]

A small parenthesis here. The investiture will, nevertheless, be a grand occasion when it takes place for Murray on a brief trip to London in early June. Arriving at Hyde Park for the mass investiture by the King of no fewer than six VCs and 444 other decorations – the largest since 1856, at the end of the Crimean War – Murray presents his card, while the hundreds of other awardees hover close by.

'What are you getting?' the English Colonel who is presiding over the affair for His Majesty asks him peremptorily in the off-hand manner of a butcher asking how many sausages and chops he would like on this day.

Murray rises to the occasion.

'The Victoria Cross, the DSO, and DSO and bar,' he replies.

'Oh, Christ,' the Colonel replies, 'you had better go first.'[73]

And he does, which already puts him well ahead of his late mate, Major Percy Black, who for his own investiture of a DSO for his derring-do at Mouquet Farm, had very nearly been run over by a bus, just outside Buckingham Palace!

'I'll be glad to get back to the battalion,' Black had said. 'A man's not safe here.'[74] Close parenthesis.

Most extraordinary?

Of those who had been in the tanks on the night – the bloody *tanks*, which had let them down so badly – there were awards of two Military Crosses, one Distinguished Conduct Medal, and three Military Medals. No, really. (Brand's notion of medals rarely being awarded when enterprises fail does not seem to apply to them.)

Not long afterwards, Jacka's view of senior officers will be further battered when he hears that, while Major Margolin had indeed recommended both him and Reg Jones for a citation for their work at Messines – a couple of months after Bullecourt – it is only Reg who receives the Military Cross, as one of five decorations for the 14th Battalion, while he gets bugger-all.

This may or not have something to do with authorship of the Tank Report, but, either way, it really feels like there are officers higher up who want him neither recognised nor promoted.

•

This fine morning, it is time for a hunt. The sky is grey, the light barely filters through the clouds, but if you look closely you can see the enemy. Not the ones hiding in their trenches, but one of those of bolder temperament who decides to be a man in No Man's land and, look, here is one who is at the head of a party who have the mettle to come and observe us. Time to teach these *schweinhunden* a lesson, and a rifle is shouldered, a sight taken and two shots are fired.

They rip through the right thigh of Bert Jacka and the Germans watching see him fall. A bold man indeed, but he has learnt that ... wait a moment, the other two Tommies next to him are charging! *Mein Gott*, they are raiding us!

Two Germans die in seconds before the rest retreat and the two Australian soldiers return to No Man's Land and the grievously wounded Bert Jacka. He is bleeding, badly. No, don't bloody stand, Bert! Lie still! The two soldiers drag Bert back to safety, and into the care of a startled medic, who realises that he might be the man who has to pronounce a hero dead.

•

The wound proves bad enough that Jacka is once more sent to the 3rd London General Hospital before, six weeks later, being discharged to recover at Perham Downs.

At least there are things there to keep him busy, beyond recovering physically and mentally from the trauma he has been through.

For Jacka, one thing is to appear at the hastily convened Dardanelles Commission, to testify to this body set up in London by Prime Minister Asquith (at the furious insistence of Winston Churchill no less) as to just what had gone wrong at Gallipoli. It is an attempt to get to the bottom of the whole disaster, and one of those who gives testimony before Jacka is none other than Colonel Neville Howse VC – Australia's first winner of the VC, back in the Boer War, who Jacka had seen up close on the evening of the first landing at Gallipoli. Howse does not mince words.

'I will recommend to my government, when the war is over, under no conceivable conditions to trust the Imperial authorities with the medical arrangements for the care of the Australian sick and wounded.'[75]

The lack of care for those first wounded on Gallipoli was not just an error or a mistake. In Howse's view it was 'criminal negligence'.[76]

Albert Jacka VC does not agree. He has seen criminal negligence in battles, but he was part of the desperate struggle to save wounded men from the first landing and he knows plans were in place; inadequate though they were to the unexpected disaster of the infamous landing. Jacka notes that the shortfall in organisation was substantially closed up in the Australian fashion, by using elbow grease, fencing wire and willing hearts.

'If at any time the arrangements did not prove sufficient it was always remedied by volunteers from infantry battalions. In those days, of course, we did not have the same ideas we have now, and everyone used his own initiative and detailed a certain number of men to assist, and the probability is that the higher command did not know what was taking place.'[77]

In Jacka's experience, the probability that the higher command don't know things is always high – unless Monash is involved.

CHAPTER TWELVE

THE BATTLE OF POLYGON WOOD

This day's battle cracked the kernel of the German defence in the salient. Every inch of ground won was vital ... Few struggles in the campaign were more desperate, or carried out on a more gruesome battlefield. The maze of quagmires, splintered woods, ruined husks of pillboxes, water-filled shell holes, and foul creeks, which made up the land on both sides of the Menin-road, was a sight which, to the recollection of most men, must seem like a fevered nightmare.[1]

John Buchan

Early September 1917, Western Front, Pompey and circumstance

The good news upon Jacka's crossing of the English Channel once more and returning to the 14th Battalion – to find them now billeted in big barns at Fontaine Les Boulans, a cobble-stoned village – is that somewhere, someone has come to their senses.

Because, as one officer of the 14th will recount, 'Margolin was so obviously incompetent,'[2] he has left the 14th Battalion, and after his recovery from his twisted knee will be assigned to command a Jewish Battalion being raised in England. The bad news is that to command the 14th, Jacka's mob, Jacka himself has been passed over.

For Brigadier General Brand professes himself of the view that what the 14th most needs after Margolin is 'another Peck', as in a deeply experienced officer of the regular army.

No Jacka!

The command is given to Lieutenant Colonel Walter John Smith, formerly of the 37th Battalion, the same officer who General Monash had been most dissatisfied with at the Battle of Messines.

Adding insult to injury is that Australia's first winner of the VC in this war, who has demonstrated both his prowess on the battlefield again and again, *and* his tactical nous, cannot even get second prize. Because at the same time as Margolin leaves, so too does his offsider, Major Otto Fuhrmann. But Jacka cannot even get *that* vacant post.

(For the record, Fuhrmann had not covered himself in glory, even as second-in-command, with the 4th Division's General Officer Commanding, Major General Sinclair-MacLagan, later noting of his performance, 'I am satisfied that it is to the best interests of the Battalion that Major Fuhrmann should leave it ... There is no doubt that as Second in Command he has failed to foster a good regimental and Brigade spirit among the Officers of the Battalion, and to bring to notice matters detrimental to discipline which have been going on in the Bn.'[3])

Oh, but it gets worse.

'[Fuhrmann] was succeeded by Major D. Thomson whose advent naturally blocked the promotion of 14th officers of long standing whose efforts had largely made the battalion what it was.'[4]

Outrageous! Pompey Elliott is so close to an eruption of fury he could be Pompei itself.[5]

Have you heard? Jacka's report on those bloody tanks at Bullecourt has been sent to Coventry, as has Jacka's career! Oh yes, Pompey has it on good authority, his own for a start, and he will say it for years to come that: 'General Birdwood ordered that Jacka's report should be expunged from the records of the AIF and Jacka himself was thence onward systematically ignored both in regard to decorations and promotions.'[6]

It is a bloody scandal, or should be. Pompey is going to take the damn thing up with Bean. By God, does he know how brilliant Jacka's report was? How all of Jacka's criticisms have been adopted and adapted to tanks in battle by Monash? And yet it is the messenger who is to be shot?

The rumours run once more about Bert Jacka and his stunted fate. Famous to the men, infamous to the top brass, the fact he is not a Major yet is a general disgrace.

Admittedly, one possibility is that Jacka is simply too valuable in his current position.

'A company under his leadership,' Brand would later note, 'was as good as an extra battalion to me in a scrap.'[7]

At least it could be noted that Brand would be aware that while Lieutenant Colonel Smith would follow orders without question, making for an easier life for him, no such courtesy would likely be extended by Jacka.

Another with a right to be put out by his lack of promotion is Captain Harold Wanliss, another high performer who also has on his resume that he has served and shone for a long stint as adjutant, and is one of the most highly regarded men in the 4th Brigade, and even wider.

Nevertheless, the view that Jacka is worthy of the position of commanding the 14th Battalion is not a universal one, even among those who know his work well, and will claim him as a friend.

'Captain Jacka was at best a company commander,' Colonel Edmund Drake-Brockman will much later state flatly. 'The other officers were majors or colonels, and were specifically appointed to command the 14th Battalion. Such appointments were in the nature of a universal practice throughout the Australian Imperial Force, and it was a procedure which was in every way proper.'[8]

Jacka's lack of promotion was a matter of ongoing fascination for Wanliss. He was sorry to see it: 'He has a higher order of brain than he is popularly credited with and in my opinion he is a born soldier with true tactical intuition and had he received fair play was capable of greater things than he was ever entrusted with. But he did not get fair play . . .'[9]

Jacka knows it too and seeks solace in a familiar corner, one he had found comfort in since childhood, the wisdom of a Minister. Most men only give a smile and nod to the Company Chaplain if they think a cup of cocoa is in the offing, but as Ministers go, Reverend Francis Rolland, aka 'King Cocoa', is as good as they get, and the man whose grandfather was the dogged Presbyterian Minister who founded Geelong College now often receives a quiet, solitary visitor.

It is Jacka. Rolland knows how bitterly disappointed he is at the appointment of Major Smith as it is a post and rank he feels he deserves. But it is not just that, and he doesn't want instruction, only an ear from someone who understands and thinks of the world beyond. This *war* is lasting forever, but *we* won't, will we?

For the question has to be asked:

Will any of us come out alive?

That includes you, padre.

Rolland listens and knows that Jacka is depressed; it is a face he won't show to his men. In the next battle Rolland knows what the men will see: 'the same cool mind, the same invincible courage, the same front line genius',[10] but here, now, is a lost man wanting to know if there is any meaning to all this. Rolland wishes he knew that too. Let us pray. (Rolland has long been fascinated with Jacka's exceptional bravery; he has realised that Jacka is simply three steps ahead of anyone else when it comes to working out what to do in the continual crisis of battle: 'His mind worked very quickly in an emergency and that he sometimes was able to sum up a situation and do the daring thing, which a slower mind could only have achieved by thoughtless impulse'.[11] The problem is what to do with that quick mind when the battle vanishes.)

In the meantime, the verdict of Jacka's mates in the *estaminet* after a pint or two when it comes to his lack of promotion is very clear: 'Jacka might do better if he's more tractable.'[12]

But that means being flexible, with occasional bowing and scraping. Impossible for Bert.

'He's got a habit of always hitting out straight from the shoulder. That is not always politic when senior officers get to hear about it.'[13]

As it happens, it is soon apparent that senior officers won't have to wait to hear about Jacka's views on important things, for he is prone to telling them outright.

For the word spreads. The 'old Brig' himself, Brigadier General Charles Brand, is coming on a personal visit to the 14th Battalion, and has requested a 2 pm parade for the 14th Battalion officers – they hope, to discuss the length and location of their leave.

And here is the old Brig now, arriving, appropriately enough, on his high horse. Brand greets them as warmly as he can – even at full heat he is still thawing, his moustache eternally on parade, present, correct and khaki – and beneath that formidable 'stache his mouth begins to talk. And talk. And talk some more, giving them a lecture on the state of the war is their treat today. Apparently, the French armies are exhausted.

Do tell? There is apparently a lot of it about.

Fortunately, however, Sir Douglas Haig has come up with a solution: pushing the Germans from the Belgian coast should do it.

Fascinating. That must be why they made him Boss Cockie of the entire British Expeditionary Force on the Western Front. Who else could have thought of that as a solution? Getting the enemy to leave occupied land, you say?

Brand senses he is losing their interest and cuts to the quick, slowly:

'Now, gentlemen, the point I am coming to is this. It has been decided by the High Command that the 4th Division shall be given a task in the upcoming battle.'[14]

'WHAT?'[15] comes a yell.

From Jacka. His fury speaks for them all. No leave? A new battle? Four fresh Australian Divisions at Sir Douglas Haig's command and he decides to add the shattered, battered, tattered, totally exhausted, bone-weary and decimated scraps of the 4th Division to his next feast?

'WHAT?' in-fucking-deed. This is not dumb insolence, it's shouting at the old Brig right now.

'I've no doubt you heard what I said, Jacka.'[16]

Oh, there's no doubt of that. Jacka glares at him furiously. If looks could kill, Jacka would be up for at least a triple homicide for the gaze he is directing at the Commander of the 4th Brigade. Brand answers his glare with more lecture:

'As I was saying before I was interrupted, our division is thought very highly of by the army commander . . .'

Oh, he should hear what we think of him!

'. . . and there is not the least doubt that you will ever cover yourselves with credit'.[17] And with that Brand stops and Jacka starts.

'Do you mean to tell me,' he says, 'that this battalion is to be flung into the line straight away, in spite of all the promises made to the men?'[18]

It is not a question; it is an insult. And Brand answers with another: 'Hullo, Jacka, what's the trouble with you? Have you the wind up?'

Now, accusing Jacka of being a coward is like accusing Goliath of being short, you can make the claim but nobody with eyes will believe it, and Jacka answers with a mocking smile.

'No, I'm only thinking *of the men*. I've been over in England swinging the lead the last week or so, and personally I don't give a damn. But I want to know *why* the promises made *to the men* have been broken. I reckon it's a damn disgrace.'[19]

The men reckon so too and Brand can see he is stuck again between a rock and a hard Jacka. The men love the man, to punish him is to ask for a mutiny. Brand doesn't dismiss his officers, he simply walks away, furious. Jacka continues the meeting without him, giving full vent to his contempt.

'These people make me sick! They go running after the "heads" volunteering for everything – "My men will do this" and "My men will do that!" They take fine care that they are not in it themselves!'[20]

Rule agrees with Jacka's point, but not his target today. Brand is not one of those 10-mile-back heroes, he is in the thick of it with them every chance he gets, and he makes damn sure that every man on his staff is there too. In any case, Rule knows that Brand is just the messenger today: 'He had no more to do with the throwing of the brigade into this coming battle than had my batman, or the cat in the colonel's billet.'[21] True enough, but Jacka's blood is up and the men's temperatures rise with him. Still, it will fall, Rule reasons. Fate will be accepted. Training and tactics for the next stunt will begin. And sure enough, orders come through and order is restored. Polygon Wood will be the place.

Now, Polygon Wood sounds like some sort of mathematical forest, but it is scarcely even a bit of brush. Before the war and the endless shelling that has since hit, it had been a delightful polygon-shaped wood, about a mile in width, with a racecourse in the middle. Now it is just a name of what once was; ground to be taken rather than enjoyed. The Australians will have to make their way across swamps and mud, open ground with no dry ground, and the only foothold you will get easily is that of your boots squelching in the mud. It is not an inviting prospect, unless you are German and on higher drier ground. Yes, the Germans are on high, and the sitting ducks on the deep slush below ... will be us. Well, there is a reason the Germans have easily held this ground for the past three years, but we must take it now and not take our time in doing so. Training will begin at once for likely scenarios of attack.

C Company trains, in the crops of all places, just outside a pretty little village nearby; D Company in a fenced field, A and B on the other side of the village. They train without their Lewis guns, which have not arrived yet. Perhaps they are on leave? No, the 13th, 15th and the 16th have theirs, but the unlucky 14th have theirs delayed. Rifles it is then, and range practice is done. Make do. All proceeds 'grumblingly', until another rum do takes place ...

The old Brig, unaware that the 14th have no Lewis guns, comes across A and B Companies training with rifles and explodes with anger before the facts can be explained to him. Rifle-range practice! Captain Harold Wanliss is summoned to be yelled at. What the hell is this? Basic training? The other battalions are using ball ammunition for battle practice, advancing in waves, as instructed, and yet here are the 14th, wasting bloody time!

'You are no good!' Brand says furiously, but that is no wonder to him. 'Your officers are a bunch of dopes! The battalion is dopey too!'[22]

Wanliss flinches; he is both a gentle man and a gentleman, and his men can see the insults cut him like a lash. Brand storms off leaving a tempest behind him. A few hours later, a rebellion rises and remains. A mutiny it is, one that will be conducted by letter. Yes, the officers all agree, they will resign their commissions *en masse*. Like a bunch of bloody dopes. Some letters are short and sweet; Rule's carries a pointed sting: 'Your aspersions are lowering the name of the unit. I feel my own spirit and morale are suffering. I do not wish to carry on any more.'[23]

So, he won't. None of them will.

For his part, Lieutenant Cecil George writes that, 'Firstly, General Brand said we were all bloody dopey in front of the NCOs and men and admitted saying he had said so.'

Which is one thing. But he had also insulted Albert Jacka VC, and even told others that the issue was caused by Jacka having 'a swelled head'.[24]

Of *all* people!

'Secondly a slur was also cast on one of our senior officers . . . The first remark to my mind infers that I am incompetent and unable to lead men in action . . . I desire to have my incompetence proved and be allowed to resign my commission . . .'[25]

The resignations mount, and the only exceptions in the 14th Battalion prove to be the two most senior officers, Colonel Smith and Major Thomson.

Sure enough, the next day Brand orders a parade of all these 'ex' officers at once. Well?

'Well, now . . .' Brand begins, uncertainly.

Yes?

'About that silly thing you fellows have done. I've flung all those resignations in the waste-paper basket.'[26]

Oh, have you now?

They are now dismissed and as soon as the formality of formation is dropped, Jacka decides to tell Brand what he needs to be told. Though incandescent with rage, he manages to compose himself enough to stay standing at rigid attention while delivering his message.

'Sir, you have insulted innocent men who cannot answer in self-defence. I demand an apology for an act unbecoming an officer and a gentleman.'[27]

Oh really? 'You have a big head!' replies Brand. 'And you are annoyed because you have not been promoted to Major!'[28]

Well, now you fucking mention it, yes he is, especially when chinless wonders like . . . and Rule rushes up to the pair and tries to stop Bert, while the old Brig threatens to arrest Jacka this very minute if he doesn't *shut his mouth*. Jacka, somewhere between mute and muttering, is led away by his fellow reinstated officers. So, Brand has thrown their resignations away? Fine. We'll resign again. And so they do, each letter a line of resignation, delivered *en masse* to a despairing Brand.

Another parade for officers is called. Jacka is against going, as they aren't officers anymore, but Rule and the others carry the day and they line up once more, only to see . . . a changed and chastened man. Brand has called them together to apologise.

'Your battalion contains some of the finest officers of this brigade,' he says, loudly. He is sorry, he was hasty, he was wrong. Can this public apology make up for his public berating?

'You officers are all that can be desired'.[29]

Good enough? Can they please fight the Germans now instead of each other? The apology will be accepted by most.

'It is not every superior,' Rule will note, 'who can recover from a mistake as the old Brig did and retain the men's respect, and one must hand him high marks for it.'[30]

And yet Jacka finds it as hard to forgive as he does to hide his chagrin. At one subsequent briefing, Brand deliberately tries to include Jacka, with a humble invitation for his opinion on the battle plan for Polygon Wood.

'I think these movements could easily be performed by the battalion, don't you, Jacka?'[31]

A pause. All eyes turn to Jacka.

'Why do you ask me?' replies the VC winner. 'If I open my mouth you threaten to put me under arrest. I'll keep my mouth shut for the present.'[32]

Bloody hell. One more sentence and he would be court-martialled, but neither Jacka nor Brand will give the other the satisfaction.

For now, there is nothing for either man to do, but follow orders, as the whole of the 4th Brigade moves up into the line once more, leaving behind the world of greenery, girls, life and love – and descending into death, darkness and destruction.

The signs are not good, for even from a distance as they approach, they are foreboding.

'The rough crosses by the road told the tale of the days,' George Mitchell pens of the experience of approaching the front. 'Shattered, smouldering ruins . . . The chill, still stink of death pervaded everything.

"All hope abandon" seemed to be the message of that region as we marched stolidly over the cobbles'.[33]

•

It is three days to the next battle, let's hope peace holds in this battalion until then.

On 24 September 1917, their formal battle orders from divisional headquarters arrive, with the objectives of their usual 'lines' – particular roads or tracks – clearly set out: *'The 4th Brigade, in conjunction with the 14th Brigade on the right, and the 13th Brigade on the left, will assume offensive operations in two stages. 1st stage (red line), 2nd stage (blue line). 16th Battalion will secure the red line. 15th and 14th Battalions on a frontage of about 500 yards will secure the blue line. 13th Battalion will be in reserve in position now occupied. The barrage will be put down 150 yards in front of our forming up line at zero.'*[34]

Zero Hour will be just a little later than a sparrow's fart, at 5.50 am on 26 September.

Late September 1917, Steenvoorde, phoney war

The old Brig is leading Jacka's mob in an imaginary battle today. Yes, training is not enough, they are going to simulate attacking and, if need be, dying. (Surely they don't have to practise dying? Doesn't everyone get it right the first time?) Brand wears a sheepskin coat and they feel like a foolish flock being herded round and exploded at the Brig's whim. An entire brigade playing at this pantomime? Jacka does not bother to contain his scorn for this *en masse* masquerade. Ted Rule joins in with gusto, but after running a hundred yards, to Jacka's great amusement, Colonel Smith rides up and tells Ted that he has been hit in the head. *Oh. Should I lie down?* Oh, Jacka has a royal treatment at the ready for just such pretend catastrophe.

'Before I knew where I was, four stretcher-bearers had me, bound up an imaginary wound, threw me on a stretcher and carried me to the rear, in spite of abuse and protest.'[35]

Your imaginary war is over, soldier. Rest well. If you get imaginary shell shock, we have a doctor here ready to pretend to treat you.

After the farce is over, all officers are on parade to hear an address from General Plumer, Commander of the Second Army. He is straight out of central casting by way of the Boer War and possibly Waterloo as well, with a monocle that he pops in for theatrical effect when he wants to have a really good stare at you. Jacka and Ted Rule are straining not to burst with laughter as he examines them suspiciously, with his massive eye staring glassily back, before Plumer treats them to a plummy lecture on the dangers they will soon face. (By which he means you.)

'After you have taken your objective you will be heavily attacked by picked German troops, who will be brought up from Lille in motor cars; whatever happens, your outpost line must hold; if need be, you must die in your post.'[36]

Oh, must we?

'It put the wind up me,' says Rule. 'For I did not too much care about dying'.[37]

Jacka is also in the 'prefer to remain alive' camp. After General Plumer finishes with a stiff salute and a final pop from his eyeglass, he disappears, thank Christ.

Well, if we are about to die, we might as well have a wash, and Jacka's mob stroll into Steenvoorde to get a hot bath. It is not hard to find where, as many houses have signs outside reading 'BAINS' so that you don't have to even ask. Ted Rule walks into his 'bath-house' and finds something straight out of Grimm's fairy tales. There is an old woman with an immense cauldron of boiling water being stirred over a fire, and in the long room in front of her are six beer barrels, split in half. These are their 'baths'! The soldiers watch her fill up the tubs and wait for her to depart so they can disrobe, and leave she does, but she comes back just seconds later!

'Now, look here, missus, you duck off out of here!'[38] says a soldier named Templeton. She shakes her head. Evidently, 'the good lady reckoned there was safety in numbers',[39] for she stays and pokes the fire. Ah. Well, farewell modesty then. Tassy Gorrell takes his clothes off in a flash, but finds that he can't fit into the tub, as he is 'all tummy', even a barrel can't hold him 'his legs were in and his rump was out'.[40]

This is getting less dignified by the minute and a naked Ted Rule tries to sink deep into his barrel as the old lady watches them, expressionless. Another soldier named Thompson takes matters into his own hands by giving her an encouraging smack on the bottom in the direction of the door. Well! She knows how to answer that: 'Entering into the spirit of the moment, she landed a mighty whack on Gorrell's backside'.[41]

With a yell, Tubby Tassy grabs his own innocent bottom with both hands and tries simultaneously to sink into the water. Archimedes could have told him this was not going to work out; it does not in spectacular fashion and as the water floods the floor, before huffing out the door, the old French tartar turns on them in disgust: '*Vous beaucoup brigands!*'[42]

Maybe, Madame, but at least now we are *clean* brigands.

26 September – 3 October 1917, Polygon Wood, third time is not the charm

There is no grandness to this next battle, and that is by design. It was in Paris last year that Lloyd George, the Welsh Wizard and British Prime Minister, has argued and won this new strategy of attack; the Allied leaders agreeing to abandon the 'decisive' grand battlefront that has seen so many thousands of men sent to their graves on useless ventures. In exchange, there will be limited attacks to wear the Germans down. From now the Allies will go after small targets, with small battles, and go after small victories while only risking small losses. Hence, Polygon Wood. It is simply an attempt to gain 1400 yards of ground. The Germans still occupy a low ridge east of Ypres, through Passchendaele and Zonnebeke, just as they have done for three long years. But if Polygon Wood falls, and the next limited battle gains the next slice of the ridge . . . one thing will follow another, and the whole ridge will eventually be in Allied hands.

So, to the first step, which is getting a foothold in Polygon Wood. Let's have a look at it. At first glance it does not look like much, just a mass of mud and slivered stumps that once were trees, a wasteland of trenches and spent artillery, a limbo waiting to become a hell again once the next battle starts. Polygon Wood might once have been glorious. But what remains has been used by the Germans as a rifle range. If there is anything likely to sober a man it is the knowledge you will literally be charging into a giant shooting gallery. As Jacka is already sober, he realises the difficulty of the task ahead immediately. The high ground is occupied by the Germans and their guns, the low ground by the Allies, and just who will have most in the lowest ground of all – six foot under – is about to be decided.

There will be no sweep to this victory, if it is that; it is just another piece that must be gained in this puzzle of war.

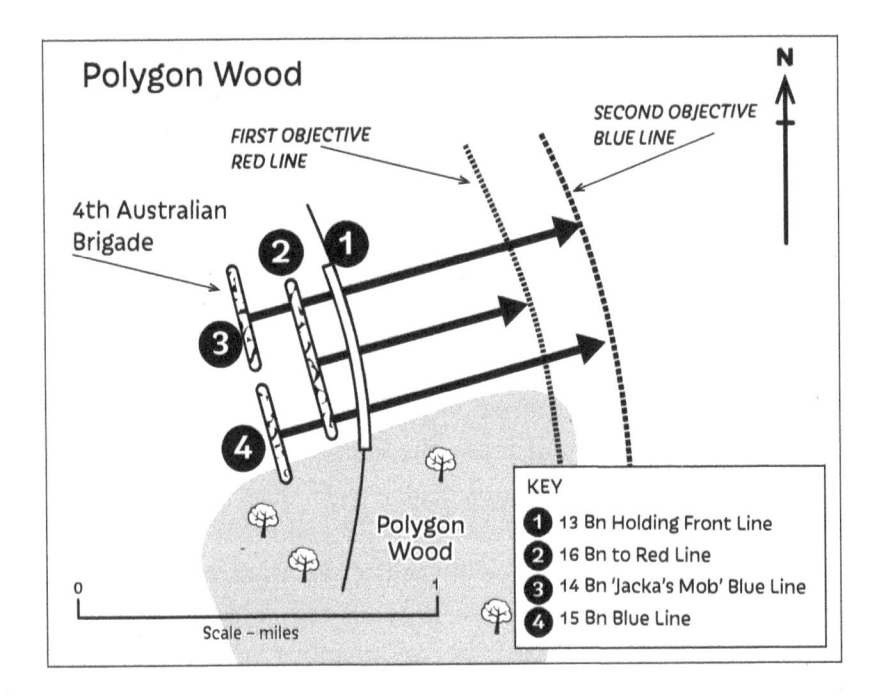

Polygon Wood

FIRST OBJECTIVE RED LINE
SECOND OBJECTIVE BLUE LINE

4th Australian Brigade

KEY
1. 13 Bn Holding Front Line
2. 16 Bn to Red Line
3. 14 Bn 'Jacka's Mob' Blue Line
4. 15 Bn Blue Line

Grand strategies don't matter to the men who have to fight the next battle, their eyes are on the Menin Road, on the wood and the town of St Julien beyond.

The 4th Division will be in the thick of it, as part of Gough's Fifth Army, which is advancing on a front of five miles. Birdwood's I Anzac Corps is advancing on a breathtakingly narrow front just 1200 yards wide.

As eventide rises, Jacka addresses his men, outlining the battle plan with his own unique commentary, each man hanging on words they know they can trust, so listen up. Boys, the going will be rough, and bloody muddy. Each one of us will have to make our way through swamps. That means no foothold is easy, and getting your feet out of the mud will take twice as long as putting them in.

Our biggest problem though will be the damn pillboxes. For in these parts, the Hun defences are literally concrete, and the troops inside them will be twitching and firing to stop us coming east. But we have this advantage: we can move and they can't. We know exactly where they are and where they will stay. If we can rush them, we've got them, and their own way out is straight retreat. And remember, this plan is just that: a plan. We respond to events; every man is to look to his next order, not just follow his last.

Jacka is brief and to the point; leaving with the customary wry observation that they should all get a good night's rest. Which they will, if they can fall asleep in the first place.

So now, at a few minutes after midnight on the day of battle, Jacka and his company – together with the rest of the 14th Battalion, and indeed the 4th Brigade – depart billets and tentatively make their way along a single track winding back by an old-fashioned shack, and make way now for a line of troops returning from a further front. Jacka's mob keep heading the other way, but it is slow going in the dark, hastening slowly across the swampy ground, past shell-holes where the road once was, but still forward in this menacingly dark twilight world, dimly lit by the usual Verey flares; not day, not night, five hours' 'march' to crawl to their starting point.

They are damned lucky to even get to the start, as by a brilliant German guess of bloody bad Australian luck, 'the whole of the back position was shelled that night by the enemy'.[43]

Miraculously, they get through it with no casualties, but it is unnerving to effectively be attacked by accident.

They have travelled the last two days in broad daylight, the darkness now signals that the front is to be their home by daybreak.

As is becoming the way of this war, each company is allotted with carefully calibrated parameters, all written down. *The 16th Battalion will capture the RED LINE, the 14th and 15th Battalions the BLUE LINE . . . Companies will form up in lines of section as arranged with the Company Commander in order from right to left 'A' 'B' 'C' 'D'. The frontage allotted to each company is 62 yards.*[44]

Out the 14th Battalion go now, side by side in two waves – Captain Harold Wanliss's A Company, Captain Patrick Hayes' B Company, Captain John Mitchell's C Company and Captain Albert Jacka's D Company. If all goes well, they are to make their way to a particular road on the map, 1500 yards away, the said 'Blue Line', and transform the ditch there into a trench capable of defence and protection as rapidly as they can. So, the side of a road will become a dugout in minutes, and at least the mud and shell craters will be an advantage here.

Arriving at the jumping-off tape, the men sink down to the ground and do what armies have learnt to do since the dawn of time: wait until the time of dawn.

'We were told to take shelter until zero time an hour later,' one soldier will recount. 'Things were so quiet ... not a shot was being fired ... As zero time drew near men conversed in subdued whispers. None knew what the day held in store for them.'[45]

The attack is due to go in at 5.50 am in the full flush of dawn.

The battle plan for Polygon Wood is simple.

The I Anzac Corps and 5th British Corps – some 110,000 soldiers in all – are to advance on a four-mile front. One thousand yards of that front is the responsibility of 4th Brigade. The 13th Battalion will hold the present line, 16th Battalion will capture the Red Line, some 800 yards ahead. Coming in the next waves, the 14th and 15th Battalions will then pass through the 16th and take the Blue Line, another 500 yards ahead, and hold it against any counter-attack.

Right? As ever, it all looks very elegant and logical on paper. There will be a two-hour barrage before battle. The operational orders state that they will advance up to the Red Line at a rate of 100 yards every six minutes – and no faster as then the artillery that protects them may start falling on them. Once again, a nice precise command to give, while to follow it will be infinitely harder.

Still, when Jacka looks out on the ground they are to advance on, 100 yards every six minutes looks like it might be a fair trot, as he notes: 'The going was very heavy in the advance ... as the terrain was a mass of shell-holes filled with water.'[46]

Forget the army, this is practically a job for the navy.

A hush falls as they wait for the artillery to begin. And, oh, how it begins.

Lance Corporal Allan McDonald of the 14th chronicles the terrifying sound: 'With a terrific scream the barrage opened. One could almost imagine that the heavens had poured tons of explosives all along the line. Every inch of ground was churned up by this wonderful creeping barrage and it seemed impossible that the foe could survive long enough under it to offer any serious resistance.'[47]

The 14th has seen, and suffered, enormous barrages before. But this transcended anything it had ever fought under – 'a gigantic thunderstorm of bursting steel hurled out of the lips of thousands of guns'.[48]

Just before 5.50 am, the whistle blows for the 16th. The 14th and 15th follow a few minutes after this. They creep behind the barrage, the adrenaline pushing them forward; the artillery warning them back; protected by hellfire that is carefully controlled.

While the 16th Battalion is in the lead, the 14th Battalion follows up hard, all of them advancing the best they can, over difficult terrain.

'The ground over which the attack took place was in frightful condition,' one Digger will note of what they see in the rising dawn. 'The whole of the ground was of a swampy nature.'[49]

Even as the 14th advance, the 16th Battalion to their front is being completely plastered by machine-gun fire from several pillboxes spraying death from the far left flank. In an instant, Jacka selects half-a-dozen men and personally leads a flanking attack against those pillboxes, acting in concert with the charging 16th.

They all know Jacka was against Brand's battle plan, refused to be a part of it, in fact, but now he tells them to trust it. They advance their own line by withstanding the German snipers and machine-gunners, and for the first time confront their challenges. Machine guns and pillboxes sprout in the front lines as thick as mushrooms in spring. The German defenders can withstand all but direct hits from the heaviest shells or – as Jacka and D Company hope to establish – attacks which get the Australians close enough to hurl well-aimed grenades into the pillbox slits.

Loudly now, quickly now, the 16th and the 14th roar together, each mad man adding up to the courage of 30 in this crazy dash. The German guns flash fierce fire, but enough Australians survive to smash the pillboxes open. The Germans inside them are either shot, stabbed or taken prisoner. Wisely, those who can, choose the third option.

The air is thick with the drifting smoke of shells, and that blend of mud and metal that makes your nostrils pinch in revulsion. Still the Australians flow forward like a tide, Jacka at the head, and slowly, bravely, the path of the Red Line is made just after eight o'clock, and now the 16th Battalion busy themselves digging in, turning lines into temporary trenches, or at least shelter from the storm of shellfire to come.

The orders of the 16th Battalion Sandgropers are clear, they are to remain stationary and dig in on the Red Line, while the Victorians of the 14th and South Australians of the 15th must sweep on through, and go on to take the Blue Line, 500 yards further on.

The barrage moves on, followed by the 14th and 15th Battalions, their first wave keeping pace as closely as they dare.

Alas, only a short time later, the iron curtain they are advancing behind, the creeping barrage, is once again paused to take out some enemy strong points. This is not perceived by the first wave of advancing troops, who only realise the situation when they are practically under the barrage!

An order is given to retire and take cover, and ultimately wave after wave turns back.

'It was a strange sight,' Captain John Mitchell will note, 'to see most of the battalion sitting smoking, waiting for the barrage to move on.'[50]

God Almighty, the retreat is catching and seems inevitable, as when the first wave starts turning back, the second and third waves start to do the same, like ripples hitting a dam wall and rebounding.

Lance Corporal McDonald is one of those who will later exult how one man can change everything: 'Things looked ugly for the moment but Captain Jacka, with consummate courage, ignoring the barrage, marched forward and signalled the troops to follow.'[51]

Well, they'd better follow their leader. Advance! Steady, steady, watch the fire ... and they follow Jacka. Two battalions follow one man, the air in front of them hot with shellfire – for once, friendly shellfire ... the sound of rifles are drowned by the roar ahead, but they can see the enemy afar and are determined to make their own marksmanship count.

At the front the only thing they get from Field HQ at the back is silence. It is so bad that, yes, messages are sent to Brigade Headquarters because they simply don't know where their bloody Battalion HQ is!

What the hell is happening? Well, as it will later turn out, Colonel Smith has changed the original plan whereby his HQ would move forward behind the troops, and instead moves the 14th Battalion HQ well back from the line of fire in a deep dugout behind the 15th's HQ – for whatever reason – and the flow of reports to Battalion HQ and orders from them to the company runners all but stops, as runners struggle to get through and then find the new position of Smith.

And it is not something that only lasts for an hour or two.

'Battalion headquarters,' Jacka will note waspishly, 'was not heard of at the front line till the end of the 2nd day of battle.'[52]

Even the most charitable observer, and that would be the Battalion Chaplain, Captain Francis Rolland, has his eyebrows permanently raised at this state of affairs, noting: 'The CO and the Adjutant were certainly very conspicuous by their absence.'[53]

It means that Jacka and his men are flying blind, without direction from Battalion HQ, and not privy to any information they might have of what the enemy is doing, or their fellow companies or battalions for that matter.

'Cut off from its nerve centre,' Rule notes, 'the 14th advanced into action at a tremendous disadvantage. Slashed about with shell and machine-gun fire, the men looked in vain to the rear for assistance and support.'[54]

As crazy as it is, it means that Jacka is essentially free to command his D Company as he sees fit, with no direction from on high – something he always fancied he was more than capable of. If necessity is the mother of invention, Jacka suddenly receives the motherlode of practical promotions.

'Instinctively knowing that his day had come,' Rule will record, 'Jacka grasped the opportunity with both hands. His friends had known that he longed for the day when he would lead D Company into the attack, but it is probable that he never dreamt of seeing the whole battalion at his heels. With a fixed purpose he set out to lift the men of the battalion up to his own standard.'[55]

Onwards!

And no matter that, this time, they are confronted by yet more pillboxes.

There is nothing more satisfying than knowing you have not just dodged death, but punched it in the face and got away with it. To charge a pillbox and live to tell the tale requires luck, a bayonet and recklessness. Luckily, the 14th has these in spades. Once you are close enough to a pillbox; you can stick your rifle right in its letter slot, and post your own direct threat. Stay in there dead or come out in a few seconds deaf, it doesn't matter to the Australians who have battered their way to these peculiar battlements. Bayonets, bullets and screams follow in quick succession and '*Hande Hoch!*' is yelled. The pillboxes empty, their dazed inhabitants cursing the retreat they didn't make, as Jacka's mob continue to advance. They have a roll on, they can feel the battle falling their way even as the artillery continues its shattering onslaught ahead.

•

Made it!

Now in possession of the Blue Line – a humble track – Jacka and his men of the 14th begin digging in, just as is happening along the entire line.

'Prisoners were in a "dopey" state,' one soldier will note, 'owing to the intensity of the shellfire . . . The whole battalion was linked up in a continuous trench on the second objective and touch was maintained with 49th Battalion on the left and 15th Battalion on the right.'[56]

But there is something else that Jacka has spotted, the road is likely a landmark already 'registered' by German artillery. When they realise the Australians have come this far, it will be their aiming point. Thus, if they do 'hold' this blue line, they will be dead men. Right, damn their orders, damn the battle plan, they must move ahead, beyond the road.

NOW! And amid the smoking shells and crackling wildfire, the scouts are sent out. Jacka is calling a meeting, all company commanders are to present themselves on the double for an improvised HQ on the battlefield.

Captains Mitchell, Hayes and Wanliss present themselves in hurried course, their panting, curious faces stare at him now as Jacka coolly states his case.

What to do? There is no protocol for breaking orders, which is what Jacka is suggesting. But sane commanders adjust to realities; and that sweeping German artillery is not going to turn to suit them. Technically? This is a meeting of equals. Each man is leading his own company. In reality, however – and in the complete absence of Colonel Smith and his 2IC, Major Thomson – there is no doubt who is in command. That would be Albert Jacka VC. And when you are in a battle, when Jacka insists on something, you lean forward and you listen. And that even goes for Captain Wanliss, as highly regarded as he is. In Australia, Wanliss is a well-educated blue-blood, from a notable family of distinguished military men and members of the legal fraternity, while Jacka is a forestry worker. But in war, in battle, Jacka is a prince among men, and Wanliss is the first to observe it.

And right now, Jacka is more than insistent. This is a matter of life or death. They know their orders, but they can see and hear the booming reality approaching them. Where are those shells heading? Where will they go next? You know it; you can *feel* the equation of disaster being written out in front of your eyes.

So we *have* to move forward.

We *have* to get off this line.

This is *precisely* where the counter-artillery of the Germans will focus their barrage, and it will slaughter our men.

We must move forward, off the obvious, and dig in.

To do otherwise is to obediently, stupidly, die. Ours *is* to reason why. *So do it, now.*

Well?

The first to agree is Wanliss. His cool assent matches Jacka's fiery pitch. What Jacka says makes sense. Let's hear your voices on it? The other commanders say aye, and all are now in a new line, following their new leader.

For the first time, Jacka is actually commanding the 14th Battalion, and making the crucial decisions.

'At Polygon Wood,' Rule will note with warmth, 'Jacka's handling of the fighting men astonished even his greatest admirers. It was a demonstration by a master for the benefit of his pupils.'[57]

Less than three years ago he had been a simple soldier, little more than a piece of flotsam on a vast sea of khaki. And yet, since that time, despite so many obstacles put in his way to prevent him rising above his station, here he is, commanding 750 men. He knows what needs to be done, and sees that it is done. With a nod, Jacka indicates that the meeting is over. We have decided what we are going to do.

Do it.

Each officer returns to his own company, and the whole battalion is soon moving off the line, and making their way forward.

They are improvising but the plan still remains, just send messages to Brand at Brigade HQ.

This has to happen, *now*. Jacka snaps the orders and the men of the 14th start moving still further forward to shell-holes they can improve into basic trenches.

For the most part it goes well, with one tragic exception.

Out on the right flank, Wanliss is set to lead the next charge, in this case trying to destroy a nearby machine gun which is cutting a swathe through them. The damn thing sounds like an instrument playing and spraying over them, but where does the tune start? The solution? Run towards the sound of fire once the latest burst is through.

Come on, boys, a push and a rush and we are done. Wanliss leaps to his feet, raises his revolver and . . . one German bullet goes into his throat, the other through his heart. The machine gun has found *him* and killed him in a murderous moment.

ON! His men charge forward regardless – getting on with the job, just as he would have wanted, getting to the next line that Jacka has designated. The 14th can see the Germans fleeing now and every instinct is to give chase, and go further still, but Jacka holds them steady here. Still others, nevertheless, are questioning why the run to this road was made. If they had dug in, where they were told to, that small road acting as their marker, perhaps Wanliss would still be alive?

Shortly afterwards, all doubts are dispelled as the Germans now bombard the road, 50 yards back, precisely where they had been! The Germans having deduced, accurately, where a logical place to dig in would be, have waited for them to dig their own grave, and then bombed it.

Holy Christ, Jacka was right!

Many of them, save Wanliss, clearly owe their lives to him.

•

Back at 14th Battalion HQ, messages are now coming through in scattershot manner: positions are held here, men have been lost there. Captain Wanliss is killed. Battalion HQ diary notes the message, but it cannot record the shockwave of loss and mourning that is felt with this news. 'There was not an officer in the 14th who was held in greater respect.'[58]

Jacka is alert for the signs of German counter-attack, and the first inkling of one comes just after one o'clock in the afternoon, from far back. Battalion HQ have received word from an airman, high in the sky, that he has seen a 'battalion of Germans approaching the far side of Broodseinde Ridge'.[59] They are coming, the only question is when.

While they wait for more German troops on foot, the main focus must be to activate the Allied artillery, situated behind them.

It is now a matter of urgency that the artillery knows of their new position, and start a barrage accordingly, right in front of them, to thwart the German counter-attack that will inevitably be hurled at them. They don't have pigeons with them, and it is too far to send a runner. So the only way it can be done is with SOS rockets. (The homing pigeons they'd started the battle with had either already gone home, or disappeared, perhaps at the claws of the trained hawks the Germans have recently unleashed in this war. In similar fashion, the Germans have positioned bitches on heat to disturb the Allies' messenger dogs.)

So, rockets it must be.

They are five-foot-long beasts and their size has one great disadvantage today, a problem that is only natural. For after crossing this battlefield ocean, the SOS rockets they have on hand are waterlogged and won't fire. Well, Jacka knows where some dry rockets might be, there are some carried by his batman. Where is he?

Oh.

'He's knocked.'[60]

Where did he fall? About 400 yards back.

Bugger.

(It is a measure of this war that whatever grief Jacka might feel at the news of the death of a good and worthy man can be quickly dwarfed by frustration that he should have died so far away.)

But.

But at least he has fallen on a dry bit of land!

(Good news. He has still been tragically killed, but the upside is the rockets are likely not wet!)

Somebody will have to go back and get them. Who?

There can only be one choice.

Jacka stands up and starts walking back in a crouched fashion, trying to make himself as small a target as possible. His luck is in, as he is indeed missed by the snipers. (Well, mostly. He does cop a flesh wound on his hand, and a bullet goes right through his tunic, but in his world neither thing counts. Barely worth mentioning.) Most importantly, he finds the dead batman, retrieves the rockets and returns with them dry and ready to fire.

Upon Jacka's return, Mitchell asks him why the hell he took that risk.

'Another man would have had trouble finding the body,' Jacka says simply, before confiding what is obvious to everyone. 'This job was *dangerous*. Had to take it on myself.'[61]

Yes, you did. Nobody else would. And he doesn't tell anyone about it! If you want to get another VC you have to start flapping your gums a little if you are the commander!

As it stands, or rather as it crouches, the whole battalion is now linked up in one continuous line of short trenches and the second objective is now theirs. All they have to do now is to hold it. Contact is maintained with the 49th Battalion on the left and the 15th Battalion on the right. All are looking ahead to see if any Germans have come over the ridge yet, for when one comes hundreds will follow.

There they are!

For now, to their front at 3.25 pm, they can see hundreds of German soldiers coming their way, taking whatever cover they can in the bare remains of what had been the wood, to get themselves into position to bring withering sniper and machine-gun fire to bear on the Australian position.

So many of them!

Yes, they will be able to shoot dozens of them, but it is obvious that with their rifles and Lewis guns alone, they will not be able to hold back this Teutonic tide.

Calmly, Jacka lights the revealed wick of the rocket like a giant firework. In a moment the signal cartridge payload ignites, and the rocket shoots a thousand feet into the air before blazing red as it slowly falls to earth, coaxed by a parachute into a graceful, notable descent. It is a signal that Battalion HQ will surely see (hell, even Field HQ might notice it). It will burn for just 35 seconds, but that will be enough. Their artillery will fire an answer that will provide their salvation, so look up . . .

. . . and they wait.

No more than five minutes later, seemingly out of nowhere, it happens. The first waves of the 2000 German soldiers of the 25th Division, preparing to go over the top, can hear an entire *cavalcade* of roaring trains coming their way, from straight out of the sky.

It couldn't be, could it?

It is!

With a shattering roar that goes on interminably, the barrage that now falls from the skies completely destroys what would have been a devastating foray by them. Their only chance of survival is to beat a retreat.

Not that that is enough, as Jacka reports: 'Our men also opened up on them with machine-gun and rifle fire and mowed them down in hundreds.'[62]

There will be at least 500 Germans killed by Jacka's mob today. As the fatal afternoon unfolds, the closest a German gets – and it is literally *one* German – is within 70 yards. His reward is to be shot, picked off by a rifle, while those far behind him suffer death from the skies.

Jacka subsequently watches the German stretcher-bearers at work. They will be left unmolested, through both decency and the fact they are carrying off defeat and death. That is the fate the Australians themselves would have suffered if they had followed orders instead of following Jacka.

At this point, the Germans – still refusing to accept that they are out-gunned, out-manned, out-soldiered and out-commanded – look set to mount yet another attack. This one will likely be concentrated on 15th Battalion just to the 14th's right, and is preceded by a massive artillery barrage right on their noggins.

Concerned, Jacka yells the order: 'Pass the word along to the battalion on the right. When the Huns advance, we'll hop out and meet the blighters with bayonet.'[63]

But will the Huns actually advance? One sign they will is the emergence of snipers suddenly picking off the unwary. Jacka brings his own gunners to bear accordingly, moving along the trenches, talking to the men, directing lines of fire and giving orders for carrying parties to keep whatever ammunition remains up to them.

'Captain Jacka's presence in the line,' one soldier will note, 'had a wonderful effect on everybody. Everything that he did was done in such a careful and painstaking manner that confidence was general throughout the line.'[64]

This time the counter-attack is nipped in the bud by both their fire on the ground and more Jacka SOS rockets calling in thunder from the skies.

This second stage of battle is through, but a third beckons surely, and the snipers are here to make you think again by blowing out the brains of some of your fellows. Blood is up and Jacka, his blue eyes searching for weakness like an eagle scanning for prey, can sense that with another push the day will be theirs, no need for a battle tomorrow. These are the last gasps of an enemy, he can feel it.

A further advance, an attack, now! This cannot be improvised, it must be requested.

'It is ours for the taking!'[65]

But Brand is worried about further German counter-attacks taking a too thinly spread line of attack. Yes, there may be a battle tomorrow to win what could have been taken today. But stick with certainties, build the odds in your favour, don't roll the dice just because you are Jacka's mob.

So the reply is a firm no. Hold your ground, don't lose it in an advance that might be cut off by a counter-attack. The two men will disagree about this order and whether it is right for as long as they both shall live – with Jacka later insisting, 'It required another battle on the 4th October to capture what was ours for the taking that day.'[66]

Either way, for now, as the day ebbs so does German activity – at least in terms of soldiers coming forward.

'The enemy's appetite for fight had by then faded,' Ted Rule will recount. 'Onlookers were therefore denied the spectacle of a hand-to-hand fight in No Man's Land between the 14th Battalion and some of the picked storm troopers of the German Army.'[67]

Yet one more artillery barrage on Australian positions descends, but as Jacka moves along the line, steadying his men, directing where the fire should go, putting ever more pep in their pop . . . there proves to be no German follow-up on the ground. Against all odds, the Australians under Jacka's command have not only taken German trenches that have previously defied all comers, but now seem to have held them.

What is more, Jacka's mob will consolidate their position for another night and day. It is Jacka himself who directs the fire from the Vickers, Stokes and Lewis guns – his intuitive orders setting up the 14th Battalion's own lattice of death to confront all German forces heading their way. The following evening at 8 o'clock they are relieved by the 45th Battalion coming forward.

Jacka's terse report tells 14th Battalion HQ, wherever they are, the situation: 'About 8 pm on the 28th the 14th was relieved by the 45th Battalion.'[68]

Casualties for the 14th Battalion number 170, comprising 40 killed, 123 wounded and 7 missing.

The battle is won and Brand immediately sends a runner forward with a message saying that he will be recommending Jacka for a DSO.

As long as they keep communicating via runners and SOS rockets, these two might get along . . .

When Colonel Smith is found and informed of what actually happened in the battle he joins in the recommendation, citing Jacka as 'the soul of the defence, personally coordinating the work of Stokes Guns, Vickers and Machine Guns in such a way that heavy losses were inflicted on the enemy'.[69]

Not to mention heavy embarrassment avoided for Colonel Smith.

Jacka is pleased with the results of his first battle in command of a company, technically a battalion, with the obvious rider that he grieves for those who have been lost, and none more than for Harold Wanliss, who he will refer to ever afterwards as 'a hero'.[70]

Jacka writes to Harold's parents; an act he typically undertakes after every battle for the fallen he has known.

'He always tried to write in a very personal manner,' Chaplain Rolland will recount. 'He would give them something special to remember and I could see that it took a heavy toll on him. But I believe that it consoled people to receive a letter from Bert Jacka himself.'[71]

As for Rolland, every life is sacred, but this one is mourned deeply. Harold Wanliss was beyond exceptional: 'Unless I was blind, he would have been Australia's leader in days when she will sorely need one.'[72]

Of all those who take the news badly — and that is everyone, for the man is revered — none will take it worse than Colonel Peck, his former battalion commander.

'Many men, many good men I have met . . .' Peck will write, 'but he was the king of them all.'[73]

The Captain and the King depart, but they must continue . . .

CHAPTER THIRTEEN

JOURNEY'S END

Lines of grey, muttering faces, masked with fear,
They leave their trenches, going over the top,
While time ticks blank and busy on their wrists,
And hope, with furtive eyes and grappling fists,
Flounders in mud. O Jesus, make it stop!

'Attack', Siegfried Sassoon

October 1917, Steenvoorde, passover

Among those in the know, Jacka's prestige has never been higher than after his successful display of leadership at Polygon Wood.

'His personal achievements in previous battles had been the admiration of his countrymen, but at Polygon Wood when the opportunity came, he displayed in addition a power of leadership, a grasp of tactics, and a military intuition that many had not given him credit for.

'It is impossible to over-estimate the value of his services during those three days in the line. He carried the left wing of the battalion forward with a magnificent dash to the second objective and there took practical control of the unit and was thereafter the guiding spirit of the storm of battle. His reckless valour, his excellent judgement, his skilful tactics, his prompt anticipation of the enemy's movements, and the force and vigour of his battle strokes gained the admiration of all ranks, and inspired everyone with the greatest confidence.

'Throughout the whole engagement he was a ubiquitous and fearless figure, the very incarnation of a great fighting soldier and a born leader of men. No more fearless or gallant soldier took part in the Great War.'[1]

Surely, such a performance is worthy of a Bar to his VC, this time, or even a DSO?

Again, alas, those pushing for proper recognition of Jacka are thwarted and when the announcements are made, he is awarded ... nothing, not even a mention in dispatches.

Captain Mitchell is one who notes how odd it is: 'The battalion received about 30 Distinguished Conduct Medals and Military Medals for the NCOs and men, but for some strange reason no officer received a decoration, not even Captain Jacka.'[2]

This is despite the fact the 14th had been in the thick of the action throughout, and one of the most powerful units involved in the entire battle, breaching the line, holding it, and then advancing it.

'It was thought by many,' Mitchell notes, 'that this was due to [Jacka's] previous argument with the brigade commander. Perhaps the brigade headquarters was not at fault as it was found later that Jacka's name was the first on their list of recommendations.'[3]

How could it be?

Even the father of Harold Wanliss, Newton Wanliss – who will become the official historian of the 14th Battalion – will record his dismay: 'At [Polygon Wood, Jacka] had the whole responsibility of the battalion on his shoulders for three days in the line. The DSO which was promised him and which he undoubtedly earned was never granted and in my opinion there was underground work used to prevent it. I won't say any more [about that].'[4]

•

Among the men, the reputation of Jacka only grows more legendary, whatever lack of official recognition there might be.

One night two Diggers are out on patrol in No Man's Land, when they realise they are being stalked by 'Fritz'.

'We should take them on,' one whispers to the other, 'and throw this bomb.'

Alarmed, his companion replies, 'Do you think I'm Bert Jacka?'

'Oh no,' says the first, before making reference to Australia's most famous sprinter, 'but you will wish you were Arthur Postle in a minute.'[5]

With this he hurls the bomb in his hand, and the two race back to their own lines, the man who had asked not to be mistaken for Bert Jacka winning by 15 yards.

When the first man relates the episode to Jacka the next day, Bert is curious.

'Why did you not run *before* you threw the bomb?'

Ah, yes.

'I had accidentally drawn the pin.'[6]

•

In the meantime, Germany needs two miracles to win the war. The first happens when a former journalist and prisoner by the name of Vladimir Ilyich Ulyanov, alias 'Lenin', leads his Bolshevik revolutionaries to topple the Tsar in Russia and establish a Communist Government – quickly concluding an armistice with Germany which will allow one million German soldiers to head to the Western Front.

The second miracle will be a little more difficult. Though America had formally entered the war on 4 April 1917, it will take time for the bulk of its forces to arrive. It is judged by German High Command that the only chance that the Germans will have to win the war will be to launch a decisive, overwhelming battle before that time, where all those soldiers who have arrived from Russia could be placed with the Western Front veterans and an attempt made to break through the British line and reach the coast.

While their manpower is still short, from October 1917 the Germans are particularly vicious with their poison gas attacks, with mustard gas causing the most devastating damage to lungs and internal organs on the inside, and shocking ulcers on the outside that make your skin fester and peel back.

On 6 November 1917 the village of Passchendaele falls to the Allies. No fewer than 310,000 casualties – of whom 12,000 Australians are mortalities – have been suffered to take it. The German lines of the Western Front have been pushed back four miles.

The strategic value of the village of Passchendaele? None, particularly, beyond having caused 220,000 casualties on the German side.

At last the 14th Battalion are allowed some precious rest, and some particularly pleasant weeks are spent around the French village of Templeux-la-Fosse, near Peronne, after which, early in the New Year, as ever . . .

In Wedderburn, Nathaniel Jacka can barely believe it, but there it is, plain as day, in *The Argus*, published on the eve of the second conscription referendum.

> After the way Australian troops have fought to uphold the honour of our little Island, Australia, by her [No] vote on conscription has dragged that same honour in the mud.'
>
> This is the opinion of Captain Jacka, V.C., written after the result of the last referendum. It settles once and for all the question as to this hero's view of conscription. When Captain Jacka won the Victoria Cross Labour officials were jubilant. He was a good unionist, they said, a stout Labour man and they bragged about the distinction as if they themselves had earned it. And when at the referendum the people were asked whether they would reinforce the Australians and increase Captain Jacka's chances of survival and safe return, the Caucus party enlisted the aid of his father as an 'anti' advocate. This was regarded as a great 'hit'.
>
> If such it was, here surely is a greater.
>
> Captain Jacka is a conscriptionist, and is 'sure It is out of pure ignorance that people voted 'No'.[7]

Nathaniel Jacka is ropable. How *could* Bert do this to him, to the *cause*?

The letter he will write to him could peel paint.

The only savage satisfaction comes the next day when, again, the referendum is defeated.

•

As Samuel Johnson said, when a man is tired of London, he is tired of life. But when a man is tired of Codford, he has probably been there for two days and one wet afternoon. That is what Ted Rule thinks and he has five months, three weeks and four more bloody days at this miserable training camp in Codford. It takes a lot to make a man miss the Western Front, but Codford can do it in spades. Yes, Ted Rule – who has been awarded the Military Medal for his brave actions at Mouquet Farm, commanding a small party to capture a German trench and 15 enemy machine guns – has been 'given' a six-month tour of duty in this fun-forsaken place; his vocation is now 'Gas Instruction Trainer'. It's a cushy job, but the strange thing is how awful it is:

'For a week or two it was a relief to think that one was out of harm's way, perfectly safe – that no parson would have one chance in a thousand of murmuring "Ashes to ashes, dust to dust" and throwing a handful of dirt at me. But the novelty soon wore off.'[8]

The sheer *banality* of safety slowly wears you down. It is different from being on leave, that is letting off steam. In Codford it is only possible to be damp. To the amazement of his superiors, Rule actually applies to be sent to France and back to the Front, as soon as possible.

There is one duty in particular that horrifies Rule, he is now the camp 'body-snatcher'. When anyone dies in training, and they do, he must arrange the burial, instruct the band, and act as chief mourner, walking behind the gun-carriage. The worst part is writing to their families, for these boys are just that, boys. They didn't die on some foreign field, they lost their lives in England, before a shot was fired or felt in anger. When Rule interviews the nurses who attended these young men as they died they invariably say the same thing: 'He kept calling for his mother.'[9] Bring back the Front.

In the early months of 1918, the 14th is assigned a portion of the Western Front near La Clytte, which they must hold against the Germans heavily entrenched on the other side of ground that would be swampy if it was not substantially frozen. In the interests of wearing the Hun down to the bun and bone, the warfare of Jacka's mob at this time is confined to launching raids, getting close enough to throw bombs into their trenches, and setting up snipers to harass them.

By this time Jacka, though exhausted, and occasionally having a revisitation of his nerves – at least in the silent watch of the night – is a master of the military art and, beyond launching and sometimes leading the raids, he also makes sure his men are well protected against similar raids from the Germans by setting up outposts in front of their own lines – with orders to shoot the first sign of movement in front of them.

Occasionally, after checking on his men in the night, Jacka goes out alone towards the German lines, a silent wolf on the hunt, looking for prey. When the Germans do the same to them – somehow evading the outposts and capturing Corporal Ernie Frost and Lance Corporal Charles Jeffries from D Company, the legend of Jacka grows still further for his reported merciless response. For when the Germans inform Frost that he and Jeffries are not the ones they want, but the lone Australian soldier who has been wreaking such havoc at night, Frost gives them fair warning that they'd be much wiser if they just left Captain Jacka alone, as 'the job might not only be unpleasant, but probably decidedly dangerous'.[10]

When the 14th Battalion is pulled out of the line on rotation with other battalions, Jacka is able to put his nocturnal skills to more benign use by stealing potatoes from a local farmer who has been robbing them blind with exorbitant prices. This works well until, with another soldier, they are out on a potato raid and what do they see, but ... potato thieves! They prove to be two 3rd Division soldiers attempting to run away with potatoes!

Outraged, Jacka yells out, 'How dare you rob our gallant allies!'[11]

He will let them go this once, but this must never happen again. And hand over your contraband!

Mercifully for Jacka it is through being away from the 14th on such excursions, including trips for supplies and training, that he is able to avoid a shocking German gas attack that severely debilitates no fewer than 16 officers of the 14th – including Lieutenant Colonel Smith – and no fewer than 250 soldiers.

Again, Jacka has hopes of being promoted to the rank of Major and being able to command the 14th Battalion. Again, he is disappointed. Again, he is not even asked to become 2IC.

4.30 am, 21 March 1918, gain land uber alles

Finally, after months of preparations, it is time for the Germans to make their move. Their million soldiers from the Eastern Front have arrived. Their tanks and artillery are in position. It is time to launch their *Kaiserschlacht*, 'Emperor's Battle' – the all-out attempt of this Spring Offensive to win the war before the full weight of the arriving American Army is felt.

This morning, before dawn, across a front 54 miles wide, extending from Arras to Barisis, south of the Oise River – with the greatest offensive power concentrated around Saint Quentin – the German artillery men of the 2nd, 17th and 18th Armies, are getting ready. Following their strict routine, the gunners working the 6608 artillery pieces and 3534 mortars – half of all German guns on the Western Front – carefully place shells and mortar bombs a safe distance to the rear of their pieces.

Over the next five hours, these men are set to fire 1,160,000 shells and some half-million mortar rounds. It is enough to make the British bombardment on the Somme two years earlier – where 1437 guns had fired 1,500,000 shells and a half-million mortar-rounds in seven days – look puny by comparison.

Among the usual shrapnel and high explosive shells the Germans have ready today are a far greater number of gas shells than usual – chlorine, phosgene and tear gas. If the last makes the enemy soldiers take off their gas masks, they will hopefully inhale the other two – which will either kill or disable them. (Of course, mustard gas would disable them more, but as it does not disperse for at least a day, it would be equally devastating to the German soldiers.)

Suddenly, off to their right, there is a streak of light arcing skywards, followed by a small crack ... and very dimly in the heavens above a large white flare explodes against the misty sky.

It is the signal the artillery batteries have been waiting for.

A shout goes up: '*Feuer frei*,' free fire, and now the gun next to *Gefreiter* Reinhard and his comrades gives an almighty blast as the first shell of the *Kaiserschlacht* roars and soars to the east. In another instant, guns all around erupt like angry volcanos, the shells disappearing as searing streaks of flame into the darkness, lobbing towards the British lines.

And again and again and again!

'*Feuer!*' '*Feuer!*' '*Feuer!*'

And *Feuer* they do, relentlessly, for the next five hours before the whistle blows and the first 300,000 of one million German soldiers go over the top. The British forces, with their backs to the French coast, must defend the best they can, preventing passage to the key railway hub and supply town of Amiens, just 30 miles to the west, and beyond that the Channel ports. And if the Germans can't get to Amiens, they should be able to at least destroy it, if they can get their artillery perched atop the town of Villers-Bretonneux.

The results are stupendous.

In a war where a good day sees the Allies or Germans advance by 50 yards, at the conclusion of the first day, the Germans have smashed the British and French lines and have advanced three miles. After the second day another four miles. Third day five miles.

No less than the fate of the war itself is in the balance!

In extremis, the call is put out for every available Allied unit to move to the front, to stem the flow.

On 25 March, after an early breakfast at 3.30 am at their billets at Neuve Eglise, followed by a march through the countryside, the 14th Battalion climb aboard a line of buses heading for battle. Reaching Bavincourt that evening, it is time to gird their loins, as they are so close now to the advancing Germans they can hear the rumbling guns in the distance, just as they have been passing people and soldiers all day who have been fleeing.

There is one charge that all soldiers except Jacka excel in; charge your glasses, gentlemen, for a toast is to be drunk. On this light evening, the sunset so drawn out it might as well be a painting instead of just looking like one, their CO is about to address them. Having sat through a few addresses by COs before, the wiser men sip, charge and recharge their glasses; they know exactly how many leaders love to hear themselves at length. But Lieutenant Colonel Henry Crowther, the new Commanding Officer of the 14th, is not such a man. When he speaks it is considered, it is clipped, and it is memorable.

His senior officers around their table, or rather the table of the charming French priest with whom they are billeted at Bavincourt, wait for him to start. Before he can, there is a noise they all hear. In the distance, perhaps six miles away, the German artillery is talking to them, jeering and sneering with shells that tell of fates to come. But here, now, a peace. Bert Jacka watches as Crowther stands – he knows that the CO was a schoolmaster in the old life, who loves the sweep and knowledge of history. Tonight he wants to make clear just *what* they are facing, *why* they are facing it, and *how* they are going to stop it!

Never in history has such a powerful army moved on such a narrow front. In fact, take all the armies of Augustus, Alexander the Great, Genghis Khan, Napoleon and Ulysses S. Grant and not one of them – and likely not even all together – would have the number of men, or remotely close to the firepower, that we now face.

'We are about to meet the enemy,' he notes. And when that meeting takes place, let it be said that 'the 14th never retreated, and that all ranks will have to stand their ground at whatever cost'.[12]

None of the listeners are more impressed than the French priest, who has not only offered his home at Bavincourt as the 14th Battalion HQ, but, on the reckoning that his cellar of wine will soon be destroyed by the advancing Germans, invited the Australians to help themselves.

•

The following morning the Commanding Officer of the 4th Division, General Ewen Sinclair-MacLagan, is grasping the extremity of the situation. The Germans have broken through around Bapaume, and now threaten Hébuterne! GHQ has called for the Australians to be thrown in to stop them and, as ever, when the best of the best is required, the 4th Brigade is chosen.

So it is that at 11.15 am, Brigadier Charles Brand is in his 4th Brigade HQ at Saulty when he receives urgent word that his 4th Brigade must 'occupy the line from Souastre to Bienvillers-au-Bois'[13] just north of the besieged town of Hébuterne and defend it at all costs.

•

And that must be Hébuterne up ahead, the village positioned some seven miles north of Albert (the town, not the short red-headed bloke in A Company). *Lieutenant Colonel* Harry Murray – for Mad Harry has had no impediments on his promotions – is soon at the head of his men jumping off the trucks some six miles from this town in the Somme Valley. Best to get out here, and proceed carefully on foot – in defensive formation, with scouts at the front and on the flanks – rather than open themselves to the possibility of an ambush when they are tightly grouped in the trucks.

Forming themselves up into company columns, the Australians of the 4th Brigade – some 3000 soldiers strong – are soon clumping down the cobbled road in the bright afternoon sunlight, not at all sure where the Germans are, and what they will be throwing at them.

Captain Albert Jacka is, as ever, with his men, moving among them as they march, checking in, chatting, sorting things as they go. Some newly anointed of the appointed become remote from the mob. Jacka is quite the opposite. He is one of them, risen but not removed.

As Private Walter Kennedy of the 4th Brigade's 15th Battalion will later recall, 'When we reached Hébuterne on the Somme, a terrible sight met our gaze, the British Army was in full retreat, indeed everything looked desperate, they [threw] us Aussies into this huge gap . . .'[14]

Panicky British officers shout as they pass: 'The Germans are in [the nearby village of] Souastre with armoured cars!'[15]

The Australians keep moving forward regardless, and they prove not to be the only ones with confidence that they will have the Germans' measure.

For as they reach Hébuterne's outskirts Captain Thomas White of the 13th Battalion notes the old folk among the French who are loading up their carts to retreat only need to take one look at the Diggers – who have legendarily fought in these parts previously – before they start unloading again.

'*Pas necessaire maintenant*,' an old man explains their actions to one of the Diggers, '*Vous les tiendrez.*'[16]

Inevitably, such words are put first into English, by those few Diggers who speak Frog, and then into rough Australian, which boils down to: 'Now that you *messieurs* are here, we don't need to go. You'll hold these bastards.'[17]

It is a widespread view among the French citizens as the Australian forces continue to flood forward.

'*Fini retreat, Madame*,' Charles Bean records one of the Diggers saying to an old lady heading west with all her worldly possessions in a wheelbarrow,[18] as he sits with his mates, cleaning their rifles. '*Fini retreat – beaucoup Australiens ici.*'[19]

As it happens, the Australians are able to take Hébuterne before the Germans on its southern flank are able to claim possession. The challenge now is to *hold* it.

•

But what of these tanks, said to be heading their way?

Colonel Harry Murray takes the lead.

Commandeering a stray platoon, he orders them to accompany him for a spot of tank-hunting.

The only solid information Murray can get comes from a hurrying British staff officer, who tells him in passing that 'the Germans are coming on in numbers',[20] and . . .

And everyone down! Get into the ditches either side of the road!

Up ahead in the distance, at the end of a long stretch of straight road, Colonel Murray can see, just behind a red car, some kind of extraordinary contraption, flanked by eight men in grey.

'If these are the tanks,' Murray thinks to himself, 'then Providence has delivered them into our hands!'[21]

The *phut phut phut* of the armoured cars' engines grows louder.

Barking instructions to his men, Murray sets up an ambush: on his signal, the Australians will shoot the soldiers flanking the tank, before having a go at the tank itself.

They steel themselves as the quiet is invaded by the roar of clanking machinery until . . .

Until Murray suddenly realises.

'Don't fire!'[22] he shouts.

There has been a mistake.

The red car? It's a tractor.

Manned by surprised-looking members of the French Agricultural Corps, retreating from the land they had been tilling around Bapaume.

Bon! Nous hold *notre* fire. They are allowed to proceed between the lines of Australian soldiers on each side of the road, 'all smiles and "*bonjours*" at knowing they now had their motors safe'[23] and never knowing just how close they had come to lying dead in a ditch.

•

With ruthless precision, from dawn on 27 March the German artillery targets Hébuterne in an effort to kill all those soldiers now standing in their way – and indeed most of the buildings are destroyed. But the cellars remain substantially intact and, as this is where most of the 4th Brigade have taken shelter, the Australian force is strong enough to continue to block German advances. Just let them come down the Rue de Serre, and see.

For the moment, concerned at just how strong the force in front of them is, the Hun does not press the attack, and merely moves units into position to make their big assault, perhaps on the morrow.

The figure, thus, now moving out towards German lines, using what cover he can to keep from view?

It is Captain Albert Jacka of D Company, trying to work out both where the Germans are, and even more importantly where the Australian forces, together with a scattering of British units, are positioned to stop them. To Jacka's horror he quickly discovers a major gap between the Australian forces of the 4th Brigade and the British 62nd Division – yes, the same mob who had been unmoving at Bullecourt – who have held their position here to the north.

It is a point of huge vulnerability for if the Germans hit there, they will almost definitely go straight through and Amiens would immediately be threatened.

It is so urgent that the gap be plugged that no sooner is Jacka back in camp than he has reported to Lieutenant Colonel Crowther and then takes his own D Company out to make sure the gap is filled – ignoring the British officer who is heard to say, 'A lot of good these few Australians will do.'[24] Crowther places the other companies on the ridge towards Gommecourt which will give them the maximum chances of stopping any marauding Germans.

'[It] was one of the neatest operations ever carried out by the 14th,' the battalion's official historian will note. 'Notwithstanding the very poor visibility and the fact that the ground crossed was hampered by old and very heavy wire entanglements, the most efficient liaison existed between the various platoons.'[25]

It is as well, for the Germans are indeed about to attack, and engage in a full-blown attack on Villers-Bretonneux in the early hours of 4 April.

The ensuing battle will be one of the Australian greats as, against all odds, the 9th Brigade, with the assistance of the British 18th Division, manage to entirely thwart the full force of the German attack.

21 April 1918, Villers-Bretonneux, a little touch of Harry in the fight

Colonel Murray certainly has a different way of going about things. Other senior officers can be very remote with their men, rarely moving among them and, when they do, are inevitably surrounded by a mob of their senior officers. But Mad Harry is not like that at all. Risen from the ranks, just like them – all in the space of three and a half years, helped in no small part by being the most decorated soldier of the forces of the British Empire during the Great War – *Colonel* Murray, if you please, is now commanding the 4th Machine Gun Battalion, with 64 Vickers medium machine guns. And every morning since they have been placed in their positions defending Villers-Bretonneux, he appears in his shirtsleeves, on a pushbike, tootling along and frequently stopping to check their positions, their morale, and their views on what should be done. Yes, he is as keen for a stink as ever.

'[He] prayed for an assault,' the Official History of the 14th Battalion records, 'satisfied that by no possible conglomeration of men and weapons could the Hun get through [his machine guns].'[26]

And on this morning Harry Murray is doing exactly that. With the Germans threatening once more, it is important that he uses his expert eye to ensure that all of the machine guns are correctly placed, with intersecting lines of fire so that there are no gaps, no weaknesses in their armour. Colonel Murray has only risen to his position because he is the best, and if he tells you to shift your machine gun or change its line of fire, it's because he knows. And they know from previous experience he has the knack of working out where the attacks will come from – land and sky.

The men like him enormously. One of the gunners, Private James Knight, will recount Murray's reaction, ducking, when a German shell lands close enough to send shrapnel blasting past them all.

'Pretty warm up here, boys,' Colonel Murray comments pleasantly.

'It must be warm when a VC ducks,' Knight replies, evenly.

'Look, me boy,' Murray says, looking him up and down. 'I'm no gamer than you are, only when I've got to be.'[27]

That's Colonel Murray. He makes no claim to be better than them. Just like Jacka, he is *one of* them.

On this morning, all is as it should be, and he departs.

•

At Cappy aerodrome on this same morning, the Red Baron is giving his final briefing. He is in a very good mood, having notched up, staggeringly, his *80th* victory just the day before. He had been so pleased with the feat that – after flying down low over the German troops so they could see it was indeed him, and letting them cheer him to the echo, throwing their hats and helmets in the air – he had landed, smacked his hands together and exulted: *'Donnerwetter!* Eighty is a respectable number.'[28]

And so it is. But not as good as 81 or 82 or . . . perhaps even *100?*

Today, of course, he must shake off the celebrations of yesterday, and focus once more on the task at hand, as must his squadron.

In the wake of Allied airborne attacks on German troops moving into position to attack Villers-Bretonneux, Baron von Richthofen is personally aggrieved, as it is the specific responsibility of his wing – his group of squadrons, *Jagdgeschwader I* – to have stopped exactly this from happening, as the *Landser*, German soldiers, came up along the Roman road towards Villers-Bretonneux. It must not happen again. Today *JG I* are to patrol along that same section of road leading west to the town, and attack any enemy aircraft seen. The German troops *must* be given protection.

•

It is a crisp, clear morning, and two hours later, driving east on the Bray–Corbie road, Bean's great friend, the AIF photographer George

Wilkins, looks up to see right ahead of him an aerial dog-fight for the ages – with as many as *30* planes involved!

One of the planes, he notes, is an entirely red tri-plane . . .

Could it be?

It is.

Rittmeister Manfred von Richthofen is now leading his squadron back to the honey-pot of Villers-Bretonneux, and they are now engaged by 14 Sopwith Camels. But what now? The Red Baron has broken away, and is pursuing a single Sopwith Camel.

•

Canadian Lieutenant Wilfrid 'Wop' May, on his first mission and with his guns jammed, has disengaged from the dog-fight unaware of just who is closing in on him from behind.

For Manfred von Richthofen's Fokker is closing in fast now, moving in for the kill, swooping on high from the Gods, hurtling downwards and accelerating all the while, embarked on a flight to the death and watching with satisfaction as the Sopwith Camel starts to loom large, fat, and ready in his gun-sights . . .

Ruhig . . . ruhig . . . ruhig . . . Steady . . . steady . . . steady . . .

Now! His finger tightens on the trigger and his twin Spandaus leap into life, his whole plane vibrating in a pleasing fashion. Amazingly, however, this time his first burst of fire doesn't bring his quarry down.

But Lieutenant May knows he is there alright, and has looked around to see 'a red triplane'[29] right on his hammer!

OH.

Holy Mother of God . . .

A wild chase ensues, with *Rittmeister* von Richthofen firing off fusillade after fusillade, only to be frustrated because this pilot never does the expected thing an experienced pilot might do. Rather, his plane appears to be nearly out of control in his panic, without ever crashing.

'I didn't know what I was doing myself,' May will recount, 'and I do not suppose Richthofen could figure out what I was going to do.'[30]

Worse for the Red Baron, the two planes have now flashed over Australian lines, as the German ace stays right on the tail of Lieutenant May as he twists and turns up the valley of the Somme River, just

50 feet above the surface of the water. Above him in turn is Captain Roy Brown, a Canadian Camel pilot who is framing to fire off a burst at him.

•

Oh . . . *God*.

Though May momentarily thinks that he has shaken the German, he is shocked to find that his pursuer has simply hopped over a hill on a riverbend, and is now coming down on him. This time, there is no escape. This time, trapped by the narrow valley sides, he can't dart to the left or to the right. He is as good as dead. The Canadian tenses, waiting for the blast he knows is coming, and even wonders if he should end it himself by jamming the stick forward and hitting the river.

•

Watching from the ground in amazement is Sergeant Cedric Popkin of the Australian 24th Machine Gun Company, of Colonel Murray's 4th Machine Gun Battalion, who now fires his Lewis Vickers machine gun . . .

'About 10.45 a.m. on the 21st April, 1918,' Sergeant Popkin will officially report, 'one of our Aeroplanes was being engaged by a German Aeroplane and was being driven down. The Planes came from an Easterly direction and when within range of my gun, were flying very low, just above the tree tops. I immediately got my gun into action and waited for our own plane to pass me, as the planes were close together, and there was a risk of hitting both. As soon as this risk was over, I opened fire . . . and observed at once that my fire took effect.'[31]

Got him!

'The machine swerved, attempted to bank and make for the ground and immediately crashed.'[32]

Yes, it is 600 yards away across open ground, but there appears to be no further German planes around, so Popkin races to the felled craft.

'The Pilot (whom I was subsequently told was Captain Baron Von Richthofen,) I saw had at least three machine-gun bullets through his body, one in his ribs at the side, and a couple through his chest, and I consider had died as a result of these wounds.'[33]

His Commanding Officer, Captain Frederick Hinton, is excited to confirm the identity of the slain pilot, and his death, and is quick to get Colonel Murray on the phone.

'That's good,' Mad Harry replies. 'Tell him to go on shooting them. That's what he's there for.'[34]

General Monash is more moved than anything when informed, and will note of what happens the next day when the Germans realise what has happened, and where:

'Richthofen's Flight, circled around overhead four or five times and then majestically flew away. Such was the requiem for this doughty warrior.'[35]

•

In the brief absence of Albert Jacka – who has been granted leave to attend the Second Army School of Instruction, an officers' training school, for those whom their commanding officers think show promise – the 14th is rotated through stints of front-line duty. On Anzac Day 1918 this sees them placed just back from the front lines to Allonville, a small village near Amiens. As they arrive at 3 am, the cool night breeze brings them the sounds of an extraordinary battle taking place to their east. What is going on?

It is the Australians, in another extraordinary feat of arms, re-taking Villers-Bretonneux which the British 8th Division had surrendered to the Germans the day before. The battle had been crucial because if the Germans had held Villers-Bretonneux their artillery would have been capable of destroying Amiens, through which 80 per cent of supplies for the British forces on the Western Front move – and so the Australians had been sent in. Mercifully, Villers-Bretonneux is recaptured meaning that, for the moment at least, Amiens – which is just under 10 miles away – is safe and the German thrust in this area is halted!

But can it hold, definitively?

By the time Jacka returns from his course on 10 May it is to find that little has changed. For the 14th Battalion is once again more or less where they had been three weeks before, and must defend Villers-Bretonneux from further German assaults. They are positioned in trenches 1000 yards to the south of the village, in Monument Wood.

The town itself has been so heavily shelled for the last *week*, it is now little more than rubble, and the trenches fare little better, as shell after shell lands and the survivors of the 14th must keep digging, particularly when the shells collapse parts of their trenches. Whensoever there is pause in the shelling, some Diggers leave the trenches to go scavenging in town and return with whatever loot they can find: from bottles of wine, to chickens, to preserved food to – and this is a favourite – ladies' silk knickers and petticoats which they purloin to replace their own filthy lice-ridden underwear!

Oh, and one more thing.

'Ladies nighties,' the newly promoted Lieutenant Ted Rule will recount, 'were quite the fashion and one of the boys lined up next morning for his breakfast arrayed in a beauty.'[36]

On the morning of 15 May, the 14th Battalion finds itself still in the line, with Jacka's D Company doing the honours, while Rule's C Company prepares to replace them. D Company is just having their breakfast of cheese and hard-tack, washed down by billy-boiled tea, when it happens.

Even above the endless chattering of the German attempts to kill them via scything machine-gun fire, suddenly many of Jacka's men hear the most frightening thing of all, a steady . . . *plop* . . . *plop* . . . *plop* . . .

'Gas! Gas!' the cry goes up. 'Gas!'

Alas, for Albert Jacka it is too late. He had not heard the distinctive sound of the gas shells, and even before the cry had gone up, he breathed in what is described by another as 'burnt-potato or onion smell . . . followed by a foul stench, a poisonous odour, that made your eyes water and your nose run instantly'.[37]

Frantically, Jacka, like every man-jack of them scrounges for the gas masks they are issued with, their unseen enemy seeping in with each breath as the frantic finding and strapping is performed by anxious hands, the yells and curses of those late to the task cutting through the deadly air; the mask is on and Jacka sucks a frantic breath, but he now . . . can *smell* it inside the mask meant to protect him! You can dodge a bullet, you can be thrown miraculously to safety by a shell, but there is no dodging gas when it's got you. Jacka totters and sits shaking, waiting for the worst to pass, or himself to do the same.

Alas, for the Victorian wood-cutter, the damage has already been done, and the die cast. The mustard gas is so thick and so widespread all around him, he simply must breathe it in, and within seconds his eyes and nose start to run, even as his throat gorges, his lungs cry out as if he has swallowed a thousand tiny needles, and his breathing becomes laboured. It is not his final words, but with what breath he has, Jacka rebukes Private Bill Fitzpatrick for not having told him immediately, when he had surely heard the plops!

All around Jacka – who is trying to work out how to vomit while still keeping the mask on – there are gurgled cries as no fewer than 18 other soldiers of the 14th Battalion suffer the same fate. All keep their masks on for an hour, until they are sure that the Germans have stopped the gas shells for now ... then up a party of men get to fill in the shell-holes and sprinkle lime about. Just as both these tasks are at their end, the Germans follow up with snipers. All jump back in their trenches except for one young fellow, determined to finish. Ted Rule counts two shots narrowly missing the lad, the third hits and kills him. The dead man is none other than big Bill Dawe, the Digger who saved Jacka's life 11 months previously when he had dared pull him down into the trench at Messines. A furious fight breaks out, as Rule's men put their gas masks on, and move forward to support D Company, continue to hold off the Germans, and evacuate those who have been hit by fire or, like Jacka, gassed.

The stench of gas is so bad in the trenches that, as night falls, Rule orders his men to keep their food and their heads out of the trench for as long as they can. Already Rule is coughing continually and many other men lose their voices, their lungs so tortured that no words can form. And these are the men well enough to stay in line.

As for Jacka and the others, they are quickly evacuated by brave stretcher-bearers wearing gas masks and brought out to the blessed fresh air, but it is too late, for the damage is done. Jacka is, in fact, so badly gassed that each agonised breath is no more than a rasping and rattling gasp. And his eyes sting so badly he fears he is blinded for the rest of his life, although on the Western Front, that may only amount to a few hours ...

By the time he gets to No. 20 Casualty Clearing Station, 10 bumpy miles away at Vignacourt, blurred smears of vision have returned, but it is touch and go as to whether he will survive. His coughing is so constant that one diagnosis is easy: bronchitis. And curing it will be even harder as a hernia from so much coughing now follows. The old schoolboy rhyme: 'It's not the cough that carries you off, it's the coffin they carry you off in,' becomes less amusing by the day.

This is a war wound that rattles long after the soldier has left the field; the young man wheezing like an old soul departing as he shocks the nurses that gaze at him now. The doctors know that only a surgery will bring relief and after that a long, long rest will be needed. That, to the army, means eight weeks. Any longer than that and the sick will start putting on airs. As for Jacka, he is just grateful to breathe without pain once more, his medical records expanding by the days as bemused doctors add up the nicks, scrapes, stitches and hypertrophy of the heart. The mighty Jacka is now officially 'disability'. 'He cannot hurry and is still weak,' a doctor's medical report notes.[38]

Is it worth sending him back to England, when he will likely die anyway?

It most certainly is when it is Jacka VC, and within three days he is sent west, and on 20 May placed on the good ship *Panama*, to make his way across the Channel to the sadly familiar 3rd London General Hospital at Wandsworth. The last time he had been here had been one year and 11 months before, and then there had been hope that his flesh wounds would heal – a hope that had been realised. But with lungs as badly affected as his, there is no such hope and the first thing is just to keep him *alive*, before restoring as much breathing as possible. His coughing is occasionally interrupted by vomiting. His eyes itch and twitch from conjunctivitis, and he, oddly, has healed first degree burns on his legs and flanks. Ah, from a previous battle? No, dozens of previous battles. Asking Jacka for his list of war wounds is like asking an English soldier to complain; he could go on forever. How long he will go on in this life seems uncertain, but surely this war, his war, must be over.

As ever when he is absent, the gap Jacka leaves behind in the 14th Battalion is enormous.

'The main prop in the battalion had been cut away,' Rule documents. 'There was not a man in the unit but knew he basked in the reflected glory of Jacka's exploits.'

And there is no replacing him.

'He set a standard that none of us could ever hope to reach.'[39]

They can only hope he will be back.

Jacka undergoes an operation on his hernia that helps, a little, but for the moment, at least, it is not enough to get him back to the 14th Battalion at the Front. The obvious thing is for Jacka to head home, but the man himself will not hear of it, and prefers to wait, counting on his recovery. There is some hope, with his official medical report from the time reading, *'Present condition – is a stone below weight. He is still pale and though he can walk well and climb hills and says he is fit, he confesses to being weak. Hernia satisfactory. Disability not permanent.'*[40]

It is a question of what the French call *'le wait and see'*, as to whether or not he will be able to return to the front lines as he wants to do.

'We get "fed up" sometimes at the front,' Jacka allows to the Melbourne *Herald*'s London correspondent, 'but after I have been a month in Blighty I want to get back among the boys again. There's a suggestion that the V.C.'s [sic] should go back to Australia to help recruiting, but, as far as I am concerned, this is not the time to go back. They ought to know what we are fighting for in Australia without being told. Besides myself there are five or more V.C.'s [sic] in the 4th Division. They are still fighting, and I think they agree with me that the only thing to do is to fight on till the job's done.'[41]

Again, he declines the offer to be sent home, and he is offered light duties at Depot No. 1 at Sutton Veny in England's rural Wiltshire, where his role is to act as Sports Officer.

Summer 1918, Hamel, strike up the orchestra, starting with the big drums

And yet, even though Jacka is not back with the 14th as he hungers to be, his influence on their fate remains profound, and nowhere more so than in the Battle of Le Hamel, which takes place just to the north-east of Villers-Bretonneux, at the height of the summer of 1918.

For, just a little over a month before, the Australian Government of Billy Hughes had finally put an Australian in charge of all Australian forces, in the person of General Sir John Monash – General Birdwood is sent to command the British Fifth Army to replace the disgraced and departed General Gough – and Monash has no sooner taken the post than he embarks on an entirely different approach.

There will be no more battle plans involving sending thousands of Diggers straight at German bunkers bristling with machine guns. There will be no more orders to attack with 12 hours' notice, making it up as they go along.

From now, all major attacks will be well thought out, repeatedly rehearsed, and based on the idea that the aim is to beat the Germans while losing as few Australian lives as possible. (It's damn nigh revolutionary in concept.)

As General Monash will later record his approach: 'The true role of infantry was not to expend itself upon heroic physical effort, not to wither away under merciless machine-gun fire, not to impale itself on hostile bayonets, but on the contrary, to advance under the maximum possible protection of the maximum possible array of mechanical resources, in the form of guns, machine guns, tanks, mortars and aeroplanes.'[42]

When it comes to those tanks, Monash wants them to be superbly well organised – with a battle plan that absorbs all the lessons of Albert Jacka's Tank Report; and their commanders to be entirely familiar with the battlefield, and present in sufficient numbers to make an impact. Happily, among the beneficiaries of the absent Jacka's legacy will be his own 14th Battalion, who in the last weeks of June have been resting in the farmlands of France, living in billets at Aubigny on the Somme, two miles north-west of Villers-Bretonneux.

•

The sunshine, the greenery, the relative peace, all make for a lovely break in an otherwise muddy and bloody war, and among the favourite activities for people like Lieutenant Ted Rule is to spend time picking strawberries in the local abandoned patches – and eating them till his nose would bleed.

Another thing the whole battalion enjoys is to head for a wash at the baths at the nearby village of Corbie.

On this day, Rule has sent C Company down to the baths, only for the Sergeant to come back, beside himself with excitement.

Poking his head into the dugout – just a few hundred yards back from the front line, within shelling range – he asks, 'Do you know there is a big stunt on, and we're in it?'[43]

No, Lieutenant Rule knows nothing about it, but upon investigation discovers that is clearly the case. In fact, the area where they are billeted 'is lousy with guns of all sizes back on the river, and tanks are hidden all over the shop'.[44]

For some, the whole thing seems quite unreal.

They are to attack the German lines at Hamel, and it will be *tanks* doing the heavy lifting.

When Monash's plan is unveiled for the officers, Ted Rule absorbs every detail, stunned by just how minutely *detailed* that detail is. And every line could have been written by the missing Albert Jacka, based on his Tank Report.

No fewer than 60 tanks will be attacking across a front of 6500 yards. And there will be no more nonsense about tanks and men proceeding to the German line without the support of artillery. '*The deployed line of Tanks [are] to advance . . . pressing close up to the barrage . . .*'

(And not just any tanks. As noted by Colonel Harry Murray, these Mark V tanks are 'greatly improved and splendidly manned', much more so than the Mark I and Mark II tanks used at Bullecourt.[45] No longer are they crewed by mechanics, but actual tank specialists.)

At Zero Hour minus eight minutes, a light barrage will start, and the tanks will begin to advance. Why minus eight minutes? Because the tanks will be positioned precisely eight minutes from the 'hop-off' tape: 'the noise of their engines being purposely drowned by aeroplanes flying over and machine guns firing'.[46]

When will Zero Hour be?

At *precisely* 3.10 am, when not only will the tanks get a little visibility, but the attacking soldiers will have just enough light to see their way pushing east, ideally with the defending German soldiers being silhouetted by the light skies of the coming sun rising behind them. For the Germans, however, the attacking soldiers will be coming out of total darkness.

At Zero Hour minus four the first wave of men will move out into No Man's Land.

At Zero Hour itself down will come a blaze of artillery that will advance 100 yards every three minutes, as will the men and tanks that follow it.

Most importantly of all, just as Jacka had insisted, tank commanders will not be laws until themselves. For, make no mistake: *Each Tank, [is] for tactical purposes, to be treated as an Infantry weapon; to be under the exclusive orders of the Infantry Commander to whom it [is] assigned.*[47]

The whole plan, Rule recognises from the first, is precise, concise and brilliant. It is a plan that has been laboured over and tweaked to perfection; not a far-off order to be followed regardless of reality. Most importantly, it is as far from the Bullecourt plan as it is possible to get.

If it works, Monash is a bloody genius. If it doesn't, well those left alive can think about what to do next.

3 July 1918, Hamel, clockwork at work

A beautiful night for a battle?

Yes. But also just a beautiful summer's night, with bursts of soft moonlight illuminating the barest wisps of mist floating up from the Somme, and the slight rustle of a breeze wafting those wisps away – even as the odd cloud passes across the face of the moon.

Precisely as Monash and his senior officers had counted on and expected – because the fact that it is like this for *nine nights out of ten* at this time of year has been carefully researched – the light breeze is blowing from west to east, coming from behind the attacking forces. This means that whatever clouds of dust are generated by the shell explosions to come on the dry soil of summer, mixed with the drifting smoke screens, will inevitably drift towards the Germans, making it difficult for Fritz to see the men and tanks who will soon be charging towards them through that genuine 'fog of war'.

•

For the 6000 men lying out behind the starting line in No Man's Land due to attack in the first wave, all is calm and quiet. Their numbers include Lieutenant Colonel Harry Murray's men of the 4th Machine Gun Battalion.

Some 200 yards behind the front ranks is the second wave, which includes Jacka's mob (they are still that, even without him), with Lieutenant Ted Rule and his mates among the many dying for a cigarette to displace this tension. (Once the battles starts, you *almost* forget about wanting a drag.)

HOLY CHRIST! Ted Rule has heard infantry barrages before, now he will be amazed if he can hear anything when this one stops. Who knows how it will end but the Battle of Hamel proper is beginning with a BANG and a ROOOOOOOAAAARRRR and a thunderous static that rips through every eardrum. Well, at least they have clear orders because God help the officer who tries to vary one with his voice now: 'Not a bit of use to try to get the men to double, for in the roar of the guns and the shells bursting ahead it was impossible to hear your own shouts.'[48]

Forward!

•

The battlefield of Hamel is the most ordered chaos that any man has seen. Jacka's mob can see the night evaporate around them, bursting shells from their artillery falling ahead just where they are supposed to, and with them 'phosphorous smoke shells, like the sun shining through a thunder cloud, which lit up places like day'.[49] By this incredible light they can see that the bloody tanks are actually where they should be! Which is waddling just behind the barrage, and just behind them are the first wave of men and just behind them ... a lot of lost Yanks, as the Americans enter the war for the first time, under no less than Australian command.

It seems that Monash has considered everything and they all flow ahead, a blast of artillery protecting tanks and Yanks alike, clockwork in motion again. So too, with Colonel Harry Murray's men of the 4th and 5th Machine Gun Battalions, both under his command for this operation, 116 machine guns in all, who fire with devastating effect.

•

In the midst of Hamel, Ted Rule is advancing fast when he sees a German head pop up from a wheat crop! It looks straight at him and BANG down he goes. Rule has shot him in a split second, like a magic trick. They come across a shelter and yell for the German soldiers to come out. Two soldiers do, they are 14- or 15-year-old boys in uniform, holding pieces of black bread out as a peace offering. If this is what the Germans are reduced to, how long can this war go on?

Lieutenant Ramsay Wood approaches Rule and the two walk over to a trench to see if they can spy any hiding Germans and CRACK. Ted turns to his left and sees Ramsay dead, a bullet through his temple. He is the best-dressed corpse Rule has ever seen on a battlefield.

In the midst of death there will still be life, and 20 minutes later, just a few yards from Ramsay's body, the Germans begin to present themselves for surrender. They give themselves up one or two at a time, appearing as if by magic and flinging their hands above their heads in defeat. In short order it is over, as the Germans surrender, *en masse*.

The incredible success of Hamel dazzles the Americans. God Almighty! Done in 93 minutes, for a gain of 2000 metres! Is it like this every time? Ah, not quite. Ted Rule is delighted and proud to overhear the dough-boys' verdict, as one says to another: 'Well, guy, these Aussies will do us, they've got plenty of guts.'[50]

Ted Rule also gets some news he can write home about: 'After Hamel I heard that I had been recommended for a decoration, but I'd had that experience before. Being recommended and getting an M.C. were two very different things'.[51]

That is another lesson that Bert Jacka taught him; but Rule is determined not to brood on it. He is alive, and by God if there are a few more battles like that, the war will be over and he will remain alive. Bless those tanks. Wonderful things, if you know what to do with them . . .

•

Though he will never make a complete recovery from being gassed, Albert Jacka can at least function again without complete exhaustion and is still doing well in England as the Sports Officer at No. 1 Command Depot, Sutton Veny.

'It was an eye-opener,' his Australian 2IC will later chronicle. 'For some reason, most of us had understood that Jacka, V.C., was of the wild, swashbuckling order, who drank heavily, swore frightfully, and used English that would shock a navvy. All were, therefore, surprised to meet a smallish, well-built man, faultlessly uniformed, clean-cut and well groomed, with an easy flow of educated English and a manner that women might describe as charming.'[52]

And if his teetotalling days are over, still he is nothing if not moderate.

'Far from heavy drinking, he occasionally took a glass of port, perhaps two, before dinner, and that was about his limit.'[53]

•

In the meantime, there are other things Jacka can do to keep his hand in. He soon hears that the locals have been having problems with thugs known as 'sandbaggers' who 'wait on dark roads, and attack men from behind, rob them, and leave them maimed and sometimes even dead'.[54]

Thugs on dark roads?

That is right up Bert's alley.

Jacka and another officer head out to see if they can get accosted, Jacka taking a cane with him to look more vulnerable, and . . . and here come two likely lads.

'Got a cigarette?'[55] one asks.

'Got none,' says Jacka and as the men loom closer they recognise him. *That is bloody Albert Jacka!* And they were going to rob him. As a matter of fact, they'll still give it a go.

'You bloody decorated hero, I'll have you on!'[56] yells one of the men and lunges at the VC winner. With a grin, Jacka throws his cane away, sidesteps his assailant and punches him in the face. Down he goes. Up he gets, and Jacka, his blue eyes flashing with pure pleasure, again punches him in the face. Down he goes. His partner in crime simply watches as he rises once more and . . . down he goes.

'I had to knock the beggar down four times before he took the count,'[57] Jacka tells Ted Rule. Yes, but why didn't you get hit? Oh, that's simple.

'Each time he hit, I ducked and walked into him.'

It is always that easy for Jacka. When Jacka learns that the man he knocked down four times is, in civilian life, a famous boxer, Rule can see him beam with delight. 'I think Jacka was really prouder of this feat than any other in his military career.'[58]

A marquee KO beats the VC any day.

•

Right now, Lieutenant Ted Rule – recently awarded a Military Cross to go with his Military Medal – is in his own hospital in London, having been, of all things, knocked over by a motorcar while on leave in England and walking past Buckingham Palace!

And he has a visitor, a . . . Mr Wanliss.

Ah, yes, him. Ted has heard that the late Harold Wanliss's father, Newton, is around.

And here he is now, an old, slightly dishevelled gentleman, who begs leave to ask a few questions, while taking copious notes.

Of course.

No sooner has the old gentleman taken a seat, however, than he fires off his first question.

'When did you see Harold last?'

Rule recounts, the best he can, that terrible day at Polygon Wood, and how one of the last things Harold had said was how much he was looking forward to getting home to Australia.

'With hungry eyes,' Rule will recount, 'he listened to every word, and no sooner was the question answered than another followed.'

Who was with Harold when he died?

Was he killed outright, or did he manage to say anything?

Did he get any medical help?

'The father was dazed with grief,' Rule chronicles, 'he thought and dreamt of nothing else but his boy. Afterwards he haunted the hospital to interview each wounded man coming from the battalion. He asked the same questions a hundred times, he heard the same answers, and was never satisfied.'[59]

•

On 31 August the still recovering sandbaggers around Sutton Veny would likely be pleased to hear that their mysterious assailant receives orders to prepare to return to his homeland 'as early as may be convenient'.[60]

As it happens it's not . . .

Convenient.

Jacka is not ready to return to Australia yet. There are many reasons, not least being that it feels wrong to be going home when all of his mates are still on the Western Front . . . and yet he is not strong enough to return there, either. There is also the issue of . . . well . . . the fierce difference of opinion he now has with his father on the issue of conscription. Taking on the German Army is one thing. Taking on Nathaniel Jacka on conscription is quite another. There will come a time, but that time is not now.

So he declines.

The AIF insist.

General Birdwood's adjutant himself officially informs him that, 'whilst very much appreciating the thoughtfulness of Captain Jacka and his self-sacrificing spirit, [the General] is of the opinion that it would be best that the decision already arrived at be adhered to'.[61]

And make no mistake.

'In arriving at this conclusion, [the General] is guided by the fact that Captain Jacka himself must realise that he is much in need of a rest when he admits that it would even be beneficial for him to remain in England for six months. In view also of the fact that the Minister has definitely expressed his wish that all V.C. winners be returned to Australia, [the General] trusts that Captain Jacka will now accept the decision without further demur . . .'[62]

Jacka demurs, with some force.

He does not wish to return, whatever might suit the government and obliges the Commanding Officer of his unit to officially write back to Birdwood on 15 September 1918, claiming estrangement and engagement as the reasons Jacka must stay:

> Jacka is very strongly opposed to returning to Australia just at the present moment for the undermentioned reasons:
> 1. He is engaged to a lady in England and has arranged to get married within the next two or three months.

(This will be news to his family, to everyone who knows Jacka, and for that matter, Jacka himself – but bloody hard to prove untrue.)

> 2. He is at the present time somewhat estranged from his father who is a strong anti-conscriptionist in Australia, Jacka being of course a conscriptionist; and he feels that if he goes out to Australia to help in the conscription campaign it will considerably widen the breach between them.

(This is a breach more honoured in the telling than in the observance, but again a nice dodge.)

> Jacka has always stated that he is fit to carry on and according to his statement to me a week or two ago, in his opinion he is quite fit (and anxious) to resume duty with his unit in the field.

If anyone is reluctant for Jacka to return to the front it is not Jacka, but rather his commander:

> I gather from other sources that there has been a certain amount of unpleasantness between him and his brigadier [Brand].
>
> I am afraid if we persist in returning Jacka to Australia merely because he is a V.C. man, we should come in for a great deal of criticism both here and in Australia ... [63]

In the face of Jacka's fierce resistance, Birdwood has no more choice than the German Army and Jacka soon receives the next letter from Birdwood's adjutant:

The General has asked me to drop you a note to let you know that your remaining in England has been approved.[64]

•

As it happens, there will shortly be no war for Jacka to return to, even if he wanted to, as at 11 o'clock on 11 November 1918 the guns on the Western Front and in the Middle East finally fall silent as the Great War comes to an end.

Wild celebrations break out across the world, and even from soldiers of *both* sides, as they realise that, against all odds, they have made it through this war. For most of the 180,000 Australians now beyond Australia, the immediate concern is to get home as quickly as possible. Albert Jacka is an exception. For one thing he still wishes some time of calm to reflect before facing the hurly-burly of home. For another, with so many of his comrades desperate to return and so few ships to take them, it is only fair that the married men with families go first, followed by married men, with single men like him bringing up the rear. It will be much later, in early September 1919, before Jacka finally leaves Perham Downs and makes his way to the docks at Plymouth to catch a ship home to Australia.

What awaits there, he is not sure, hoping only that the memory of that ancient first VC at Gallipoli may have slipped from the public mind . . .

CHAPTER FOURTEEN

HOME IS THE SOLDIER

The anguish of the earth absolves our eyes
Till beauty shines in all that we can see.
War is our scourge; yet war has made us wise,
And, fighting for our freedom, we are free.

'Absolution', Siegfried Sassoon

That is what Jacka is. His bearing, speech, appearance and courage are true to the Australian type ... Other VC winners have come home without great display, but in the general mind of the people Jacka is the symbol that stands for them all.[1]

The Herald (Melbourne), 20 October 1919

Late 1919, Melbourne, hail the conquering hero

Given a choice, Albert Jacka VC would arrive home anonymous as a lost dog. He would just wander down the gangplank and disappear into the crowd, home and away. And he had been hoping that the passage of time would do the trick. After all, he had won the VC nudging towards *five* years ago, in May 1915. The 1920s are nearly upon them, and the war has been *over* for nearly a year. Surely, he will be left alone to get on with his life and there won't be too much fuss?

But only a man who has not been in Australia for years, let alone Melbourne, could think this. Jacka's presence on the ship *Euripides* had been spotted in South Africa and the news flashed to a waiting nation in late September, giving it plenty of time to prepare. '*Captain Albert Jacka, the first Australian to win the Victoria Cross, and the recipient of many additional distinctions for gallantry, is returning* to Australia on the S.S. Euripides, *which is due at Cape Town today. He is expected to reach Melbourne about October 23.*'[2]

Expected he is, and reach Port Melbourne he does, whereupon a visitor comes aboard to shake Jacka's hand. To his astonishment it is the Governor-General of Australia, Sir Ronald Ferguson. In ancient Greece, Euripides was famed for writing tragedies, but even he would not be equal to conjuring up the horrific scenario now befalling one soldier aboard the SS *Euripides*. Captain Jacka is going to be celebrated against his will! For following the Governor-General are Senator Russell, the Acting Minister for Defence, along with Mr Wise, the Assistant Minister for Defence, and a Mr Trumble who is apparently the Secretary for Defence. (The soldiers on board have no idea who the last three fellows are, as they have been away for a while, actually defending things.) These grandees are followed by . . . the grinning countenance and khaki moustache of the State Commandant, Brigadier General Charles Brand!

It is a trap! It is sabotage! It is too late to stop and a polite order is given to Captain Jacka to get ready for public parade . . . via a shiny new motorcar, driven by Dr Weigall, the President of the Royal Automobile Club. As cab drivers go, he's not bad and three other grinning Diggers jump in the car with the mournful Jacka and prepare to wave. The old Brig poses for an official photograph (he is smiling broadly, Jacka is not), and then retreats to join the Governor-General in his own car and . . . they are off.

By God! It is not just a throng around the ship, for as they motor through Port Melbourne they can see that the streets are lined with schoolkids, housewives and working men, all standing and cheering! Well, the returning men wave back and Jacka joins them wholeheartedly. These people have stopped their lives for just a moment to see him. There is no point trying to talk them out of it, just wave! The houses they drive past have bunting on them, there are signs written in paint and chalk for them to see: 'JACKA WILL DO US'[3] says one. The calligraphy is not exactly steady, but neither is Jacka by this point. By God, this is something! He is not just a soldier now, not just known to the ranks, he is a bona-fide *celebrity*, who could look Dame Nellie

Melba in the eye and not blink. No, more than that, he is a symbol. The applause and cheers are not just for him, they are for every brave boy who left and never came home, every son, husband, father, brother and mate. The roar continues to grow just as the crowd does, as they all lean forward to get a better look at him as he passes.

'They saw a rather short young man of 26, with a fair-complexioned, boyish face, and bright eyes that spake determination, mingled with extreme embarrassment at the warmth of the popular welcome. Jacka may be daring, resourceful and gallant, but he has most pronounced the attribute of modesty, if not shyness. As regards his own deeds the Sphinx could not maintain a more rigid silence. He refused point blank to be "interviewed," and would say nothing of himself for publication or other use.'[4]

As they come into the city they see men running out of their offices and shopgirls happily deserting their posts just to see Jacka! But which one is he? The short one, with blue peepers, look hard! Ah yes, he is the one 'hiding bashfully among his fellows'.[5]

His fellow Diggers obligingly point as they wave. He's THIS one! Dr Weigall drives on proudly and now slowly, guided by necessity as the reporter for the *Herald* will note on the paper's entire top half of the front page on the morrow, 'neath the headline:

WELCOME OF WELCOMES FOR JACKA, V.C.
MELBOURNE PAYS SPONTANEOUS TRIBUTE TO AUSTRALIA'S MOST POPULAR HERO

Roman Triumph Through Thronged Streets

When Albert Jacka won the Victoria Cross at Courtney's Post in 1915, he became the symbol of the spirit of Anzac. Through the long campaigns that followed, he carried on the splendid tradition. Today Melbourne remembered these things and the welcome it extended to him was a notable and spontaneous tribute . . .

As the car passed Melbourne suspended business for a few moments to indulge in a happy festival of hero worship. Through a narrow lane of cheering people the motor car passed. Smiles were on every face, greetings were on every lip, and every hand signalled, 'Put it there'.[6]

As they enter Bourke Street, the girls who toil in the giant drapery workhouses have temporarily *stopped* toiling and one girl is brave enough to rush up and leap on the car, to fling her arms around her hero and give him a passionate kiss.

'That's for Sister Susie!'[7] she says, referring to the popular 1914 song 'Sister Susie's Sewing Shirts for Soldiers' as the crowd roars its approval. The Diggers in the car roar too, because she has made a mistake!

'Their deputy had not kissed Captain Jacka but a delighted and bashful Digger in his car. Everybody was satisfied, however – particularly Jacka's understudy.'[8]

Good Lord, they can't enter Swanston Street, because there is no more street, just crowd! *Make way! Make way!* No way, Dr Weigall, they all want to see Jacka. The car inches its way to the Town Hall, a rolling riot of happiness and shouted celebration following and greeting them at once. Awaiting Jacka and the Diggers are their comrades already returned, the men of the 14th, some in uniform, some already back on civvy street, all assembled here to yell for Jacka. And they come armed, with flowers! Hundreds of flowers, thousands of damn flowers – roses, poppies, daisies, carnations and gardenias – all raised and at the ready, now thrown in an attack of colour and celebration as Jacka is here! A brass band plays 'Over There', the words that all know and every soldier chants:

So prepare, say a prayer
Send the word, send the word to beware
We'll be over, we're coming over
And we won't come back till it's over, over there

Well, it is all over, over there, but the celebration here will not stop, as ex-Majors and current Privates continue to throw their garlands – Majors and Privates, incidentally, who are observed to be chatting happily with each other, as 'all distinctions of rank were forgotten in the joy of the day'.[9] It is a triumph, the kind Roman emperors enjoyed, and Jacka will just have to suffer through it. The Lord Mayor, Alderman Cabena, is waiting to give a very long speech, but he will have to wait a very long time before giving up entirely, as he can see from where he stands on the portico that Jacka's car will be racing snails at this rate just to reach the assembled pooh-bahs waiting at the Town Hall. The *Herald*'s reporter gleefully records what follows:

PELTED WITH FLOWERS

> Driven by Dr. R. E. Weigall, president of the Royal Automobile Club, the car crept beneath the portico – and vanished. That was the impression which was given, for a human wave engulfed it. The Lord Mayor looked down, not upon Captain Jacka, but the shoulders of the returned men who greeted him. They swarmed over the car, and pelted him with roses and flowers, they cheered and shouted welcome, and on every side men and women craned their necks or stood on tip-toe to see the man of the hour.[10]

Jacka's car is lost under a mass of adoration. The entire population of Melbourne seems to be in Collins and Swanston streets together, and they swarm now towards the last sighting of the car, because Jacka must be in there somewhere!

'Surging, jostling and shouting, taking all the pushing and buffeting in the best of spirits, they sought a glance of the soldier, an opportunity to pat him on the back, shake his hand, or in some other way express their feelings.'[11]

But they can't even see him! The lucky beggars who are near the car grab onto it, anxious to hold their place, but Jacka still can't be spotted, lost under the hail of flowers and humanity. It is an incredible scene, or it would be, if they could see it.

'Stand him up – let's have a look at him!'[12] bellows one voice, and then the cry is taken up by others who can't see, 'STAND HIM UP!'[13] And up he stands, for about five seconds, knocked over by a huge roar and his own embarrassment.

Dr Weigall is roaring now, there are a dozen people thumping and jumping on his beautiful car, trying to touch Jacka. *Christ, this is getting dangerous!* The hood is broken, the car springs are forced so flat that tyres jam against the mudguards – they are stuck! The wheels won't move, can't move, until the crowd does. The cars that are following now start to HOOOOOOT and HOOOOOONK which only adds to the scene, no, the reality of chaos. Dr *HOOOOOT* Weigall has

HOOOOOONK begged the crowd to move, they won't listen, so now he lets his fists do the talking. Yes, the until recently dignified President of the Royal Automobile Club is going to punch this mob into submission, one man at a time!

And it is not just the men.

'The energy and strength shown by the women in the crowd was surprising . . .' the *Herald* will report. They must get to him.[14]

When will the police arrive? Oh, they are already here, lost in the massive crowd that *HOOOOOOT* nobody can control. Well, one *HOOOOOOOOONK* man is making some headway, Dr Weigall has now booted several worshippers off his car and pushes a couple more before his automobile becomes mobile once more! Slowly they move off, the cheers turning to loud lamentation.

'But I haven't even seen him!' shouts one woman. A group of women rush towards Jacka's car now, the police won't hold *them* back, how could they? Many of them wear badges proudly saying 'Duty Done', some say 'In Memoriam', they are not giggling shopgirls; they are women who want to see the man who fought alongside their sons. They will never see those men again, they *must* see this one. *And there he is!* Waving now, as the car makes its way, in slow triumph, street by street, all the way to St Kilda, coated with cheers and flowers, both mounting as the morning goes on and on.

By the time they get to the Finalisation Depot, where Jacka is given medical checks and clearance to go on leave – if not yet officially demobbed – he has had far more than enough. He is *shaking*. The *Herald*'s reporter observes that Jacka is clearly 'in a state of nervous tension. Everywhere he looked, everywhere he moved, there were admiring people cheering lustily and straining hard at the barriers that they might grasp his hand. Excited women shrieked in his ears and flags fluttered in his face as he moved along the walk to the depot entrance.'[15]

None there knows that Jacka once suffered shell shock, it is a secret kept from all but his closest comrades. He is their hero, and the thought that their yells and roars are making him sweat and shake does not occur to them.

Finally, the official party is away from the crowds and inside the depot.

'Thank heaven that's over,'[16] Jacka says.

But it isn't, not quite, for as Jacka and the Diggers march down a hall to greet the phalanx of more officials readying their discharge, they are greeted by 'a knot of charming little V.A.D.'s [sic]',[17] the Voluntary Aid Detachment; consisting of the very thing that unnerves Jacka most: attractive young Australian women! Unlike the Sister Susies, the VADs *know* which one he is and are very anxious to make his acquaintance. Captain Edwin Wright, the staff officer for invalid soldiers, notices that Jacka appears distressed and suggests the traditional British solution: 'Would you like a cup of tea?'[18]

Jacka is grateful for any suggestion to desert his female fans and follows the Captain into an anteroom. (The women watching him go note that Captain Jacka is wearing pink socks! They are not exactly regulation, but then Jacka has never followed regulations particularly closely.) Unfortunately, on entering the anteroom, Jacka realises that it contains not just tea but even more VADs!

A delightful little table has been readied for him to have his tea while watched. 'Captain Jacka will have a cup of tea, Miss,' says Captain Wright and Jacka blushes furiously. 'I don't want *any* tea!' he blurts before backing towards the door and whispering into Wright's ear: 'Get me a car! Let me escape!'[19] Wright nods and moves off to arrange it. Jacka is left waiting with Lieutenant Mills, an aide to the old Brig, and a photographer approaches now, to no avail. No photos. Another journalist tries another tack: 'Congratulations on your remarkable war record!'[20]

'I'm not going to say anything,' says Jacka, and he slips from the building, racing to a car with Lieutenant Mills. The press rush after him, peppering him with dozens of questions, all getting the same answer: 'I've got nothing to say!'[21]

Will Jacka really say nothing? The journalists beg Brigadier General Brand to make him talk.

'He was one of the Fourth Brigade,' replies an amused Brand. 'They were *doers*, not talkers.'[22]

But there is one journalist, from the *Herald*, who has done his homework and knows just the question that might set Jacka off. He was the face on 10,000 recruitment posters, but his own father led a campaign against conscription and ... and now Jacka does answer, loudly and heatedly: 'I was in favour of conscription.'

And he has one thing more to say about the inaccuracies of the press: 'It was stated that I was in Malta. I was never near the place.'[23]

And with that, Jacka is driven back to the *Euripides* and safety from civilians. The *Herald* notes that 'Captain Jacka was adjutant of the *Euripides* and will go on to Sydney with the vessel.'[24]

That he will, but he won't get off the bloody vessel. This madness won't be repeated.

Now, when it comes to being mad, Dr Weigall has a bone to pick with the general public. 'Nobody was better pleased than I to see the public show of appreciation,' he says, but, 'It would be only fair if a little more self-control was used. Cars which are built to carry five cannot be expected to carry 40!'

No, apparently not. 'The women were as bad as the men! I do not wish to make any complaint, but if unruly demonstrations are repeated and the public show no respect for cars, motorists will have to decline to undertake the transport of such characters!'[25]

Dr Weigall need not worry, there won't be another character like Jacka.

18 October 1919, Wedderburn, Victoria, homecoming

It is an hour before midnight when the quiet knock comes on the door. No fewer than 1753 days and nights have passed without that knock coming. A sleepy Nathaniel Jacka opens the door to be overwhelmed with joy: Bert is home at last, in his weeping mother's arms in a moment, and every light burns bright now as brothers, sister, and never seen nieces and unknown nephews are brought forth to hug him. Home. Home with nobody knowing save those who matter most. It is the moment Jacka has dreamt of for five long years. It is the moment his parents feared would never come. Home safe, at last.

Father and son have quarrelled across oceans. The issue of conscription has divided them when separate, but now they are together and young Bert, little Bert, his boy, falls into Nathaniel's arms. Hang politics, hang the war; my boy is home. They will never quarrel again; at least not in the damn newspapers. Home, and hugs and tears at end at last, in a waking dream to bed.

But even in your hometown, you will awake to find yourself famous. Wedderburn wants to honour their most famous son, tonight, and a reluctant Jacka has no choice but to agree. He is their blue-eyed boy, literally. A guard of honour, led by Lieutenant McHugh, escorts the uniformed Jacka into the packed Institute Hall, where 70 returned men of the area wear their uniforms once more in the stifling heat. The Ladies Welcome Home Committee have prepared this welcome for months and dammit they will have it. But something is clearly wrong.

The guest of honour is shaking and sweating even among old friends. 'I'm suffering from a nervous breakdown,' says Jacka simply.[26] To these people, he can say what he has tried to deny for so long. The wounds of war come out in peace for him; and the strain, the shock, each day it appears anew. This evening is a torture to him, but it is one he will endure, with their help and understanding.

To the formalities, Miss Ida Mortcroft stands and raises a glass, the tinkling of a fork tapped against it brings silence: 'The toast is to our guest, our hero and our friend.'[27]

Hear, hear!

And now the local MP, in the time-honoured manner of all local MPs, rises to say a few expected words.

'May I say, to support the toast, that we have gathered to honour the bravest man the world has ever known!'

Hear, hear! Bravo!

The bravest man in the world is sweating through his uniform, shaking in fear with panic gripping him in this safest of havens. Two more speeches follow from local worthies. There is also a brief impromptu speech from an ex-Sergeant in the crowd, who feels he must speak, and tells the story of how he had been shot at Gallipoli out in No Man's Land, only for Bert to walk out, throw him over his shoulder and walk back! Like so many, he owes his life to Jacka. *Cheers!* It is another deed that Jacka has never mentioned, one that another man would dine out on for life.

More speeches, more thanks flow. Oh, to be a drinking man and just float through this thing, but no, now Jacka must rise stone sober and the applause rings out, ROARS OUT, on and on and on, all stand and shout their acclaim. He gestures for them to sit and at last they are silent and still, gazing up at him.

'Well,' says Jacka after a long pause. 'I am about to commence the greatest feat of all – responding to the compliments that have been paid to me.'

Laughter. (But, oh, he means it, look at him now, swaying in place. But continue he must and does.)

'No words can express my feelings on this occasion. I was farewelled in company with three others five years ago. Two of those never returned. The other has.'[28]

Silence now and a nod from the soldier Jacka singles out with a glance. Absent friends are present now for all. No fewer than 53 young men left this small town and surrounds to go to war, and will never see Australia again. They died half a world away, for their world to live. The strain and pain of loss is etched in Jacka's face as he tries to get out the next sentence that will drag them past this grief.

'Now . . .' he falters.

Come on, Bert! All in the hall will the shaking hero on.

'Now I am back . . . after winning the V.C. and . . . other things.'

Those who were there know; those who weren't never will. So many things that can never be said, never forgotten either.

'It's not that I deserve these distinctions, I only . . . I only took advantage of the opportunity. My comrades were soldiers of the first water. We *all* enlisted in the common cause. I'm no different from any other "Digger".'

Yes, he is, but they know exactly what he means.

'I don't mean to live in Wedderburn again, I've . . . I've joined an importing and exporting business in Melbourne, but I will always, *always* come here any chance I get.'[29]

And Jacka nods and sits to more roars and applause. Their boy! Reverend Jager proposes a toast to all returned men and all drink their health heartily (even the teetotallers).

The evening concludes with the presentation of a medal, not from the King, not from the government, but from the Ladies of Wedderburn. It is a medal they give to every son of the town who returns to them;

with a solid gold mounting from the Bendigo mines. The medal shows a Digger on a shield, circled by a boomerang and wattle, a kangaroo and emu. It could hardly be more Australian unless it was surrounded by corks, but this one is slightly different – it has a miniature Victoria Cross attached to it. Bert Jacka thanks them warmly and thanks God even more profusely that this evening is over. It is kind, it is lovely, it is over! To a final roar he exits, into the night, out of his uniform and into freedom.

Truly home, at last.

•

Or is he?

Every night that Bert is with them is marked by two things: the persistent and hacking cough that those who have inhaled mustard gas must endure, and the sound of Bert restlessly walking around in the wee hours. Not only does he find it extremely difficult to sleep, but what sleep he does get is blighted by nightmares of a horror that only former soldiers know, and front-line soldiers at that. Once more he has jumped into the shell-hole. Once more the fat Hun has lined him up and is about to shoot him. Once more he has ducked and lunged, thrusting his bayonet deep into the man's intestine. Once more the shocked Hun is staring at him with that devastating, haunting expression of one who knows he has only seconds to live, that he will never see again, know again, embrace again, everything he holds dear in this world before – *ach, meine Mutter,* oh, my mother – he falls dead at the feet of the man who has killed him, who has taken him away from his family, who has left him dead in a ditch in France.

Jacka wakes. And coughs. And walks.

Others in this situation – and there are tens of thousands of returned Diggers suffering much the same – drink, to dull the pain.

Bert Jacka remains a teetotaller.

•

It is no easy thing for one so marked by the war, so defined by it in the public mind, to settle back into the quiet civilian life he craves, but as with everything, Jacka does his best.

He settles back in Melbourne in the New Year, in a tenement in St Kilda not far from the waters of Port Phillip Bay.

What now?

Well, on the ship home he had talked extensively and deep into the night with two of his former subalterns from the 14th, Lieutenants Reg Roxburgh and Ernie Edmonds. From an old-time Melbourne business family, Roxburgh had suggested that the three of them – with Bert contributing his famous name and organisational abilities, and Edmond his experience before the war as a salesman – go into business together and now they do exactly that. Financially, Jacka's stake in the business is funded by a reported £200 in backpay from his time in service, boosted by the £500 long ago promised and given by the businessman John Wren for the first winner of the VC in the Great War, while Wren also backs the 26-year-old with more money now. Wren, in his early sixties, and of Irish Catholic stock, had laid down the foundation stone of his fortune 30 years earlier by running an illegal SP bookie operation from a room in the back of a Collingwood hotel. From there he had been into everything. If it hadn't fallen off the back of a truck, it was in parliament, and Wren owned it either way. He was an enormous supporter of the returned Jacka from the first – despite their different strands of religion.

Roxburgh, Jacka & Co. Pty. Ltd., Importers and Exporters, is soon open for business at 475 Collins Street, selling electrical goods.

With the business established, and his digs at St Kilda secured, there is one obvious thing lacking for Albert Jacka to build the future he had imagined for himself.

Her name proves to be Vera Carey and one morning when he is getting into the lift at the Olderfleet building (that grand piece of chocolate-box gothic that looks as though it has won second place in a design-your-own-European-castle competition) the petite 21-year-old 'bombshell' rushes in to give the national hero a kiss. One thing leads to another, and not long after Jacka organises a job for her as a typist in the business, he proposes.

One problem for them both in these times when one's religion is often a defining feature is that she is a Catholic, while he is Anglican. It means, for starters, that Jacka's family do not approve and, instead of what might well have been a large public wedding for Victoria's favourite son, they are married quietly on 17 January 1921 in East St Kilda's principal Catholic church, St Mary's. The wedding is so quiet, in fact, that there is no newspaper coverage, and it is not clear if any of the Jacka family attends. The best man role is fulfilled by Vera's brother, James, who is only 18 years old, and has only met Bert a few times.

Domestic life begins with Bert leaving their home at Murchison Street, St Kilda, to go to the store in Collins Street, where he is one of the principal attractions to bring potential customers into the store and enable them to ever after boast that they had bought their latest electrical goods from Bert Jacka VC himself. In the evenings he returns home, where he and Vera are happy for only a short time.

Tension in the nation at large is reflected in their own home. The most Protestant institution is the secretive Freemasons, and the fact that Jacka is a revered member does not sit easily with Vera Jacka. East Kilda's Masonic Lodge, which backs on to their own property, is a flashpoint in point, and one night Vera infuriates Bert by singing a most secret Masonic hymn! How on earth does she know this? Has Jacka been singing in his sleep? No, she simply stood in their yard and overheard the tune!

Despite their desires, they are not blessed with a child, which might have made settling down a little easier.

In the absence of domestic bliss, Jacka is drawn to old Army mates.

One he frequently catches up with is his old mate Ted Rule, who, though he has gone back to his farm near Shepparton, always visits Bert when he is in Melbourne.

The funny thing about Ted? All of them had just known him as a soldier and an officer, and though he was often seen to be scribbling in his diary, none of them had known him to be a writer. And yet, after copies of parts of his diary had been sent to Charles Bean by Harold Wanliss's father, Newton – who has been compiling the Official History of the 14th Battalion – Bean has written to Ted and encouraged him to turn the whole thing into a narrative book!

Another one Jacka keeps in touch with is the man Charles Bean will describe as 'the most distinguished fighting officer of the AIF': Harry

Murray VC, DSO (and Bar), DCM, four mentions in dispatches and the *Croix de Guerre*. True, Harry's life has turned briefly scandalous by his running off to New Zealand with his wife's niece – a woman nearly 24 years younger than him. *Smith's Weekly* breaks the story, and follows up: 'Colonel Harry Murray's dramatic flight from Blairmach Station, Western Queensland, some weeks ago with Miss Nelly Cameron, his wife's niece, published exclusively in *Smith's Weekly* last week, created sensation throughout Australia. Letters poured in from all quarters expressing sorrow that Australia's greatest soldier so voluntarily outlawed himself. Diggers, mostly, sympathised with him . . .'[30] At least his reputation is in part salvaged when they both return and, after he and his first wife divorce, the two are married in 1927 and have two children.

Jacka becomes involved in efforts of the newly established Returned Services League to look after the welfare of those who, with their families, are struggling because of their war service. The St Kilda branch of the RSL, where Jacka serves as Treasurer, becomes one of the strongest in the nation and is known as 'the Hero's Club' because, as its most famous member, Jacka is naturally the very public face of the institution. Providing cheap food and drink for veterans, it organises and hosts dances, fetes and sporting outings. It is a club of camaraderie, for men who experienced something unique together and now find their homes strangely foreign. It may be termed a league or a club, but really it's like a mess that has survived the war; a place where blokes who fought can mix with their own kind, where no explanations are needed and the past's daily intrusion into the present – that dark thing that lurks in so many of them – is understood.

Activities with the RSL inevitably bring Jacka back into contact with Sir John Monash, which includes the two of them marching side by side every year in the annual Anzac Day marches down Collins Street. (In strict contrast to Jacka's growing closeness to Monash is his public disdain for the likes of General James McCay, the Butcher of Fromelles as he is known, who had not only ordered his men over the top in that disastrous battle, but refused a truce with the Germans the following day that might have saved hundreds of Australian lives.

When the two find themselves on the same stage for a fundraiser for the RSL, Jacka refuses to shake McCay's hand.)[31]

There are some battles that will never be over, but the fight for funds unites the highest and lowest born in fundraising marches and parades to raise a monument to the dead.

The most significant of such marches comes in 1927 when, on the occasion of the visit to Australian shores of the Duke of York (later King George VI), Jacka and Monash march together – equals in the eyes of the public, despite Jacka never rising above the rank of Captain – in the front ranks of the extraordinary 30,000 who turn out to parade before His Royal Highness at the site of the old Federal Parliament House.

Monash has had his own struggles settling into post-war civilian life. Despite being among the most brilliant Generals of the Great War, he has not been offered command of the Australian Army in peacetime, nor given a post commensurate to one of his prestige. Through a combination of anti-Semitism and Prime Minister Billy Hughes' fear that Monash might become a political rival – Monash is never promoted to full General. Further, he is never given the obvious role of Victorian Governor, and the only major post he can secure is as Chairman and General Manager of Victoria's State Electricity Commission.

Jacka is dismayed at the lack of acclaim for the man who had saved more lives than any other Australian officer. Monash gained the eternal respect of his men simply by caring for them, and pursuing tactics that did not involve thoughtless slaughter as a starting point.

For the first time testing the powers of fame, beyond selling enlistment – Jacka organises, with the help of *The Age*, a public dinner at the Melbourne Town Hall specifically to celebrate the former commander. 'I think he'd like an address from us better than anything else.'[32]

Oh, and the Prime Minister is invited too, although as one wag remarks, preference will be given to soldiers first! (Luckily Mr Stanley Bruce MC and *Croix de Guerre avec Palme* is a returned soldier himself so he will safely make the cut, as will the Federal Treasurer, Dr Earle Page, a former military surgeon.) This dinner will formally mark what they all know: that Monash is owed a debt by them all. 'It is felt that the Diggers should recognise in this way the work accomplished during the war by the leader of the Australians.'[33]

Come Anzac Day, 700 are seated in Town Hall, and after a minute's silence, Sir John receives a 'communique' from 'HQ': The soldiers would like more beer, immediately. This is an organisational challenge he is able to meet and a night of buoyant speeches, celebration and commemoration follows.[34]

Senator Drake-Brockman, once commander of Percy Black's 16th Battalion, seconds the toast, and a simple Digger, Sydney Fowler, sums up the men's tribute to Monash with one word – 'dinkum'. That's what he was to them, and what they will be for him, forever. 'You are one of Australia's greatest sons,'[35] Fowler concludes, and the applause for Monash will not finish for several minutes, try as he might to get it to stop. Finally, Monash stands and speaks to them all: 'I have never sought praise, nor am I pleased by adoration, but I am deeply conscious of the honour you confer on me.' *Wild applause.* 'I have never wanted more than the sincere esteem and respect of my comrades who were on active service with me, and the confidence of the people of Victoria.'

He has both.

'The honour done to me is greater, as you have chosen Anzac Day on which to do it. Anzac Day is becoming a day of mourning, but I don't think it should be. The keynote of Anzac Day should be the note of pride in what was accomplished on that day.'[36]

Sir John then tells the story of the great victories of 1918 that ended their war and closes with an exhortation to all: 'Continue your allegiance, with the Returned Services League and adopt a definite objective.'[37]

Purpose and the future, gentlemen, not just the past. Speaking of which, there are some funds that have to be raised ...

It is through such efforts that Jacka becomes more involved with a project that Monash is pushing hard: the building of the Shrine of Remembrance in Kings Domain, up from the Royal Botanic Gardens. He and Monash both speak extensively at public functions – Jacka using lantern slides to show the battlefields they were fighting in – urging the public to donate, just as they strong-arm mayors, Legacy and RSL clubs, together with state politicians.

To the surprise of many, Jacka proves to be a compelling speaker.

'Thousands of young Australians were killed then and at later times,' he is chronicled by *The Argus* as saying at the Theatre Royal, 'and they had set for us traditions that we must live up to. It is for us now to do something to keep evergreen the memory of those fine men who had died.'[38]

(Applause.)

Thank you, but your applause is not enough. We need your money, and we need you to be generous.

•

Jacka's domestic life improves, a little, when in 1927, he and Vera are able to adopt a baby girl; her father is a Digger by the name of Smith, who Jacka had known in the war.[39] The story will later be told that, at a function at Government House in 1927, Vera is able to ask the Duchess of York herself whether she might name the little girl after the Duchess's own daughter born the year before, Princess Elizabeth, and does indeed receive the royal blessing. Vera is thrilled, and immensely enjoys such occasions, such as the next year when, together with all the VC winners and their wives, the couple are invited to the 10th anniversary commemoration of Armistice Day at Government House.

And yet things remain tense at home, and difficult for Jacka on the health front as his lungs continue to ail.

As the economy starts to stall in the late 1920s, so too does his business – now Jacka, Edmonds & Co., after the departure of Roxburgh due to alcoholism, likely brought on by war trauma. Though by now the business has expanded to four stores that has meant taking on a lot of debt, which becomes increasingly difficult to manage – most particularly after the stock-market crash of late October 1929. Inevitably, the business must close, leaving Jacka and Edmonds in great debt, and people out of work. In a gesture of great generosity, John Wren again steps forward, this time paying off the debts, amounting to nigh on £20,000.

The situation for returned veterans everywhere, not just Jacka and Edmonds, becomes ever more grim. Jacka has just been elected as a councillor of St Kilda Council, so a great deal of his efforts from now go to the council putting greater resources to looking after the destitute, with a special nod to the veterans who seem to be doing it toughest of all.

What now?

The course is not obvious, beyond meeting his responsibilities to provide an income for Vera and Betty. Yes, Jacka has come away with some assets, including the house they own in Murchison Street, East St Kilda, but they will not be able to hold it for long unless he has a salary.

Not long after, at the instigation of Jacka, the 14th Battalion's colours are officially handed over to St Kilda Council for permanent display in the foyer of the St Kilda Council building. And an option appears.

Why not stand for the office of the Mayor of St Kilda, which actually comes with a relatively handsome annual salary of £500? Jacka accepts the invitation and, after winning the election, from 25 August 1930 onwards is officially Lord Mayor Albert Jacka VC, MC & Bar.

Unofficially, he will be known as the 'Lemonade Mayor'[40] for the fact that his teetotalling ways continue.

Immediately, Jacka proposes an innovative program to aid the unemployed with government-created work. The government takes in taxes from the employed, so why not use that revenue to make work for the unemployed? Imagine if '1 million pounds were set aside to give 40,000 men 10 weeks' work at, say, 2 pounds 10 shillings a week'?[41] There would be money flowing back into the community. It is the sort of program that President Franklin Delano Roosevelt will soon be using on a massive scale to combat the Depression in America; at the moment it is just a notion floated by the Mayor of St Kilda.

Work, pay, dignity; all can be achieved with some thought and sympathy. It is well covered by the press, and Jacka is quoted by the *Sun*, in October 1929.

'Almost every day I meet men with whom I served abroad,' he says, 'and men who were unable to go to the war, down and out, for want of work ... Something must be done to help them; the amount of distress and unemployment in Melbourne is a tragedy.'[42]

22 January 1931, St Kilda, freedom in speech

Disorder in the court! In the old abandoned St Kilda courthouse, the old abandoned men of the Great War are gathering. The unemployed are having a meeting today, and each speaker will literally be in the dock. The old prisoners' box is where they must stand, and the dimly lit court hears voices of anger ring out, 15 minutes each – they have nowhere to go and they are all here at once to be heard. The windows of this court are broken, there is a boarded-up hole in the wall, and all the furniture and fixtures have been stripped. It is on its bare bones, and so are they. In the centre of these desperate men today is the new Mayor of St Kilda, Albert Jacka VC. He was asked to speak at 10.30 am, but forgoes his place so the men may speak first. One by one they rise, by midday they have not begun to finish.

An argument now breaks out about whether their 'cause' is being hijacked by Communists. An Irish voice rings out from the back of the court: 'Oi've been in two revolutions and, begorra, Oi don't want to be in another.'

Cheers! But a socialist in the crowd objects, very briefly, before the Digger next to him speaks for the first time: 'Shut up, or hop out!'

He shuts up. But the next two speakers are *both* Communists, who proceed to argue with each other about which comrade has betrayed the workers the most. The crowd begins to jeer the second speaker but one man now leaps to the front. It is Jacka.

'Men,' he says, 'you agreed to hear him for fifteen minutes; now hear him.'

It is the right thing, be quiet and listen. You don't have to agree, but give him his fair go. And when Bert Jacka asks you to pipe down, you *know* you'd better.

Finally, it is Jacka's go, and all fall silent to hear him now. This small man in front of them was once the mightiest man in the whole of the army; his quiet voice now holds the whole of the court.

'Gentlemen, I can understand your feelings, because I grew up in the country. I worked there from daylight until dark. I am a working man. I know of the hardship people are suffering, even in a place like St Kilda.'

Jacka tells them of his own anger at seeing the women and children of the unemployed being evicted from their homes. He has found them new homes where he could; given them a week's rent from public funds, but it is just one week, he is just one man, just one mayor. Everyone must be in this new fight together.

'The best we can do,' says Jacka simply, 'is proceed with the same normal conduct and discipline as in the past.'

Yes, it's true the council's funds are overdrawn, but meat, bread and groceries will be handed out to every family in St Kilda who needs them; for as long as his term lasts. But there is one body that comes in for a shellacking.

'I must say that I am disappointed with the Victorian Government,' Jacka adds. 'It has not done as much for the unemployed as the St Kilda Council even.'

If you are to be evicted, let him know, personally.

'Evictions are bad and likely to cause trouble.'

If you own your house and you are in debt and can't pay your rates, let him know that, too. Help is coming, hope is here already; if you are afraid, you are not alone. The meeting has one last piece of business: 'A vote of thanks to Cr. Jacka was carried.'[43]

No, one more word from Jacka: 'I've placed a motor truck at the disposal of the unemployed; to collect surplus, unsold vegetables from market gardeners.'[44] Now is not the time to be proud; it is time to survive.

Alas, both his reduced circumstances and his frantic business as Lord Mayor sees increasing pressure placed on the marriage. Even though Vera hugely enjoys the role as Lady Mayoress, when his term finishes in August 1931 – he decides not to continue in the top spot for the strain it puts on his health – she takes Betty and moves into new premises, helping to support herself by working as a hostess at the famous Hotel Australia in Collins Street, welcoming patrons and making sure they needn't drink alone.

Jacka is crushed, and ill.

As crook as he is, however, he still attends the funeral of Sir John Monash when the great man tragically dies of a heart attack in October 1931 at the age of 66.

For 'neath appropriately sombre leaden skies, on Sunday, 11 October 1931, no fewer than 300,000 people – a stunning one-third of the entire population of Melbourne – form up in funeral garb to pay their last respects.

As for Monash's own memorial, his own tombstone, it is no flowery or grand tribute: it reads at his own request just this: '*John Monash*'.

17 January 1932, Melbourne, death of a salesman

How long does it take before a battle is over? Not in your mind, but in your body? At least 13 unlucky years in this case, because it is 1931 and Albert Jacka has just been diagnosed with an illness caused by German gas, bronchitis. Just before Christmas, with blood in his urine and dangerously high blood pressure, his doctor diagnoses him as 'suffering from a severe degree of nephritis [kidney disease] with cardiac vascular degeneration. Rest in bed and vigorous treatment essential.'[45]

The monetary result? He is given a 20 per cent disability pension, all of which will go to his estranged wife, Vera, and beloved little daughter, Betty.

The practical result is that he is going to die – though not just of bronchitis, or a weakened heart, those two ailments diagnosed by Dr Crowe of the Repatriation Commission. Rather, it is expected he will die of pulmonary fibrosis, the 'direct sequels of gassing on service'.[46] Jacka accepts the pension and brushes off the diagnosis, just as he will dismiss the theory of his family that he is suffering lead poisoning as a result of stopping so many bullets. Yes, he is crook, but, look, he has been worse. (After all, according to the press, he's already been dead.)

The only reason he consented to get checked out in the first place was for his young daughter, Betty. For now, he continues to sell the soap, literally. Yes, he has accepted a position as salesman and 'commercial traveller' for the Anglo Soap Company. There is no time for pride, only practicality. He has a family to feed, and a job to do. Still, when the news trickles out to old comrades, they are stunned and angered that it has come to this. His mates are incredulous.

Albert Jacka VC?

'. . . selling soap to grocers, travelling from shop to shop,' Ted Rule will note. 'Our bright particular star would have to wait patiently while bacon and butter were distributed to sundry customers before receiving a bland "Not today, thank you", or "Overstocked already".'[47]

It is a bleak picture, a terribly trivial pursuit for a man of his great capacities, and yet Jacka himself doesn't necessarily see it like that. Before the war, he had been laying out fencing in the Victorian hinterlands, unnoticed. After the war he had done what he could. The fact that the public notice this time doesn't concern him. Ted Rule knows that at least one wealthy old soldier reaches out to him, offering discreet help that will never be known by any. No, is the firm reply. Jacka is not a charity case; he has a job. As Mayor, he saw real poverty and still sees it, as acting chairman of St Kilda Council. He also sees to it, in December 1931, that mixed bathing should be permitted in the Ladies Baths! Progress is here, there is no time to live in the past.

At a council meeting on 14 December, those attending get a shock. Jacka looks as though he has aged 10 years in a night. His blue eyes look watery and weary. *Anything wrong, Bert?* All fine. Today's mission for Jacka is to have a new council job, repairing Elwood Park Kiosk, granted to the unemployed of St Kilda. They *need* the jobs; they *need* the dignity and this council can give them both. Arguments on both sides are respectful, but the strain is showing on Jacka to even get out polite sentences. Just after the meeting is adjourned, to the shock of all, he collapses and is rushed to Caulfield Military Repatriation Hospital.

Jacka's very fame soon presents a real problem.

'Councillor Unsworth, St Kilda, phoned,' an administrative officer at the Repatriation Commission records, 'regarding the above mentioned ex-soldier, [Albert Jacka] who is in Ward 5 at the Repatriation General Hospital, Caulfield. He states that the Ward is noisy and Jacka is more or less held up as an exhibit by other patients to visitors and these conditions are against his recovery. Councillor Unsworth desires to know if he can make arrangements to transfer Jacka to the Alfred Hospital, where it would be possible for him to make arrangements for him to be in a single Ward . . .'[48]

The papers are quick to pick up the story and Jacka's name flashes again around the nation:

CAPT. JACKA'S GAME FIGHT

Father's Hopes: 'Has A Chance,' He Says

While Captain Albert Jacka, V.C., is fighting for his life in the Caulfield Repatriation Hospital, a member of his family is constantly at his bedside.

Today his father, Mr Nathaniel Jacka, of Bealiba Street, Caulfield, who spends most of the day with his son, told of his hopes that Captain Jacka will pull through. 'I believe he has a fighting chance,' Mr Jacka said. 'The crisis in his illness came last Thursday night. None of us expected him to get through it, but he is still living. I would not care to say that he is getting stronger, but to me he seems easier. The doctors evidently think he has little hope of recovery, but I feel instinctively that there is still a chance.'[49]

Ted Rule is at work, as it happens, in the same office as three other men from the old 14th Battalion, when his desk phone rings and the voice of the operator breaks through: 'Hello, hello, Melbourne calling, just a moment please.'

A second later a voice with a military clip comes over the line: 'Hello, is that you, Hill?'

'No,' says Rule, 'but if you hang on a moment I'll get him.'[50]

Ernie Hill is fetched very easily, he is sitting across the room from Rule, and he holds the phone to his ear as the voice barks bad tidings that Rule also easily hears.

'Captain Mitchell speaking, I've rather unpleasant news for you.'

The doctors think that, whatever his father says, Jacka will in fact be very likely dead within two days.

'If he passes out, it has been decided to give him a military funeral, and we're making arrangements accordingly.'[51]

The pall bearers at this stage are all to be men who landed with Jacka at Gallipoli, of which Hill is one.

'There's no need to tell you that we expect all 14th men in your locality to attend. I'm afraid the funeral may be as early as Sunday.'

So that's that.

Someone who remains of a different mind is Nathaniel Jacka, who sits now with his silent son, praying for him to come round. The wasted, wan figure on the bed wakes for a moment, looks at his father and says: 'Hello Dad, how are you?'[52] It is the same thing he has said every time he has come into consciousness – never surprised, just pleased. Nathaniel makes the same reply each time: 'I'm alright, son. How are *you* feeling?'

'Not so bad,' his boy replies.

The doctors disagree, but Jacka Senior holds to his last thread of hope.

'He wants to get better and that is half the victory won,' he tells one reporter. 'He still has his fighting spirit, and while a man has that there is no reason to despair.'[53]

The reason Jacka still has that spirit is visiting him now. She is five years old, little Betty dressed up in her best to see her father. 'Dad's bed is very high,'[54] she thinks, and this is a particular memory she will carry of him in future years: her sick father on white sheets on a white bed, and being lifted up as she is now, for a kiss. (What Betty doesn't see are the daggers thrown at her mother Vera, every eye an accusation as she glides in with the daughter so seldom seen. The strong word is that she is already seeing another fella, even *living* with him, and there is a word for women like that – an even worse one than *Catholics*.)

Still, stilted smiles are put on until Vera and Betty leave.

Jacka fades in and out of consciousness; he is drifting between this world and the next. In this hell, heaven must indeed be close.

But even in this state, he draws the attention of all. Indeed,

JACKA FIGHTING DEATH
V.C. – Yet You Let Him Down

MELBOURNE, Saturday. Blind, racked with pain, conscious only at intervals, Captain Jacka, Australia's first V.C., still lies at point of death.

FIGHTING in the dark! Opening exhausted eyes to a wall of blackness through which no light shines! Single handed, Jacka won the greatest war award of the British Empire. Single handed, he is fighting the greatest enemy. For doctors will say no more, and only his iron will keeps this Victoria Cross winner alive.

At his bed, in military hospital, a father and a wife watch, haggardly.

Outside, the world goes on. It can never stop, and it takes no heed of those who sicken and fight – and die. Over the rumble of traffic and the rustle of crowded streets comes no voice, saying: 'He won the Victoria Cross – yet you let him down!'

JOBS FOR OTHERS

That is the truth. Victoria Cross winner, and Mayor of St Kilda, Jacka had been unemployed for months. The strain of his financial worries, added to the ravages of war gas, brought him to his sick bed. He may never leave it.

Jobless through the winter months, while still Mayor of St. Kilda, Jacka, fighting his own battle alone, found employment through his council for hundreds of men who otherwise would have faced dire want.

As for himself, well, he was up against it. Then he got a job as a soap salesman. Still with a smile. There are many men in Melbourne today, placed through him, who will remember his hardships, and will say a prayer for what he did for them.

THIS IS COURAGE!

Things got worse for Jacka, V.C. He had to leave his home. His plucky wife, at first without telling him, went to work as a waitress at the Hotel Australia in Melbourne. Jacka tried to sell his soap. Then his illness came, and the whole world crashed about the little family. In his fever and his blindness, with bodily disfigurements and agonising rash from war gas; with kidneys terribly diseased and lungs assailed, Jacka fights Death.

All day his father sits with him: at three in the morning his wife bathes him and tends him. Through the hours, in the hideous darkness, a V.C. whom Australia chose to forget for practical reward fights the good fight.

'He won the Victoria Cross – yet you let him down!'[55]

Every day, Ted Rule and Ernie Hill phone Captain Mitchell, every day the news is the same.

'He's holding his own, but there's no hope.'

'How could there be?' thinks Rule. 'After all the gas he's swallowed in France and the way he was knocked about in beating the Germans off Pozières summit.'[56]

But he *lived* then, he came back then ... Telegrams flood in from old soldiers around the world; sending their best wishes, which are read to the boy by his father.

'I'm still fighting, Dad,'[57] Jacka says. And fight he does, even as his body weakens to the point where the only movement it can produce are tremors of pain. Finally, on the late morning of Sunday, 17 January 1932 – with his estranged wife, Vera, called to the hospital for the end – his once mighty heart ceases to beat.

A telegram is sent to Hill and the other prospective pall bearers, not with news of death, but orders that say the same: 'LEAVE IN THE MORNING'.[58] A last duty calls for the men of the 14th, their finest is to be buried.

19 January 1932, Melbourne, fall out

Aching baking heat of 110 degrees Fahrenheit. Bushfires are sweeping Victoria, and the smoke hangs in a heavy pall even over the city itself. Yet still the crowds line up outside Anzac House on Collins Street in their thousands to see the great man, this embodiment of all that is Anzac, lying in repose.

Gnarled old Diggers looking down – many of them old before their time – can't help but recall Jacka in his prime, unable to believe that the great man is dead. And they remember so many things, in such detail, like it was yesterday.

Bill Howard is there, and he remembers the extremity of that situation at Gallipoli, with the Turks having breached the trenches and Jacka shouting cheerily, 'Hello, Bendigo,' before jumping out into No Man's Land and then down on the unsuspecting Turks.

Gazing upon his coffin, Percy Bland is thinking of his terror when going out into No Man's Land at Gallipoli with Jacka for three nights until he spotted the Turkish machine-gunner and guaranteed his obliteration. And what about the time they'd been trekking back from the

Bullecourt disaster and Bert had given that Pommy cavalry officer what-for?

Ted Rule is present, front and centre, and inevitably his mind goes back to the charge at Pozières, the vision of Jacka and half-a-dozen others charging wildly at 80 Germans, and the carnage that resulted.

Bill Jacka can't shake the memory of his brother Albert's face being like a lump of lard in the immediate aftermath of that same battle.

Jacka's heartbroken father, Nathaniel, who watched his boy die in hospital from damage done far away, is comforted by Bert's siblings; the only ones who still think of him as a sweet, shy boy, not the famed legend he has become.

Newton Wanliss, the father of the late, great, Captain Harold B. Wanliss DSO, is overcome with grief and, though, of course he never served with Bert, as Official Historian of the 14th he knows more of his history than most. He has read the letters and diaries of the men who served with his son and Jacka, he even coaxed terse prose accounts from a reluctant Jacka as to what actually occurred in the fog of battles past. Now Jacka has joined history, and Harold, and Newton Wanliss is sorry indeed to witness it.

The Reverend Francis Rolland – now the revered headmaster of Geelong Grammar – is presiding over the service.

Religion is ritual at any funeral or memorial service, but there is one part of the service that strikes at the heart; that must be personal: the eulogy. Mr Rolland asks Allan McDonald, who has previously served as a Sergeant in the 14th Battalion, to deliver it now.

McDonald fought side by side with Jacka at Polygon Wood, he saw him command battalions, saw him win a battle, saw greatness in its truest form. McDonald has been writing the eulogy since before Jacka died, praying that he would live. It cannot say everything, but it will give something of what this man was, the best of the best, in war and peace.

'With heavy hearts we meet today to pay tribute to the greatest fighting soldier the AIF produced, Captain Jacka. To those who knew him best he was more than a fighting man. He was a friend and a source of inspiration when fear was about us; he was one of the most gallant men that one could conceive, a man who helped to make Australian history. A few short months ago our association held a reunion in this building. Never will any of us forget that night and the appeal that he made for the unemployed, and particularly for the unemployed "Digger". He is enshrined in our hearts, a dauntless leader, an incomparable soldier, and sincere, loyal, and trusted friend.'[59]

Members of the congregation weep, some of them men, and some of them members of the most recent organisation that Jacka had led, the St Kilda Unemployed Organisation. The wreath on his coffin has been provided by them, many of their members donating a precious shilling they could ill afford, to honour him.

No man could ask for a better or simpler verdict on his life, and every man and woman who hears it knows that it is deserved. His fate may not have been fitting, but he defied fate so many times on the battlefield, it's only fair it defied him in the end. And now Jacka is about to be enshrined not just in words but in fact; a city is waiting to see the glorious dead be led through their streets.

Albert Jacka is destined for St Kilda Cemetery today, but not before respects are paid, and so deep is the respect of the crowd that files past his coffin that Captain Mitchell can tell another hour at least – no, another two hours now – of delay must be expected. A full three hours is needed before at last the crowds are cut off and the lying in repose ends. It must end. The heat, the sweat, the bronzed soldiers burning outside to bear him, the thousands more who line Swanston Street, look like waves of wheat as they sway to stay up in this heat. Ceremonial and stately funerals are bloody hard in the heat of an Australian January, but they have a job to do today for Jacka and they will get his body in the ground with reverence, even if it kills them.

Jacka's pall bearers today have one notable thing in common. They are Bill Dunstan VC, Robert Grieve VC, Alby Lowerson VC, William Joynt VC, Rusty Ruthven VC, Albert Borella VC, Mick Moon VC and Issy Smith VC. Each man is a hero, and they are all carrying a legend, the greatest legend of them all, the one the papers are calling Australia's greatest front-line soldier.

Slowly, carefully, his coffin – 'covered with a Union Jack and the original pennant of his colours of the 14th Battalion'[60] – is placed upon the gun carriage that will bear Jacka through the streets this last time. To head the procession are the men of the 14th Battalion; many a time they marched with Jacka, many a time he led them, today the last for both.

'Through a city whose roar had faded to a murmur,' the *Herald* notes, 'and between solid phalanxes of people who stood bare-headed in the blistering sun, the funeral procession moved off.'[61]

The sun scorches down as the procession leaves Anzac House and moves down Collins Street, and now the crowds crane to see the coffin borne high, those looking down from office block windows see simply the Union Jack, the colours of the 14th, a slouch hat and his unsheathed bayonet. At Swanston Street and Russell Street the crowds flow forward, silently swarming as close as they can to see Jacka's coffin. (So vast are the crowds that mounted police have had to intervene, using their horses to force a laneway between the ever-pressing mourners, all wanting to get as close as they can, some wanting to touch the carriage and even the coffin itself!)

The Diggers march slowly; those they fought for, those their friends died for are watching.

'Every window,' the *Herald* reports, 'in shop and office was populous with clerks, shopgirls and the crowd flooded over the Swanston Street intersection and packed the parapets of the Town Hall and other adjacent buildings. For an hour the sun beat down mercilessly on the files of people who pressed forward to the tram tracks. It did not deter them from paying a last tribute of respect to a great soldier.'[62]

Old hands from the 13th, 15th and 16th – the men of the mighty 4th Brigade – follow the procession now; falling in at Russell Street. (Why, four soldiers have travelled down from Queensland in a day just for the honour.) But here too is new blood, fresh faces from the current 14th Battalion, the drummers and firing party that march now with the men who once held their roles when they were young, a thousand years ago in 1914.

Melbourne stops. The trams halt. The old Stewart Dawson building is being demolished today, but it stands for a few moments more, as the silent workers face the procession. The quiet is broken by the RSL band playing the mournful pomp of the 'Dead March'. They turn into

Swanston Street, that great artery of the city, and the vast crowd can see 800 Diggers now, their medals glinting in the searing sun, old soldiers in suits following Jacka. There is more than one man struggling in this heat, but they can bear it because they must. All wore one uniform, all fought in one war, the Great War, the last one, but how different they are now as they march behind their hero.

'Some of them, lame and worn-looking, walked with difficulty over the tram tracks. Personal discomfort was forgotten in a general desire to honour "poor old Bert". There were "Diggers" in faultless suits who swung canes jauntily as they strode along. There were others who were collarless and whose boots were falling to bits, those who had been overwhelmed in the war after the war.' (*Yes, Jacka was one of them, and they march for him today.*) 'There were frail men, prematurely aged, with greying hair and eyes that had lost their old-time brightness.'[63]

All walks of life march together. Old men who should look younger. Young men who remember those absent today, who fell out before Jacka, half a world away. They all fought with Jacka, their spirits are here today, you can feel it. The heat blows in gusts now; the wind is no relief, yet none begs off, none fall out. On they march – *far and near and low and louder, on the roads of earth go by* – as a city watches.

As soon as the gun carriage bearing Jacka is sighted, hats are doffed, leading to a most arresting and moving sight.

'A plain of felt hats turned in a flash to a plain of pink glistening foreheads as every head was bared at the approach of the gun carriage.'[64]

Eight horses pull the carriage forward, atop them are soldiers of the 3rd Divisional Artillery. As they pass Princes Bridge at 3.10 pm, the band strikes up Chopin's haunting 'Funeral March' and women begin to weep openly as the swell of the music matches the poignant sight of a single coffin leading so many silent hundreds.

There is one splash of military colour in a following open-topped car. It is the old Brig, make that Brigadier General Charles Brand, who leads a glorious group of officers from the Army, Navy and Airforce. Two cars precede them, containing nothing but flowers, wreaths and bunches bought and brought by the people; a beautiful moving garland that catches many a throat as it passes.

Work on the uncompleted Shrine of Remembrance stops as Jacka approaches: 'At the Shrine the Diggers' escort came to attention on either side of the road, and the gun carriage passed through.'[65]

Nearby, on the balconies of the Homeopathic Hospital, nurses stand with their patients on crowded balconies; the staff of the Defence Department stand at attention as Jacka's coffin passes their barracks. And now, most moving of all, at St Kilda junction, 200 unemployed men of St Kilda join the procession. Their battle continues, though their General lies dead at their head.

As Chapel Street joins Dandenong Road, the 14th Battalion Band joins the procession to relieve the RSL players; and 500 more returned soldiers join as the procession swells and swelters. At 4.30 pm, far later than expected for a crowd far bigger than any imagined, the gravesite is reached at St Kilda Cemetery and the long halt begins. A guard of honour – not of soldiers, but children – waits. The children of St Kilda, selected from each school, stand to attention as Jacka's coffin passes them, the last post before journey's end. A massive crowd gathers around the grave itself in all directions, and Ted Rule wonders how on earth this part will be pulled off.

For there in front of them, beside a gravestone now veiled in a Union Jack, is the old Brig. How strange this life is, for Jacka's old sparring partner and *bête noire* is now tasked by duty to serve and seal his memory to this fantastic crowd. By God, in the days when he and Jacka used to go at each other, they could clear a room! But will the old Brig be able to command this multitude? A silence settles over the masses now as this last eulogy is to be delivered. Brand's voice rings out.

'Looking on . . .' His voice breaks instantly with the strain and emotion, and he pauses.

Go on? Every man and woman watching wills it.

'Looking on his grave, every citizen will say, "Here lies one of Australia's greatest front-line soldiers". The unemployed of St Kilda will say, "Here lies one of our best friends". Captain Jacka will be remembered. He had handed down the torch of honesty, justice, courage . . .'[66]

And now Brand breaks off once more. Courage; the word does not do Jacka's insane bravery justice, but it will have to do for now.

'He was an inspiration,' Brand continues. 'When danger threatened, he fought the nation's battles in the line but fought the men's battles out of the line.'[67] And out of line he bloody was, but Brand admired him still and now that Jacka has gone all such petty quarrels fall away. A great man has fallen, a great warrior who died a humble salesman. Attention must be paid. Ted Rule hears a voice whisper behind him now: 'I never heard the old man make such a speech.'[68] True, but he never had such a man to make a speech about. When his graveside eulogy is over, with a final flourish, Brand pulls off the Union Jack and salutes Jacka's Australian tombstone. Gradually, all shuffle forward to pay homage and to read the words newly carved of the newly dead:

> CAPTAIN
> ALBERT JACKA
> V.C., M.C. AND BAR
> 14TH BATTALION A.I.F.
> THE FIRST AUSTRALIAN V.C.
> IN THE GREAT WAR
> 1914–1918
>
> A GALLANT OFFICER
> AN HONOURED CITIZEN
> DIED 17TH JANUARY 1932
>
> AGED 39 YEARS[69]

'God Save the King' is sung and the services are over at last. Ted Rule, his pen true as ever, records the scene as the giant crowd recedes: 'The spell was broken. Men gathered in little groups and renewed old friendships whose flavour, like that of old wine, had even improved with age.'[70] The old comrades talk of – what else? – Jacka. His fortune, his fate, his unique manner. Old tales are told and new ones learnt. Rule is particularly taken with one story of Jacka as Mayor. He was up on a dais making a formal speech at a stuffy function when he suddenly caught sight of an old comrade from the 14th at the back of the crowd in front of him. Jacka stopped in the middle of a sentence and said with a grin: 'Hello, Syd!' then continued with the rest of his Mayoral address. Afterwards, Jacka was walking past a table when he heard a comment about this moment: 'What an odd thing to do!' Jacka stopped and answered: 'I haven't seen this old soldier since we were in France together. The address *could* be delayed for a second; the greeting *couldn't*!'[71]

Did he really lose all his money? Have your heard about his wife? Selling soap door to door? Why didn't somebody help him? Oh, many tried but Jacka would not let them. Once he was offered a seat in Parliament, he would be a landslide man if ever there was one, but Jacka would not hear of it.

'If I did accept,' Jacka had sagely noted to one close friend, 'they'd say, "Look at Jacka – failure in business, climbs into a safe job as an M.P.!"'

Typical Jacka. No other like him. *Extraordinary bloke. Do you remember the time at Gallipoli that* . . . and the talk turns to the glories of the past, glories no other matched, and they talk together of what they never speak of separately; for nobody else understands the Great War. They head on to the pub, to drink to their favourite teetotaller, but later Ted Rule finds himself walking back to the cemetery, alone. There, in the blessed cool of night, he sits on a marble slab and thinks of Jacka. What was it all for? What did it all mean? These questions are too deep for a Digger. Jacka is six foot deep now; but his memory is alive, ringing in the heads of his old friends. The nation knew the legend; they knew the man. The most amazing thing is they were one and the same.

EPILOGUE

'Safe quit of wars, I speed you on your way
Up lonely, glimmering fields to find new day,
Slow-rising, saintless, confident and kind—
Dear, red-faced father God who lit your mind'

'To His Dead Body', Siegfried Sassoon

They were far and away the most famous lines to emerge from the Great War, written by Laurence Binyon in his 1914 poem, 'For the Fallen':

They shall grow not old, as we that are left grow old:
Age shall not weary them, nor the years condemn.
At the going down of the sun and in the morning
We will remember them.

So it proved for Albert Jacka, even if his death from war wounds did not occur for well over a decade after the war was over. He would indeed be remembered – as this book is testimony – to this day.

So gigantic was the presence of Jacka in the lives of so many, his death left a massive gap that precious memories flooded to fill.

What though, of the most significant figures in his life, who grew old without him?

Jacka's estranged wife, and now widow, Vera, it must be said, was a rarity among his intimates in that she did not appear to mourn him for long, if at all. She had, after all, seen him just a couple of times in the year before he died, and both were brief visits to the hospital. But in the public outpouring of grief at his death, she waited no more than a day before launching an appeal for herself. Among the first to donate to it are members of the St Kilda Unemployed Organisation. They also 'canvass members of the public to make their own donations, to the fund being raised to help Mrs Jacka'.[1]

Over £2000 was raised.

The *Herald* also throws its weight behind the appeal, with a strong report:

A COTTAGE FOR MRS JACKA
HERALD APPEAL
V.C.'S WIDOW NEEDS HELP
£25 STARTS FUND

Worn out by financial worries, reduced to desperate need and torn with anxiety about the welfare of a courageous wife who had struggled on through the economic fight with him, Captain Albert Jacka, V.C., Australia's foremost frontline soldier, died in indigent circumstances. Today, Mrs Jacka, weary and jaded from days and nights watching at the bedside of her husband, sits in their little home at St Kilda, surrounded by a mass of telegrams of condolence from all parts of Australia, but with the bleak future ahead of having to subsist on an ordinary pension of £2 -2/6 a week . . .

Directors of The Herald and The Weekly Times Ltd. feel among those thousands there are many who have the means and would welcome an opportunity to pay an even more tangible tribute to the memory of Australia's first V.C. They can do this by helping to provide a home for Mrs Jacka.

The Herald, therefore, has decided to start a fund for the contribution of £25 for the provision of a cottage for her . . .

Jacka often in his last days expressed to his wife appreciation of the way she had struggled on gamely with him.

A pathetic feature of his illness, however, was that for some time before his death his sight had failed, and he was unable to see his wife's face or even hand as she held it before his eyes.[2]

It was not mentioned that Vera Jacka had already moved in with her new beau, a wealthy businessman, Frank Duncan. They would marry seven months later, though never moved into the house the public bought for her, which would see the newspaper extend more than a wisp of wasp in her direction:

CAPT. JACKA'S WIDOW MARRIES

A letter from Melbourne tells of the handsome widow of Capt. Jacka. V.C., who died in January of this year, being married again. It will be remembered that the Digger was out of work at the end and, although Mayor of his borough, was so hard up that his wife, with commendable grit, went to work in a city restaurant to keep the pot boiling. The public, who would not help the gallant Digger, rushed to the widow's aid and collected £1200. They bought her a little house, 'in grateful remembrance of her soldier husband.' It was adorned with wisteria and the pretty widow, in deep black, completed the picture. Her stay, however, was brief. She rented the little home, went to reside at a guest house and the people who gave of their pounds and pennies for the home marvelled thereat. The secret is now out, for recently Mr. F. Duncan, of Clifton Hill, led her to the altar and she became Mrs. Duncan.[3]

Vera Jacka would also neglect to tell the Department of Defence she had remarried, which sees an official take a dim view of an article he spies in *Truth* newspaper on 1 October 1932: 'Mr F. (Frank) Duncan, of Clifton Hill, a well-known Melbourne businessman was quietly married in Melbourne this week to Mrs Albert Jacka, widow of the late Captain Jacka VC ... The happy pair left for Sydney where they are at present spending their honeymoon.'[4]

The official scribbles a note on the newspaper clipping – 'I understand the marriage took place at St Patrick's Church Melbourne on 29/9/32. O/C desires you to verify in order to stop payment of her [war widow's pension of £4 -4/6 a week]'[5] – and it is put in her file as she is advised the pension is stopped.

At least ...

'Payment in respect of your child (one pound per fortnight) will continue.'[6]

For many decades, on the anniversary of Jacka's death, the surviving men of the 14th Battalion and the 4th Brigade, those who fought with Jacka and those who only knew him by legend, gathered in Melbourne and marched slowly to his grave, for a service to honour the first VC of the Great War. Initiated by Newton Wanliss in 1941, the 'pilgrimage was led by 100 former members of the 14th Battalion,'[7] as the core of the large crowd with them.

By 1947, a special speaker was announced in *The Argus*.

JACKA PILGRIMAGE

> The 14th Battalion and 4th Brigade Association will hold their annual pilgrimage to the grave of the late Captain Albert Jacka, VC, at the St Kilda Cemetery at 3 pm on Sunday next. Members will assemble and march from the corner of Williams and Dandenong Roads at 2.45 pm. Major-General C. H. Brand will be the speaker.[8]

(Brand is 74 at this stage, but still marching for Jacka, and still speaking warmly of him.)

Throughout the years, it was a common sight to see progressively older men standing in front of his grave with their heads bowed – old Diggers from the 14th, who happened to be passing through Melbourne, taking the time to pay their respects at Bert's grave.

Wider Australia would also honour him.

In St Kilda, the main road was renamed Jacka Boulevard, 50 years after his death, in recognition of his military achievements, and what he had done in his role as Mayor of St Kilda.

In Canberra, the suburb of 'Jacka' was christened in 2001.

•

The legend of Albert Jacka VC would live on, powered by his feats, the pride of his comrades and, most particularly, the books, starting with ... *Jacka's Mob*. For yes, even as Ted Rule's expanded diary on his experiences in the Great War is about to go to print under the title *These Australians* – Charles Bean will call it 'easily the best memoir that exists of the life of our infantry in France'.[9]

Rule's publisher decides to capitalise on the wave of public sentiment for Jacka and rename it for the fallen VC hero. Jacka's deeds and derring-do are, after all, intimately woven through the whole account, as are insights into the kind of man he was.

Published in 1933, it is an immediate bestseller, and will be revered through the years as a classic account of what the Great War was like.

The reverence with which Jacka would continue to be regarded will see defenders flood forward on the rare occasion when anyone would dare take a pot-shot.

The classic example came in 1950 when ABC Radio put out a play which portrayed Jacka as a borderline illiterate, an uncouth savage who just happened to be handy with gun in hand.

Australia leaned in, as two actors took on the role of Jacka and his brother Bill.

> Jacka: I get tired of it myself. But, Bill, we've got no education, you know that. It looks as if we'll be toiling all our lives like this, unless we make an effort to get somewhere.
> Bill *(scornful)*: You mean go to school?
> Jacka: Yes, I know that, at our age, school sounds silly. That's all right if you've ever been there, but we haven't. Why, I can just about read and write, and enough arithmetic to count up how many logs at two bob a log earns a quid, and I'll be 21 this year.[10]

Led by Bill himself, the Jacka family took a very dim view of the play, characterising it as a 'mass of inaccuracies and misstatements, and, in parts ... most offensive and belittling'.[11]

The general manager of the ABC, Mr Charles Moses, initially tried to defend the broadcast, insisting that it was no less than a 'eulogy of Captain Jacka', but the President of the 14th Battalion Association, Hugh Jackson, was having none of it, with his kindest remark being that it was 'utter trash'.[12]

The matter was even raised in Federal parliament, by a former comrade, now parliamentarian, Allan McDonald, a Liberal from Victoria – who in his eulogy for Jacka two decades earlier had called

Jacka 'the greatest fighting soldier the AIF produced'. McDonald was visibly moved as he defended the great man now.

'This broadcast depicted them as illiterate yokels,' he thunders, 'something we cannot speak of in a too disparaging form. Bill and Bert Jacka were employed by the Victorian Forestry Commission. They were not chopping wood. Bert Jacka was named the greatest fighting soldier of The First A.I.F. The least we can do is to see that those false conceptions are removed.'

Now openly sobbing, McDonald continued in a faltering voice: 'He always will be to me a most faithful friend.'[13]

In the face of the outcry, the ABC ended up apologising. Those who fought alongside Jacka will go on speaking his name with reverence, their own fates varying.

Ted Rule returned to his farm and orchards outside Shepparton. He was a pioneer of fruit drying plants and served as President of the Northern Victoria Fruitgrowers' Association. He married Muriel Tuck, remaining devoted to each other as Muriel battled dementia from the 1940s onwards. A pillar of the community (despite thrashing all in the community on any tennis court available) and a regular member of the Shepparton Methodist Church, he was a beloved local character noted for his wit and kindness. Ted Rule died in 1958 on the Mornington Peninsula, where he had been advised to retire by doctors concerned about a skin complaint that still plagued him from the trenches of the Great War. *The Shepparton News* eulogised him as a 'soldier of extraordinary calibre and a gentleman in the truest sense of the word'. Muriel survived him by five years. Rule's wonderful book *Jacka's Mob* stands among the best of war memoirs, a candid, funny and touching portrait of what life was actually like for the soldiers who fought. It is an immortal work; and invaluable to anyone who wants to understand the real Australian experience of the First World War.

Harry Murray, VC, CMG, DSO lived as a grazier in Queensland for the rest of his days. However, in 1939, at the age of 59 years, he saw the way the wind was blowing and re-enlisted! H. Murray joined the names in the militia of the 26th Battalion, 11th Brigade at Townsville. As he had guessed, after the Second World War commenced, the unit became part of the 2nd Australian Imperial Force; with Murray as Commander, until General Blamey personally stepped in to suggest that perhaps a younger man might be better suited to fight in this conflict. Instead, Murray commanded the Volunteer Defence Corps, 23rd Queensland Regiment, until the end of the war. In 1956, Murray and his wife travelled to London to participate in the centenary celebration of the Victoria Cross. They visited France, but Murray could not bring himself to walk the battlefields of yesteryear. On 6 January 1966, as Nell, his second wife, drove from the family cattle station, Glenlyon, at Richmond, Queensland, a tyre blew out and the car rolled on the Leichhardt Highway near the town of Condamine. Murray was in the passenger seat, and though seemingly not badly hurt, he was taken to the local hospital where he died the next day, of heart failure.

Charles Brand, CB, CMG, CVO was knighted at Buckingham Palace before returning to Australia in 1919. He was mentioned in dispatches eight times during the Great War, a testament to his selfless bravery. He remained with the Australian Army, being made a Brigadier General on 1 April 1920. Brand personally supervised the visit of the future King George VI, when he and the Duchess of York attended the opening of the new Federal Parliament in Canberra in 1927. Evidently, Brand took a liking to this new building and decided to join it, retiring from the military in 1933 to run for parliament himself. He won a seat in the Senate for the United Australia Party in 1934, which he held until 1947. Commendably, his primary concern as a politician was the welfare of returned soldiers, from the First World War and then, sadly, the Second. (He also made the papers by insisting that the term 'brass hat', directed at him by a fellow Senator in 1945, was unparliamentary language. How times have changed . . .) The old Brig died at his home in Toorak in 1961, at the age of 87. He was survived by his wife and two daughters. His portrait hangs today in the Australian War Memorial, Canberra.

General Sir Hubert Gough, GCB, GCMG, KCVO was another to make 'old bones', but they were bitter ones. Perhaps deservedly, Gough was made a public scapegoat and symbol of the British military bungling in the Great War, with even Douglas Haig describing many of Gough's decisions as stupid. So blackened was his name that Lloyd George pointedly did not invite him to celebrations of the Armistice, one of only three senior officers to meet such a fate. Despite the support of Winston Churchill, Gough had his career buried by being appointed Chief of the Allied Military Mission to the Baltic in 1919. His task there was to support the White Russians in their doomed war against the revolution, which was made difficult by rumours (spread by the White Russians) that he was in the pay of the Bolsheviks! He was sacked by October and retired. His remarkable run of unsuccess continued with a failed run at parliament as a Liberal candidate in 1922. His attempts to become a pig and poultry farmer did not bring fortune; neither did a brief spell attempting to market American wallpaper paste to Britain. He found his metier as a floating company director, looking grim at board meetings for Siemens Brothers and Caxton Electrical among many others. Inevitably, much of his energies post-war went into trying to rehabilitate his reputation, involving pen battles with Haig, Lloyd George and F.E. Smith. Gough wrote in the introduction to the book *The Fifth Army in March 1918*: 'Why my country failed to realise or to appreciate the splendid valour and great results achieved by the men of the Fifth Army is a difficult and perhaps a delicate matter for me to touch upon.'[14]

Gough was knighted in 1937, and he died at home in 1963, aged 92, one of the longest lived of the British Commanders of the Great War.

William Birdwood, GCB, GCSI, GCMG toured Australia and New Zealand during 1920 to wild acclaim, much to the chagrin of Australian Generals like Monash who found themselves second-class heroes in their own land. 'Birdy' was the symbol of victory for Australians, all defeats and drawbacks forgotten. He then returned to the Indian Army and became Commander-in-Chief in 1925. Retiring from the forces in 1930, there was a pronounced push to make him the Governor-General of Australia (he did have experience at the General part), but Prime Minister Scullin had the wisdom to give the role to the brilliant judicial mind of Sir Isaac Isaacs, the first Australian to become the Head of State. Instead, Birdy was made the Master of Pembroke College, Cambridge. Split between academia and the army, his autobiography was entitled *Khaki and Gown*, presumably to the despair of his publisher. He was made Baron Birdwood of Anzac and Totnes in 1938. The Baron had already revisited Anzac Cove in 1936, conducting one of the first major remembrances on the site itself.

Birdwood died in May 1951 at Hampton Court Palace, aged 85. To this day, the Australian Government pays for his gravesite to be maintained.

Bill Jacka was transformed by his experiences in the First World War into a great radical. In 1936 a pamphlet headlined 'The Truth about Anzac' was put out by a Communist organisation, and it carried a plea by Bill that the Australian people should 'unite in a determined refusal to do the bidding of a small minority that thrives on the business of war. To the returned soldiers, the mothers and fathers, and the splendid young men and women who have grown up since: the last slaughter, I appeal, as one who took part in the Gallipoli campaign, to let the rulers of Australia know that you will not tolerate a repetition of what occurred 21 years ago, that you will not allow your determination and heroism to be prostituted by the masters of the old world, whose only God is profit. Display your courage in refusing to fight in imperialist war, under any pretext whatever.'[15] Bill himself became Mayor of Footscray in 1941, at which point a red flag soon flew from Footscray Town Hall! (Well, they were our allies at the time.) Among his mayoral achievements was the launch of an appeal entitled 'Food For Russia Week'.[16] He died in 1978, aged 81.

Major John Peck left the 14th to serve under John Monash, proving his worth immediately at the Battle of Messines by personally conducting reconnaissance, despite heavy bombardment, to determine the precise position of the front. Peck's perpetual humour and good cheer hid one truth from his men and his commanders: he was a very ill man, but on 2 September 1918 his bluff was discovered. He was evacuated to a hospital and diagnosed with chronic nephritis, the same condition that would end his life in 1928. Once the war was over, Peck remained in the army and studied in England to master the supply and transport lessons learnt in the Great War. With his typical enthusiasm, Peck even qualified as a chef at Aldershot and set about transforming the way the mess was organised in the Australian Army. Under Peck's reign, army cooks now had to complete a ten-day culinary school and obtain a certificate of competency before being allowed to serve any servings. His later career included time as Chairman of the New Guinea Expropriation Board and an appointment to the Victoria Barracks (Brisbane) as General Staff Officer. His early passing was lamented by his friends and colleagues, who were invariably both; one noting that Peck's greatest military gift was to say nasty things nicely, his wit making the rub of life go smooth.

Lieutenant George Mitchell ended the war that rarest of creatures; a man who had served four years in the front lines and never been wounded. Born not to settle down, he tried his hand in various states at growing potatoes, became a real estate agent, a journalist, a motor car salesman, a garage owner, and finally, when all else failed, an author. His brilliant memoir, *Backs to the Wall*, at last gained him profit and a profile in 1937. He followed it up with a pointed novel about an imagined invasion of Australia entitled *The Awakening*. In 1940, he literally wrote the handbook for front-line soldiers, suitably titled 'Soldier in Battle'.

Mitchell won the seat of Oxley in the NSW Legislative Assembly in 1941, but due to being on active service in the Second World War, only sat for three days himself before losing the next election in 1944. In July 1941, at the age of 45, he married the 20-year-old Thelma Bell, a stenographer from New Zealand. In 1942, Mitchell trained and led guerilla forces in Western Australia who lived off the land and spent their days improbably searching for Japanese soldiers. On 11 May 1945, Mitchell landed troops under fire at Dove Bay, New Guinea, a full 30 years after his first amphibious landing under fire at Gallipoli! Finally in retirement, Mitchell listed his hobbies as swimming, experimenting and writing. He was certainly wonderful at the last of these three. George Mitchell died in 1961, aged 66.

Major Otto Fuhrmann returned to Australia to be the deputy librarian at the Supreme Court of Victoria, the same position he had held before war broke out. In 1921 he authored and published a book on High Court procedural acts and rules. That same year he became the private secretary to Prime Minister Billy Hughes, but could only stand the job and Hughes for seven months before resigning. Happily, Fuhrmann was then asked to serve as private secretary for the far more gregarious Sir Joseph Cook at Australia's High Commission in London. This he did for the next 16 years, helping to establish an Australian diplomatic service worthy of the name and liaising extensively with the League of Nations. Fuhrmann's later positions included being appointed consul-general in Shanghai, running the Eastern Group Supply Council in India for five years and ministerial service in Tel Aviv. He died in 1961, aged 72.

Private Martin O'Meara VC, tragically, never recovered from the trauma of war, the things he had seen and done, and though he got back to Australia, he was immediately put into Claremont Hospital for the Insane. His diagnosis in 1919 makes sobering reading: 'Delusional Insanity, with hallucinations of hearing and sight, is extremely homicidal and suicidal, and requires to be kept in restraint. He is not hopeful of his recovery in the near future.'[17] He was transferred to a soldiers' hospital for long-term care. There he remained until he was returned once more to the asylum shortly before his death in December 1935, aged 50.

Betty Jacka, Jacka's adopted daughter, grew up quite removed from his legacy. When the author Robert Macklin tracked her down in the 1990s, she told him of how growing up with a new stepfather, Frank Duncan, changed everything. 'Duncan already had a family from a previous marriage,' she explained. 'I had a happy life as the youngest member of a large family. My husband and I lived overseas for a few years because we liked to travel. We came home to have our family. We've had a pleasant and uneventful life together. The far past of my life hasn't entered my head for many a long year. I prefer to keep it that way.'[18] Her mother, Vera Franklin, died in Melbourne in 1962.

The **Reverend Sir Francis William Rolland** continued as the headmaster of Geelong Grammar for a quarter-century, along the way becoming Moderator of the Presbyterian Church of Victoria, and Chairman of the Headmasters' Conference of Australia, before retiring in 1945. In a very active retirement, he spearheaded the training of deaconesses in Victoria and the teaching of religion in state schools. A witty and charming man when not in the pulpit, Sir Francis specialised in bon mots delivered during his school speeches, such as: 'A headmaster's work consists mainly of interruptions to it.'[19] Sir Francis also memorably once explained that many headmasters think their students are bad, until they meet the boy's parents. He received an OBE in 1953, a CMG in 1955, and was knighted in 1958. He died in Melbourne, in January 1965, aged 86.

•

And beyond his actual Victoria Cross now displayed at the Australian War Memorial, the legacy of Albert Jacka VC himself?

He is certainly remembered, a century on, if not quite revered the way he should be – and not just because of his extraordinary achievements. For me, the wonder of the story of Albert Jacka is how it is so emblematic of the experience of so many of his generation – his story is theirs, only more so.

He was the shell-shocked, shaking soldier who nevertheless summoned an almost supernatural calm on the battlefield. He was the man who, though he had never been to high school let alone university, had a brain that functioned faster in crisis than the titled and the privileged who commanded him. He was a man plucked from normality who, confronted by cataclysmic events beyond his wildest imaginings, nevertheless accomplished extraordinary things. In his specific case, he was one who, according to the hardest and truest markers of all – his own comrades – deserved no fewer than four VCs.

So great were his achievements that though the VC he received made him famous, he in turn added to the lustre of the Victoria Cross. This, *this* is what a holder of the Victoria Cross looks like, these are the things he achieved. It was already a medal almost mystical in its resonance for the British; Jacka was the first to make it so for Australians, too.

He was also one whose greatness was not confined to the war, who despite being the most famous man in Australia was most concerned for the welfare of his fellow veterans, a man who fought for the unemployed and the desperate as the horrors of the Great Depression began to bite.

Equally emblematic, alas, of the experience of so many of his generation, is that he was also the father who died too young, never knowing the joy of seeing his daughter grow up.

But, what a man, what a legacy.

It has been a privilege to write this book and try to bring his life, *to* life.

Vale, Bert, and bravo.

NOTES

Abbreviations

AWM   Australian War Memorial
NAA   National Archives of Australia
OHA   *Official History of Australia in the War of 1914–1918*
SLV   State Library of Victoria

Epigraph

1 *The Cessnock Eagle and South Maitland Recorder*, 19 February 1932, p. 3.
2 *The Advertiser*, 18 January 1932, p. 9.
3 Rule, *Jacka's Mob*, Military Melbourne, Prahran, 1999, p. 121.
4 Wanliss, *Reveille*, 31 January 1931.

Chapter one   Jacka v Jacko

1 Ashmead-Bartlett, *Uncensored Dardanelles*, Hutchinson & Co., London, 1929, p. 37.
2 *Daily Herald* (Adelaide), 31 July 1914, p. 5.
3 Bean, *Official History of Australia in the War of 1914–1918*, Vol. I, Angus & Robertson, Sydney, 1941, p. 252.
4 Macklin, *Jacka VC: Australian Hero*, Allen & Unwin, Sydney, 2006, p. 2.
5 Bean, *OHA*, Vol. I, p. 252.
6 Winter, *25 April 1915: The Inevitable Tragedy*, University of Queensland Press, St Lucia, 1994, p. 94.
7 Winter, *25 April 1915*, p. 95.
8 Örnek and Toker, *Gallipoli: The Front Line Experience*, Currency Press, NSW, 2005, p. 19.
9 Bean, *OHA*, Vol. I, p. 254.
10 Author's note: This hope recorded in Norris, War Narrative, 'There and back', 11 April 1914 – 18 November 1916, MLMSS 2933, item 3, p. 29.
11 Bean, *OHA*, Vol. I, p. 270.

12 Macklin, *Jacka VC*, p. 50.
13 Eşref, R., 'Anafarta Kumandanı Mustafa Kemal ile Mülakat' [Interview with Mustafa Kemal, Commander of the Anfarta Group], in Martı, M. (ed.), *Çanakkale Hatiraları*, Cilt III, Istanbul: Arma Yayınları, 2005, p. 28.
14 Eşref in Martı (ed.), *Çanakkale Hatiraları*, p. 28.
15 Wanliss, *The History of the Fourteenth Battalion, A.I.F.*, The Naval and Military Press Ltd. and The Imperial War Museum, England, 1929, p. 15.
16 Wanliss, *The History of the Fourteenth Battalion*, p. 15.
17 'Wanliss Papers', Source Records of 14th Battalion History by Newton Wanliss, AWM 224 MSS 143, item 3 A.
18 Wanliss, *The History of the Fourteenth Battalion*, p. 17.
19 Grant, *Jacka, VC: Australia's Finest Fighting Soldier*, Macmillan in Association with the Australian War Memorial, Melbourne, 1989, p. 20.
20 Diary of Captain Jacka, AWM 224 MSS 143 A, item 4.
21 Author's note: The presence of the machine guns is disputed by some. The accounts vary. I have found the most credible accounts include those in the first landing coming under fire from machine guns.
22 Diary of Captain Jacka, AWM 224 MSS 143 A, item 4.
23 Diary of Captain Jacka, AWM 224 MSS 143 A, item 4.
24 *Western Mail*, 26 April 1934, p. 2.
25 *Western Mail*, 26 April 1934, p. 2.
26 *Western Mail*, 26 April 1934, p. 2.
27 *Western Mail*, 26 April 1934, p. 2.
28 Ashmead-Bartlett diary and papers, State Library of New South Wales, 1915–1917A 1583.
29 Hamilton, *Gallipoli Diary*, Vol. I, Edward Arnold, London, 1920, p. 143.
30 Hamilton, *Gallipoli Diary*, Vol. I, p. 142.
31 Hamilton, *Gallipoli Diary*, Vol. I, p. 142.
32 Bean, *OHA*, Vol. I, p. 460.
33 Hamilton, *Gallipoli Diary*, Vol. I, p. 144.
34 Hamilton, *Gallipoli Diary*, Vol. I, p. 144.
35 Percy Bland interview, AWM Oral History Recording, Accession No. S01169, September 1993.
36 Diary of Captain Jacka, AWM 224 MSS 143 A, item 4.
37 Marks, war diary, 7 August 1914 – 21 December 1918, State Library of New South Wales, MLMSS 2879.
38 *Reveille*, 1 December 1936.
39 *The Argus*, 17 July 1915, p. 6.
40 *Bendigonian*, 10 February 1916, p. 4.
41 *Bendigonian*, 10 February 1916, p. 4.
42 Diary of Captain Jacka, AWM 224 MSS 143 A, item 4.
43 Diary of Captain Jacka, AWM 224 MSS 143 A, item 4.

44 *The Herald*, 24 April 1926, p. 13.
45 Author's note: Jacka will later recall it as a Vickers, and that's the gun they used through most of the war, but they hadn't yet had their Maxims replaced by Vickers.
46 *The Herald*, 24 April 1926, p. 13.
47 Diary of Captain Jacka, AWM 224 MSS 143 A, item 4.
48 Diary of Captain Jacka, AWM 224 MSS 143 A, item 4.
49 Diary of Captain Jacka, AWM 224 MSS 143 A, item 4.
50 Stanley, *Quinn's Post*, Allen & Unwin, Sydney, 2005, p. 27.
51 Bean, *OHA*, Vol. II, Angus & Robertson, Sydney, 1924, p. 133.
52 Bean diaries, May 1915, AWM 38, 3DRL 606/8/1, p. 12.
53 Bean, *Bean's Gallipoli: The Diaries of Australia's Official War Correspondent*, Allen & Unwin, Sydney, 2007, p. 131.
54 Bean, *OHA*, Vol. II, p. 136.
55 Bean diaries, May 1915, AWM 38, 3DRL 606/8/1, pp. 19–20.
56 Bean, *OHA*, Vol. II, p. 138.
57 Bean, *OHA*, Vol. II, p. 138.
58 Bean, *OHA*, Vol. II, p. 139. Author's note: It is normal for a third or so of any large force (like the corps size force that was defending Anzac Cove) to have jobs that do not put them in the trenches with a rifle.
59 Bean, *OHA*, Vol. II, p. 137.
60 McCarthy, *Gallipoli to the Somme: the story of C. E. W. Bean*, John Ferguson, Sydney, 1983, p. 148.
61 McCarthy, *Gallipoli to the Somme*, p. 148.
62 Bean, *OHA*, Vol. II, p. 140.
63 Bean, *OHA*, Vol. II, p. 138.
64 Barwick, war diary, 22 August 1914 – September 1915, p. 127, MLMSS 1493/Box 1/Item 1.

Chapter two   Death or glory

1 Wanliss Papers, Letter, Wanliss to Bean about Jacka, 1 March 1923, AWM 224 MSS 143, item 3.
2 Bean, *OHA*, Vol. II, p. 133.
3 Macklin, *Jacka VC*, p. 65.
4 Wanliss, *The History of the Fourteenth Battalion*, p. 41.
5 Laffin, *Damn the Dardanelles! The Story of Gallipoli*, Osprey, London, 1980, p. 81.
6 Author's note: This quote comes from an interview conducted by historian Dr Peter Williams with a 12th Australian Infantry Battalion veteran, in Hobart, 1980.

7 Hatwell, *No Ordinary Determination: Percy Black and Harry Murray of the First AIF*, Fremantle Press, Fremantle, 2014, p. 76.
8 Records of C. E. W. Bean, Official Historian, Diaries and Notebooks, AWM 38 3DRL 606/8/1, p. 24.
9 Hogue, *Trooper Bluegum at the Dardanelles*, Andrew Melrose, London, 1916, p. 115.
10 Hogue, *Trooper Bluegum at the Dardanelles*, p. 75.
11 Mitchell, *Backs to the Wall*, Allen & Unwin, Sydney, 2007, p. 23.
12 Wanliss Papers, AWM 224 MSS 143, item 3 A [reported speech].
13 Wanliss Papers, AWM 224 MSS 143, item 3 A.
14 Bean, diary, AWM 38, 3DRL 606/8/1.
15 Wanliss Papers, AWM 224 MSS 143, item 3 A.
16 Wanliss, *The History of the Fourteenth Battalion*, pp. 42–43.
17 Records of C. E. W. Bean, AWM 38 3DRL 606/8/1.
18 *The Tamworth Daily*, 11 August 1915, p. 2.
19 Records of C. E. W. Bean, AWM 38 3DRL 606/8/1.
20 Bean, diary, AWM 38, 3DRL 606/8/1.
21 Bean, diary, AWM 38, 3DRL 606/8/1.
22 War Letters of General Monash, 1934, Vol. I, AWM RCDIG0000569.
23 *The Tamworth Daily*, 11 August 1915, p. 2.
24 *Bendigonian*, 10 February 1916, p. 4.
25 Bean, 'Albert Jacka', *Reveille*, 31 January 1932, p. 2.
26 Records of C. E. W. Bean, AWM 38 3DRL 606/8/1.
27 Records of C. E. W. Bean, AWM 38 3DRL 606/8/1.
28 Jacka, war diary, AWM MSS143 A Item 4, 19 May, p. 10 [or at least the reverse side of p. 5, as Jacka has marked it in his diary].
29 Barwick, diary, MLMSS 1493/Box 1/Item 1, p. 127 (of original, facsimile).
30 Bean, *OHA*, Vol. II, p. 143.
31 Dolan, *Gallipoli Air War: The Unknown Story of the Fight for the Skies Over Gallipoli*, Pan Macmillan, Sydney, 2013, p. 198.
32 Dolan, *Gallipoli Air War*, p. 198.
33 Grant, *Jacka, VC*, p. 35.
34 Diary of Captain Jacka, AWM 224 MSS 143 A, item 4.
35 Wanliss, *The History of the Fourteenth Battalion*, p. 44.
36 Macklin, *Jacka VC*, p. 67.
37 Hamilton, *Gallipoli Diary*, Vol. I, p. 249.
38 Fahrettin Altay Paşa, 'Fahrettin Altay'ın Çanakkale Hatıraları', Martı, M. (ed.), Cilt III, Arma Yayınları, Istanbul, 2005, p. 30.
39 Collection relating to the service of Chaplain Andrew Gillison, 1914–1915, AWM 3DRL/6277.
40 Bean, *Gallipoli Mission*, AWM, Canberra, 1948, p. 58.

41 Author's note: The correct spelling for this saying in Modern Turkish is: 'Uğurlar ola. Güle güle gideceksiniz, güle güle geleceksiniz.'
42 Herbert, *Mons, Anzac and Kut*, Edward Arnold, London, 1919, p. 119.
43 Bean, Despatch, *Commonwealth Government Gazette*, No. 7, 13 January 1916, p. 92.
44 Bean, Despatch, 13 January 1916, p. 92.
45 Bean, diary, AWM 38, 3DRL 606/8/1, p. 13.
46 *The Age*, 23 February 1924, p. 18.
47 *The World's News*, 18 November 1916, p. 2.
48 Bean, diary, AWM 38, 3DRL 606/7/1, 'Simpson. Donkey man, 3rd amb. Hit May 19', p. 108.
49 *The Farmer and Settler*, 10 September 1915, p. 3.
50 Moorehead, *Gallipoli*, Wordsworth Editions, Hertfordshire, 1998, p. 176.
51 Diary of Captain Jacka, AWM 224 MSS 143 A, item 4.
52 Percy Bland interview, AWM S01169.
53 Percy Bland interview, AWM S01169.
54 Diary of Captain Jacka, AWM 224 MSS 143 A, item 4.
55 William Fitzpatrick interview, AWM Oral History Recording, Accession No. S01181.
56 Hamilton, *Gallipoli Diary*, Vol. I, p. 318.
57 Hamilton, *Gallipoli Diary*, Vol. I, p. 331.
58 Hamilton, *Gallipoli Diary*, Vol. I, p. 331.
59 Kipling, 'For All We Have and Are', *The Times*, 2 September 1914.
60 Hamilton, *Gallipoli Diary*, Vol. II, pp. 16–17.
61 *The London Gazette*, Supplement 29240, 23 July 1915, p. 7279.
62 *Wedderburn Express and Korongshire Advertiser*, 30 July 1915, p. 2.
63 *Wedderburn Express and Korongshire Advertiser*, 30 July 1915, p. 2.
64 *The Korong Vale Lance and North West Advertiser*, 17 July 1915, p. 2.
65 *Examiner*, 29 July 1915, p. 7.
66 *Bendigonian*, 10 February 1916, p. 4.
67 Macklin, *Jacka VC*, p. 72.
68 Cutlack, *War Letters of General Monash*, Angus & Robertson, Sydney, 1934, p. 60.

Chapter three   The days of their discontent

1 Kipling, 'Epitaphs of a War', 1919, *Rudyard Kipling's Verse Inclusive Edition 1885–1926*, Hodder & Stoughton, London, 1927, p. 380.
2 Mitchell, *Backs to the Wall*, p. 168.
3 3rd Australian Light Horse Brigade War Diary, AWM 4, 10/3/7 – August 1915, p. 82.

4   3rd Australian Light Horse Brigade War Diary, AWM 4, 10/3/7 – August 1915, p. 82.
5   War Letters of General Monash, Vol. I, 1934, AWM RCDIG0000569.
6   Birdwood, *Khaki and Gown*, Ward, Lock & Co., Melbourne, 1941, p. 273.
7   Barwick, diary, MLMSS 1493/Box 1/Item 1, p. 146 (of original/facsimile).
8   Bean, *OHA*, Vol. II, p. 502.
9   *The West Australian*, 26 August 1915, p. 7.
10 Oral, *Gallipoli 1915: Through Turkish Eyes*, Türkiye İş Bankası Kültür Yayınları, Istanbul, 2007, p. 244.
11 Fewster (ed.), *Gallipoli Correspondent*, George Allen & Unwin, Sydney, 1983, p. 146.
12 Bean, diary, AWM 38 3DRL 606/11/1 p. 34.
13 Fewster (ed.), *Gallipoli Correspondent*, p. 146.
14 Monash, diary, 6 August 1915, Monash Papers, SLV, MS 13875, Box 4083/1, p. 103.
15 Birdwood, *Khaki and Gown*, p. 273.
16 Bean, *OHA*, Vol. II, p. 532.
17 Wanliss, *The History of the Fourteenth Battalion*, p. 53.
18 Wanliss papers, AWM 224 MSS 143 A.
19 Perry, *Monash*, Random House, Australia, 2014, p. 222.
20 Bean, *OHA*, Vol. II, p. 654.
21 Bean, *OHA*, Vol. II, pp. 654–655.
22 Bean, *OHA*, Vol. II, p. 659.
23 Longmore, *The Story of the Old Sixteenth*, Naval and Military Press, Uckfield, (first edition 1929, but no publication date for this edition), p. 76.
24 Hatwell, *No Ordinary Determination*, p. 89.
25 Hatwell, *No Ordinary Determination*, p. 89.
26 14th Battalion War Diary, April to August 1915, 8 August, AWM 4 23/31/8.
27 Grant, *Jacka, VC*, p. 43 [reported speech].
28 Bean, *OHA*, Vol. II, p. 734.
29 Collection relating to the Service of Chaplain Andrew Gillison, 1914 – 1915, AWM 3DRL/6277.
30 Records of C. E. W. Bean, AWM 38 3DRL 606/8/1.
31 Hatwell, *No Ordinary Determination*, p. 95.
32 Hatwell, *No Ordinary Determination*, p. 95.
33 Diary of Captain Jacka, AWM 224 MSS 143 A, item 4.
34 Ashmead-Bartlett, *The Uncensored Dardanelles*, p. 196.
35 Ashmead-Bartlett, *The Uncensored Dardanelles*, p. 196.
36 Ashmead-Bartlett, *The Uncensored Dardanelles*, p. 202.
37 Ashmead-Bartlett, *The Uncensored Dardanelles*, p. 197.
38 Younger, *Keith Murdoch*, HarperCollins, Sydney, 2003, p. 58.
39 Younger, *Keith Murdoch*, p. 58.

40 *The Advertiser* (Adelaide), 19 August 1915, p. 7.
41 Ashmead-Bartlett, *The Uncensored Dardanelles*, p. 196.
42 War Letters of General Monash, Vol. I, 1934, AWM RCDIG0000569.
43 Rule, *Jacka's Mob*, p. 2.
44 Wanliss, *The History of the Fourteenth Battalion*, p. 75.
45 Rule, *Jacka's Mob*, p. 2.
46 Papers of Captain F. B. Stanton, 14th Battalion, WM 2 DRL 155, 12/11/3116.
47 Rule, *Jacka's Mob*, p. 2.
48 Rule, *Jacka's Mob*, p. 2.
49 Percy Bland interview, AWM S01169.
50 Rule, *Jacka's Mob*, p. 3.
51 Rule, *Jacka's Mob*, p. 4.
52 Rule, *Jacka's Mob*, p. 4.
53 Rule, *Jacka's Mob*, p. 5 [reported speech].
54 Rule, *Jacka's Mob*, p. 5.
55 Rule, *Jacka's Mob*, p. 5.
56 Rule, *Jacka's Mob*, p. 5.
57 Hatwell, *No Ordinary Determination*, p. 97.
58 Rule, *Jacka's Mob*, p. 8 [reported speech].
59 Rule, *Jacka's Mob*, p. 11.
60 Perry, *Monash*, p. 232.
61 Author's note: After Winston Churchill, who was likely inspired by T. S. Eliot, 'in my end is my beginning' from *Four Quartets*.
62 Derham, *The Silence Ruse: escape from Gallipoli; a record and memories of the life of General Sir Brudenell White*, Cliffe Books, Armadale, 1998, p. 33 (Special Army Order, Headquarters Dardanelles Army, 18 December 1915).
63 Letter from Arthur Valentine Steel (1st Battalion AIF) to Marie and George Steel, January 1916, courtesy of Steel family of Wangaratta, and I thank them for allowing me to publish it.
64 Rule, *Jacka's Mob*, p. 11.
65 Rule, *Jacka's Mob*, p. 11.

Chapter four   From Cairo to Calais

1 Bean, 'Fight for Pozières Ridge', *The West Australian*, 10 August 1916, p. 7.
2 Bean, *Official History of Australia in the War of 1914–1918*, Vol. III, *The Australian Imperial Force in France, 1916*, Angus & Robertson, Sydney, 1929, p. 135.
3 Rule, *Jacka's Mob*, p. 14.
4 Rule, *Jacka's Mob*, p. 14.
5 Author's note: Edgar Rule relied on his memory to write *Jacka's Mob*, and consequently some of the facts are distorted. Though in the book Twomey is

recorded as being a Sergeant at this time, in fact he had not yet been promoted and was still a Private.
6. Rule, *Jacka's Mob*, pp. 14–15.
7. Rule, *Jacka's Mob*, p. 15.
8. Albert Williams, undated manuscript, AWM MSS 1337, p. 61.
9. Bean, *OHA*, Vol. III, pp. 48–49.
10. Athol Dunlop, diary, 9 February 1916, AWM PR00676, pp. 45–46.
11. Letter from Clarence Collier to parents, 12 April 1916, AWM 1DRL/206, p. 1.
12. Apcar de Vine, diary, 13 February 1916, AWM 1DRL/0240, p. 102.
13. Ellis, A. D., *The Story of the Fifth Australian Division, being an Authoritative Account of the Division's Doings in Egypt, France and Belgium*, Hodder & Stoughton, London, 1920, p. 37.
14. Sloan, Liutenant Colonel Hannibal, *The Purple and the Gold*, Halstead Press, Sydney, 1938, p. 257. Author's note: In the original account, the words 'fuck' and 'c-nt' are completely dashed out, in respect of the sensibilities of 1938. I have restored them on the grounds they are the only two words that fit, and our contemporary sensibilities are less exacting.
15. Bean, diary, dated February to March 1916, AWM 38 3DRL 606/40/1, pp. 16–17.
16. Masefield, *The Battle of the Somme*, William Heinemann, London, 1919, p. 222.
17. Macklin, *Jacka VC*, p. 94.
18. Carlyon, *The Great War*, Macmillan, Sydney, 2014, p. 171.
19. Perry, *Monash*, p. 247.
20. Perry, *Monash*, pp. 247–249.
21. Monash, *Australian Victories in France in 1918*, Hutchinson & Co., London, 1920, p. 294.
22. Lecture Notes Relating to Albert Jacka, AWM PR84/333.
23. Wanliss, *The History of the Fourteenth Battalion*, p. 95.
24. Letter, Harold Elliott to George Henderson, 12 April 1916, AWM PR01279, p. 3.
25. Pedersen, *Fromelles*, Pen and Sword Books, South Yorkshire, 2002, p. 31.
26. Wanliss, *The History of the Fourteenth Battalion*, p. 95.
27. Williams, AWM MSS 1337, p. 25.
28. Rule, *Jacka's Mob*, p. 15.
29. Rule, *Jacka's Mob*, p. 15.
30. War letters of General Monash, 26 April 2016, Volume 1, 24 December 1914 – 4 March 1917.
31. Rule, *Jacka's Mob*, p. 15.
32. Rule, *Jacka's Mob*, p. 15.
33. Letter, Goldy Raws to family, 30 May 1915, AWM 2DRL/0481, p. 14.
34. William Fitzpatrick interview, AWM No. S01181.
35. Rule, *Jacka's Mob*, p. 121.

36 William Fitzpatrick interview, AWM No. S01181.
37 Grant, *Jacka, VC*, p. 57.
38 Grant, *Jacka, VC*, p. 57.
39 Wanliss Papers, AWM 224 MSS 143 A, item 5.
40 Williams, AWM MSS 1337, p. 72. Author note: In fact, the usual sign was '8 *chevaux* or 40 *hommes*'.
41 Rule, *Jacka's Mob*, p. 17.
42 Harry Preston, diary, 2 April 1916, AWM 2DRL/0811, p. 55.
43 Harry Preston, diary, 2 April 1916, AWM 2DRL/0811, p. 55.
44 Bean, *OHA*, Vol. III, p. 205.
45 Grant, *Jacka, VC*, p. 61.
46 Rule, *Jacka's Mob*, p. 109.
47 *Northern Star*, 8 September 1916, p. 8.
48 *Northern Star*, 8 September 1916, p. 8.
49 Masefield, *The Battle of the Somme*, pp. 13–14.
50 Monash, Personal Files, Book 13, 1 July – 16 August 1916, AWM 3DRL/2316.
51 Monash, Personal Files, AWM 3DRL/2316.
52 Monash, Personal Files, AWM 3DRL/2316.
53 Monash, Personal Files, AWM 3DRL/2316.
54 Monash, Personal Files, AWM 3DRL/2316.
55 Australian Red Cross Society Wounded and Missing Enquiry Bureau Files, 1914–18 War, Robert David Julian, 14th Battalion, AWM 3DRL/0428.
56 Australian Red Cross, Robert David Julian, AWM 3DRL/0428.
57 Monash, Personal Files, AWM 3DRL/2316.
58 *Northern Star*, 8 September 1916, p. 8.
59 Rule, *Jacka's Mob*, p. 22.
60 Rule, *Jacka's Mob*, p. 22.
61 Rule, *Jacka's Mob*, p. 23.
62 Wanliss, *The History of the Fourteenth Battalion*, p. 123.
63 War Letters of General Monash, 1934, Vol. I, AWM RCDIG0000569.
64 Rule, *Jacka's Mob*, p. 24.
65 Rule, *Jacka's Mob*, p. 24.
66 Sweeting, 'Charles Henry Brand (1873–1961)', *Australian Dictionary of Biography*, Volume 7, 1979.
67 Rule, *Jacka's Mob*, p. 24.
68 Rule, *Jacka's Mob*, p. 24.
69 Letter, Pompey Elliott to Charles Bean, 17 August 1926, AWM 38 3DRL 606/243B/1, p. 116.
70 Letter, Pompey Elliott to Charles Bean, p. 116.
71 Bean, *OHA*, Vol. IV, Angus & Robertson, Sydney, 1936, p. 439.
72 Bean, *OHA*, Vol. III, p. 468.

73 Letter, Walker to Bean, 13 August 1928, in Bean Papers, AWM 38 3DRL7953/34, Part 1, p. 2.
74 Bean, diary, 21 July 1916, AWM 38 3DRL 606/52/1, p. 36 (p. 40 of PDF), p. 38 (p. 41 of PDF).
75 Hartnett, *Over the Top*, Allen & Unwin, Sydney, 2011, p. 64.
76 Barwick, diary, 21 July 1916, item 3, p. 272.
77 Barwick, diary, 21 July 1916, item 3, pp. 272–73.

Chapter five The Valley of the Somme

1 Extract from a private and confidential letter written by Charles Bean to 14th Battalion historian Newton Wanliss, 1923, AWM43 [A414].
2 Bean, *OHA*, Vol. III, p. 537.
3 Bean, *OHA*, Vol. III, p. 537.
4 Preston, 'John Leak's V.C.', *Reveille*, 1 August 1935, p. 30.
5 Preston, 'John Leak's V.C.', *Reveille*, 1 August 1935, p. 30 [reported speech changed to direct speech].
6 Preston, 'John Leak's V.C.', *Reveille*, 1 August 1935, p. 30.
7 Ben Champion, diary, 23 July 1916, AWM 2DRL/0512, p. 90.
8 Ben Champion, diary, 23 July 1916, AWM 2DRL/0512, pp. 90–91.
9 Rule, *Jacka's Mob*, p. 25.
10 Rule, *Jacka's Mob*, p. 25.
11 Captain R. Hayes, Bullecourt, manuscript, AWM 224 MSS 143 A, item 7.
12 Letter, Gordon Maxfield to his father, 13 October 1916, AWM 1DRL/0489, p. 2.
13 'Albert Cathedral', awm.gov.au/collection/C169800.
14 Barwick, Flora, Archie Barwick – condensed diary, 1921, transcribed by Flora A. Barwick in 1995, collection.sl.nsw.gov.au/record/n88EexBn, p. 61.
15 Rule, *Jacka's Mob*, p. 26.
16 Grant, *Jacka, VC*, p. 69.
17 Bean, diary, 4 August 1916, AWM 38 3DRL 606/54/1, pp. 109–10.
18 Wanliss, *The History of the Fourteenth Battalion*, p. 135.
19 Haig, *War Diaries & Letters*, Weidenfeld & Nicolson, London, 2005, p. 215.
20 Rule, *Jacka's Mob*, p. 26.
21 Rule, *Jacka's Mob*, p. 26.
22 Fiveash, 41st Battery, 13th Field Artillery Brigade, diary, AWM MSS1217, p. 106.
23 Rule, *Jacka's Mob*, p. 26.
24 Rule, *Jacka's Mob*, p. 26.
25 Mitchell, *Backs to the Wall*, p. 39.
26 *Snowy River Mail*, 29 September 1916, p. 3.

27 Letter, Frank Miller to Mr Finlay, 30 November 1916, AWM 224 MSS 143 A, item 6.
28 *The Bendigo Independent*, 3 October 1916, p. 7.
29 *The Sun*, 17 October 1916, p. 1.
30 Grant, *Jacka, VC*, p. 70.
31 Papers of Private William Bourne, Wallet 1, AWM PR 03573.
32 Rule, *Jacka's Mob*, p. 27.
33 Rule, *Jacka's Mob*, p. 27.
34 Rule, *Jacka's Mob*, p. 27.
35 *Mortlake Dispatch*, 15 November 1916, p. 2 [reported speech].
36 Rule, *Jacka's Mob*, p. 28.
37 Rule, *Jacka's Mob*, p. 28.
38 Rule, *Jacka's Mob*, p. 29.
39 Rule, *Jacka's Mob*, p. 28.

Chapter six Attack!

1 Rule, *Jacka's Mob*, p. 121.
2 *The Land*, 29 January 1932, p. 16.
3 Wanliss, *The History of the Fourteenth Battalion*, p. 138.
4 *Mortlake Dispatch*, 15 November 1916, p. 2.
5 Wanliss, *The History of the Fourteenth Battalion*, p. 135.
6 Bean, *OHA*, Vol. III, p. 715.
7 Rule, *Jacka's Mob*, p. 29.
8 Jack Sheldon, *The German Army on the Somme 1914–1916*, Pen and Sword, South Yorkshire, 2005 p. 231.
9 Author's note: Charles Bean states in Volume III of his *Official History of Australia in the War of 1914–1918* that Jacka and his small cohort of men were sheltering in a deep dugout during the lengthy German bombardment on the night of 6 August 1916. He further writes that as the Germans were passing over, they rolled a bomb down the shaft, after which Jacka rushed up, firing at the German bomber up the stairway. Edgar Rule's book, *Jacka's Mob*, published four years after Bean's Official History, tells a similar tale – although Rule's original diary entry for this action has the Germans merely sweeping past. Albert Jacka, while recovering from his wounds after Pozières, was interviewed at length on the events surrounding his actions on the morning of 7 August 1916. He makes no mention of sheltering in a deep dugout, and states emphatically that he and his men had been sheltering in a shell-hole, that he himself had been splashed by shell shrapnel during the bombardment. Neither does Jacka mention a bomb being rolled down, or himself rushing up to fire upon Germans above. Jacka's account describes the Germans at this point as sweeping past without detecting them.

10 *The Herald*, 14 October 1916, p. 12.
11 *The Bendigo Independent*, 3 October 1916, p. 7.
12 *The Herald*, 14 October 1916, p. 12.
13 Letter, Frank Miller to Mr Finlay, 30 November 1916, AWM 224 MSS 143 A, item 6.
14 *The Sun*, 17 October 1916, p. 1.
15 *Daily Advertiser*, 7 October 1916, p. 1 [reported speech].
16 Letter, Frank Miller to Mr Finlay, 30 November 1916, AWM 224 MSS 143 A, item 6.
17 *Daily Advertiser*, 7 October 1916, p. 1.
18 Macklin, *Jacka VC*, p. 117.
19 Letter, Frank Miller to Mr Finlay, 30 November 1916, AWM 224 MSS 143 A, item 6.
20 *The Herald*, 14 October 1916, p. 12.
21 Wanliss, *The History of the Fourteenth Battalion*, p. 139.
22 *The Northern Champion*, 1 November 1916, p. 6.
23 Notes on Bayonet Training, Army War College, Government Printing Office, Washington, 1917, p. 22.
24 Hogue, *Trooper Bluegum at the Dardanelles*, p. 259.
25 *The Sun*, 17 October 1916, p. 1.
26 Rule, *Jacka's Mob*, p. 30.
27 Rule, *Jacka's Mob*, p. 29.
28 Rule, *Jacka's Mob*, p. 29.
29 Wanliss, *The History of the Fourteenth Battalion*, p. 139.
30 *The Northern Champion*, 1 November 1916, p. 6.
31 *The Argus*, 2 October 1916, p. 8.
32 *The Northern Champion*, 1 November 1916, p. 6.
33 *Inglewood Advertiser*, 24 October 1916, p. 3.
34 *The Northern Champion*, 1 November 1916, p. 6.
35 Letter, Frank Miller to Mr Finlay, 30 November 1916, AWM 224 MSS 143 A, item 6.
36 *Mortlake Dispatch*, 15 November 1916, p. 2.
37 *Mortlake Dispatch*, 15 November 1916, p. 2.
38 Rule, *Jacka's Mob*, p. 29.
39 Rule, *Jacka's Mob*, p. 29.
40 Macklin, *Jacka VC*, p. 120.
41 Macklin, *Jacka VC*, p. 124.
42 *The Sun*, 17 October 1916, p. 1.
43 Wanliss, *The History of the Fourteenth Battalion*, p. 141.
44 Benjamin Leane, diary, 8 August 1916, AWM 1DRL/0412.

45 Pegram, Thesis, *Surviving the Great War: Australian Prisoners of War on the Western Front, 1916–18*, Research School of Humanities & Arts, ANU College of Arts & Social Sciences, 24 July 2017.
46 Hatwell, *No Ordinary Determination*, p. 131.
47 Hatwell, *No Ordinary Determination*, p. 111.
48 Hatwell, *No Ordinary Determination*, p. 111.
49 Hatwell, *No Ordinary Determination*, p. 133.
50 Hatwell, *No Ordinary Determination*, p. 133.
51 Hatwell, *No Ordinary Determination*, p. 134.
52 Hatwell, *No Ordinary Determination*, p. 141.
53 Hatwell, *No Ordinary Determination*, p. 141.
54 *The Herald*, 14 October 1916, p. 12.
55 *The Herald*, 14 October 1916, p. 12.
56 *The Sun*, 17 October 1916, p. 1.
57 *The Sydney Morning Herald*, 16 August 1916, p. 11.
58 *The Age*, 17 August 1916, p. 5.
59 Wanliss, *The History of the Fourteenth Battalion*, p. 140.
60 Macklin, *Jacka VC*, p. 121.
61 *The London Gazette*, Supplement 11074, 14 November 1916.
62 Bean, *OHA*, Vol. III, p. 720.
63 Rule, *Jacka's Mob*, Angus and Robertson, Sydney, 1933, p. 94.
64 Macklin, *Jacka VC*, p. 122.
65 Records of C. E. W. Bean, AWM 38 3DRL 606/55/1 – August 1916, p. 152.
66 Rule, *Jacka's Mob*, p. 35.
67 Records of C. E. W. Bean, AWM 38 3DRL 606/55/1 – August 1916, pp. 83–84.

Chapter seven   Glittering prizes

1 Percy Bland interview, AWM S01169.
2 Rule, *Jacka's Mob*, 1933, p. 121.
3 Letters from Albert Jacka relating to his wounding at the Battle of Pozières and recommendation for the Distinguished Service Order, 1916, Wallet 1 of 1, AWM 2021.22.136.
4 Macklin, *Jacka VC*, p. 124.
5 Fitzhardinge, *The Little Digger, 1914–1952: William Morris Hughes, A Political Biography*, Vol. II, Angus & Robertson, Sydney, 1979, p. 182.
6 Fitzhardinge, *The Little Digger*, p. 182.
7 Power, *The Les Darcy American Venture*, self-published, New Lambton, NSW, 1994, p. 41.
8 Conscription Referendums, 1916 and 1917, NAA.
9 Horne, *In Search of Billy Hughes*, Macmillan Australia, Melbourne, 1979, p. 76.

10 Horne, *In Search of Billy Hughes*, p. 79.
11 Rule, *Jacka's Mob*, p. 48.
12 *Daily Sketch*, 8 September 1916, p. 2.
13 Rule, *Jacka's Mob*, p. 48.
14 Rule, *Jacka's Mob*, p. 48.
15 *The Age*, 3 November 1916, p. 8.
16 Letters from Albert Jacka, AWM 2021.22.136.
17 Personal records of Capt. Jacka, AWM 88/190.
18 *The Gazette*, All Awards and Accreditation Notices.
19 Personal records of Capt. Jacka, AWM 88/190.
20 Personal records of Capt. Jacka, AWM 88/190.
21 *The Sun*, 30 September 1916, p. 1 [reported speech].
22 *Rudyard Kipling's Verse Inclusive Edition 1885–1926*, Hodder & Stoughton, London, 1927, p. 559.
23 Arthur Tulloh interview, AWM Oral History Recording, Accession No. S01203.
24 Arthur Tulloh interview, AWM S01203.
25 *The London Gazette*, Supplement 11074, 14 November 1916.
26 *Reveille*, 31 January 1932.
27 'Bar to V.C.: Jealousy's Pull Against Jacka', *Reveille*, 31 October 1929, p. 2.
28 *Reveille*, 31 October 1929, p. 2.
29 Wanliss, 'A.I.F. Celebrities (9): Captain Jacka V.C., M.C. & Bar', *Reveille*, 30 April 1931, pp. 7–8.
30 Grant, *Jacka, VC*, pp. 81–82.
31 Rule, *Jacka's Mob*, p. 49.
32 Rule, *Jacka's Mob*, p. 49.
33 Rule, *Jacka's Mob*, p. 49.
34 Rule, *Jacka's Mob*, p. 49.
35 *The Herald*, 19 October 1916, p. 12.
36 *Hamilton Spectator*, 28 October 1916, p. 4.
37 Lawriwsky, 'The Truth about Albert Jacka, Our First War Hero', *Quadrant* online, 25 April 2024.
38 *The Australian Worker*, 2 November 1916, p. 14.
39 Rule, *Jacka's Mob*, pp. 54–55.
40 Rule, *Jacka's Mob*, p. 48.
41 Wanliss, *The History of the Fourteenth Battalion*, p. 169.
42 Rule, *Jacka's Mob*, p. 62.
43 Grant, *Jacka, VC*, p. 95.
44 Percy Bland interview, AWM S01169.
45 Bean, *OHA*, Vol. IV, p. 253.
46 Anne Devereaux, *Playing Your Part – the diary of William Devereaux, D Coy 14th Battalion AIF*, privately published, p. 75.

47 *Smith's Weekly*, 3 December 1932, p. 18.
48 Incinerator Kate, Great War Forum, March 2012.
49 Rule, *Jacka's Mob*, p. 55.
50 Grant, *Jacka, VC*, p. 127.
51 Rule, *Jacka's Mob*, p. 61.
52 Rule, *Jacka's Mob*, p. 61.
53 Rule, *Jacka's Mob*, p. 61.
54 Wanliss, *The History of the Fourteenth Battalion*, p. 169.
55 Hartnett, *Over the Top*, p. 51.
56 Arthur, *Forgotten Voices of the Great War*, Random House, London, 2003, p. 94.
57 Carlyon, *The Great War*, 2014, p. 174.

Chapter eight Recover, return, revenge

1 *Reveille*, 31 January 1932, p. 3.
2 14th Battalion War Diary, March 1917, AWM 4, 23/31/29.
3 Wanliss, *The History of the Fourteenth Battalion*, pp. 186–187.
4 Rule, *Jacka's Mob*, p. 68 [reported speech].
5 14th Battalion War Diary, April 1917, Appendix 5, AWM 4 23/31/30.
6 Watson, *A Company of Tanks*, William Blackwood and Sons, London, 1920, p. 45.
7 Bean, *OHA*, Vol. IV, p. 261 [reported speech].
8 Watson, *A Company of Tanks*, pp. 44–45 [reported speech].
9 14th Battalion War Diary, April 1917, AWM 23/31/30.
10 Bean, *OHA*, Vol. IV, p. 278.
11 Bean, *OHA*, Vol. IV, p. 278.
12 David Dunworth, officer in 15th Battalion, AWM 224 MSS 143 A, item 7.
13 Captain D. R. MacDermid, AWM 224 MSS 143 A, item 7.
14 Dunworth, AWM 224 MSS 143 A, item 7.
15 Carlyon, *The Great War*, 2014, p. 285.
16 Hatwell, *No Ordinary Determination*, p. 109.
17 *The Argus*, 29 April 1921, p. 7.
18 Hayes, Bullecourt, AWM 224 MSS 143 A, item 7.
19 14th Battalion War Diary, April 1917, AWM 23/31/30.
20 *Western Mail*, 29 July 1937, p. 9.
21 Sgt C. H. Mayer, AWM 224 MSS 143 A, item 7.
22 Rule, *Jacka's Mob*, p. 75 [reported speech].
23 *Western Mail*, 29 July 1937, p. 9.
24 14th Battalion War Diary, April 1917, AWM 23/31/30.
25 Rule, *Jacka's Mob*, p. 75.
26 Rule, *Jacka's Mob*, p. 75.

27 *Daily Mercury*, 22 January 1932, p. 3.
28 Rule, *Jacka's Mob*, p. 75.
29 16th Battalion War Diary, April 1917, AWM 4, 23/33/17.
30 Guppy, CQSM, 14th Battalion, Bullecourt, from his diary, AWM 224 MSS 143 A, item 7.
31 Records of C. E. W. Bean, AWM 38 3DRL 606/247/1, p. 27.
32 Bean, *OHA*, Vol. IV, p. 279.
33 Macklin, *Jacka VC*, p. 150.
34 Hayes, Bullecourt, AWM 224 MSS 143 A, item 7 [reported speech].
35 14th Battalion War Diary, April 1917, AWM 4 23/31/30, Appendix 7.
36 Watson, *A Company of Tanks*, p. 47.
37 Watson, *A Company of Tanks*, p. 48.
38 14th Battalion War Diary, April 1917, AWM 4 23/31/30, Appendix 7.
39 14th Battalion War Diary, April 1917, AWM 4 23/31/30, Appendix 7.
40 Records of C. E. W. Bean, AWM 38 3DRL 606/247/1.
41 White, *The Fighting Thirteenth: A History of the Thirteenth Battalion AIF*, Naval and Military Press, Uckfield, reprint (original publication date 1924), p. 93.
42 Letter, Corporal J. Grieves to Wanliss, AWM 224 MSS 143 A, item 7.
43 Percy Bland interview, AWM S01169.
44 Wanliss, *The History of the Fourteenth Battalion*, p. 193.
45 Percy Bland interview, AWM S01169.
46 Percy Bland interview, AWM S01169.
47 Percy Bland interview, AWM S01169.
48 Percy Bland interview, AWM S01169.

Chapter nine   Bullecourt blunders

1 *The Land*, 29 January 1932, p. 16.
2 Bean, *OHA*, Vol. IV, p. 286.
3 Bean, *OHA*, Vol. IV, p. 285 [reported speech].
4 Records of C. E. W. Bean, AWM 38 3DRL 606/247/1, p. 11.
5 Records of C. E. W. Bean, AWM 38 3DRL 606/247/1, p. 13.
6 Records of C. E. W. Bean, AWM 38 3DRL 606/247/1, p. 13.
7 Rule, *Jacka's Mob*, p. 82.
8 *Reveille*, 1 December 1936.
9 *Reveille*, 1 December 1936.
10 Watson, *A Company of Tanks*, pp. 57–58.
11 Bean, *OHA*, Vol. IV, p. 287.
12 Watson, *A Company of Tanks*, pp. 57–58.
13 Watson, *A Company of Tanks*, pp. 57–58.
14 Mitchell, *Backs to the Wall*, p. 129.

15 Rule, *Jacka's Mob*, p. 76.
16 Rule, *Jacka's Mob*, p. 76.
17 Rule, *Jacka's Mob*, p. 75.
18 Australian Red Cross Society Wounded and Missing Enquiry Bureau Files, 1914–18 War, Captain Alfred Williamson, 14th Battalion, AWM 1DRL/0428.
19 Australian Red Cross, Williamson, AWM 1DRL/0428.
20 Rule, *Jacka's Mob*, p. 76.
21 Letter, Private L. Dunphy (14th Battalion) to Wanliss, 25 June 1923, AWM 224 MSS 143 A, item 7.
22 Mitchell, *Backs to the Wall*, p. 89.
23 Mitchell, *Backs to the Wall*, p. 89.
24 14th Battalion War Diary, April 1917, AWM 23/31/30.
25 Hayes, Bullecourt, AWM 224 MSS 143 A, item 7.
26 14th Battalion War Diary, April 1917, AWM 4 23/31/30 [reported speech].
27 14th Battalion War Diary, April 1917, AWM 4 23/31/30, Appendix 9 [reported speech].
28 14th Battalion War Diary, April 1917, AWM 4 23/31/30, Appendix 9.
29 Rule, *Jacka's Mob*, p. 77.
30 Rule, *Jacka's Mob*, p. 77.
31 Records of C. E. W. Bean, AWM 38 3DRL 606/247/1 [reported speech].
32 Bean, *OHA*, Vol. IV, p. 291.
33 Watson, *A Company of Tanks*, p. 57 [reported speech].
34 Watson, *A Company of Tanks*, p. 57.
35 Watson, *A Company of Tanks*, p. 57.
36 Watson, *A Company of Tanks*, p. 57.
37 Guppy, diary, AWM 224 MSS 143 A, item 7.
38 Bean, *OHA*, Vol. IV, p. 347.
39 Hayes, Bullecourt, AWM 224 MSS 143 A, item 7.
40 14th Battalion War Diary, April 1917, AWM 4 23/31/30, Appendix 9. Narrative of events 11 April.
41 Lucy, *There's a Devil in the Drum*, Faber & Faber, London, 1938, p. 223.
42 Rule, *Jacka's Mob*, p. 77.
43 *Reveille*, 1 December 1936.
44 Bean, *OHA*, Vol. IV, p. 347.
45 Percy Bland interview, AWM S01169.
46 Mitchell, *Backs to the Wall*, p. 128.
47 *Reveille*, 1 December 1936.
48 Records of C. E. W. Bean, AWM 38 3DRL 606/247/1.
49 Watson, *A Company of Tanks*, p. 42.
50 Records of C. E. W. Bean, AWM 38 3DRL 606/247/1 [reported speech].
51 Records of C. E. W. Bean, AWM 38 3DRL 606/247/1 [reported speech].
52 Records of C. E. W. Bean, AWM 38 3DRL 606/247/1 [reported speech].

53 Letter, Dalitz to Wanliss, 6 March 1924, AWM 224 MSS 143 A, item 7.
54 Records of C. E. W. Bean, AWM 38 3DRL 606/247/1.
55 Carlyon, *The Great War*, Picador, Sydney, 2010, p. 337.
56 Boland, B Company, 14th Battalion, AWM 224 MSS 143 A, item 7.

Chapter ten   'Come on, boys!'

1 Bean, *OHA*, Vol. IV, p. 544.
2 Mitchell, *Backs to the Wall*, p. 129.
3 Mitchell, *Backs to the Wall*, p. 129.
4 Hayes, Bullecourt, AWM 224 MSS 143 A, item 7.
5 Bean, *OHA*, Vol. IV, p. 315 [reported speech].
6 Bean, *OHA*, Vol. IV, p. 315.
7 48th Battalion War Diary, April 1917, 23/65/15, Appendix [reported speech].
8 Mitchell, *Backs to the Wall*, p. 128.
9 Records of C. E. W. Bean, AWM 38 3DRL 606/247/1.
10 Records of C. E. W. Bean, AWM 38 3DRL 606/247/1.
11 Percy Bland interview, AWM S01169.
12 *Reveille*, 1 December 1936.
13 White, *The Fighting Thirteenth*, p. 91.
14 White, *The Fighting Thirteenth*, p. 91.
15 White, *The Fighting Thirteenth*, p. 91.
16 *Reveille*, 1 December 1936.
17 *Reveille*, 1 December 1936.
18 Bean, *OHA*, Vol. IV, p. 296.
19 *Reveille*, 1 December 1936.
20 Boland, AWM 224 MSS 143 A, item 7.
21 Boland, AWM 224 MSS 143 A, item 7.
22 16th Battalion War Diary, April 1917, AWM 4, 23/33/17.
23 Letter, Sgt D. Blackburn, 14th Battalion, Lewis gunner, to Wanliss, 10 April 1924, AWM 224 MSS 143 A, item 7.
24 Hayes, Bullecourt, AWM 224 MSS 143 A, item 7.
25 Papers of Captain F. B. Stanton, 14th Battalion, AWM 2 DRL 155, 12/11/3116.
26 *Reveille*, 1 December 1936.
27 *Reveille*, 1 December 1936.
28 Records of C. E. W. Bean, AWM 38 3DRL 606/247/1.
29 Dunworth, AWM 224 MSS 143 A, item 7.
30 Dunworth, AWM 224 MSS 143 A, item 7.
31 Bean, *OHA*, Vol. IV, p. 291.
32 *Reveille*, 1 December 1936.
33 *Reveille*, 1 December 1936.
34 Hayes, Bullecourt, AWM 224 MSS 143 A, item 7.

NOTES • 431

35 Australian Red Cross, Williamson, AWM 1DRL/0428 [reported speech].
36 14th Battalion War Diary, April 1917, AWM 1 23/31/30, Appendix 9.
37 Rule, *Jacka's Mob*, p. 78.
38 Watson, *A Company of Tanks*, p. 58.
39 14th Battalion War Diary, April 1917, AWM 4 23/31/30, Appendix 9.
40 *Reveille*, 31 January 1932.
41 Watson, *A Company of Tanks*, p. 58.
42 Watson, *A Company of Tanks*, p. 58.
43 Watson, *A Company of Tanks*, pp. 58–59.
44 Mitchell, *Backs to the Wall*, p. 130.
45 Records of C. E. W. Bean, AWM 38 3DRL 606/247/1.
46 Bean, *OHA*, Vol. IV, p. 316.
47 14th Battalion War Diary, April 1917, AWM 4 23/31/30, Appendix 9 [reported speech].
48 Bean, *OHA*, Vol. IV, p. 317.
49 Bean, *OHA*, Vol. IV, p. 317.
50 Wanliss, *The History of the Fourteenth Battalion*, p. 202.
51 *Reveille*, 1 December 1936.
52 *Reveille*, 1 December 1936.
53 Letter, Dunphy to Wanliss, 25 June 1923, AWM 224 MSS 143 A, item 7.
54 Records of C. E. W. Bean, AWM 38 3DRL 606/247/1.
55 14th Battalion War Diary, April 1917, AWM 4 23/31/30, Appendix 9 [reported speech].
56 14th Battalion War Diary, April 1917, AWM 4 23/31/30, Appendix 9 [reported speech].
57 14th Battalion War Diary, April 1917, AWM 4 23/31/30, Appendix 9 [reported speech].
58 14th Battalion War Diary, April 1917, AWM 4 23/31/30, Appendix 9 [reported speech].
59 14th Battalion War Diary, April 1917, AWM 4 23/31/30, Appendix 9 [reported speech].
60 *Reveille*, 1 December 1936.
61 Falls, *Military Operations France and Belgium 1917*, Macmillan and Co., London, 1940, p. 868.
62 *Reveille*, 1 December 1936.
63 *Reveille*, 1 December 1936.
64 *Reveille*, 1 December 1936.
65 Guppy, diary, AWM 224 MSS 143 A, item 7.
66 Guppy, diary, AWM 224 MSS 143 A, item 7.
67 White, *The Fighting Thirteenth*, p. 97.
68 White, *The Fighting Thirteenth*, p. 97.
69 Carlyon, *The Great War*, 2014, p. 304.

70 Letter, Blackburn to Wanliss, 10 April 1924, AWM 224 MSS 143 A, item 7 [reported speech].
71 Carlyon, *The Great War*, 2014, p. 304.
72 Carlyon, *The Great War*, 2014, p. 304.
73 *Reveille*, 1 December 1936.
74 *Reveille*, 1 December 1936.
75 *Reveille*, 1 December 1936.
76 Carlyon, *The Great War*, 2014, p. 304.
77 Carlyon, *The Great War*, 2014, p. 304.
78 Carlyon, *The Great War*, 2014, p. 305.
79 *Reveille*, 1 December 1936.
80 White, *The Fighting Thirteenth*, p. 97.
81 White, *The Fighting Thirteenth*, p. 97.
82 Percy Bland interview, AWM S01169.
83 Letter, Blackburn to Wanliss, 10 April 1924, AWM 224 MSS 143 A, item 7.
84 Rule, *Jacka's Mob*, p. 79.
85 Mitchell, *Backs to the Wall*, p. 134.
86 Mitchell, *Backs to the Wall*, p. 97.
87 George Dean Mitchell, The AIF Project, UNSW Canberra Australia.
88 *Reveille*, 1 December 1936.
89 *Reveille*, 1 December 1936.
90 *Reveille*, 1 December 1936.
91 *Reveille*, 1 December 1936.
92 Guppy, diary, AWM 224 MSS 143 A, item 7.
93 Percy Bland interview, AWM S01169.
94 *Reveille*, 1 December 1936.
95 *Reveille*, 1 December 1936.
96 *Reveille*, 1 December 1936.
97 Percy Bland interview, AWM S01169.
98 Percy Bland interview, AWM S01169.
99 Percy Bland interview, AWM S01169.
100 Hayes, Bullecourt, AWM 224 MSS 143 A, item 7.
101 Rule, *Jacka's Mob*, p. 75.
102 Wanliss, *The History of the Fourteenth Battalion*, p. 207.
103 Rule, *Jacka's Mob*, p. 80.
104 Rule, *Jacka's Mob*, p. 81.
105 Sgt R. N. MacDonald, 14th Battalion, AWM 224 MSS 143 A, item 7.
106 Boland, AWM 224 MSS 143 A, item 7.
107 Hayes, Bullecourt, AWM 224 MSS 143 A, item 7.
108 Percy Bland interview, AWM S01169.

Chapter eleven   The aftermath

1. William Shakespeare, *King John*, Act V, Scene 2.
2. Arthur Tulloh interview, AWM S01203.
3. *The Argus*, 29 April 1921, p. 7.
4. Wanliss, *The History of the Fourteenth Battalion*, p. 207.
5. Wanliss, *The History of the Fourteenth Battalion*, p. 207.
6. Records of C. E. W. Bean, AWM 38 3DRL 606/247/1, Bean to Wanliss, 8 May 1924.
7. *The Queenslander*, 20 December 1934, p. 19.
8. Macklin, *Jacka VC*, p. 166.
9. Macklin, *Jacka VC*, p. 161.
10. Rule, *Jacka's Mob*, p. 81.
11. Rule, *Jacka's Mob*, p. 82.
12. Grant, *Jacka, VC*, p. 114.
13. Bean, *OHA*, Vol. IV, p. 349.
14. Bean, *OHA*, Vol. IV, p. 349.
15. Historic Hansard, Australian Senate, 28 April 1921 [reported speech].
16. Percy Bland interview, AWM S01169.
17. Hayes, Bullecourt, AWM 224 MSS 143 A, item 7.
18. Mitchell, *Backs to the Wall*, p. 138.
19. Mitchell, *Backs to the Wall*, p. 138.
20. Watson, *A Company of Tanks*, p. 71.
21. Rule, *Jacka's Mob*, p. 81.
22. Rule, *Jacka's Mob*, p. 81.
23. Rule, *Jacka's Mob*, p. 81.
24. Rule, *Jacka's Mob*, p. 81.
25. 14th Battalion War Diary, April 1917, AWM 4 23/31/30, Appendix 9.
26. Records of C. E. W. Bean, Diary of Captain E. J. Rule, AWM 38 3DRL 606/245/1, p. 55.
27. Bean, *OHA*, Vol. IV, p. 351.
28. Watson, *A Company of Tanks*, p. 70.
29. *Reveille*, 1 December 1936.
30. *Reveille*, 31 January 1932.
31. Records of C. E. W. Bean, AWM 38 3DRL 606/247/1, p. 57.
32. Historic Hansard, Australian Senate, 28 April 1921 [reported speech].
33. Historic Hansard, Australian Senate, 28 April 1921 [reported speech; tenses changed].
34. Historic Hansard, Australian Senate, 28 April 1921.
35. Macklin, *Jacka VC*, p. 165. Author's note: The rumours of who authored this report and who suppressed it reverberated for the remainder of the war and into the decade beyond. I note that General White will later deny any such

thing occurred, telling Bean that any expunging was not known to him and he found such an action to be improbable. I have tried to reflect the current beliefs of those involved, but I think that this report created embarrassment rather than any conspiracy. Jacka himself did not learn the truth of this matter until Pompey Elliott raised it under privilege in parliament five years after the war concluded; and I believe that this may have been the first time Jacka learnt that other names were put as the authors of his report. It is remarkable how many of Jacka's contemporaries were of the fixed belief that Jacka's authorship of this report, and its suppression, doomed his chances for any further promotion or official honour.

36 Australian Imperial Force Unit War Diaries 1914–1918 War, General Staff Headquarters, 4th Australian Division, Part 2 – April 1917, AWM 1/48/13, p. 26.
37 Rule, *Jacka's Mob*, p. 83.
38 Rule, *Jacka's Mob*, p. 83.
39 Rule, *Jacka's Mob*, p. 83.
40 Wanliss, *The History of the Fourteenth Battalion*, p. 216.
41 Grant, *Jacka, VC*, p. 114.
42 Mitchell, *Backs to the Wall*, p. 68.
43 Rule, *Jacka's Mob*, p. 105.
44 *The Land*, 29 January 1932, p. 16.
45 Private W. H. Boyes, 14th Battalion, Passchendaele, Letter to Wanliss, 31 March 1925, Wanliss Papers, AWM 224 MSS 143 A, item 9.
46 Sgt J. Malseed, 14th Battalion, Letter to Wanliss, 6/2/25, Wanliss Papers, AWM 224 MSS 143 A, item 8.
47 Rule, *Jacka's Mob*, p. 122.
48 Passingham, *Pillars of Fire: The Battle of Messines Ridge June 1917*, Spellmount, Port Stroud, 2012, p. 90.
49 Rule, *Jacka's Mob*, p. 88.
50 Grant, *Jacka, VC*, p. 124.
51 Wanliss Papers, AWM 224 MSS 143 A, item 12, p. 2.
52 Deayton, *The Battle of Messines 1917*, Australian Army Campaigns Series 18, Army History Unit, Canberra, 2017, p. 4.
53 Gilchrist, '7 June 1917, The Battle of Messines', Anzac Memorial.
54 Mitchell, *Backs to the Wall*, p. 186.
55 Mitchell, *Backs to the Wall*, p. 198.
56 Wanliss, *The History of the Fourteenth Battalion*, pp. 221–222.
57 Wanliss Papers, AWM 224 MSS 143 A, item 8.
58 Macklin, *Jacka VC*, p. 176.
59 Rule, *Jacka's Mob*, p. 95.
60 Rule, *Jacka's Mob*, p. 95.
61 Wanliss, *The History of the Fourteenth Battalion*, p. 222.

62 Macklin, *Jacka VC*, p. 177.
63 Westerman, 'AIF Battalion Commanders in the Great War, The 14th Infantry Battalion – a Case Study', *Stand To!*, Journal of the Western Front Association, January/February 2017, No. 108, p. 21.
64 Rule, *Jacka's Mob*, p. 87.
65 Rule, *Jacka's Mob*, p. 87.
66 Rule, *Jacka's Mob*, p. 87.
67 Rule, *Jacka's Mob*, p. 87.
68 'Jacka's Mob': Review by Dr C. E. W. Bean, *Reveille*, 1 May 1933, p. 30.
69 *London Gazette*, Supplement 5983, 18 June 1917 thegazette.co.uk/London/issue/30135/supplement/5983.
70 Macklin, *Jacka VC*, p. 159.
71 Macklin, *Jacka VC*, p. 160.
72 Macklin, *Jacka VC*, p. 160.
73 *Western Mail*, 18 June 1942, p. 63.
74 Hatwell, *No Ordinary Determination*, p. 151.
75 *The Brisbane Courier*, 20 November 1919, p. 7.
76 'Major General Neville Reginald Howse', awm.gov.au/collection/P11026078.
77 Grant, *Jacka, VC*, p. 131.

Chapter twelve   The Battle of Polygon Wood

1 *The Sydney Morning Herald*, 22 September 1919, p. 8.
2 Grant, *Jacka, VC*, p. 124.
3 Westerman, 'AIF Battalion Commanders in the Great War', *Stand To!*, p. 21.
4 Wanliss, *The History of the Fourteenth Battalion*, p. 233.
5 Historic Hansard, Australian Senate, 28 April 1921.
6 Records of C. E. W. Bean, AWM 38, 3DRL 606/8/1, p. 56.
7 *Reveille*, 31 January 1932.
8 Historic Hansard, Australian Senate, 28 April 1921.
9 Biographical Indexes of Dr Bean for War 1914–1918, Jacka file, AWM 43, Wanliss to Bean, 5 March 1923.
10 Grant, *Jacka, VC*, pp. 124–125.
11 Grant, *Jacka, VC*, p. 125.
12 'Euripides', *Reveille*, November 1929, p. 12.
13 'Euripides', *Reveille*, November 1929, p. 12.
14 Rule, *Jacka's Mob*, p. 109.
15 Rule, *Jacka's Mob*, p. 109.
16 Rule, *Jacka's Mob*, p. 109.
17 Rule, *Jacka's Mob*, p. 109.
18 Rule, *Jacka's Mob*, p. 109.
19 Rule, *Jacka's Mob*, p. 109.

20 Rule, *Jacka's Mob*, p. 109.
21 Rule, *Jacka's Mob*, p. 109.
22 Rule, *Jacka's Mob*, p. 109.
23 Rule, *Jacka's Mob*, p. 110.
24 Grant, *Jacka, VC*, p. 124.
25 Wanliss Papers, AWM 224 MSS 143 A.
26 Rule, *Jacka's Mob*, p. 110.
27 *The Land*, 29 January 1932, p. 16.
28 Grant, *Jacka, VC*, p. 123.
29 Rule, *Jacka's Mob*, p. 110.
30 Rule, *Jacka's Mob*, p. 110.
31 Rule, *Jacka's Mob*, p. 110.
32 Rule, *Jacka's Mob*, p. 110.
33 Mitchell, *Backs to the Wall*, p. 32.
34 4th Infantry Brigade, war diary, 1914–18 War, September 1917, AWM 23/4/24.
35 Rule, *Jacka's Mob*, p. 111.
36 Rule, *Jacka's Mob*, p. 111.
37 Rule, *Jacka's Mob*, p. 111.
38 Rule, *Jacka's Mob*, p. 111.
39 Rule, *Jacka's Mob*, p. 111.
40 Rule, *Jacka's Mob*, p. 111.
41 Rule, *Jacka's Mob*, p. 111.
42 Rule, *Jacka's Mob*, p. 111.
43 Letter, J. Mitchell, 14 Battalion, C Coy, Polygon Wood, to Wanliss, 16 January 1925, Wanliss Papers, AWM 224 MSS 143 A, item 8.
44 14th Battalion War Diary, AWM 4 23/31/35, Part 1, September 1917.
45 Wanliss Papers, AWM 224 MSS 143 A, item 8.
46 Wanliss Papers, Jacka to Wallis, 18th July 1931, AWM 224 MSS 143 A.
47 Wanliss Papers, AWM 224 MSS 143 A, item 8, Letter from Lance Corporal Allan McDonald.
48 Wanliss, *The History of the Fourteenth Battalion*, p. 240.
49 Mitchell to Wanliss, AWM 224 MSS 143 A, item 8.
50 Mitchell to Wanliss, AWM 224 MSS 143 A, item 8.
51 Wanliss Papers, Letter from McDonald, AWM 224 MSS 143 A, item 8.
52 Wanliss Papers, Letter, Jacka to Wanliss, 18 July 1931, AWM 224 MSS 143 A.
53 Rolland to Wanliss, August 1931, quoted by Grant, *Jacka, VC*, p. 142.
54 14th Battalion War Diary, AWM 4 23/31/35, Part 1, September 1917.
55 Rule, *Jacka's Mob*, p. 112.
56 Mitchell to Wanliss, AWM 224 MSS 143 A, item 8.
57 Rule, *Jacka's Mob*, p. 112.
58 Mitchell to Wanliss, AWM 224 MSS 143 A, item 8.

59 C. E. W. Bean, *OHA, Volume V – The Australian Imperial Force in France: December 1917–May 1918*, Angus & Robertson, Sydney, 1937, p. 829.
60 Mitchell to Wanliss, AWM 224 MSS 143 A, item 8.
61 Rule, *Jacka's Mob*, p. 112.
62 Wanliss Papers, Letter from Jacka to Wanliss, Polygon Wood, AWM 224 MSS 143 A, item 8.
63 Rule, *Jacka's Mob*, p. 112.
64 Mitchell to Wanliss, AWM 224 MSS 143 A, item 8.
65 Letter, Jacka to Wanliss, 18 July 1931, AWM 224 MSS 143 A.
66 Macklin, *Jacka VC*, p. 192.
67 Rule, *Jacka's Mob*, p. 112.
68 Wanliss Papers, Letter from Jacka to Wanliss, Polygon Wood, AWM 224 MSS 143 A, item 8.
69 Recommendation Files for Honours and Awards, 1914–18 War, 14th Battalion, AWM 28.
70 Hunter, 'Many good men have I met – but he was the king of them all', AWM, 26 September 2017.
71 Macklin, *Jacka VC*, p. 194.
72 Bean, *OHA*, Vol. V, p. 828.
73 Bean, *OHA*, Vol. V, p. 828.

Chapter thirteen   Journey's end

1 Wanliss, *The History of the Fourteenth Battalion*, p. 245.
2 Mitchell to Wanliss, AWM 224 MSS 143 A, item 8.
3 Mitchell to Wanliss, AWM 224 MSS 143 A, item 8.
4 Wanliss Papers, Letter, Bean to Wanliss about Jacka, 1 March 1923, AWM 224 MSS 143, item 3.
5 *Daily Mercury*, 22 January 1932, p. 3.
6 *Daily Mercury*, 22 January 1932, p. 3.
7 *The Argus*, 19 December 1917, p. 8.
8 Rule, *Jacka's Mob*, p. 113.
9 Rule, *Jacka's Mob*, p. 113.
10 Wanliss, *The History of the Fourteenth Battalion*, p. 260.
11 White, *Reveille*, 29 February 1932.
12 Wanliss, *The History of the Fourteenth Battalion*, p. 266.
13 4th Infantry Brigade War Diary, March 1918, AWM 23/4/30, p. 8.
14 Kennedy, 'From Anzac Cove to Villers-Bretonneux', Unpublished Memoir, AWM PR02032, p. 63.
15 Bean, *OHA*, Vol. V, p. 122.
16 White, *The History of the Thirteenth Battalion, A.I.F.*, 13th Battalion A.I.F. Committee, Sydney, 1924, p. 122.

17 White, *The History of the Thirteenth Battalion*, p. 122.
18 Author's note: Though Bean doesn't specifically indicate it was an old lady with a wheelbarrow on this occasion, diaries and letters indicate them as the most common sight they saw at this late stage, as most families and younger people had already gone, and that is indeed what fits with the comment.
19 Bean, *OHA*, Vol. V, p. 177.
20 Bean, *OHA*, Vol. V, p. 123.
21 Bean, *OHA*, Vol. V, p. 124.
22 Bean, *OHA*, Vol. V, p. 124 [reported speech].
23 White, *The History of the Thirteenth Battalion*, p. 122.
24 Wanliss, *The History of the Fourteenth Battalion*, p. 266.
25 Wanliss, *The History of the Fourteenth Battalion*, p. 271.
26 White, *The Fighting Thirteenth*, p. 136.
27 Hatwell, *No Ordinary Determination*.
28 Guttman, *Sopwith Camel vs Fokker Dr I Western Front 1917–1918*, Osprey, Oxford, 2008, p. 65.
29 Guttman, *Sopwith Camel vs Fokker Dr I*, p. 68.
30 McGuire, *The Many Deaths of the Red Baron*, Bunker to Bunker Publishing, Calgary, 2001, p. 143.
31 Statement by No. 424 Sgt Popkin, 24th Australian Machine Gun Company, War Diary, April 1918, AWM 4/24/24.
32 Statement by Popkin, AWM 4/24/24.
33 Statement by Popkin, AWM 4/24/24.
34 Records of C. E. W. Bean, AWM 38 3DRL06/270, Part 3/1.
35 Macdougall, *War Letters of General Monash*, Duffy and Snellgrove, Sydney, 2002, p. 182.
36 Rule, *Jacka's Mob*, p. 119.
37 MacDonald, *To the Last Man*, Penguin Books, London, 1999, p. 82. Author's note: The quotation refers to a bombardment several weeks before 17 April, but accurately describes the sounds and smells of gas bombardments in 1918.
38 Albert Jacka, NAA, Series No. B73, 1040503.
39 *Reveille*, 31 January 1932.
40 Albert Jacka, NAA, Series No. B73, 10450503.
41 *Inglewood Advertiser*, 4 October 1918, p. 2.
42 Monash, *Australian Victories in France in 1918*, p. 96.
43 Rule, *Jacka's Mob*, p. 130.
44 Rule, *Jacka's Mob*, p. 130.
45 *Reveille*, 1 December 1936.
46 Rule, *Jacka's Mob*, p. 131.
47 Monash, *Australian Victories in France in 1918*, p. 50.
48 Rule, *Jacka's Mob*, p. 132.
49 Rule, *Jacka's Mob*, p. 132.

50 Rule, *Jacka's Mob*, p. 131.
51 Rule, *Jacka's Mob*, p. 135.
52 *The Land*, 29 January 1932, p. 16.
53 *The Land*, 29 January 1932, p. 16.
54 *The Land*, 29 January 1932, p. 16.
55 Rule, *Jacka's Mob*, p. 122.
56 Rule, *Jacka's Mob*, p. 122.
57 Rule, *Jacka's Mob*, p. 122.
58 Rule, *Jacka's Mob*, p. 122.
59 Rule, *Jacka's Mob*, p. 147.
60 Macklin, *Jacka VC*, p. 214.
61 Albert Jacka War Record, NAA M91031.
62 Albert Jacka War Record, NAA.
63 Albert Jacka War Record, NAA.
64 Albert Jacka War Record, NAA.

Chapter fourteen Home is the soldier

1 *The Herald*, 20 October 1919, p. 1.
2 *The Argus*, 27 September 1919, p. 20.
3 *The Herald*, 20 October 1919, p. 1.
4 *The Age*, 21 October 1919, p. 7.
5 *The Herald*, 20 October 1919, p. 1.
6 *The Herald*, 20 October 1919, p. 1.
7 *The Herald*, 20 October 1919, p. 1.
8 *The Herald*, 20 October 1919, p. 1.
9 *The Herald*, 20 October 1919, p. 1.
10 *The Herald*, 20 October 1919, p. 1.
11 *The Herald*, 20 October 1919, p. 1.
12 *The Herald*, 20 October 1919, p. 1.
13 *The Herald*, 20 October 1919, p. 1.
14 *The Herald*, 20 October 1919, p. 1.
15 *Weekly Times*, 25 October 1919, p. 41.
16 *The Herald*, 20 October 1919, p. 1.
17 *The Herald*, 20 October 1919, p. 1.
18 *The Herald*, 20 October 1919, p. 1.
19 *The Herald*, 20 October 1919, p. 1.
20 *The Herald*, 20 October 1919, p. 1.
21 *The Herald*, 20 October 1919, p. 1.
22 *The Herald*, 20 October 1919, p. 1.
23 *The Herald*, 20 October 1919, p. 1.
24 *The Herald*, 20 October 1919, p. 1.

25 *The Herald*, 20 October 1919, p. 1.
26 *The Age*, 30 October 1919, p. 8.
27 *The Age*, 30 October 1919, p. 8.
28 *The Age*, 30 October 1919, p. 8.
29 *The Age*, 30 October 1919, p. 8.
30 *Smith's Weekly*, 21 November 1925, p. 3.
31 Pedersen, *Fromelles*, p. 113.
32 *The Age*, 23 February 1924, p. 18.
33 *The Herald*, 23 February 1924, p. 1.
34 *The Sun*, 26 April 1924, p. 2.
35 *The Sun*, 26 April 1924, p. 2.
36 *The Sun*, 26 April 1924, p. 2.
37 *The Sun*, 26 April 1924, p. 2.
38 *The Argus*, 18 May 1928, p. 16.
39 Lawriwsky, 'The Truth about Albert Jacka', *Quadrant* online, 25 April 2024.
40 Lawriwsky, 'The Truth about Albert Jacka', *Quadrant* online, 25 April 2024.
41 St Kilda Council minutes, September 1931.
42 *The Sun*, 22 October 1929, p. 3.
43 *The Herald*, 29 July 1931, p. 10.
44 *The Herald*, 29 July 1931, p. 10.
45 Jacka, Albert, VC, MC and Bar, NAA: B73, C91031.
46 Macklin, *Jacka VC*, p. 262.
47 *Reveille*, 29 February 1932.
48 Jacka, Albert, VC, MC and Bar, NAA: B73, C91031.
49 *The Herald*, 14 January 1932, p. 1.
50 Rule, *Jacka's Mob*, p. 149.
51 Rule, *Jacka's Mob*, p. 149.
52 *The Herald*, 14 January 1932, p. 1.
53 *The Herald*, 14 January 1932, p. 1.
54 Macklin, *Jacka VC*, p. 263.
55 *The Sun*, 17 January 1932, p. 1.
56 Rule, *Jacka's Mob*, p. 149.
57 *The Herald*, 14 January 1932, p. 1.
58 Rule, *Jacka's Mob*, p. 149.
59 *The Argus*, 20 January 1932, p. 6.
60 *The Newcastle Sun*, 19 January 1932, p. 4.
61 *The Herald*, 19 January 1932, p. 1.
62 *The Herald*, 19 January 1932, p. 1.
63 *The Herald*, 19 January 1932, p. 1.
64 *The Herald*, 19 January 1932, p. 1.
65 *The Herald*, 19 January 1932, p. 1.
66 Rule, *Jacka's Mob*, p. 150.

67 Rule, *Jacka's Mob*, p. 150.
68 Rule, *Jacka's Mob*, p. 150.
69 Captain Albert Jacka V.C., Monument Australia.
70 Rule, *Jacka's Mob*, p. 150.
71 Rule, *Jacka's Mob*, p. 151.

Epilogue

1 *The Sun*, 23 January 1932, p. 4.
2 *The Herald*, 20 January 1932, p. 1.
3 *Coffs Harbour Advocate*, 25 October 1932, p. 3.
4 Jacka, Albert, VC, MC and Bar, NAA: B73, C91031.
5 Funeral of Albert Jacka, NAA: B1535, 746/1/33.
6 Funeral of Albert Jacka, NAA: B1535, 746/1/33.
7 'Visit to V.C.'s Grave', *Reveille*, February 1941, p. 11.
8 *The Argus*, 13 January 1947, p. 4.
9 Grant, *Jacka, VC*, p. 45.
10 *The Herald*, 1 June 1950, p. 16.
11 *Advocate (Burnie)*, 27 May 1950, p. 1.
12 *Advocate (Burnie)*, 27 May 1950, p. 1.
13 *Maryborough Chronicle*, 26 May 1950, p. 5.
14 Sparrow, *The Fifth Army in March 1918*, John Lane, London, 1921, p. xii.
15 Fox, *The Truth About ANZAC*, Victorian Council Against War and Fascism.
16 *The Argus*, 6 November 1941, p. 7.
17 O'Meara, The AIF Project, UNSW 2024.
18 Macklin, *Jacka VC*, p. 271.
19 Heritage Guide to Geelong College, 'Sir Francis Rolland'.

BIBLIOGRAPHY

Books

Arthur, Max, *Forgotten Voices of the Great War*, Random House, London, 2003
Ashmead-Bartlett, Ellis, *Uncensored Dardanelles*, Hutchinson & Co., London, 1929
Barwick, Flora, Archie Barwick – condensed diary, 1921, transcribed by Flora A Barwick in 1995, collection.sl.nsw.gov.au/record/n88EexBn
Bean, C. E. W., *Bean's Gallipoli: The Diaries of Australia's Official War Correspondent*, Allen & Unwin, Sydney, 2007
Bean, C. E. W., *Gallipoli Mission*, Australian War Memorial, Canberra, 1948
Bean, C. E. W., *Official History of Australia in the War of 1914–1918, Vol. I, The Story of ANZAC from the outbreak of war to the end of the first phase of the Gallipoli Campaign, May 4, 1915*, eleventh edition, Angus & Robertson, Sydney, 1941
Bean, C. E. W., *Official History of Australia in the War of 1914–1918, Vol. II, The Story of ANZAC from 4 May 1915 to the evacuation of the Gallipoli Peninsula*, Angus & Robertson, Sydney, 1924
Bean, C. E. W., *Official History of Australia in the War of 1914–1918, Vol. III, The Australian Imperial Force in France, 1916*, Angus & Robertson, Sydney, 1929
Bean, C. E. W., *Official History of Australia in the War of 1914–1918, Vol. IV, The Australian Imperial Force in France 1916–1918*, Angus & Robertson, Sydney, 1936
Bean, C. E. W., *Official History of Australia in the War of 1914–1918, Vol. V, The Australian Imperial Force in France during the Main German Offensive, 1918*, Angus & Robertson, Sydney, 1937
Birdwood, W.R., *Khaki and Gown*, Ward Lock & Co., Melbourne, 1941
Carlyon, Les, *The Great War*, Macmillan, Sydney, 2014
Carlyon, Les, *The Great War*, Picador, Sydney, 2010
Cutlack, F. M. (ed.), *War Letters of General Monash*, Angus & Robertson, Sydney, 1934
Deayton, Craig, *The Battle of Messines 1917*, Australian Army Campaigns Series 18, Army History Unit, Canberra, 2017
Derham, Rosemary, *The Silence Ruse: escape from Gallipoli; a record and memories of the life of General Sir Brudenell White*, Cliffe Books, Armadale, 1998

Dolan, H., *Gallipoli Air War: The Unknown Story of the Fight for the Skies Over Gallipoli*, Pan Macmillan, Sydney, 2013
Ellis, A. D., *The Story of the Fifth Australian Division, being an Authoritative Account of the Division's Doings in Egypt, France and Belgium*, Hodder & Stoughton, London, 1920
Falls, Captain Cyril, *Military Operations France and Belgium 1917*, Macmillan and Co., London, 1940
Fewster, Kevin (ed.), *Gallipoli Correspondent, the Frontline Diary of C.E.W. Bean*, George Allen & Unwin, Sydney, 1983
Fitzhardinge, L. F., *The Little Digger, 1914–1952: William Morris Hughes, A Political Biography*, Vol. II, Angus & Robertson, Sydney, 1979
Grant, Ian, *Jacka, VC: Australia's Finest Fighting Soldier*, Macmillan in association with the Australian War Memorial, Sydney, 1989
Guttman, Jon, *Sopwith Camel vs Fokker Dr I, Western Front 1917–1918*, Osprey, Oxford, 2008
Haig, Douglas, *War Diaries & Letters 1914–1918*, Weidenfeld & Nicholson, London, 2005
Hamilton, Sir Ian, *Gallipoli Diary*, Vol. I, Edward Arnold, London, 1920
Hamilton, Sir Ian, *Gallipoli Diary*, Vol. II, E. Arnold, London, 1920
Hartnett, H. G., *Over the Top*, Allen & Unwin, 2011, Sydney
Hatwell, Jeff, *No Ordinary Determination: Percy Black and Harry Murray of the First AIF*, Fremantle Press, Fremantle, 2014
Herbert, A., *Mons, Anzac and Kut*, Edward Arnold, London, 1919
Hogue, *Trooper Bluegum at the Dardanelles*, Andrew Melrose, London, 1916
Horne, Donald, *In Search of Billy Hughes*, Macmillan Australia, Melbourne, 1979
Laffin, John, *Damn the Dardanelles! The Story of Gallipoli*, Osprey, London, 1980
Longmore, Captain C., *The Story of the Old Sixteenth*, Naval and Military Press, Uckfield (first edition 1929, but no publication date for this edition)
Lucy, John, *There's a Devil in the Drum*, Faber & Faber, London, 1938
MacDonald, Lyn, *To the Last Man: Spring 1918*, London, Viking, 1998
Macdougall, Tony (ed.), *War Letters of General Monash*, Duffy and Snellgrove, Sydney, 2002
Macklin, Robert, *Jacka VC: Australian Hero*, Allen & Unwin, Sydney, 2006
Martı, M., (ed.), *Çanakkale Hatiraları*, Cilt III, Arma Yayınları, Istanbul, 2005
Masefield, *The Battle of the Somme*, William Heinemann, London, 1919
McCarthy, Dudley, *Gallipoli to the Somme: the story of C.E.W. Bean*, John Ferguson, Sydney, 1983
McGuire, Frank, *The Many Deaths of the Red Baron*, Bunker to Bunker Publishing, Calgary, 2001
Mitchell, George, *Backs to the Wall*, Allen & Unwin, Sydney, 2007
Monash, Sir John, *Australian Victories in France in 1918*, Hutchinson & Co., London, 1920

Moorehead, Alan, *Gallipoli*, Wordsworth Editions, Hertfordshire, 1998
Notes on Bayonet Training, Army War College, Government Printing Office, Washington, 1917
Oral, H., *Gallipoli 1915: Through Turkish Eyes*, Türkiye Iş Bankasi Kültür Yayınları, Istanbul, 2007
Örnek, T. and Toker, F., *Gallipoli: The Front Line Experience*, Currency Press, NSW, 2005
Passingham, Ian, *Pillars of Fire: The Battle of Messines Ridge June 1917*, Spellmount, Port Stroud, 2012
Pedersen, Peter, *Fromelles: French Flanders*, Pen and Sword Books, South Yorkshire, 2004
Perry, Roland, *Monash*, Random House, Australia, 2014
Power, Bob, *The Les Darcy American Venture*, self-published, New Lambton, NSW, 1994
Rule, Edgar John, *Jacka's Mob*, Angus and Robertson, Sydney, 1933
Rule, Edgar John, *Jacka's Mob*, Military Melbourne, Prahran, 1999
Sheldon, Jack, *The German Army on the Somme 1914–1916*, Pen and Sword Books, South Yorkshire, 2005
Sloan, Lieutenant-Colonel Hannibal, *The Purple and the Gold*, Halstead Press, Sydney, 1938
Sparrow, Walter Shaw, *The Fifth Army in March 1918*, John Lane, London, 1921,
Stanley, Peter, *Quinn's Post*, Allen & Unwin, Sydney, 2005
Wanliss, Newton, *The History of the Fourteenth Battalion, A.I.F.*, The Naval and Military Press Ltd. and The Imperial War Museum, England, 1929
Watson, Major William, *A Company of Tanks*, William Blackwood and Sons, London, 1920
White, T. A., *The Fighting Thirteenth: A History of the Thirteenth Battalion AIF*, Naval and Military Press, Uckfield, reprint (original publication date 1924)
White, T. A., *The History of the Thirteenth Battalion, A.I.F.*, 13th Battalion A.I.F. Committee, Sydney, 1924
Winter, Denis, *25 April 1915: The Inevitable Tragedy*, University of Queensland Press, St Lucia, 1994
Younger, R. M., *Keith Murdoch: Founder of a Media Empire*, HarperCollins, Sydney, 2003.

Journal and magazine articles

'Bar to V.C.: Jealousy's Pull against Jacka', *Reveille*, 31 October 1929
Bean, C. E. W., 'Albert Jacka', *Reveille*, 31 January 1932
Bean, C. E. W., Despatch, *Commonwealth Government Gazette*, No. 7, 13 January 1916
Bean, C. E. W., 'Fight for Pozières Ridge', *The West Australian*, 10 August 1916

Bean, C. E. W., 'Jacka's Mob': Review, *Reveille*, 1 May 1933
'Euripides', *Reveille*, November 1929
Preston, Harold, 'John Leak's V.C.', *Reveille*, 1 August 1935
'Visit to V.C.'s Grave', *Reveille*, February 1941
Wanliss, Newton, 'A.I.F. Celebrities (9): Captain Jacka V.C., M.C. & Bar', *Reveille*, 30 April 1931
Wanliss, Newton, *Reveille*, 31 January 1931
Westerman, William, 'AIF Battalion Commanders in the Great War, The 14th Australian Infantry Battalion – a Case Study', *Stand To!*, Journal of the Western Front Association, January/February 2017, No. 108, westernfrontassociation.com/media/6159/stand-to-108.pdf
White, T. A., *Reveille*, 29 February 1932

Newspapers

The Advertiser (Adelaide)
Advocate (Burnie)
The Age
The Argus
The Australian Worker
The Ballarat Star
The Bendigo Independent
The Bendigonian
The Brisbane Courier
The Cessnock Eagle and South Maitland Recorder
Coffs Harbour Advocate
Daily Herald (Adelaide)
Daily Mercury
Daily Sketch
Examiner
The Farmer and Settler
Hamilton Spectator
The Herald (Melbourne)
Inglewood Advertiser
The Korong Vale Lance and North West Advertiser
The Land
The London Gazette
Maryborough Chronicle
Mortlake Dispatch
The Newcastle Sun
The Northern Champion

Northern Star
The Queenslander
Smith's Weekly
Snowy River Mail
The Sun
The Sydney Morning Herald
The Tamworth Daily
Wedderburn Express and Korongshire Advertiser
Weekly Times
The West Australian
Western Mail
The World's News

Archives/State collections

Official diaries

3rd Australian Light Horse Brigade War Diary, AWM 4, 10/3/7
4th Infantry Brigade, Australian Imperial Force Unit War Diaries, 1914–18 War, September 1917, AWM, Item No. 23/4/24
14th Infantry Battalion War Diary, AWM 4 23/31/8
14th Battalion War Diary, 1914–18 War, AWM 4, Item No. 23/31/28, 29, 30
16th Battalion War Diary, AWM 4, Item No. 23/33/17
24th Australian Machine Gun Company, War Diary, AWM 4/24/24, Statement by No. 424 Sgt Popkin
Australian Imperial Force unit diaries 1914–1918 War, General Staff Headquarters, 4th Australian Division, Part 2 – April 1917, AWM 1/48/13

Other

Ashmead-Bartlett, Ellis, Diary and Papers, State Library of New South Wales, 1915–1917A 1583
Barwick, Archibald, war diary, 22 August 1914 – September 1915, MLMSS 1493/Box 1/Item 1, archival.sl.nsw.gov.au/Details/archive/110336342
Bean, C. E. W., diaries, notebooks and folders, AWM 38 3DRL 606, awm.gov.au/collection/RCDIG1066752
Champion, Ben, diary, AWM 2DRL/0512, awm.gov.au/collection/RCDIG0000977
de Vine, Apcar, diary, AWM 1DRL/0240
Dunlop, Athol, diary, AWM PR00676
Dunworth, David, officer in 15th Battalion, AWM 224 MSS 143 A, item 7
Gillison, Chaplain Andrew, Collection, 1914–1915, AWM 3DRL/6277 awm.gov.au/collection/C2725508
Guppy, A., diary, AWM 224 MSS 143 A, item 7

Jacka, Captain Albert, diary, AWM 224 MSS 143 A, item 4

Leane, Benjamin, diary, 8 AWM 1DRL/0412, awm.gov.au/collection/RCDIG0001007

Marks, diary, 7 August 1914 – 21 December 1918, State Library of New South Wales, MLMSS 2879

Monash, Sir John, diary, Monash Papers, SLV, MS 13875, Box 4083/1

Preston, Harry, diary, AWM 2DRL/0811

Letters

Bean to Wanliss, Private and Confidential letter, March 1923, AWM 43 [A414]

Blackburn, Sgt D., to Wanliss, 10 April 1924, AWM 224 MSS 143 A, item 7

Boyes, Private W. H., letter to Wanliss, 31 March 1925, Wanliss Papers, AWM 224 MSS 143 A, item 9

Collier, Clarence to parents, 12 April 1916, AWM 1DRL/206

Dalitz, Private C. to Wanliss, 6 March 1924, AWM 224 MSS 143 A, item 7

Dunphy, Private L. to Wanliss, 25 June 1923, AWM 224 MSS 143 A, item 7

Elliott, Harold to George Henderson, 12 April 1916, AWM PR01279

Elliott, Pompey to Charles Bean, 17 August 1926, AWM 38 3DRL 606/243B/1

Grieves, Corporal J. to Wanliss, AWM 224 MSS 143 A, item 7

Jacka, Albert, letters relating to his wounding at the Battle of Pozières and recommendation for the Distinguished Service Order, 1916, Wallet 1 of 1, Australian War Memorial, AWM 2021.22.136, awm.gov.au/collection/C2778933

Malseed, Seargeant J., 14th Battalion, to Wanliss, 6/2/25, Wanliss Papers, AWM 224 MSS 143 A, item 8

Maxfield, Gordon to his father, 13 October 1916, AWM 1DRL/0489

Miller, Frank to Mr Finlay, 30 November 1916, AWM 224 MSS 143 A, item 6

Mitchell, Sergeant J. to Wanliss, 16 January 1925, AWM 224 MSS 143 A, item 8

Monash, General John, War Letters of General Monash, 1934, Volume I, s3-ap-southeast-2.amazonaws.com/awm-media/collection/RCDIG0000569/bundled/RCDIG0000569.pdf

Raws, Goldy to family, 30 May 1915, AWM 2DRL/0481, awm.gov.au/collection/RCDIG0001092

Steel, Arthur Valentine Steel (1st Battalion AIF) to Marie and George Steel, January 1916, courtesy of Steel family of Wangaratta

Walker, Harold to Charles Bean, 13 August 1928, in Bean Papers, AWM 38 3DRL 7953/34, Part 1

Other items

Australian Red Cross Society Wounded and Missing Enquiry Bureau Files, 1914–18 War, Robert David Julian, 14th Battalion, AWM, 3DRL/0428,

BIBLIOGRAPHY • 449

s3-ap-southeast-2.amazonaws.com/awm-media/collection/RCDIG1049316/document/5636987.PDF

Australian Red Cross Society Wounded and Missing Enquiry Bureau Files, 1914–18 War, Captain Alfred Williamson, 14th Battalion, AWM 1DRL/0428, s3-ap-southeast-2.amazonaws.com/awm-media/collection/RCDIG1064222/document/5651736.PDF

Bean, *Official History 1914–18 War*, Records of C. E. W. Bean, Official Historian, Diaries and Notebooks, AWM 38, Item No. 3DRL 606

Boland, B Company, 14th Battalion, AWM 224 MSS 143 A, item 7

Bourne, Private William, Papers, Wallet 1, AWM PR 03573

Devereaux, Anne, *Playing Your Part – The Diary of William Devereaux, D Coy 14th Battalion AIF*, p. 75, privately published

Fiveash, Herbert, 41st Battery, 13th Field Artillery Brigade, diary, AWM MSS 1217

Funeral of Albert Jacka, NAA: B1535, 746/1/33

Hayes, Captain R., Bullecourt, AWM 224 MSS 143 A, item 7

Howse, Major General Neville Reginald, awm.gov.au/collection/P11026078

Kennedy, Walter, 'From Anzac Cove to Villers-Bretonneux', Unpublished Memoir, AWM PR02032

MacDonald, Captain D. R., AWM 224 MSS 143 A, item 7

MacDonald, Sgt R. N., AWM 224 MSS 143 A, item 7

Mayer, Sgt C. H., AWM 224 MSS 143 A, item 7

Monash, Personal Files, Book 13, 1 July – 16 August 1916, AWM, Collection No. 3DRL/2316

National Archives of Australia, Albert Jacka, Series No. B73, Item No. 1040503

National Archives of Australia, Jacka, Albert, VC, MC and Bar, Series No. B73, Item No. C91031

National Archives of Australia, Jacka's Official War Record, Series No. B73, Item No. M91031

Norris, Sam, War Narrative, 'There and back', 11 April 1914 – 18 November 1916, MLMSS 2933/Item 3, p. 29, acms.sl.nsw.gov.au/_transcript/2011/D12052/a2769.htm

Personal records of Capt. Jacka, AWM 88/190

Recommendation Files for Honours and Awards, 1914–18 War, 14th Battalion, AWM 28

St Kilda Council minutes, September 1931

Stanton, Captain F. B., Papers, WM 2 DRL 155, 12/11/3116

Wanliss Papers, Source Records of 14th Battalion History by Newton Wanliss, AWM 224 MSS 143 A

Williams, Albert, undated manuscript, AWM MSS 1337

Interviews

12th Australian Infantry Battalion veteran, interview conducted by historian Dr Peter Williams, Hobart, 1980

Bland, Percy, interview conducted by David Chalk, AWM Oral History Recording, Accession No. S01169, September 1993, s3-ap-southeast-2.amazonaws.com/awm-media/collection/S01169/document/9163200.PDF

Fitzpatrick, William, interview conducted by David Chalk, AWM Oral History Recording, Accession No. S01181, s3-ap-southeast-2.amazonaws.com/awm-media/collection/S01181/document/9170338.PDF

Tulloh, Arthur, interview conducted by David Chalk, AWM, Accession No. S01203 awm.gov.au/collection/S01203

Online sources

Captain Albert Jacka V.C., Monument Australia, monumentaustralia.org.au/themes/people/military/display/33518-captain-albert-jacka-v.c.

Conscription Referendums, 1916 and 1917, National Archives of Australia, naa.gov.au/help-your-research/fact-sheets/conscription-referendums-1916-and-1917#1916

Fox, L. P., 'The Truth About ANZAC', Victorian Council Against War and Fascism, reasoninrevolt.net.au/objects/pdf/d0887.pdf

The Gazette, All Awards and Accreditation Notices, thegazette.co.uk/awards-and-accreditation/content/100073

Gilchrist, Dr Catie, '7 June 1917, The Battle of Messines', Anzac Memorial anzacmemorial.nsw.gov.au/our-stories/our-stories/7-june-1917-battle-messines

Heritage Guide to Geelong College, 'Sir Francis Rolland', gnet.tgc.vic.edu.au/wiki/rolland-the-very-rev-sir-francis-william-kt-cmg-obe-mc-ma-dd.ashx

Historic Hansard, Australian Senate, 28 April 1921 historichansard.net/senate/1921/19210428_senate_8_95/

Hunter, Claire, 'Many good men have I met – but he was the king of them all', AWM, 26 September 2017, awm.gov.au/articles/blog/harold-boyd-wanliss-and-the-battle-of-polygon-wood

Incinerator Kate, Great War Forum, March 2012, greatwarforum.org/topic/176179-incinerator-kate/page/2/

Lawriwsky, Michael, 'The Truth about Albert Jacka, Our First War Hero', *Quadrant* online, 25 April 2024, quadrant.org.au/magazine/2024/04/the-truth-about-albert-jacka-our-first-war-hero/

Lecture Notes Relating to Albert Jacka, AWM PR84/333 s3-ap-southeast-2.amazonaws.com/awm-media/collection/AWM2018.785.10/bundled/AWM2018.785.10.pdf

Mitchell, George Dean, The AIF Project, UNSW Canberra Australia, aif.adfa.edu.au/showPerson?pid=210467

The London Gazette, Supplement 5983, 18 June 1917 thegazette.co.uk/London/issue/30135/supplement/5983

The London Gazette, Supplement 11074, 14 November 1916, thegazette.co.uk/London/issue/29824/supplement/11074

O'Meara, Martin, The AIF Project, UNSW 2024, aif.adfa.edu.au/showPerson?pid=228342

Sweeting, A. J., 'Charles Henry Brand (1873–1961)', *Australian Dictionary of Biography*, Volume 7, 1979 adb.anu.edu.au/biography/brand-charles-henry-5338

Theses

Pegram, Aaron, Thesis, *Surviving the Great War: Australian Prisoners of War on the Western Front, 1916–18*, Research School of Humanities & Arts ANU College of Arts & Social Sciences, 24 July 2017, web.archive.org/web/20200218150915id_/openresearch-repository.anu.edu.au/bitstream/1885/136647/1/Pegram%20Thesis%202017.pdf

Poems

Kipling, Rudyard, 'Epitaphs of a War', 1919

Kipling, Rudyard, 'For All We Have and Are', *The Times*, 2 September 1914

Rudyard Kipling's Verse Inclusive Edition 1885–1926, Hodder & Stoughton, London, 1927

INDEX

I Anzac Corps 92, 128, 199, 221, 291, 320, 322
II Anzac Corps 92, 291, 297
4th Brigade AIF xi
   Bullecourt 193, 194, 199, 203, 217, 218, 222, 228, 232, 236, 240–4, 247, 260, 270–3, 278, 281
   Gallipoli 6, 16, 17, 33, 35, 56, 58, 60, 61, 64, 71
   Jacka's funeral 394
   Polygon Wood 312, 316, 317
   Western Front 92, 97, 100, 101, 107, 112, 133, 137, 155, 159, 186, 297, 344
4th Division AIF 84, 87, 97, 107, 114, 117, 169, 297
   Polygon Wood 320
   Pozières 123, 125, 128, 130, 155
   VCs awarded to 355
13th Battalion AIF xi
   Bullecourt 194, 203, 223, 224, 228, 232, 250–5, 260
   Gallipoli 69, 79
   Jacka's funeral 394
   Polygon Wood 317, 321, 322, 323
   Pozières 156, 158
14th Battalion AIF xi
   A Company 102, 103, 294, 314, 322
   B Company 96, 126, 130, 132, 133, 136, 294, 299, 314, 322
   Bullecourt 203, 211–13, 217, 218, 222–78

   C Company 136, 137, 226, 294, 314, 322, 352
   company commanders 294
   Crowther in command 342–3
   D Company 75–80, 85, 89, 102, 103, 291–5, 314, 322, 325, 340, 346, 352
   dividing 85–6
   Egypt 84–92
   evening lectures 190
   Fuhrmann in command 291–2
   Gallipoli 5, 6, 15–35, 42, 46, 55, 56, 60, 63–71, 80, 81
   Hamel 356–61
   Intelligence Officer 181, 194–6, 204–12, 230, 237, 284, 293
   Jacka passed over for command 292, 305–6, 308
   Jacka Pilgrimage 402
   Jacka's funeral 393, 394
   Jacka's homecoming 369
   Jacka's mob vii, 178, 228, 297, 299, 308, 339, 402
   Margolin in command 296–7, 302, 308
   Messines 295–302
   Peck in command 180–90, 287–92, 297, 308
   Polygon Wood 313–34
   Pozières 123–39, 147–64
   Villers-Bretonneux 347, 351
   Western Front 96–100, 105, 107, 123–64, 179, 184, 190–6, 203, 296, 337, 339

15th Battalion AIF
  Bullecourt 194, 203, 219, 224, 228, 232
  Gallipoli 66
  Jacka's funeral 394
  Polygon Wood 322–6, 330, 332
  Pozières 147, 150
16th Battalion AIF xi
  B Company 87, 155, 251
  Bullecourt 194, 205, 206, 217, 223, 224, 228, 232, 235, 238–56, 265, 278
  Gallipoli 8, 18, 66, 67, 87
  Jacka's funeral 394
  Margolin and 296
  Mouquet Farm 155–6
  Polygon Wood 317, 321–4

Aarons, Captain Daniel 242, 245, 263–4
ABC Radio play about Jacka 403–4
Allenby, General 193, 221
American Army 340, 359, 360
Anderson, Lieutenant Herb 185
Anderson, Sergeant Fred 110
Anglo Soap Company 386
Anzac Day 94, 289, 351, 379, 381
Appleton, Lieutenant Frank 136, 147, 150, 162
Armistice Day 365
  10th anniversary commemoration 382
Arras 193, 196, 197, 200, 202
Ashmead-Bartlett, Ellis 1, 11, 65, 71, 72, 73
Asquith, Lord 72, 307
Australian Imperial Force 32, 84, 210
  1st Australian Infantry Brigade 61
  1st Australian Tunnelling Company 296
  1st Battalion 119
  1st Brigade 119
  1st Division 5, 11, 87, 92, 97, 114, 117, 118, 122, 123, 124, 292
  2nd Battalion 124

2nd Division 84, 87, 92, 97, 114, 123, 125, 127, 130, 133, 137, 292
3rd Brigade 119, 180
3rd Division xi, 87, 113
4th Australian Field Hospital 155
4th Brigade see 4th Brigade AIF
4th Division 84, 87, 97, 107, 114, 117, 123, 125, 128, 130, 155, 169, 297, 320
4th Infantry Battalion 92
4th Machine Gun Battalion xi, 347, 350, 359, 360
5th Division 114, 115, 292
5th Machine Gun Battalion 360
8th Light Horse 64
10th Battalion 30
10th Light Horse 64
11th Battalion 2, 3, 4, 16
12th Brigade 192, 203, 204, 232, 239–41, 247, 249, 254, 259, 270, 272, 278
13th Battalion see 13th Battalion AIF
13th Brigade 317
14th Battalion see 14th Battalion AIF
14th Brigade 317
15th Battalion see 15th Battalion AIF
15th Brigade 115
16th Battalion see 16th Battalion AIF
19th Battalion 100
24th Machine Gun Company 350
26th Battalion 125, 184
28th Battalion 125, 136, 138, 184
29th Brigade 72
37th Battalion 302, 309
45th Battalion 333
46th Battalion 84, 85, 86, 203, 227, 233, 243, 255, 259
47th Battalion 203
48th Battalion 136, 144–7, 150, 152, 155, 203, 217, 219, 227, 239, 247–9, 270, 299
49th Battalion 163, 330

INDEX • 455

50th Battalion 299
51st Battalion 190, 194

Bain, Sergeant Major 67
Banyard, Sergeant 85, 86
Barwick, Private Archie 120, 127
Bean, Charles vii, xi, 84, 86, 88, 344, 348, 378
   Bullecourt 182, 202, 225, 233, 247, 260, 279, 281, 283
   Gallipoli 25–7, 31, 36, 45, 61–3, 69
   on Jacka vii, 121, 162, 164, 173, 304
   on Murray 378
   Pozières 84, 105, 114, 117–19
Beck, Sergeant Frank 148, 151
Bell, Thelma 408
Belshazaar, Major 76
Binyon, Laurence 399
Birdwood, General Sir William 90
   Bullecourt 202, 261, 281–2, 288
   denying Jacka awards and promotion 305, 309
   Fifth Army 356
   Gallipoli 2, 11–13, 25, 46, 51, 58, 60, 63, 72, 81–2
   life after war 406–7
   Polygon Wood 320
   wanting Jacka to return home 363–5
   Western Front 128, 130, 199, 291, 296
Black, Major Percy xi
   B Company 16th Battalion commander 87, 155, 251
   Bullecourt 205–6, 241, 245, 249, 251, 254, 261
   Distinguished Service Order 205, 305
   Gallipoli 8, 18, 56, 67, 70, 71, 83
   Jacka compared 292
   Mouquet Farm 155–7, 205, 305
   Western Front 155–7, 188
Blackburn, Sergeant 252, 253, 269
Blamey, Colonel 117, 118

Bland, Private Percy 48–9, 133, 218, 219, 269, 274, 277, 281, 391
Boland, Sergeant 276
Borella, Albert VC 393
Bourne, Private William 135, 146
Boyle, Lieutenant Henry 32
Bradley, Lieutenant Henry 207, 209, 210, 212
Braithwaite, Major General Walter 13
Brand, Brigadier General Charles xi, 113
   Bullecourt 200, 203, 210, 212, 217, 234, 260, 261, 264, 269, 273, 280, 282
   insulting Jacka and men 313–16, 364
   Jacka Pilgrimage 402
   Jacka's funeral 395, 396–7
   Jacka's homecoming 367, 372
   life after war 405
   opinion of Jacka vii, 310, 397
   Polygon Wood 311–17, 323, 328, 332
   recommending Jacka for award 162, 173, 305, 333
   visit to 14th Battalion 311–16
   Western Front 113, 117, 131–2, 180, 186, 296, 343
Bridges, Major General William 11, 46
British Army
   2nd Division 106
   4th Cavalry Division 193, 265
   8th Division 351
   10th Hampshire Regiment 69
   12th Division 106
   25th Division 297
   62nd Division 218, 232, 239, 249, 260, 262, 264, 265, 292
   Australians' view of officers 88
   East Lancashire Regiment 106
   Fifth Army xi, 117, 190, 192, 197, 199, 202, 221, 292, 320
   Heavy Branch Machine Gun Corps 224, 230
   Monash's criticism of 73

British Army (*continued*)
  Third Army 192, 196, 202, 221, 292
  Western Front 105–7
Broadmeadows Camp 17, 35
Brown, Captain Roy 350
Bruce, Stanley 380
Buchan, John 308
Buchman, Ken 253
Bullecourt xi, 190, 193–295, 392
  aftermath 278–89
  casualties 278, 293
  Jacka's Tank Report 284–9, 306, 309, 356
  second attack on 292–3
  tanks 196–260, 269–70, 281–9, 306, 357

Cabena, Alderman 369
Cairo 84–92
  officer training 89–92
  Wazza 95
Cameron, Nelly 379, 405
Canadians 164
  Newfoundland Regiment 106
  Villers-Bretonneux 350–1
Carey, James 378
Carey, Vera *see* Jacka, Vera
Carroll, Private Horace 146, 151
Carter, Lieutenant Lionel 144, 145, 155
Caulfield Military Repatriation Hospital 387, 388
Champion, Lance Corporal Ben 122–3
Churchill, Winston 307, 406
Codford training camp 338–9
conscription 166–8, 177, 338, 363, 364, 373
Cook, Sir Joseph 409
Corrigan, Lieutenant Colonel Jack 169
Courtney's Post 17, 18, 20, 24, 26, 27, 31–42, 51, 68, 79, 368
Cowrey, Sergeant Jim 33
Cox, General Herbert 63, 90, 91, 94, 169

Crabbe, Lieutenant Keith Wallace 19, 33–9, 41, 46, 68, 70
Crowe, Dr 386
Crowther, Lieutenant Colonel Henry 342–3
Curtin, John 177

Dalitz, Sergeant Major Alwin 244
Danman, Private Harry 112
Dardanelles Commission 307
Dare, Lieutenant Colonel Charles xi
  Gallipoli 23, 66, 68, 69
  Jacka's award recommendation 161–3, 173
  opposing Jacka becoming officer 89, 90, 91
  return to England 180, 186
  Western Front 102, 103, 161–3, 169, 180
Dawe, Bill 300, 301, 353
De Arango, Lance Corporal Stephen 35, 36, 38, 110
De Robeck, Admiral John 13
Distinguished Conduct Medal
  Black 56
  Bullecourt, awards after 306
  Jacka not receiving 306, 336
  Mitchell 271
  Murray 56, 379
  Polygon Wood, awards after 336
Distinguished Service Order (DSO)
  Black 205, 305
  Jacka deserving 173, 283, 333, 335, 336
  Jacka told he'd won 169
  Murray 305, 379
  Wanliss 392
Dix, Flotilla Commander Charles 2
Dobbie, Lieutenant Henry 136, 147, 150, 151
Drake-Brockman, Colonel Edmund 205, 206, 251, 257, 285, 310

putting name to Jacka's report 287–9
  Senator 381
Duncan, Frank 400, 401, 409
Dunphy, Private 263
Dunstan, Bill VC 393
Dunworth, Captain David 147, 150, 203, 254
Durack, Fanny 127
Durrant, Lieutenant Colonel James 271
dysentery 51

Earle, Walter 49
Edmonds, Lieutenant Ernie 185, 377, 382
Eibel, Lieutenant Henry 254
Elliott, General Pompey 115, 116, 288, 309
Enver, General 24
estaminets 187–8, 302
Evans, Private William 254

Fanshawe, Lieutenant General Robert 261
Ferguson, Sir Ronald 367
Finlay, Private Jack 146, 148, 152
Fisher, Andrew 1, 52–3
Fitzpatrick, Private Bill 49, 95–6, 353
Fowler, Sydney 381
Freemasons 378
Fromelles 114, 115, 117, 164, 379
Frost, Corporal Ernie 340
Fuhrmann, Major Otto 96, 180, 309
  14th Battalion commander 291–2
  avoiding fighting 111, 136, 161, 292
  life after war 409
  Pozières 111, 136, 146, 147, 161–3, 292

Gallipoli 1–83
  Anzac Cove 24–8, 44, 51, 59, 72, 74–8
  August Offensive 51, 57, 66, 90
  casualties 12, 42, 63, 66, 67, 72, 80, 164
  commemoration 94

Courtney's Post 17, 18, 20, 24, 26, 27, 31–42, 51, 68, 79, 368
Dardanelles Commission 307
evacuation 79–83
Hill 60 68–73
Hill 971 64–8
Lone Pine 60–4, 72, 92
Quinn's Post 17, 23, 24, 27, 30, 79
'Shrapnel Gully' 17
speech on the beach 58–61
Suvla Bay 65–6, 68, 72
trenches 14, 15, 17, 18, 67, 77
Garcia, Sergeant 109
gas warfare 101, 119, 225–6, 340, 341, 352–4, 376
Gayning, Sergeant Bill 80
George, Lieutenant Cecil 315
German Army
  2nd Army 341
  17th Army 341
  18th Army 341
  25th Division 331
  27th Württemberg Division 221
  123rd Württemberg Regiment 229, 235
  124th Württemberg Regiment 213, 229, 235, 240
  Bullecourt 193–277
  Kaiserschlacht 340–2
  Polygon Wood 329–33
Gibbs, Philip 298
Gill, Lloyd 290
Gillison, Captain Reverend Andrew 6, 43, 49, 69–70, 82
Godley, General Alexander
  Gallipoli 11, 12, 47, 50, 61, 62, 65, 67, 68, 72
  Western Front 101, 291
Gorrell, Tassy 318, 319
Gough, General Hubert xi
  Allied Military Mission to the Baltic 406

Gough, General Hubert (*continued*)
  Bullecourt 190, 192–204, 221–4, 261, 264, 273, 279–82, 287, 288
  disgraced 356, 405–6
  life after war 405–6
  Polygon Wood 320
  Pozières 117, 118, 122, 130
Green, Private Sidney 78
Grieve, Robert VC 393
Guppy, Sergeant Les 266, 272

Haig, Field Marshal Douglas 116, 130, 312
  Bullecourt 192, 193, 198, 199, 200, 222, 262
  opinion of Gough 280, 406
Haking, General Richard 115
Hamel 355–61
Hamilton, General Sir Ian 12–16, 46, 47, 50, 51, 58, 65, 67, 68, 72
Hamilton, Lieutenant Bill 32, 33, 41
Hardress Lloyd, Lieutenant Colonel John 197
Harington, General Charles 296
Hayes, Captain Patrick 322, 327
Hayes, Captain Robert 126, 256, 277, 281
'Heavy Ponderers' 87
Hébuterne 343–6
Henderson, Lieutenant Bob 158, 159
Hersing, Kapitänleutnant Otto 47
Hill, Lieutenant Ernie 293, 388, 390
Hindenburg Line 182, 190, 193–211, 217, 225, 238, 240, 251, 256, 261, 279, 285
Hinton, Captain Frederick 351
HMS *Queen Elizabeth* 5, 13, 15, 31
HMS *Triumph* 47–8
Hoggart, Captain Bill 19
Holmes, Major General William 201, 216, 217, 273, 282, 287, 288

Howard, Lance Corporal Bill 19, 27, 35, 36, 37, 41, 55, 391
Howard, Major Harry 116
Howe, Lieutenant 'Snowy' 3
Howse, Colonel Neville 9–10, 307
Hughes, Billy 161, 166, 356, 380, 409
Hummerston, Captain Horace 263

Incinerator Kate 183–4, 284, 289–90
Indian Brigade 62
Isaacs, Sir Isaac 407

Jacka, Albert xi
  adopted daughter 382–6, 389, 409
  adoration of his men 294–5
  boxing prowess 302–4, 361–2
  Bullecourt 185–219, 223–46, 257–9, 264, 269, 274–5, 280–7, 392
  character 22, 34, 36, 46, 89, 95–6, 144, 187, 189, 220, 278, 292, 311, 361
  company commander 75–6, 79–80, 85, 89, 102, 291, 293–4, 310, 322
  conscription, view on 167–8, 177–8, 338, 363, 364, 373
  Courtney's Post attack 31–42, 51, 68, 368
  death 391
  deserving of awards 161–3, 173, 305–6, 336
  dividing 14th Battalion 85–6
  Egypt 84–96
  forestry worker xi, 38, 404
  France 99
  funeral xiii, 391–8
  Gallipoli 6–83, 297, 365, 391
  gassed 352–4, 361, 376, 386
  hero status 56–7, 74–7, 159–61, 166, 178, 306, 336, 355, 366–73
  homecoming 366–76
  illness 385–91
  import export business 375, 377, 382

INDEX • 459

Intelligence Officer 181, 194–6, 204–11, 230, 237, 284
legacy of 410–11
life after war 376–91
London General Hospital 157, 165–6, 307, 354
marriage to Vera 377–8
Mayor of St Kilda 383–7, 390, 397, 401, 402
mental suffering 174–6, 179
Messines 295–302, 353
Military Cross 173, 278, 305, 411
Monument Wood 351–2
news of VC at home 51–7, 160–1
officer training 89–92, 351
opinion of officers 88–9, 96, 103, 275
passed over for promotion 292, 308–11, 340
Polygon Wood 313–36, 392
Pozières 131–64, 173, 392
preparation for battle 297, 320–1
presentation of VC 170–1
promotion to Captain 189
Rechabite 7, 50, 54, 95
recommendations for medals 39, 41, 46, 68, 70, 161–3, 173, 302–6
refusing to return home 363–5
return to Australia 366–98
RSL Treasurer 379
rumours of death 168–9
Sports Officer, Sutton Veny 355, 361
St Kilda Council 382–6
Tank Report 284–9, 306, 309, 356
teetotaller 187, 302, 376, 398
Victoria Cross vii, xi, 51–7, 89, 154, 160, 285, 338, 365, 366, 368, 390
Villers-Bretonneux 347–55
Western Front 102–3, 111–64, 179, 185–246
wounds 151, 153–5, 157, 306–7, 354
writing to families of the fallen 334
Jacka, Betty 382–6, 389, 409

Jacka, Bill 80, 153–5, 165, 178, 392, 403, 407
Jacka Boulevard, St Kilda 402
Jacka (Canberra suburb) 402
Jacka, Edmonds & Co 382
Jacka, Nathaniel 53, 177–8, 338, 363, 372, 373, 388–9, 392
Jacka Pilgrimage 402
Jacka, Vera 377–8, 382–6, 389, 391, 399–401, 409
'Jacko' (Turks) 20, 24, 43
Jackson, Hugh 403
Jager, Reverend 375
jam-tin bombs 19, 37, 95
Janton, Katherine *see* Incinerator Kate
Jeffries, Lance Corporal Charles 340
Jones, Captain Reg 294, 299, 300, 302, 305
Jorgensen, Lance Corporal Sidney 137, 141, 152
Joynt, William VC 393
Julian, Lieutenant Robert 109

Kemal, Colonel Musafa 4, 24
Kennedy, Major General Alfred 265
Kennedy, Private Walter 344
Kerr, Lieutenant Jack 263
Keyes, Commodore Roger 14
King George V 170–1, 305
King George VI 380, 405
Kipling, John 172
Kipling, Rudyard 50, 58, 171–2
Knight, Private James 348

Law, Lieutenant Oswald 147
Leane, Colonel Raymond 'Bull' 2, 136, 155, 217, 248, 260
Leane, Major Benjamin 155, 217
Lemnos 5, 41, 51, 70
Lenin, Vladimir 337
Lloyd George, David 319, 406
Lone Pine 60–4, 72, 92

Loughran, Captain 71
Lowerson, Alby VC 393

MacDermid, Captain Donald 203, 294
Macklin, Robert 409
Malseed, Sergeant John 294
Mannix, Cardinal 167
Margolin, Major Eliazar 296–7, 302–3, 306, 308, 309
Masefield, John 88
May, Lieutenant Wilfrid 'Wop' 349–50
Mayor of St Kilda 383–7, 390, 397, 401, 402
McCay, General James 92, 94, 115–17, 379–80
McDonald, Allan 323, 324, 392, 403–4
McHugh, Lieutenant 374
McKinley, Lieutenant 226
McNally, Private James 36–8
Melba, Dame Nellie 367
Messines 295–302, 309, 353, 407
Military Cross
  Bullecourt, awards after 306
  Jacka 173, 278, 305, 411
  Jacka not receiving 306, 336
  Jones 306
  Polygon Wood, awards after 336
  Rule 362
Military Medal
  Bullecourt, awards after 306
  Jacka not receiving 306, 336
  Polygon Wood, awards after 336
  Rule 338, 362
Miller, Corporal Ken 252–3
Miller, Private Frank 134, 146, 148, 152
Mills bombs 95, 103, 111, 126, 147, 152, 244, 251, 254
Mills, Lieutenant 372
Mitchell, Captain John 322, 324, 327, 330, 336, 388, 390, 393
Mitchell, Lieutenant George 30, 58, 133, 293

Bullecourt 219, 225–8, 239, 241, 243, 247, 259, 270–1, 281
  Distinguished Conduct Medal 271
  life after war 408
  Messines 299
  never wounded in war 408
  Polygon Wood 316
Monash, General Sir John xi, 307, 309, 379–81
  3rd Division commander 113, 291, 300, 302, 351
  adopting Jacka's Tank Report 289, 309, 356
  commanding all Australian forces 356
  criticism of Bullecourt debacle 279, 289
  Egypt 90–1, 94, 96
  funeral 385–6
  Gallipoli 6, 16, 33, 35, 46, 47, 55–67, 73, 80
  Hamel 356–8
  Jacka keeping in touch with 379, 380
  lack of acclaim 380
  support for Jacka becoming officer 90–1
  Western Front 101–2, 110, 112–14
Moon, Mick VC 393
Morgan, Lieutenant Tom 271
Mortcroft, Ida 374
Moses, Charles 403
Mouquet Farm 155–9, 205, 305, 339
Murphy, Sergeant William Patrick 15–16
Murray, Lieutenant Colonel 'Mad Harry' xi
  4th Machine Gun Battalion xi, 347, 350–1
  A Company 13th Battalion commander 87, 156, 249, 268
  after WWI 378–9, 404–5
  Bullecourt 239–42, 249–56, 260–74, 280, 284
  death 405
  Distinguished Service Order 305, 379

Gallipoli 8, 18, 30, 56, 67, 70, 78–9, 83
Hamel 357, 359–60
Jacka compared 292
Jacka keeping in touch with 378–9
life after war 379
Marseilles 98
Messines 305
military career 404–5
Mouquet Farm 156–9
opinion of Jacka 278
Victoria Cross 188, 223, 268, 305, 379
Villers-Bretonneux 347–8
Western Front 156–9, 188, 189, 300, 343, 345
Murray, Nell 379, 405

New Zealanders
Gallipoli 3, 5, 7, 11, 12, 58, 63, 66
Western Front 92, 297, 298
Nicholls, Bill 253
Noreuil 190, 192, 206, 215, 224, 234
Northcote, Private 148, 159

O'Meara, Private Martin VC 176, 409
Orr, Captain Bob 238, 240, 241, 277

Page, Earle 380
Pasha, Kiazim 29
Passchendaele 319, 337
Pearce, George Foster 52
Pearce, Sergeant John 109
Peck, Lieutenant Colonel John xi
14th Battalion commander 180–90, 257–8, 287–92, 297, 308, 334
army cooking, transforming 408
Bullecourt 196, 200–1, 203, 205, 210, 214, 223, 231, 257–8, 280
Gallipoli 4
Jacka and 181, 186, 189, 190, 285
life after war 407–8
Messines 407
putting name to Jacka's report 287–9

Pentland, Lieutenant William 233, 243–4, 255
Perham Downs, Wiltshire 174–6
Pittendreigh, Corporal Robert 70
Plumer, General 318
Poliness, Private Frank 35, 36, 39
Polygon Wood 313–36, 392
Popkin, Sergeant Cedric 350
Postle, Arthur 336
POWs 278
Pozières 105, 114, 117–64, 173, 190, 192, 196, 392
Preston, Private Harry 99
Princess Elizabeth 382

Rabett, Lieutenant Colonel Reginald 261
Raff, Elsie 8, 54, 187
Rankine, Major Robert 33, 66
Rechabites 7, 50, 54, 95
Red Baron 191–2, 348–51
Reinhard, Gefreiter 341
Returned Services League (RSL) 379–81
Ribemont 179, 180, 183, 189–90, 289
Richards, Lieutenant 259
Richthofen, Manfred von see Red Baron
Robertson, Brigadier General James 225, 249
Rolland, Reverend Francis 310–11, 325, 334, 392, 410
Roosevelt, Franklin 383
Rose, Captain John 30
Roxburgh, Jacka & Co Pty Ltd 377, 382
Roxburgh, Lieutenant Reg 377, 382
Royal Flying Corps 174, 191
Rule, Captain Edgar (Ted) vii, xi
after war 378, 386, 390–1, 404
Bullecourt 208, 218, 225–7, 231–2, 239, 269, 275, 280, 282, 293
Codford training camp 338–9
death 404
diary 378, 402–3
Egypt 84, 85, 94, 96

Rule, Captain Edgar (Ted) (*continued*)
   Gallipoli 74–8, 83
   Hamel 356–7, 359, 360
   Jacka's funeral 396, 397, 398
   Jacka's Mob book vii, xv, 402, 404
   London hospital 362
   Military Cross 362
   Military Medal 338
   Monument Wood 352, 353
   on Jacka vii, 161–3, 168, 174, 289–96, 304, 305, 313, 355, 362, 386
   on Margolin 296
   on Peck 180–1
   Polygon Wood 313–18, 325, 328, 333, 362
   Pozières 123, 128, 132, 136–42, 150–3, 392
   Western Front 99, 102, 111–14, 136–42, 192
Rule, Muriel 404
Russell, Senator 367
Ruthven, Rusty VC 393
Rutland, Lieutenant John 20–1

'sandbaggers' 361–2, 363
Sassoon, Siegfried 295, 335, 366, 399
Scullin, James 406
Second Army School of Instruction 351
Shirtley, Lieutenant William 'Bluey' 192, 271
Short, Corporal 277
Simpson and his donkey 47
Sinclair-MacLagan, General Ewen 309, 343
Smith, Colonel Walter 302, 309, 310, 311, 315, 317, 325, 327, 334, 340
Smith, F.E. 406
Smith, Issy VC 393
Smith, Lieutenant Quinton 22
Smith, Private 'Combo' 3
Smith, Sergeant Charlie 111
Somme Valley 104–7, 112, 114, 121–39

SS *Euripides* 366, 367, 373
SS *Transylvania* 97
St Kilda Cemetery 393, 396, 402
St Kilda Council 382–6
   Jacka as Mayor 383–7, 390, 397, 401, 402
St Kilda Unemployed Organisation 393, 400
Stanton, Captain Fred 76, 232, 238, 240, 252, 253, 277
Stopford, General 60, 62, 67, 68
stretcher bearers 7, 9, 63, 110, 276
Suez Canal 92–4
Sutton Veny Command Depot 355, 361

tanks
   Bullecourt 196–260, 269–70, 281–9, 306, 357
   Hamel 357–8
   Jacka's report on 284–9, 306, 309, 356
Taylor, Private Clarence 146, 151
Templeton 318
Thompson, Lieutenant Stanley 142, 150, 319
Thomson, Major D 309, 315, 327
Thursby, Rear Admiral Cecil 14
Trumble, Mr 367
Tuck, Muriel 404
Tulloh, Private Arthur 96, 171–2, 278
Turkish Army, Gallipoli 4–83
   5th Ottoman Army 4
   2nd Division 24
   9th Division, 27th Regiment 4
   19th Division 4, 24
   57th Infantry Regiment 4
   armistice 42–5
   present to Australians 44–5
Turnbull, Reg 177–8
Twomey, Private 85–6

Unsworth, Councillor 387

Victoria Cross 171
  duty of recipients 355
  Howse 9, 307
  Jacka vii, xi, 51–7, 89, 170–1, 278, 285, 338, 365, 366, 368, 390
  Jacka deserving more vii, 160–3, 173–4, 278, 283, 304, 305, 335, 411
  Jacka standing for all winners 366
  Murray 188, 223, 268, 305, 379
  O'Meara 176
  pall bearers at Jacka's funeral xiii, 393
  presentation by King 170–1
  soldiers from Pozières receiving 174
Villers-Bretonneux 342, 347–51
Villers-Stuart, Major 25

Wadge, Lieutenant Frank 176, 207, 209, 210
Wadsworth, Captain William 238, 258
Walker, General Harold 'Hooky' 27, 46, 117, 118
Wallace-Crabbe, Lieutenant Keith *see* Crabbe, Lieutenant Wallace
Wanliss, Captain Harold xiv, 102–3, 187–8, 190, 334, 336, 362, 392
  Bois Grenier trench raid 107–12
  Bullecourt 203, 207, 211, 217, 257
  Jacka and 102–3, 294, 310, 327, 334
  passed over for promotion 310
  Polygon Wood 314, 322, 327–9, 334, 362
Wanliss, Newton vii, xv, 29, 121, 192, 336, 362–3, 378, 392, 402
Warloy 123–6
Watson, Major William xi
  Bullecourt 197–9, 201, 214–16, 224–5, 234, 236, 259, 282, 283

Wedderburn, Vic 7, 53, 178, 338, 373
  conscription debate 177–8
  farewell from 7–8
  homecoming to 373–6
  news of VC in 53–4
Weigall, Dr R.E. 367–71, 373
Western Front 73, 87, 95, 100–365
  Armistice Day 365
  arrival of 14th Battalion 97–100
  Bullecourt 190, 193–295
  casualties 73, 104, 106–7, 117, 133, 164, 196, 278, 293, 337
  Fromelles 114, 115, 117, 164, 379
  gas 101, 119, 225–6, 340, 341, 352–4
  Messines 295–302, 309, 407
  Mouquet Farm 155–9, 205, 305, 339
  Polygon Wood 313–36, 392
  Pozières 105, 114, 117–64, 190, 192, 196
  Somme Valley 104–7, 112, 114, 121–39
  Ypres 297, 319
White, Captain Thomas 344
White, General Cyril Brudenell 26, 81, 82, 119, 199, 202, 222
Wilkins, George 348–9
Williams, Private Billy 143, 146, 148, 152
Williams, Private Henry 93
Williamson, Captain Alf 'Lofty' 36, 226–7, 238, 240, 256–7, 272, 277
Wilson, Private 277
Wilson, Sam 49
Wise, Mr 367
Wood, Lieutenant Ramsay 360
Wren, John 54–5, 382
Wright, Captain Edwin 372
Wyatt, Captain Wilfred 212, 216, 225, 230